Educating for Responsible Management
Putting Theory into Practice

PRME Principles for Responsible
Management Education

**Greenleaf Publishing/PRME Book Series –
For Responsibility in Management Education**

Other books in the Principles for Responsible Management Education (PRME) Series:

Inspirational Guide for the Implementation of PRME: Placing Sustainability at the Heart of Management Education
June 2012; ISBN 978-1-90920-101-9 (pbk)

Inspirational Guide for the Implementation of PRME. Second Edition: Learning to Go Beyond
September 2013; ISBN 978-1-90609-313-6 (pbk)

Inspirational Guide for the Implementation of PRME: UK and Ireland Edition
Edited by Alan Murray, Denise Baden, Paul Cashian, Alec Wersun and Kathryn Haynes
September 2014; ISBN 978-1-78353-124-0 (pbk); ISBN 978-1-78353-125-7 (hbk)

Learning to Read the Signs, 2nd Edition: Reclaiming Pragmatism for the Practice of Sustainable Management
F. Byron (Ron) Nahser
August 2013; ISBN 978-1-90609-379-2 (pbk); ISBN 978-1-90764-390-3 (hbk)

Socially Responsive Organizations and the Challenge of Poverty
Edited by Milenko Gudić, Al Rosenbloom and Carole Parkes
July 2014; ISBN 978-1-78353-059-5 (hbk)

Responsible Management Education and the Challenge of Poverty: A Teaching Perspective
Edited by Milenko Gudić, Carole Parkes and Al Rosenbloom
December 2015; ISBN 978-1-78353-257-5 (hbk)

Anti-Corruption: Implementing Curriculum Change in Management Education
Wolfgang Amann, Ronald Berenbeim, Tay Keong Tan, Matthias Kleinhempel, Alfred Lewis, Ruth Nieffer, Agata Stachowicz-Stanusch and Shiv Tripathi
September 2015; ISBN 978-1-78353-510-1 (pbk); ISBN 978-1-78353-473-9 (hbk)

Responsible Business: The Textbook for Management Learning, Competence and Innovation
Oliver Laasch and Roger Conaway
August 2016; ISBN 978-1-78353-505-7 (pbk); ISBN 978-1-78353-486-9 (hbk)

Integrating Gender Equality into Business and Management Education: Lessons Learned and Challenges Remaining
Edited by Patricia M. Flynn, Kathryn Haynes and Maureen A. Kilgour
May 2015; ISBN 978-1-78353-225-4 (hbk)

Overcoming Challenges to Gender Equality in the Workplace: Leadership and Innovation
Edited by Patricia M. Flynn, Kathryn Haynes and Maureen A. Kilgour
July 2016; ISBN 978-1-78353-546-0 (pbk); ISBN 978-1-78353-267-4 (hbk)

EDUCATING FOR
RESPONSIBLE MANAGEMENT

Putting Theory into Practice

Edited by **Roz Sunley** and **Jennifer Leigh**

Routledge
Taylor & Francis Group

LONDON AND NEW YORK

 **PRME** Principles for Responsible
Management Education

**Greenleaf Publishing/PRME Book Series –
For Responsibility in Management Education**

First published 2016 by Greenleaf Publishing Limited

Published 2017 by Routledge
2 Park Square, Milton Park, Abingdon, Oxon OX14 4RN
711 Third Avenue, New York, NY 10017, USA

Routledge is an imprint of the Taylor & Francis Group, an informa business

British Library Cataloguing in Publication Data:
A catalogue record for this book is available from the British Library.

ISBN-13: 978-1-78353-346-6 [pbk]
ISBN-13: 978-1-78353-386-2 [hbk]

Contents

Foreword

Wayne Visser

It is not unjust, in my opinion, to place a large portion of blame for the last global financial crisis—and more generally for unsustainable capitalism—squarely onto the shoulders of management education. The ubiquitous MBA programmes that churn out tens of thousands of executive graduates every year have done little to question the short-term, shareholder-value, profit-maximization dogma of decades past. Indeed, most still celebrate and reinforce the philosophy espoused by US economist Milton Friedman in 1970 when he claimed that "the social responsibility of business is to make profits".

But the world has changed. We face serious global challenges—from climate change and biodiversity loss to income inequality and corruption—and many of these continue to get worse, not better. Management education is, belatedly and slowly but surely, starting to wake up and smell the crisis, not least due to the laudable efforts of initiatives such as the UN Global Compact, Principles for Responsible Management Education (PRME) and, most recently, the UN Sustainable Development Goals. The journey of a thousand miles has indeed begun with the first step, but there remains a long road ahead.

I make these observations as a complicit insider-outsider, who has been involved with responsible management education in 46 universities in 17 countries over the past 20 years. This includes current roles at the University of Cambridge's Institute for Sustainability Leadership in the UK, where I am a Senior Associate and Tutor on their Master's programme, and the Gordon Institute of Business Science (GIBS) in South Africa, where I am an Extraordinary Professor teaching their MBAs and the Founder Director of their Integrated Value Lab.

What I have seen first-hand over the years is a gradual evolution of management education through similar stages as I have observed in corporate social responsibility (CSR) around the world, from defensive, charitable and promotional approaches, towards more strategic and transformative modes. For clarity, these are described briefly in Table 1. Seen from this perspective, *Educating for Responsible Management* is a timely travel guide for our journey of maturation, as it explores how business schools can navigate through to stages 4 and 5.

Table 1 **Stages of evolution in management education**

Stage of maturity	Keywords	Typical practices
1. Defensive	Compliance, risk	Links ethics to corporate governance or legal context
2. Charitable	Voluntary, philanthropic	Offers optional business ethics module
3. Promotional	Marketing, branding	Offers optional CSR or sustainability module
4. Strategic	Management, codes	Has CSR or sustainability as a core, compulsory module
5. Transformative	Integration, innovation	Has integrated social, ethical and environmental considerations into all management subjects; emphasizes systemic leadership, futures thinking, eco-innovation, social entrepreneurship, inclusive business and circular economy

This is not the first book on responsible management education, but a number of features make it stand out. First, the chapters are presented as a collaborative dialogue between academics and practitioners. As a "pracademic" myself, I see enormous value in straddling both worlds, thereby providing a much needed space for convocation and creativity between the ivory tower and the boardroom. *Educating for Responsible Management* is proof that this approach is essential to producing relevant, emergent, applied research at its best.

Second, the editors have ensured that the book focuses on the *process* of responsible management education, more than the *content* (which other books have covered before). This is critical if we are to inculcate more transformative approaches in our business schools, since, as the writer and poet Ben Okri observes, "form endures longer than content".[1] And it is precisely the form of education, as much as the content, that has kept management students' minds trapped in outmoded ways of seeing the world.

Conversely, it is innovation in form—in the *way* we teach as much as *what* we teach—that is most likely to bring about the much needed paradigm shift in management education. This was confirmed by pedagogical research I did for the Cambridge Institute for Sustainability Leadership, which found that education using experiential learning and action research was far more likely to result in significant changes in executive thinking and practice on sustainability. Or, as the editors of

---

1 Okri, B. (2011). *A Time for New Dreams*. London: Ebury Digital.

this book put it: it helps move business students "out of the comfort zone—into the learning zone".

The third and final distinguishing feature of *Educating for Responsible Management* is that the authors not only present the "how", but also wrestle with the "why" and "so what" of their proposals. They realize that until management educators can answer the sceptics and critics of CSR and sustainable enterprise—in terms of why this is a better approach, not just for society and the planet, but also for business—all our efforts, PRME inspired or otherwise, will be like shifting deck chairs on the *Titanic*.

This touches on the essence of our reformation challenge for management education, which is finding credible ways to question, re-assess, re-imagine and redirect the purpose of business. In this sense, we are in the midst of a pivotal existential crisis in management education. I congratulate the authors of this book for tackling this collective challenge that we face so bravely, intelligently, honestly and passionately. And I heartily recommend *Educating for Responsible Management* to anyone who is concerned about business, society and nature surviving and thriving in the coming decades.

Dr Wayne Visser
Cambridge, UK
May 2016

The Six Principles of PRME

Source: www.unprme.org/about-prme/the-six-principles.php

As institutions of higher education involved in the development of current and future managers we declare our willingness to progress in the implementation, within our institution, of the following Principles, starting with those that are more relevant to our capacities and mission. We will report on progress to all our stakeholders and exchange effective practices related to these principles with other academic institutions:

Principle 1 | Purpose: We will develop the capabilities of students to be future generators of sustainable value for business and society at large and to work for an inclusive and sustainable global economy.

Principle 2 | Values: We will incorporate into our academic activities and curricula the values of global social responsibility as portrayed in international initiatives such as the United Nations Global Compact.

Principle 3 | Method: We will create educational frameworks, materials, processes and environments that enable effective learning experiences for responsible leadership.

Principle 4 | Research: We will engage in conceptual and empirical research that advances our understanding about the role, dynamics and impact of corporations in the creation of sustainable social, environmental and economic value.

Principle 5 | Partnership: We will interact with managers of business corporations to extend our knowledge of their challenges in meeting social and environmental responsibilities and to explore jointly effective approaches to meeting these challenges.

Principle 6 | Dialogue: We will facilitate and support dialog and debate among educators, students, business, government, consumers, media, civil society organizations and other interested groups and stakeholders on critical issues related to global social responsibility and sustainability.

We understand that our own organizational practices should serve as example of the values and attitudes we convey to our students.

1

Introduction

Jennifer S.A. Leigh
Nazareth College, USA

Roz Sunley
University of Winchester, UK

> Provide leaders for tomorrow who have been educated to think critically,
> to act ethically and always to question.
>
> *Louise Richardson, New Vice Chancellor of Oxford University at her instal-*
> *lation, January 2016*

This edited collection profiles cutting-edge approaches to teaching and learning for
the Principles for Responsible Management Education (PRME) that move beyond
current discussions of sustainability and corporate social responsibility *content*, to
include a wider lens that highlights the *process of educating* the next generation of
responsible managers within and beyond the boundaries of higher education. The
completion of this book coincides with the release of the newly negotiated United
Nations Sustainable Development Goals or Global Goals. These inter-governmen-
tally created goals released on 25 September 2015 follow up on the Millennium
Development Goals (MDGs), and form an ambitious backdrop for all nations,
sectors, industries and organizations. This inspirational goal architecture offers an
exceptional opportunity to fundamentally rethink management education.

Writers from around the world share their ideas and experience of the six Principles of the PRME (see page 10). A unique aspect of this book is that each chapter
integrates original content from academic authors, together with commentary from
practising managers. This collaborative approach allows integration of academic
and business voices on education for responsible management, in essence modelling the PRME Principles 5 and 6, Partnership and Dialogue. In this introduction

we begin by demonstrating the Principles through the book's fundamental framework, and discuss briefly the global need for management education reform. After discussing the book's theory-practice structure, we share the genesis of the book and then the subsequent themes that emerged across the chapters. We use these themes, as well as the PRME Principles, to introduce the chapters. With this thematic and Principles framework the chapters appear more than once, indicating the multi-dimensional character of the teaching and learning innovations.

Starting with **Principle 5**, our book models Partnership explicitly as the authors "interact[ed] with managers of business corporations to extend our knowledge of their challenges in meeting social and environmental responsibilities, and to explore jointly effective approaches to meeting these challenges" (PRME, 2015, p. 170). When crafting this new model of scholarship we sought to bring research and teaching practice to practitioners for their perspective, and practitioners to research in order to understand the opportunities and challenges instructors face. The depth of interactions in these chapters varied from co-authorship to consultation and testimonial to joint action research and co-instruction. These book chapters represent varied responses to effective approaches to "meeting these challenges" through minor and radical changes in our classroom practices.

We engaged **Principle 6** by requesting the integration of academic and managerial perspectives in each chapter. This chapter structure of co-authorship "facilitate[d] and support[ed] dialogue and debate among educators, students, business,...civil society organizations,...and other stakeholders on critical issues related to global social responsibility and sustainability" (PRME, 2015, p. 170). In this book we move the dialogue beyond the business case for responsible management education (RME) to a conversation about *how* to educate managers and leaders, and the value of the numerous experiential, engaged and ethics focused approaches for learners. In the conclusion we reflect more on this approach and its upsides and downsides.

While many academic journals, websites, conferences and teaching resources testify to growing interest in PRME, attention has been focused on the initiative itself rather than how management educators prepare themselves, their students, the learning environment and their teaching resources for this arena of learning. Little is known about the pedagogical frameworks that underpin educating for PRME, or their assessment by practising managers. As growing numbers of academic institutions sign up to PRME—600 and counting—it is important that management educators understand that a variety of pedagogical approaches and strategies can provide effective learning experiences for PRME related topics beyond traditional instruction such as lectures and case studies. This text aims to provide comprehensive and detailed coverage of innovative pedagogical approaches being used around the world, drawing together leading thinkers and management educators in this field, to share their practice, primary research and scholarship on this topic.

Global needs

The urgency for management education reform is evident in recent global agreements such as COP21 and the United Nations' 21 October 2015 release of their 2030 agenda for people, planet, prosperity, peace and partnership which highlighted their 17 Sustainable Development Goals and 169 targets (United Nations, 2015). Their report titled *Transforming our World: The 2030 Agenda for Sustainable Development* outlines their aspirations: "We envisage a world in which every country enjoys sustained, inclusive and sustainable economic growth and decent work for all" (UN, 2015, p. 4). The UN acknowledges the fundamental role of commerce; however this vision will require a new level of commitment, dedication and collaboration:

> Private business activity, investment and innovation are major drivers of productivity, inclusive economic growth and job creation. We acknowledge the diversity of the private sector, ranging from micro-enterprises to cooperatives to multinationals. We call upon all businesses to apply their creativity and innovation to solving sustainable development challenges (UN, 2015, p. 29).

Article 12 of the COP21 agreement signed in December 2015 suggests "climate change education, training, public awareness, public participation and public access to information" are essential if this global framework is to be effective.

It is clear that now, more than ever, the global community is looking towards business and education to play their role in creating a just and fair economy, which in turn increases the urgency and relevance of management education reform. PRME offers business schools a systematic and holistic framework to revise both content and process. The book's 15 chapters with 44 contributing authors and practitioners, representing many places including Aotearoa (the nation also known as New Zealand), Colombia, India, Italy, Spain, South Korea, the United States and the United Kingdom, provide a truly international perspective on new ways forward.

Our book fosters a deeper understanding of the interdisciplinary nature of responsible management education. It goes beyond traditional management functions to explore a deeper more holistic formation of individuals who, as the next generation of global leaders, will be called cognitively, emotionally and behaviourally to respond to the complex challenges of our world. We argue that responsible management content is no longer enough, but that we must radically broaden the way in which we inspire and enrich the education of our future business leaders.

Structure of the book

To embody Principles 5 and 6, this book incorporates two types of chapter structure to capture the dual voices of academic educators and practising managers:

- Academic authors with practitioner commentary
- Co-authorship between academics and practitioners

These blended voices approaches seek to support a new model of academic writing that bridges the theory–practice divide, with conversation across practice lines. The practice voices in the chapters critically reflect on the utility of a particular academic idea, and draw out subsequent implications for teaching practice in higher education.

The book is designed for responsible management educators, deans, faculty developers and corporate trainers. Responsible management educators will benefit from the leading practices profiled in the chapters, all of which include sections with guidance for individual interpretation in the classroom. Anyone engaged in innovative pedagogy will find inspiration in the various models from around the globe. Deans supporting curricular reform will gain a deeper understanding of how practitioners view the relevance of the various pedagogical practices detailed in the book. We believe this academic–practitioner partnership in each chapter directly addresses the ongoing issue of relevance in the responsible management domain. Additionally, we hope it can help academic administration understand the benefits of such pedagogical practices and the resources needed to construct these learning environments. Lastly, we believe that corporate trainers will benefit from understanding the challenges inherent in responsible management education, which may stimulate new approaches in their own professional work.

Origins of the book

The vision and genesis of this book occurred in a small coffee shop in Copenhagen, following a Research in Management Learning and Education Unconference attended by both editors. We quickly entered an intense dialogue that evidenced Jennifer's broad scholarship of PRME and Roz's passion for practical pedagogy, which this book now reflects with the help of all our contributing authors.

The process has been somewhat akin to what is known in software development as the principle of "scrum", in that the book has developed iteratively and holistically with writers contributing their ideas towards the vision of a book on educating *for* responsible management, rather than content *about* the topic.

Emergent themes about responsible management teaching

Teaching responsible management (RM) topics is much more than curating the newest interdisciplinary knowledge on the various complex issues facing business in the 21st century. This book provides clear evidence that responsible management education (RME) requires us as educators to utilize more experiential and engaged approaches to help guide our learners and emerging leaders. We believe we must begin with the problem or responsibility focus, which then leads us to the appropriate teaching approaches, instead of taking RME and inserting it into our normal teaching protocols. The minimal training and attention given to pedagogy in many institutions, which is amplified by reward systems endorsing narrow disciplinary scholarship over investment in teaching, often thwarts change. Despite these barriers we see academics from all over the globe, and at all stages of their careers, innovating and experimenting with new RME teaching and learning methods and philosophies.

As we read the first drafts of the chapters at an intensive editing retreat we were excited by the emergence of several shared themes within the chapters—none of which was scripted within the strictures of the initial call. We share these themes below as a means of introducing the chapters. Following this section we classify chapters by PRME Principles for readers seeking this focus.

Out of the comfort zone—into the learning zone

It appears to be a fundamental process that RME topics, and the often purposefully disruptive teaching and learning processes highlighted in the book, move students out of their comfort zone and attempt to push them into a learning zone. This can also be a place of discomfort for instructors as students adjust to new boundaries of learning.

- This theme begins in Chapter 3 by Sunley and Coleman, "Establishing a foundational responsible learning mind-set for business in the 21st century", which discusses a pilot class where the instructor purposefully integrates liberal education practices into a first year undergraduate orientation course, which results in some students embracing, and some contesting, the need for more authentic engagement with their learning.

- Humphries, Casey-Cox and Dey in Chapter 4 titled "Choosing food yet consuming plastic: Learning to notice the difference in management education" catapult both instructors and students into the learning zone of Radical Human Ecology theory and an experiential exercise focused on modern lifestyles and plastic.

- Swamy and Keegan share in Chapter 12, "Developing responsible managers through service-learning at Goa Institute of Management, India", that service-learning in Goa, India continues to be a pedagogy for pushing student and academic boundaries.

- "Experiential learning through shared responsibility and risk" by Wagenberg and Gutiérrez in Chapter 5 brings moving students out of their comfort zone to the course level with a semester long entrepreneurship class where investment funds come from their personal funds in order to create higher accountability.

- Lastly, Tyran and Garcia in Chapter 14 protest the systematic omission of socioeconomic and cultural class issues in management education within their chapter "Management education and social class: Can managers do more to encourage social equality and meritocracy in the workplace?"

These chapters collectively contest fundamental assumptions about teaching and learning and disrupt the traditional roles of teachers and learners. Fortunately, the practitioner commentaries repeatedly validate the relevance of this approach in order to prepare 21st century responsible managers. Pushing, prodding and provoking students is not for the meek, as discussed in these chapters. It requires a high level of emotional and social intelligence on the part of instructors as well as modelling an element of risk taking.

Risk taking

Traversing into the learning zone away from our habitual practices, as instructors and students, requires risk taking. Despite institutional disincentives, academics in these chapters demonstrate creative risks in contesting the normative teaching and learning practices through themes discussed above and below. Humphries, Casey-Cox and Dey in Chapter 4 ask us to take risks by modelling how to bring our full identities into the classroom, which in their case includes their family roles as mothers, grandmothers and as social justice activists. Wagenberg and Gutiérrez in Chapter 5 detail their experiences of financial risk taking with their personally funded entrepreneurial student start-up companies in Colombia. Sunley and Coleman in Chapter 3 foster structured risk taking that pushes first-year students ("freshers") off campus and into the wider community. With risk comes reward, as it introduces more emotion into learning. Thus, we observe that RME educators seeking risk need high levels of emotional intelligence to manage their own and students' affective needs. Moving out of one's comfort zone by taking risks inherently evokes ambiguity.

Ambiguity

In numerous student quotes and practitioner comments throughout the book we see the challenge and need for RME to embrace ambiguity as a part of learning. This is typified by "It's been an incredible ride that brought forth just as many questions as there were answers". This quote from the Pragmatic Inquiry method is an example described in Kelley and Nahser's Chapter 8 "Integrating PRME principles in practice through pragmatic inquiry: A sustainable management case study", which purposely embraces the unknown as they put students in the proverbial "driver's seat". Similarly, Swamy and Keegan's self-study (Chapter 12) on service-learning in India pointedly highlights uncertainty experienced by both faculty and students in this pedagogy. While new pedagogies sometimes create discomfort for all partners in the learning equation, we observe that RME educators can productively leverage ambiguity for richer learning experiences. This stance, however, requires that instructors release the need for certainty as a subject matter expert embodied in the traditional professorial role and become more facilitators of student engagement with learning.

Engagement

The above qualities highlight that the type of RME advocated for in this book requires entirely new levels of engagement for the institution, faculty and students. Several chapters addressed this topic from various vantage points at the field, institutional, curricular, delivery platform and conceptual levels. First, the survey of RM educators conducted by Forray, Leigh, Goodnight and Cycon presented in Chapter 16, "Teaching methods and the Kolb learning cycle: Pedagogical approaches in the Principles for Responsible Management Education domain", provides a broad landscape of engagement practices in the RME field based on an experiential learning model. Second, at the institutional level, we noted the more interdisciplinary, intentional and innovative the curriculum, the more stakeholders needed to be considered, as is seen in Chapter 10, titled, "The Daniels Compass: Global business education for management professionals". This chapter by Mayer and Hutton catalogued the evolution of an RME curriculum at the University of Denver business school starting in the 1990s. This systematic engagement is also addressed in the change-focused chapter (15), titled "The drivers, barriers and enablers of institutionalizing responsible management education" by Warin and Beddewela, which identified the engagement levers needed for institutionalization. Third, we noted in Chapter 14 the logistical creativity needed for global digital engagement as actualized through Chapter 13 "The Global Integrative Module: A competency based online learning experience to help future managers understand complex global social challenges" by the international team Iñesta, Valencia, Rovira, Caporarello, Choi, Statler, Mària, Sayeras, Serlavós, Marin, Obeso, Wilson, & Gessi.

From a conceptual perspective, we discovered that many chapters conceived engagement comprehensively from a holistic stance: Chapter 11, Heaton, Schachinger and Lazlo's consciousness-based education; Chapter 9, Rimanoczy's sustainability mind-set; Chapter 4, Humphries, Casey-Cox and Dey's notion of leveraging multiple identities in the classroom; Chapter 8 Kelley and Nahser's Pragmatic Inquiry process; and Chapter 3, Sunley and Coleman's being-knowing-doing model. These approaches envisioned RME engagement as a multi-dimensional teaching and learning process that considers cognition, emotion and action or "Head, Heart, and Hands" in tandem. These chapters underscore the need for a deeper and more integrative learning process—one that incorporates our cognitive, emotional and behavioural dimensions. The models, practices and sensibilities require a holistic approach where we bring our whole selves to the learning—instructors and students alike.

Interdisciplinary intersections and integration

Those engaging in RME have, and will continue to push and disrupt discrete disciplinary notions. These chapters testify to the fact that RM educators must learn alongside their students as new discoveries are made in the natural and social sciences and historic and contemporary insights, with the humanities informing our notions of business and society. Example chapters that illustrate this disciplinary variety include wisdom traditions and management education seen in Heaton, Schachinger and Laszlo (Chapter 11), introductory business and behavioural ethics described in Manwaring, Greenberg and Hunt (Chapter 6), virtual classrooms and social impact project teams (GIM) detailed by Inesta *et al.* (Chapter 13), intersections between business and liberal arts featured in Chapter 3 by Sunley and Coleman, and curricular revisions that demand interdisciplinary courses recorded in Mayer and Hutton (Chapter 10). These disciplinary fusions forecast what we see as the forefront of what is needed and desired in RME.

Mind-sets

The educational mavens and mavericks showcased in this book model a different teaching and learning mind-set or teaching philosophies, "narrative description[s] of one's conception of teaching, including the rationale for one's teaching methods" (Beatty *et al.*, 2012, p. 100). Teaching philosophies incorporate many dimensions that include our deeply held ideas about who we are (ontology), what we know (epistemology), what we value (axiology), the teacher's role, the student's role and educational goals.

First, in terms of knowledge, this new RME mind-set moves beyond the exclusive basis of traditional empirically based positivist knowledge from the sciences and social sciences to holistic consideration that knowledge can originate from numerous sources including experts, individuals' reason, sensory experiences or one's intuition (Beatty *et al.*, 2012). Second, the authors in this book are keen to prepare students for responsibilities that are unknown in their entirety, ones that must increasingly address "super wicked problems". These unique global challenges are vexing to solve due to incomplete information, changing parameters, under conditions where time is running out, there is no central authority in charge of the issues, and those attempting to address the problem are also contributing to it (Levin *et al.*, 2012). Examples of super wicked problems include global warming, economic inclusion, refugee diasporas and obesity. Third, explicit in the shared mind-set of these educators is the value of RME content and process—how learning moments are developed and created. For the process orientation, most chapters in this book reconceive the instructor role as a facilitator and the student role as an engaged learner. Lastly, in all instances the chapters' multifaceted instructional goals go beyond exclusive RME content coverage and focus on innovative learning processes intended to prepare students for tackling complex organizational and societal challenges.

Chapter structure: the PRME framework

In this section we offer a reading menu of sorts based on the principles. When we initially structured the book we anticipated broad coverage of all six Principles for Responsible Management Education through the lens of teaching practice and below we divide the chapters according to them for those who have particular interest in specific principles. What developed as we read the chapters is that many cover more than one principle, so our classification speaks to what we see as the primary contributions; however we acknowledge some overlap in the categorization that follows.

We refer the readers to the PRME Principles included at the beginning of the book (page x), which form the basic organizing framework. Each chapter follows a general pattern starting with a connection to a main PRME Principle. This is then followed by a description of the innovation or study and then ends with an implications for practice section. A more extensive discussion of the history of PRME and related research, written by Hayes, Parkes and Murray is provided in Chapter 2.

Principle 1: Purpose

Heaton Schachinger and Laszlo in Chapter 11, "Consciousness development for responsible management education", argue that to better assist students with generating sustainable value, educators need to place more attention on psychological differences researchers call consciousness development. Manwaring, Greenberg and Hunt with practitioners Augsburger and Houlker, in "Walking the talk: Empowering undergraduate business students to act on their values" (Chapter 6), discuss strategies for this principle because in their view teaching productive ways to deal with ethics challenges is fundamental for responsible leadership. Wagenberg and Gutiérrez, in "Experiential learning through shared responsibility and risk", explore how the fundamental teaching philosophy and instructional design choices in an entrepreneurship course could be revised in order to enable effective learning experiences for responsible leadership. Humphries, Casey-Cox and Dey, in "Choosing food yet consuming plastic: Learning to notice the difference in management education" (Chapter 4), push our traditional notions of theory and practice by utilizing personal experience as activists and consumers, concepts from Radical Human Ecology, and indigenous Maori traditions to provoke our notions about purpose and a sustainable global economy for all peoples.

Principle 2: Values

Mayer and Hutton provide an in-depth case study from their institution's ongoing journey towards identifying shared responsible management values throughout their curriculum in "The Daniels Compass: Global business education for management professionals" (Chapter 10). Tyran and Garcia along with practitioner Debbie

Ahl in "Management education and social class: Can managers do more to encourage social equality and meritocracy in the workplace?" push us to consider the role of social class as a critical and often ignored responsible management dimension.

Principle 3: Methods

Sunley and Coleman's ideas in "Establishing a foundational learning mind-set for business in the 21st century" (Chapter 3) argue that developing a foundational responsible mind-set starts with an undergraduate student taking personal responsibility for his or her own learning and provide an educational framework for responsible learning as the basic infrastructure for Principle 3. Rimanoczy in her chapter titled "A holistic learning approach for responsible management education" offers a responsible management model called the "sustainability mind-set" that addresses foundational questions proposed by Principle 3: What are the learning methodologies most appropriate to develop responsible managers? Iñesta *et al.* provide an innovative process and environment in their competence-based responsible management module where students work together in multicultural teams via an online learning ePlatform to present social impact solutions to global social challenges. Kelley and Nahser in "Integrating PRME principles in practice through pragmatic inquiry" introduce their integrative, interdisciplinary teaching method "Pragmatic Inquiry" which is rooted in the tradition of American Pragmatism and holds that learning and the discovery process begin with the recognition that there is a challenge or opportunity that is not being met with existing capacities.

Principle 4: Research

Four chapters focus on Principle 4, Research, covering a wide range of levels. Hayes *et al.* (Chapter 2) provide a review of the PRME literature to date including discussion of journal articles, chapters and relevant RME books and textbooks. From Warin and Beddewela (Chapter 15 we learn more about drivers, barriers and enablers to the process of institutionalizing RME into current business school curricula within the UK. Forray *et al.*'s research in Chapter 16 provides descriptive insights to the most common and least common pedagogical practices used in RME classrooms. Lastly, Swamy and Keegan (Chapter 12) conduct a self-study of service-learning expectations and outcomes of a service-learning course in Goa, India.

Principle 5: Partnership

The unique theory–practice model of this book allowed all authors to interact to some extent, and a handful to a large extent, with managers of businesses and organizations. These exchanges have allowed us to extend our pedagogical knowledge with a deeper understanding of their challenges in meeting social and environmental responsibilities. We note the following chapters as ones that mod-elled a deep partnership in developing the ideas for the book where new ideas were developed through conversation and co-authorship. First, Sunley and Coleman in Chapter 3 blended their knowledge to explain the relevance and strategies for increasing personal responsibility for learning. Next, Glaser and Sunley in Chapter 7 "Thinking Conversational Intelligence for sustainable business relationships in an age of digital media", partnered to bring a well-known practitioner communication model into the higher education classroom—thus offering us a practice to [what we're teaching] theory connection. Third, Wagenberg (entrepreneur) and Gutierrez (academic) in Chapter 5 share their reflections on the entrepreneurship class they co-taught with the intent of developing responsible managers and social impact. Lastly, Swamy and Keegan in Chapter 12 bring us their collegial insights and analysis of service-learning in India.

Principle 6: Dialogue

Following again from our fundamental design of academic–practitioner co-authorship each chapter speaks directly to Principle 6. The book's design allows for a variety of dialogue models as described above in the chapter structure. In the introduction section for each chapter the authors explain the different voices and when and where they appear in the chapter. This allows readers to look for these sections. Our dialogue includes perspectives from consultants, managers in small companies, non-profits, social enterprises and large corporations. Despite the range of sectors and organizational size, the perspectives of these managers rein-force the value of seeking dialogue and debate on critical issues related to global social responsibility and sustainability.

Final thoughts

The final chapter provides commentary for the future of responsible management education. First, we begin with a synthesis of the key theoretical traditions seen in the chapters and the implications for management education. Second, we share our insights as editors and authors in light of these themes and the book's intended purpose. Last, we provide implications for action or further research.

A final comment: as part of preparing this book for a global audience we real-ized that there are a variety of different teaching terms that we take for granted in our different higher education contexts. While we have pushed authors to define key practices, we would like to note a few important terms you will see commonly in our book. In Canada and the US learning is often structured into semesters (13–15 weeks) and called a course. In the UK learning can be structured into terms or semesters, with teaching programmes split into different courses or modules.

Those who assist academics with teaching in the North American context are often called teaching assistants (TAs), in the UK context, associate, or hourly paid lecturers can offer additional teaching support. In the European context they are called tutors.

This book testifies to the breadth and diversity that constitute responsible management education in the 21st century. To equip and empower our business leaders of the future, we really do need to educate for critical thinking, ethical behaviour and questioning minds.

References

Beatty, J., Leigh, J., & Lund Dean, K. (2012). Philosophy rediscovered: Exploring the connections between teaching philosophies, educational philosophies, and philosophy. *Journal of Management Education, 33*(1), 99-114.

Levin, K., Cashore, B., Bernstein, S., & Auld, G. (2012). Overcoming the tragedy of super wicked problems: Constraining our future selves to ameliorate global climate change. *Policy Sciences, 45*(2), 123-152. doi: 10.1007/s11077-012-9151-0.

PRME (Principles for Responsible Management Education) (2015). *Inspirational Guide for the Implementation of PRME: UK and Ireland Edition.* Sheffield: Greenleaf Publishing.

Richardson, L. (2016). Louise Richardson: educate students to "prevent next financial crisis". *Times Higher Education.* Retrieved from: https://www.timeshighereducation.com/news/louise-richardson-educate-students-prevent-next-financial-crisis

United Nations (2015). Transforming our world: The 2030 agenda for sustainable development. United Nations Sustainable Development Knowledge Platform. Retrieved from http://www.un.org/ga/search/view_doc.asp?symbol=A/RES/70/1&Lang=E

2

Development of responsible management education and the Principles for Responsible Management Education in context

Ross Hayes, Carole Parkes and Alan Murray
Winchester Business School, University of Winchester, UK

Research into the teaching of subjects broadly relating to ethical issues in business and management has a long history. Over the last three decades, in particular, research output has increased in volume in line with the growing awareness among researchers of political, institutional and societal shortcomings. This awareness focuses, among other things, on the limitations of the planet to sustain compound economic growth forever on the one hand, and on the other the continuing injustices delivered to the vulnerable and powerless by, arguably, the world's most powerful institution—the institution of business.

UNESCO's Education for Sustainable Development (ESD) and its focus on the Decade of ESD (2005–2014) provided an impetus for educational institutions to examine their provision of (especially) teaching in this area, and to raise awareness among senior management, faculty and students of the many complex issues embodied within the concept of sustainable development. At the same time, a growing number of academic journals emerged in the field of corporate responsibility and sustainability and in the area of education for sustainable development, which added to the range and volume of writing in these areas.

The purpose of this chapter is threefold. First, it is to offer insight into the background and rationale of the PRME initiative; second it is to trace the development and progress of PRME worldwide; and third, it is to review the broader responsible management education literature, beginning before the 2007 launch of PRME.

Context: why and how did PRME emerge?

It is worth noting that 2006/2007 marked the end of an era, which began in the late 1980s, of unprecedented growth with low inflation in most Western countries. This was, of course, due to the exceptionally rapid developments of economies in China, particularly, but also in other countries in the developing world, spurred on by the relentless pursuit, by Western companies, of cheaper manufacturing opportunities, matched by the globalization of financial markets and rapid improvements in IT.

By the same time, however, a weight of evidence was also emerging which linked the damage being done to the Earth's biosphere by industrial activity. Whether by UN (UNEP, 2005), academics (Meadows *et al.*, 2004), or NGOs (WWF, 2006), all the evidence pointed to human behaviour as the cause of the problem. Climate change had been studied systematically since the establishment of the United Nations Framework Convention on Climate Change (UNFCCC) at the Rio Summit in 1992 and since then the Intergovernmental Panel on Climate Change (IPCC) has reviewed the evidence every six years or so. In February 2007, on publication of its *4th Assessment Report*, it pronounced that the link between climate change and industrial activity was "unequivocal" (IPCC, 2007).

The United Nations Global Compact (UNGC), seen as a response to some of these perceived global problems facing the world, had been announced in 1999 by Kofi Annan and established a year later. Over the next few years it launched a number of initiatives designed to combat some of the worst social and environmental issues identified (Rasche *et al.*, 2013). The UN Global Compact sought to develop partnerships among a number of agencies, including the private sector, civil society organizations and educational establishments. One of the partner organizations that has taken massive strides in this area since 2007 is the Principles for Responsible Management Education (PRME) initiative. Conceived by the Head of the Global Compact Networks as "Global Corporate Citizenship and Academia: A Global Convergence", the concept paper circulated in 2006 by Manuel Escudero outlined a new vision for schools of business and management to meet the changing demands of the decades to come. The paper highlighted the failure of traditional approaches to be able to prepare graduates to respond to demands for a more responsible way of managing companies. In particular he identified business education as the key to creating responsible managers:

> Business education: the academic sector can play a strategic role as change agents, educating the managers of today and tomorrow, incorporating the values of responsible corporate citizenship into their education activities.

1. The development of a) new teaching materials, b) case studies, c) technical tools, d) capacities, and e) skills for future responsible leaders is crucial for both the long-term mainstreaming of global corporate citizenship in business, as well as for the advancement of responsible business education.

2. The academic sector can train professionals to act as generators of sustainable value both for business and society, willing to endeavor for an inclusive and sustainable global economy.

3. The sector could strive to embed curricula and educational disciplines in universal values of global corporate citizenship: from marketing to financial analysis, from operations to business strategies, from accounting to international analysis, or from microeconomics to legal studies (Escudero, 2006).

Little was Escudero to realize how visionary his observations would be in the years to follow. The "end of an era", of course, occurred when the financial crisis fractured financial systems across the world. Some banks failed, some were taken largely into state ownership, interests rates reached all-time lows, and "austerity" became the byword in liberal economies as public services bore the brunt of budget cuts designed to pay for the cost of saving the banking system. Among those facing blame for the crisis were business schools, which stood accused of perpetuating a flawed focus on growth, profit and greed, seen by many as the root causes of the financial crash.

PRME was seen by the pioneer schools and engaged faculty as the ideal opportunity to challenge colleagues and senior faculty to take a fresh look at how curriculum development is, so often, a term used for rearranging subjects and topics that remain largely unchanged for years. PRME's six point focus offered the opportunity for an examination to be undertaken not just into the curriculum, but also into research topics, the manner in which schools engage with wider society, and to engage with the private sector—a priority on the agenda of the Global Compact.

Establishing PRME: the first steps

Following the circulation of Escudero's letter, a PRME Task Force was convened comprising 60 deans, university presidents and official representatives of leading business schools and academic institutions, charged with developing a set of principles (see page 10) to lay the foundation for a global platform for responsible management education. It was supported by five academic institutions—AACSB International (the Association to Advance Collegiate Schools of Business), EFMD (the European Foundation for Management Development), the Aspen Institute Business and Society Program, EABIS (the European Academy of Business in Society) and GRLI (the Globally Responsible Leadership Initiative)—and the student-led organization, Net Impact.

The Principles were first published at the 2007 UN Global Compact Leaders Summit in Geneva, Switzerland attended by more than 1,000 business, civil society and government leaders. UN Secretary-General Ban Ki-moon set out the potential benefits of the PRME in his closing remarks: "The Principles for Responsible Management Education have the capacity to take the case for universal values and business into classrooms on every continent" (Ban Ki-moon, 2008).

At its inception, the central commitment for any institution participating in the PRME initiative was the regular sharing of information with its stakeholders on the progress made in implementing the six principles through a "Sharing Information on Progress" (SIP) report. The SIP's main objective has been to serve as a public vehicle for information on responsible management education but can also be seen as an effective tool for developing a learning community among signatories (for learning, teaching and research) and facilitating stakeholder dialogue.

Collective activities: working groups and regional chapters

To support the implementation of PRME at individual institutions, there have been a number of collective activities through the development of PRME Working Groups, Regional Chapters and PRME Champions. The Working Groups have focused on particular issues under the PRME agenda and include: Gender Equality, Poverty—a challenge for Management Education, Anticorruption in Curriculum Change, 50+20—Management Education for the World Joint Project, Business for Peace, Sustainable Leadership in an Era of Climate Change, and Sharing Information on Progress (SIP). The Working Groups have been active in publishing reports, books and online resources to support teaching, learning and research in their area of specialism.

The regional PRME Chapters were officially set up at the 3rd Global Forum in 2012 (see below), alongside the Rio+20 Earth Summit, with the aim of rooting PRME within different national, regional, cultural and linguistic contexts, and facilitating the growth and engagement of PRME with respect to implementing the six principles. PRME Chapters develop their own internal arrangements and activities, while committing to: providing a platform for dialogue, learning and action on responsible management and leadership education and research; increasing the visibility of PRME and its signatories in the region; adapting the six principles into the local context; and developing and promoting activities linked to the Principles. There are currently eight established regional PRME Chapters: Brazil, Central & Eastern Europe, DACH (German-speaking countries), Latin America & Caribbean, MENA (Middle East and North Africa), Nordic, North America and UK & Ireland; and six emerging Chapters: Australia/New Zealand, Iberia (Spain & Portugal) and India, plus three PRME Chapters for the Asia region focusing on East Asia (China,

Japan, South Korea), the ASEAN region and South Asia (Pakistan, Bangladesh and Sri Lanka). The Chapters organize meetings, conferences and other events and activities to support the implementation of the Principles in their regions.

Global developments: forums and summits

PRME is the first organized relationship between the United Nations and management-related academic institutions, business schools and universities and since its official launch in 2007, the initiative has grown to around 650 institutions from over 80 countries across the world. Over this time, PRME has held a series of Global Forums and Summits aimed at developing responsible management education in a number of areas. These began in 2008 with the 1st Global Forum for Responsible Management Education (New York) that welcomed 270 participants from 45 countries around the world, consolidated the establishment of the Principles and set out the expectations for the development of PRME.

The 2nd Global Forum in 2010 was held alongside the 10th Anniversary of the Global Compact (New York) and reported that there were now 300 business school signatories to PRME from 62 countries. The First SIP Analysis Report (2008–2010) was presented together with an Inspirational Guide to Implementing PRME in Executive Degree programmes, the establishment of the first Working Group (Poverty as a Challenge to Management Education) and the aspiration of 1,000 signatories by 2015 was set.

In 2011, the PRME Summit (Brussels) explored each of the PRME Principles in turn, with keynote speakers and inputs drawn from the Global Compact business community. Participants used these inputs to reflect on current practice and develop action plans for business schools.

In 2012, the 3rd Global Forum (Rio de Janeiro) took place alongside the Rio+20 Earth Summit and focused on the Contribution of Higher Education and Management Schools to the "Future We Want" agenda. PRME signatories had grown to over 400 and a range of initiatives and outcomes were presented. These included: the 50+20 Management Education for the World, an Anti- Corruption Toolkit for Curriculum Change, the Gender Equality Global Resource Repository, The Fighting Poverty through Management Education: Challenges, Opportunities and Solutions Report; an Analysis of the first 100 SIP Reports; an MBA Global Student Survey; Reports on Leadership and Business Skills in a Rapidly Changing World; and the first *Inspirational Guide to the Implementation of PRME* (a collection of 63 case stories from 47 institutions, representing 25 countries across Asia, Oceania, the Americas, Europe, the Middle East and Africa; PRME, 2012).

By the time of the 2013 PRME Summit, held in Bled, Slovenia, 91 new institutions had become signatories to PRME (since Rio+20), totalling more than 500 active signatories. In order to enhance accountability, the SIP policy of delisting signatories (in line with Global Compact policy) for continued failure to submit their SIP reports was implemented (resulting in 27 signatories being delisted as signatories). A 2nd *Inspirational Guide for the Implementation of PRME* with 27 case stories focusing on inspiration, innovation, implementation and impact was published. The regional PRME Chapters in Asia, Australasia, Latin America, Brazil, UK and Ireland, German-speaking Europe (Switzerland, Austria and Germany), Nordic countries, and the Middle East and North Africa presented reports on their progress, together with reports from the active PRME Working Groups. These included: the PRME Working Groups on Anti-Corruption in Curriculum Change, Gender Equality, Poverty, a Challenge for Management Education, and Sharing Information on Progress (SIP). EFMD and AACSB announced new accreditation standards to embed a focus on social responsibility and sustainable development, to complement changes implemented by CEEMAN (the Central and East European Management Development Association) and AMBA (the Association of MBAs). There was also a Platform for Sustainability Performance in Education, a new partnership of higher education institutions (HEIs) with UN agencies of a comparable reporting and assessment tool for improving sustainable performance in HEIs, plus the launch of a "sustainability literacy test" for assessing the sustainability-related knowledge of students.

Recent developments: PRME champions and the "Network of Networks"

Finally in 2013, PRME launched a two year pilot of the Champions group of 30 experienced and engaged PRME signatories that are committed to working collaboratively to develop and promote activities that address shared barriers to making responsible management education a reality. The PRME Champions group is modelled after the Global Compact's LEAD initiative, which gathers corporate sustainability leaders from all regions and sectors to collaborate on driving change. The Champions group is globally and proportionally representative, according to the makeup of the larger PRME community (i.e. balance of regions and type of academic institution). The PRME Champions group began its first official cycle in January 2016.

In 2015 The Global Forum/6th PRME Assembly (New York) saw an additional 137 new signatories since Bled in September 2013. Jonas Haertle, Head of the PRME Secretariat described PRME as a "Network of Networks", noting that:

> the PRME initiative, now in its eighth year, is a thriving network and a truly global platform for learning and action…[comprising] over 600 institutions in over 80 countries, all of which have heeded our call to "place sustainability at the heart of management education".

The main focus of the Forum was to set out the "path forward for management education and business to take a leading role in shaping and achieving the global sustainable development RME agenda and the SDGs" (Sustainable Development Goals) (PRME, 2015). In terms of the development of PRME, it was noted that 18 PRME Chapter and Regional Meetings have been held (since 2013), the number of regional PRME Chapters now reached 12 around the world and new resources and tools had been launched, such as the Anti-Corruption Toolkit developed by the PRME Working Group on Anti-Corruption in Curriculum Change with the support of the Siemens Integrity Initiative, and the PRME Chapter UK & Ireland region-specific *Inspirational Guide for the Implementation of PRME* (Murray *et al.*, 2014). Also in this time, many collaborative efforts had taken place including the PRME Champions' meeting with the Global Compact Board, the Principles for Responsible Investment (PRI) Advisory Council and ambassadors at UN Headquarters to discuss the historic opportunity that business has to shape and advance the post-2015 development agenda.

At the 2015 PRME Global Forum new PRME work streams were launched on Business for Peace, Business and Human Rights, and Climate Change, Resilience and Environment Protection. The Forum also saw the launch of the AIM2Flourish project, which was initiated at the 2014 Business as an Agent of World Benefit conference. The PRME Advisory Committee—which enables signatory institutions and the different constituencies of PRME to directly influence the strategic direction of the PRME initiative—met, and committed to work together with the PRME Steering Committee to jointly revise the strategy, in light of learnings from the initial eight years of PRME and in an effort to focus the work of PRME for the coming three to five years.[1]

By tracing the lineage of the PRME initiative we can see that, while interest grew slowly, over the past few years there have been a number of exciting developments involving increasing numbers of academics from around the world. Working Groups, initially established to create networks of scholars with similar interests, have utilized these networks to collaborate on a number of books. It is not our intention to review the contents of these books in this chapter; rather, we now turn to the subject of responsible management education (RME) in the widest sense and review some of the literature in this field.

The emergent RME literature

Although publications relating to PRME only emerged some years after the initiative was announced, research into the provision of RME in the form of "ethics-based" courses and programmes has a much longer pedigree. For example, the

---

1 Further information on all aspects of PRME can be found at: www.unprme.org

connection between unethical behaviour in business, especially in relation to corporate failures, drew attention to the role auditors play in overseeing practices designed to avoid such failures. Questions were asked (and still are when such issues occur) about why certain practices or procedures were allowed to continue or why valuations were so drastically wrong when clean audit reports were issued sometimes only a few weeks or months before the scandal hit. The inference was, and is, that auditors, for many reasons, fail to confront corporate boards and decline to sign off on questionable practice. This has led to a number of studies looking at the role of accounting education in this process.

In one study Gray *et al.* (1994) posit connections between higher levels of moral reasoning and "deep" learning; contrasting this notion with the "shallow" learning techniques employed in the accounting programmes of the time (and of the present, many would argue). They suggested that accounting students needed to be exposed to ethical issues in their programmes of study in order to prepare for difficult moral choices likely to challenge them in their future careers. On a similar theme, Sikka *et al.* (2007), in the context of audit failure and fraud, examined accounting textbooks for evidence of engagement, among the various topics of study, in ethical issues or possible dilemmas. From a selection of 43 texts from financial accounting, management accounting and auditing, the authors found a disappointing lack of focus on any critical aspect of accounting, such as the political and institutional structures that resist any notion of change despite any evidence in favour of change.

Fassin (2005, p. 265) lists the major business scandals over recent decades: "fraud", "unfair competition", "unfair communication", "non-respect of agreements", "unfair attitude towards, and treatment of, stakeholders by the abuse of power, [and] in conflicts of interest: personal interest vs stakeholder interests", which have all led to increasing distrust in business and a greater pressure for more transparency, accountability and change of underlying values. Thus, even before the financial crash of 2007/2008 there was disquiet that business education focused too narrowly on management practices designed to maximize returns as the primary aim, making greed the natural consequence, and greed being seen by many as the underlying catalyst for what was to come (Grey, 2002; Pfeffer and Fong, 2002). And after each successive environmental, social or economic scandal there are increasing pressures for business schools and other institutions in higher education to change the values they are imparting to students.

The nature of business school research has also come under scrutiny and the primacy of quantitative research, characterized by the statistical analysis of large data sets, has been challenged. Indeed the paper by Dunne *et al.* (2008) provided an analysis of articles published in "top" journals noting the research questions and methods employed, and highlighting the paucity of research examining contemporary social issues.

Thus, it behoves those of us in schools of business and management to seriously reflect on our own practice and consider the nature of our teaching, at least, as changing the research culture would seem to us to be a much more ambitious and long-term project.

The emergent PRME literature

As a result of the popularity of the PRME and the influence it is starting to have on the actions of business schools, a number of prominent management journals have devoted space to looking at the implementation of the initiative. For instance, the *Journal of Management Education* devoted a special issue looking at Principle 3 (Method) and Principle 4 (Research) (Forray and Leigh, 2012). Such research is useful as it provides much needed guidance as the PRME relies on self-regulation for implementation. As such, much of this research has focused on: models that can be used in different contexts to aid implementation (Dickson *et al.*, 2013), case studies of success stories (Parkes and Blewitt, 2011) and change management literature looking at how to overcome traditional academic barriers to successfully embed the PRME across the six principles. Solitander *et al.* (2012), for instance, look at the barriers to implementing PRME at strategic, structural and cultural levels at business schools in France and Finland. Blasco (2012), focusing on Principle 3, also highlighted barriers to implementation at the curriculum level by arguing for a need to understand the hidden curriculum. Such research is useful because as the PRME (2016) website notes "no one school has yet to successfully demonstrate broad scale implementation". The idea that business schools have experienced resistance and barriers to implementing the PRME initiative highlights a number of issues with implementation.

Beyond these implementation concerns, PRME has faced some criticisms related to institutional adoption of RME and the implicit priorities of the six principles themselves. Regarding the first, Rasche and Gilbert (2015) looked at why the rhetoric of responsible management education does not match the reality. They went on to argue that external stakeholders put pressure on business schools to be seen as responding to their concerns but, at the same time, internal barriers prevent radical change (e.g. academic culture). Therefore, "decoupling" (of public statements and internal actions) can be used in the form of outwardly promoting responsible management education, without the type of commitment needed to make the rhetoric a reality. Similarly, a paper by Louw (2015) argued that a key problem with PRME is that the six principles are incorrectly presented as value-free and uncontested. For example, Louw (2015) takes issue with Principle 5, "Partnership", which is exclusive to corporate (as opposed to other, e.g. worker) interests; thus, for Louw (2015), privileging the same group that caused that recent global financial crisis. Clearly if PRME is to enjoy the type of change its proponents hope, further research needs to address some of these concerns. Regarding the second broad critique, Davis (2015) highlights more fundamental issues with what he calls the "missing" ontology and "hidden" ethics of PRME. In particular, positioning

PRME at an institutional level and adopting a form of "systems thinking" to implementation is seen as problematic.

Finally, in looking forward to the 2015 Sustainable Development Goals (see below), there is a developing, wider agenda for PRME and a developing literature on some of the challenges of moving towards a more inclusive and sustainable world that the goals represent. This includes publications on PRME in relation to some of the most marginalized voices through the inclusion of indigenous peoples (Verbos and Humphries, 2015) and the PRME Working Groups on Poverty and Gender Equality (Gudic *et al.*, 2014, 2015; Flynn *et al.*, 2015).

Insights into the RME pedagogical literature

Solitander *et al.* (2012) consider pedagogy as the method and practice of teaching covering course content and curriculum development. We have already highlighted the criticism of many current programmes for focusing too much on profit maximization, shareholder value, individualism and disregarding the wider role of business in society, a theme further explored in Burchell *et al.* (2015). In addition, it has been argued that traditional management curricula emphasized hard skills (e.g. thinking about management rationally and logically) and ignored softer skills (e.g. empathy for others), which are needed when making ethical decisions and understanding management from a stakeholder perspective (Mintzberg, 2004).

In terms of the dominant teaching approach, the strong focus on a teacher-centred approach whereby teachers attempt to impart their knowledge to students who are seen as containers to be filled with knowledge has been criticized by Pfeffer and Fong (2002, p. 85): "The problem is that when students are relieved of any sense of responsibility for their learning and much involvement in the learning process, the evidence is that they learn much less". This notion is evident in one of the most popular teaching methods: the case study. A number of scholars are critical of this teaching method on the grounds that: it suggests that there is one best way to solve business problems; problems can be solved in a rational and logical manner; the needs of business often come before other social actors and are not problematized; and in many cases students have no knowledge or experience of the problems they are encountering (Bennis and O'Toole, 2005; Contardo and Wensley, 2004; Swiercz and Ross, 2003). It has been argued that the traditional form of management pedagogy has, therefore, led to a situation in which business schools were and are producing "critters with lopsided brains, icy hearts, and shrunken souls" (Leavitt, 1989, p. 39).

Underlying this traditional form of management pedagogy has been a realist ontology, which presents management as a neutral discipline, which can be understood and practised as a natural science, where phenomena to be researched have an objective reality (Grey *et al.*, 1996). In Table 2.1, we outline the "traditional" model, and contrast it with what a "responsible" model might look like.

Table 2.1 **Difference between traditional and responsible forms of management pedagogy**

Source: table created by authors, using material from Canto de Loura (2014), Choo (2007), Ghoshal (2005) and Grey *et al*. (1996).

Area of pedagogy	"Traditional" management pedagogy	"Responsible" management pedagogy
Course content	Textbook learning Key values: profit maximization, individualism, greed is acceptable, competition	Experiential learning Key values: stakeholder view of business, ethical compass, collaboration
Curriculum	Hard skills Teacher-centred Disciplinary Descriptive and prescriptive	Hard and soft skills Student-centred Inter/Intra and multidisciplinary Reflective and reflexive
Teaching methods	Passive	Active
Underlying philosophy	Positivist view of management	Emancipatory/critical view of management
Intended outcome	Focused on improving position of a small number of elites Orthodox	Outcome of education is focused on improving society for all Transformational

This suggests the need for a guiding philosophical stance which recognizes that business and management are not separate from the global challenges confronting humanity today (e.g. poverty, war, climate change), the complexity of global issues and the possibility for business to help with many social issues. Indeed, early adopters of PRME and the RME agenda more widely into management pedagogy have recognized the weaknesses with the traditional pedagogy by suggesting responsible forms of management pedagogy, which include the following:

- Introducing course content—whether through stand-alone courses or more holistically throughout all management programmes—which looks at how management classes might respond to a broader range of sustainable, ethical and social issues. For example, Subrahmanyan and Gomez-Arias (2016) discuss how they attempted to integrate poverty into marketing classes; and Brumagim and Cann (2012) look at how to adapt Maslow's hierarchy of needs for the purposes of teaching sustainable development.

- Starting to build a curriculum which, where possible, is multidisciplinary (e.g. philosophy, geography, psychology, sociology) and includes key "sustainability" concepts such corporate social responsibility (Gardiner and Lacey, 2003; Stubbs, 2013) and the "triple bottom line" (Elkington, 1998; Wu *et al.*, 2010) across all areas of management.

- Including more experiential forms of learning, which have become popular ways of highlighting key sustainable and ethical issues (Baden and Parkes, 2013; Parkes and Blewitt, 2011; Rasche and Escudero, 2009; Sobczak and Mukhi, 2015), focused on providing experiential, transformative, reflexive and active forms of education. Kolb (1984, p. 38) defines experiential learning as "the process whereby knowledge is created through the transformation of experience". Examples of this form of learning include: internships, home-stays, overseas travel and guest speakers (Domask, 2007).

Moving forward: the new agenda for responsible management education

At the PRME Global Forum in 2015, a Transformational Model for PRME implementation was introduced. The model builds on experience accumulated since the launch of PRME and draws on concrete examples from individual PRME schools. It is described as a "strategic journey", in different stages, that evolves over time through a process of continuous improvement. It also acknowledges the complexities and variety of business and management schools. Therefore, the stages of the model are presented as a "living document", created for and by the PRME community and to be reviewed and developed over the coming years.

In 2017, PRME will reach its tenth anniversary and the agenda for responsible management education in the next decade is likely to be dominated by the agreements made at the United Nations in September 2015 when the Sustainable Development Goals were formally adopted.

Sustainable Development Goals

The Sustainable Development Goals (SDGs) replace the Millennium Development Goals (MDGs). Yet, unlike the MDGs, the development of the SDGs has been in partnership with stakeholders that are seen as central to their implementation and this includes educational institutions. In a declaration issued at the conclusion of the 2015 PRME Global Forum for Responsible Management Education, participants not only reaffirmed support for PRME, made commitments to enhance the quality of the PRME initiative individually, institutionally and collectively as a community but also called for governments, business leaders, accrediting bodies, rankings providers and UN system entities to support management educators in their key role in developing future leaders and helping to achieve the SDGs.

Throughout the development of the proposed SDGs, higher education institutions, and management schools in particular, have emerged as one of the core focus areas in discussions on the required architecture for achieving the goals. In her closing statement at the PRME Global Forum, Susana Malcorra, Chef de Cabinet, spoke on behalf of UN Secretary-General Ban Ki-moon, saying: "Today, I am encouraged to see the progress you have made—individually, at your academic institutions, and as a community" and recognizing that "as educators, researchers, and thought leaders, your role [in achieving the SDGs] is essential".

The 17 Sustainable Development Goals (and their associated 169 target areas) cover: poverty, food, health, education, women, water, energy, economy, infrastructure, inequality, habitation, consumption, climate, marine ecosystems, ecosystems, institutions for peace, and sustainable development. Working towards achieving the SDGs provides a range of complex challenges for responsible management education moving forward, not only in curriculum design and pedagogy, building partnerships within and across communities locally and globally but also in radically reimagining the way in which responsible management education is conceived and delivered.

At the time of writing, PRME has just completed a Strategic Review involving many of its key stakeholders. The process of the review aimed to consider what has (or has not) been achieved over the last decade but importantly what needs to be the focus and approach in moving forward with Agenda 2030 and the SDGs. This book argues that in order to inspire and enrich the education of our future leaders, a more holistic education that enables leaders as individuals and/or as business and community leaders to go beyond traditional management boundaries and to understand, think, behave and act in a truly interdisciplinary way is critical.

Bibliography

Baden, D. & Parkes, C. (2013). Experiential learning: Inspiring the business leaders of tomorrow. *Journal of Management Development, 32*(3), 295-308.

Ban Ki-moon (2008). *A Global Initiative, A Global Agenda*, Principles for Responsible Management Education, United Nations Global Compact. Retrieved from www.unprme.org/resource-docs/PRMEBrochureFINALlowres.pdf

Bennis, W. & O'Toole, J. (2005). How business schools lost their way. *Harvard Business Review, 83*, 96-104.

Blasco, M. (2012) Aligning the hidden curriculum of management education with PRME: An inquiry-based framework. *Journal of Management Education, 36*(3), 364-388.

Brumagim, A. L. & Cann, C. W. (2012). A framework for teaching social and environmental sustainability to undergraduate business majors. *Journal of Education for Business, 87*, 303-308.

Burchell, J., Kennedy, S. & Murray, A. (2015). Responsible management education in UK business schools: Critically examining the role of the United Nations Principles for Responsible Management Education as a Driver for Change. *Management Learning, 46*, 479-497.

Canto de Loura, I. (2014). Dilemmas in sustainability: a pedagogical approach to raise awareness on the key role businesses play to practice and promote sustainability. *Journal of Management Development, 33*(6), 594-602.

Choo, K. L. (2007). Can critical management education be critical in a formal higher education setting? *Teaching in Higher Education,* 12, 485-497.

Contardo, I. & Wensley, R. (2004). The Harvard Business School story: avoiding knowledge by being relevant. *Organization,* 11, 211-231.

Davis, P. (2015). *Problematising The United Nations' Principles for Responsible Management Education Initiative: the Challenges of Missing Ontologies and Hidden Ethics.* Retrieved from https://www.academia.edu/8530011/Problematising_The_United_Nations_Principles_for_Responsible_Management_Education_Initiative_the_Challenges_of_Missing_Ontologies_and_Hidden_Ethics

Dickson, M. A., Eckman, M., Loker, S. & Jirousek, C. (2013). A model for sustainability education in support of the PRME. *Journal of Management Development,* 32(3), 309-318.

Domask, J. J. (2007). Achieving goals in higher education: An experiential approach to sustainability studies. *International Journal of Sustainability in Higher Education,* 8, 53-68.

Dunne, S., Harney, S. & Parker, M. (2008). The responsibilities of management intellectuals: A survey. *Organization,* 15, 271-282.

Elkington, J. (1998). *Cannibals with Forks: The Triple Bottom Line of 21st Century Business.* Gabriola Island, BC: New Society Publishers.

Escudero, M. (2006). Global corporate citizenship and academia: A global convergence. Concept paper. New York: United Nations.

Fassin, Y. (2005). The reasons behind non-ethical behaviour in business and entrepreneurship. *Journal of Business Ethics,* 60, 265-279.

Flynn, P., Haynes, K., & Kilgour, M. (2015). *Integrating Gender Equality into Business and Management Education Lessons Learned and Challenges Remaining.* Sheffield: Greenleaf Publishing.

Forray, J. M. & Leigh, J. S. (2012). A primer on the Principles of Responsible Management Education intellectual roots and waves of change. *Journal of Management Education,* 36(3), 295-309.

Gardiner, L. & Lacey, P. (2003). Integrating "business in society" into mainstream business education. *European Business Forum,* 74-76.

Ghoshal, S. (2005). Bad management theories are destroying good management practices. *Academy of Management Learning and Education,* 4, 75-91.

Gray, R. H., Bebbington, J. & McPhail, K. (1994). Teaching ethics and the ethics of teaching: educating for immorality and a possible case for social and environmental accounting education. *Accounting Education,* 3, 51-75.

Grey, C. (2002). What are business schools for? On silence and voice in management education. *Journal of Management Education,* 26, 496-511.

Grey, C., Knights, D. & Wilmott, H. (1996). Is a Critical Pedagogy of Management Possible? In French, R. & Grey, C. (eds.), *Rethinking Management Education.* London: Sage.

Guidic, M., Rosenbloom, A. & Parkes, C. (Eds.) (2014). *Socially Responsive Organizations and the Challenge of Poverty.* Sheffield: Greenleaf Publishing.

Guidic, M., Parkes, C., & Rosenbloom, A. (Eds.) (2015). *Responsible Management Education and The Challenge of Poverty: A Teaching Perspective.* Sheffield: Greenleaf Publishing.

IPCC (2007). *Fourth Assessment Report.* Geneva: WMO/Intergovernmental Panel on Climate Change.

Kolb, D. A. (1984). *Experiential Learning: Experience as the Source of Learning and Development.* Englewood Cliffs, NJ: Prentice-Hall.

Leavitt, H. J. (1989). Educating our MBAs: On teaching what we haven't taught. *California Management Review,* 31.

Louw, J. (2015) "Paradigm Change" or no real change at all? A critical reading of the UN Principles for Responsible Management Education. *Journal of Management Education,* 39(2), 184-208.

Meadows, D., Randers, J. & Meadows, D. (2004). *Limits to Growth: The 30-Year Update.* London: Earthscan.

Mintzberg, H. (2004). *Management not MBAs: A Hard Look at the Soft Practice of Managing and Management Development.* Harlow: FT/Prentice Hall.

Murray, A., Baden, D. Cashian, P., Wersun, A., & Haynes, K. (Eds.) (2014). *Inspirational Guide for the Implementation of PRME* (UK and Ireland ed.). Sheffield: Greenleaf Publishing.

Parkes, C. & Blewitt, J. (2011). "Ignorance was bliss, now I'm not ignorant and that is far more difficult": Transdisciplinary learning and reflexivity in responsible management education. *Journal of Global Responsibility,* 2, 206-221.

Pfeffer, J. & Fong, C. (2002). The end of business schools? Less success than meets the eye. *Academy of Management Education and Learning,* 1(1), 78-95.

PRME (2012). *Inspirational Guide for the Implementation of PRME: Placing Sustainability at the Heart of Management Education.* Leeds: GSE Research.

PRME (2015, June 25). Management education, business and government leaders met at PRME Global Forum to celebrate and reaffirm commitment to sustainable development. Retrieved from http://www.unprme.org/news/index.php?newsid=363#.VwYLROIrLDc

PRME (2016). PRME Champions. Retrieved from http://www.unprme.org/working-groups/champions.php

Rasche, A. & Escudero, M. (2009). Leading change: The role of the Principles for Responsible Management Education. *Journal of Business and Economic Ethics,* 10(2), 244-250.

Rasche, A. & Gilbert, D. U. (2015). Decoupling responsible management education: Why business schools may not walk their talk. *Journal of Management Inquiry,* 24(3), 239-252.

Rasche, A., Waddock, S. & McIntosh, M. (2013). The United Nations Global Compact: Retrospect and prospect. *Business and Society,* 52, 6-30.

Sikka, P., Haslam, C., Kyriacou, O. & Agrizzw, D. (2007). Professionalizing claims and the state of UK professional accounting education: Some evidence. *Accounting Education,* 16, 3-21.

Sobczak, A. & Mukhi, U. (2015). The role of UN Principles for Responsible Management Education in stimulating organizational learning for global responsibility in business schools: An interview with Jonas Haertle. *Journal of Management Inquiry,* 1-7.

Solitander, N., Fougere, M., Sobczak, A. & Herlin, H. (2012). We are the champions: Organizational learning and change for responsible management education. *Journal of Management Education,* 36, 295-309.

Stubbs, W. (2013). Addressing the business-sustainability nexus in postgraduate education. *International Journal of Sustainability in Higher Education,* 14, 25-41.

Subrahmanyan, S. & Gomez-Arias, T. (2016). Responsible management education and the challenge of poverty: A teaching perspective. In Gudic, M. & Parkes, C. (eds.), *Responsible Management Education and the Challenge of Poverty: A Teaching Perspective.* Sheffield: Greenleaf Publishing.

Swiercz, P. M. & Ross, K. T. (2003). Rational, human, political and symbolic text in Harvard Business School case studies: A study of structure and content. *Journal of Management Education,* 27, 407-430.

UNEP (2005). *Millennium Ecosystem Assessment - Living Beyond Our Means - Statement from the Board.* New York: United Nations Foundation.

Verbos, A.K., & Humphries, M.T. (2015). Indigenous wisdom and the PRME: Inclusion or illusion? *Journal of Management Development,* 34(1), 90-100.

Wu, Y.-C. J., Huang, S., Kuo, L. & Wu, W.-H. (2010). Management education for sustainability: A web-based content analysis. *Academy of Management Learning and Education,* 9, 520-531.

WWF (2006). *Living Planet Report 2006.* Gland, Switzerland: WWF International.

3

Establishing a foundational responsible learning mind-set for business in the 21st century

Roz Sunley
Winchester Business School, UK

Michael Coleman
IBM, UK

Introduction

This chapter is premised on the notion that responsible management begins with individuals taking personal responsibility for themselves. Despite many examples of good teaching practice (Palmer and Zajonc, 2010; Colby *et al.*, 2011) there is still a prevailing assumption that education *about* responsible management, with its intrinsic values and ethics, is sufficient to encourage professional responsibility in future business careers. We argue that developing a foundational responsible mind-set starts with an undergraduate student taking personal responsibility for his or her own learning, and seeing responsibility as working from "inside out", rather than being imposed as an "add on" to learning. This chapter discusses an educational framework for responsible learning as the basic infrastructure for Principle 3 of the Principles for Responsible Management Education (PRME), with its focus on effective learning experiences for responsible managers and leaders.

The chapter explores the introduction of a new professional development course for first year undergraduates in a UK business school that aims to challenge the prevailing instrumental approach to management education. The primary voice in the chapter is Roz Sunley from the University of Winchester, and this is complemented with the insights of Michael Coleman, an IBM Learning Manager. He provides a critical commentary on this approach, using notions of "relevance, rigour and life preparation", derived from Hardy and Everett in their book *Shaping the Future of Business Education* (2013). These key terms, "relevance, rigour and life preparation", are integral to business education that is fit for purpose in a rapidly changing world.

Relevance refers to the need for business education to continue to meet the evolving needs of society; this is particularly pertinent as IBM published a report in June 2015 entitled *Pursuit of Relevance: How Higher Education Remains Viable in Today's Dynamic World* (Zaharchuk *et al.*, 2015). Rigour concerns the level of challenge and probity of academic study, what Zajonc (2010) calls a community of inquiry where diverse perspectives are encouraged and debated. Life preparation denotes the ability to manage knowledge, innovation, disruptive technologies and people, as a "more informed and better thinking citizen" (Everett and Page, 2013, p. 2). We argue the complexities of relevance, rigour and life preparation mean there is a need for business leaders with a more multidisciplinary mind-set, who understand themselves as life-long learners, creative problem solvers and good citizens, who can make a difference in the world.

We begin with a short review of some recent discussions about contemporary management and integrative education and the relevance of a foundational responsible mind-set as the cornerstone of responsible management education. The chapter then presents two models. The first is the Relational Model of Learning that illustrates the different dimensions of a student's "learning self", with elements of being, knowing and doing, that influence his or her commitment to learning. The second is the Learning-Engagement model that highlights how students can be encouraged to move from instrumental learning to deeper engagement, which is fundamental to a *foundational responsible learning mind-set*. We continue with the practical challenges of planning, creating and running an innovative course that equips and empowers students to move out of the comfort zone of instrumental learning into more responsible learning in a fusion of social, cultural and academic contexts. We provide student commentary on this creative new addition to management studies, before final consideration is given to the opportunities and challenges of implementing this pedagogical blend.

Review of business management and integrative education

The content and practice of management education continues to be debated as some contend it still fails to address new global realities that require a keener focus on integrative thinking, values and an ability to cope with uncertainty and ambiguity.

The Carnegie Foundation for the Advancement of Teaching published findings from a study of undergraduate business education in 2011 in which they clearly defined two concerns. The first related to the need for students to understand complexity and ambiguity "in managing knowledge and personnel"; the second highlighted the need to "understand and responsibly engage with the challenges that come along with business's growing interdependence with other institutional sectors and realms of society" (Colby *et al.*, 2011, p. 50). However despite this focus on personal responsibility and engagement, Cowden and Singh (2013, p. 57) contend "a commoditized Sat-Nav[1] education system" is becoming increasingly prevalent as instrumental forms of teaching and learning are demanded by heavily indebted students, who want the shortest possible route to accredited outcomes. We contend an instrumental pedagogy offers students little preparation for unexpected challenges in complex business environments, and does little to counter the growing trend of passive learners around the world.

Hardy and Everett (2013) argue for a fusion of practical and theoretical learning by synthesizing what is best in business disciplines with more liberal arts approaches, to provide students with a broader education for life. They argue for multidisciplinary "cognitive dexterity" (p. 6) in courses that embrace "critical thinking, cultural literacy and professional acumen" (p. 5). This strongly supports a curriculum expounded by the American Academy of Arts and Sciences in 2013 as providing "opportunities for integrative thinking and imagination, for creativity and discovery, and for good citizenship". Robinson (2011, p. 166) argues "creativity is essentially human and it holds the constant promise of alternative ways of seeing, of thinking and of doing". From these sources, we see the learning individual in the 21st century faces new challenges that require vision, flexibility, curiosity, an ability to cope with uncertainty, and a willingness to step out of traditional comfort zones.

While business educators reflect on the need for more integrative education, it is also being proposed by key educationalists. Barnet (2007, p. 153) wants education "for the formation of human beings" while Palmer and Zajonc (2010) suggest higher education in the 21st century needs to go beyond a "values curriculum", and embrace a more holistic approach that reflects all the dimensions of what it means to be human; who we are (being), how we know (knowing) and what we do (volition). Like those authors, we argue that wider dimensions of the "learning self" need to be acknowledged and explicitly encouraged as the basis for the development of a foundational responsible mind-set, because this provides the cornerstone for responsible management and leadership.

---

1 "Sat-Nav" is a global positioning system (GPS)

Relational Model of the Learning Self

The Relational Model of the Learning Self derives from a Celtic knot or trefoil that symbolizes the process of human spiritual growth (see Fig. 3.1). It is based on the doctoral research of the academic author (Sunley, 2005), and provides the first part of the pedagogy and praxis for an approach to responsible management education. This approach encompasses the cognitive (knowing), affective and social (being) dimensions of learning, and asks students to step outside the narrow confines of their comfort zone (doing) and embrace their own *lived* experience in new learning contexts. This echoes Zajonc's call for an approach that "recognizes the whole human being and his or her place in community and in the world" (2010, p. 60).

Figure 3.1 **Relational Model of the Learning Self**

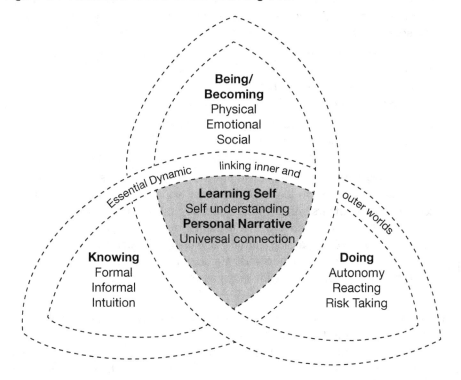

There is no preferred pathway or virtuous loop in this first model, as it is only intended as a reflective mirror to an individual's developing learning and personal narrative. It also offers an interpersonal lens through which to better understand how our connections with others can be based on different elements of the model such as through mutual action or formal learning situations. The Learning Self is never in perfect balance as presented in the theoretical model, as it is constantly being reshaped by forces outside his or her control, and is in a process of continual internal change and transformation. For example, excessive working hours can result in the "doing" section of the model becoming disproportionate and unbalancing an individual's developing personal narrative, because there is little time to nurture the whole person, or stop to reflect on learning that is taking place. Box 3.1 describes the different elements of this relational model.

Box 3.1 **Elements of the Relational Model of the Learning Self**

The model includes four main elements:

Being/Becoming (ontology): The developing physical, emotional and social selves reveal different aspects of the whole person at different times. These are not always clearly visible to the self or others, and are always in the process of "becoming". Learning is an embodied, cognitive, affective and social experience that involves the whole "being" of a person.

Knowing (epistemology): The development of knowledge can be acquired formally, through education, and informally through life experience, alongside an intuitive or instinctive knowledge (Polanyi, 1983) that is also part of a person's developing story.

Doing (volition): Individuals are actors in their own narratives (Freire, 1996) and take responsibility for their own actions. They can react to experience or make autonomous decisions, which can include taking risks.

Essential dynamic: The connecting artery in this model links and vitalizes the whole, while bridging the inner and outer worlds, reflecting a universal connection with others and the world. Just as healthy arteries are essential for a flourishing heart, so too this essential dynamic fuelled by energy, curiosity and positive learning attitude is vital in a developing learner. It is represented by a dotted line to illustrate how an individual impacts on the world and how outside forces influence a person's narrative.

We know theoretical models are not without challenge. Support for this first model can be found in Barnet (2007) who contends individuals have to make an "ontological commitment" (p. 16) to being learners. This goes beyond cognition, and includes "the idea of will" (p. 18). Students demonstrate their "will" in a "surface" or "deep" orientation to their studies and this provides the "foundation of educational energy" (p. 20). In this relational model, energy animates the vitalizing artery that connects the learning self to all the different elements. In Box 3.2 we turn to Michael Coleman's perspectives, which will appear throughout the chapter.

Box 3.2 **Relevance, rigour and life preparation**

Although I am drawing on my experiences as an IBM learning professional, these are my personal reflections.

While learners bear the prime responsibility for their learning mind-set, leaders and curriculum designers also carry a responsibility to provide a supportive learning environment.

Relevance

The model of the Learning Self resonates well with my own experience. I offer colleagues the opportunity to invest time working on something they find personally interesting, without the expectation of any immediate return on this investment. This encourages individuals to engage in an open learning process (doing) with the possibility of new ideas (knowing) by following their own intrinsic interests (being). New insights often lead to answers to problems that arise in the future.

Rigour

Perhaps one of the greatest challenges lies in helping more outcome-focused learners and managers see the relevance and importance of devoting time and energy to pursuing learning for its own sake, without the benefits clear up front. Enquiry-based learning offers opportunities for wider perspectives to be explored and appreciated.

Life preparation

Developing this learning mind-set early on as part of a degree programme will, I believe, produce graduates with a better chance of thriving in a rapidly changing world where they will regularly meet disruptive new ideas and management processes.

At the beginning of the chapter we contested the premise that education *about* responsible management is sufficient to develop future responsible leaders. Instead, we argue that developing the necessary professional skills and mind-set begins with students (who will become future employees and managers) taking personal responsibility for their own learning, and seeing responsibility not as imposed from outside, but emerging from the core of their (responsible) learning selves. This leads to consideration of a second model that illustrates how students can be equipped and empowered to transition their learning selves from instrumental learning to a foundational responsible learning mind-set.

Foundational responsible learning mind-set

Given the many challenges of responsible management, this provides fertile ground for fostering students' wider learning and helping them develop a foundational responsible mind-set as a precursor to responsible leadership. Muff (2012) highlights the importance of "learning attitude" as a factor for business success, and we contend the first step to demonstrating a "learning attitude" and an ability to take responsible ownership in the work place is being able to take responsibility for one's own learning. This requires movement away from didactic teaching environments to those in which students are empowered to experiment and take ownership of their own learning; these are reflected later in this chapter.

Barnet contends "the authentic student is one who 'takes hold' of her educational experience in her own way" (2007, p. 51), or in our terms, develops a foundational responsible learning mind-set. The Learning-Engagement model that follows demonstrates this potential educational journey. Although the model is particularly relevant to first year undergraduates, it also has resonance with adult learners returning to education, whose memory and experience of education may be rooted in less active learning and more didactic teaching methods. This second model reflects the value that writers such as Freire (1996), Palmer (1998), and Gibbs and Coffey (2004) give to active learning, and supports Barnet's contention (2007) about the need for individual "authenticity", which starts with being actively involved and engaged in one's own learning. Barnet calls this "a will to learn"; we term this a responsible learning mind-set.

Figure 3.2 **The Learning-Engagement model**

Source: adapted from Pixton *et al*. (2014).

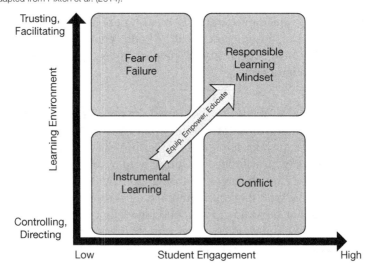

In this second model of Learning-Engagement (see Fig. 3.2), the aim is to equip, empower and engage students to develop confidence in their own abilities as independent and responsible learners. The vertical axis represents the learning environment that ranges from a controlled and directing learning space to a more trusting, facilitative zone. Levels of student engagement are represented along the horizontal axis. This model is relevant to students and teachers in that both are required to move from a comfort zone of experience and practice.

This model provides the pedagogical foundation for a new first year, mandatory academic and professional skills course, created by the academic author, designed to bridge the knowledge and skills gap between secondary and tertiary education. In the description below, the various sections are described and linked to the first Learning Self Model. In Box 3.3 we turn to Michael Coleman's comments on the relevance, rigour and life preparation offered in this second model.

Instrumental learning

High control—teacher/Low engagement—student
With increasing pressures on secondary education to meet national and international educational targets and standards (Cowden and Singh, 2013), many first year undergraduates begin higher education with little self-engagement with learning, as their prior experience has been one of being "taught to the tests" (Mansell *et al.*, 2009). This early experience fails to equip students for the next stage of their learning journey in higher education. Buckley *et al.* (2015) suggest new undergraduates can therefore initially feel unsupported at university as they have little understanding of the demands of independent study or how to self-manage their time.

In this quadrant, students are dependent on teacher direction for what they need to know and do.

Responsible learning mind-set

Low facilitation—teacher/High engagement—student
The shift to a responsible learning mind-set is recognizable by a student's personal engagement with their own learning and the contribution they make to the learning of others. Barnet and Coate (2005, p. 128) suggest engagement "is a relational concept; it indicates an identity…between the student and the act of learning". We argue this can sometimes be as much about attitude as aptitude and attainment. In this learning zone, students have increased self-awareness and are beginning to understand metacognition and self-efficacy as part of a more holistic sense of their own learning narratives.

If this can be achieved, students recognize and value elements of being, knowing and doing as an integral part of their learning selves.

However this learning journey is not without challenge and for some students a fear of failure can limit their openness to a less directive learning space.

Fear of failure

Low facilitation—teacher/Low engagement—student
In a more autonomous and trusting learning space, some students can experience feelings of insecurity and fear of failure. They lack self-efficacy and are unaccustomed to having freedom to choose. They are still waiting to be told what to do (Pixton *et al.*, 2014) and want secure scaffolding to help them embrace new ways of learning. Students may also challenge the need to study anything other than what they perceive as immediately pertinent to their chosen subject discipline (and ultimate employment), given the burden of student debt that now accompanies higher education in the UK (Cowden and Singh, 2013).

This quadrant reflects the challenges facing responsible management learning and the commonplace anxiety that many students experience of being fearful and not knowing what choices to make.

However some students relish new freedoms and delight in being able to pursue their own interests, but this can also sometimes lead to conflict.

Conflict

High control—teacher/High engagement—student
This arises when students want to exercise their new-found confidence in independent learning, but are prevented from developing personal responsibility for their learning by a teacher's restrictive pedagogy and continuing need for control. According to Felman (2001, p. 152), "restrictive pedagogy comes from the belief that we are teaching solely the subject matter, rather than the actual reality that we are teaching human beings". In practice this can lead to student demotivation and frustration.

This quadrant highlights the potential conflict between students becoming more confident in themselves and their engagement with learning, and the limitations of what they can do as a result of continuing teacher direction.

Box 3.3 **The value of a responsible learning mind-set**

Relevance

Like many professionals, the learning content I am responsible for often features terminal tests of understanding. This can be a great way of helping validate what learners have understood about information covered. All too often though the mere presence of an assessment awakens the instrumental learner mind-set, and sets the test up as the goal rather than the learning. I am now beginning to question whether we need to find a new way that helps learners validate the learning, rather than the test becoming the focus of the quest.

Rigour

Moving from the safe harbour of instrumental learning to a responsible learning mind-set requires conscious teaching design and a supportive learning environment. In my work-based experience a key element of such a transition is ensuring regular opportunities for reflection. Building in project time that allows colleagues to periodically pause and reflect on the process, diverse perspectives and their learning, as a community of inquiry, can offer insights that inform the ongoing strategy. This reflection and review can also open up people's willingness to try new things.

Life preparation

In an era of Big Data, business leaders are not short of information, but they may be lacking the mental models and insights needed to ask the right questions to turn data into actionable insights or "knowledge". Early in my IBM career I had the opportunity to shadow a senior manager. I remember how well he was able to process the information he was given, but he also had an impressive ability to notice what he was not being told and ask insightful questions as a result. In hindsight, he modelled a high level of personal engagement and facilitated the learning of others, which are features of a multidisciplinary mind-set and key elements of a responsible learning mind-set.

Adopting a responsible learning mind-set enables students to build a broader perspective and curiosity leading them to more effectively question information that will equip them to make more effective decisions.

Designing the new course

Institutional context

In my UK university, with its growing business school, a new undergraduate business management degree was introduced in 2014 with the explicit aim of integrating critical reasoning, multiple framing and personal reflection (Colby *et al.*, 2011) into the curriculum. An innovative undergraduate first year, second semester course was designed that incorporates liberal arts principles, encouraging students to step outside the narrow confines of management to embrace other disciplines. While these elements might not be out of place in one of the new liberal arts degrees springing up in the UK, this multidisciplinary approach is unusual in British business schools.

Pedagogical context

This 12 week academic and professional skills course builds on more traditional foundational skills such as accessing and referencing academic journals. It was created with the deliberate intention of encouraging students out of their usual instrumental learning comfort zones, to become more confident, independent learners by the end of their first year; that is, with a foundational responsible learning mindset. It was rooted in the premise that valuing the reality of each student's individual learning journey is key to equipping and empowering independent learners.

Brabazon's view echoes a fundamental assumption of the course: "comfortable students are not good scholars. Comfortable students are consumers of learning… downloading information is a distinct experience from being challenged, critiqued unsettled and probed" (Brabazon, 2007, p. 98). It was anticipated this course would generate some learner, and possibly tutor, discomfort, with its explicit aim of challenging students to make more choices and take more responsibility for their learning; with little certainty about outcomes for both tutors or students. This reflects Barnet's contention that "the educational voyages that we wish our students to embark upon are bound to cause ontological discomfort. Far from such discomfort being uncommon however, it is difficult to imagine that it could be avoided" (2007, p. 76).

However, it was important to scaffold learning to minimize fear of failure and any potential for "disassociated learning" (Cowden and Singh, 2013, p. 86) as a result of asking students to "bring mind, body and self into the classroom" and embrace their own lived experiences in new learning contexts.

The chapter will now explore the format, content and student outcomes from this new course, which provides a breadth and depth of challenge to help students start to make explicit connections across business, the humanities and social sciences. It involves intentional creativity, fun, innovation, risk taking, personal engagement, teamwork and serious play to help students move from instrumentalism to a responsible learning mind-set as part of their developing personal narrative.

The rationale for this focus is that as students prepare for a world of relentless change and complexity, higher education needs to equip them with "creative thinking skills, openness to change, flexibility and the ability to cope with challenging tasks" (Barak, 2009, p. 345). Industry leaders, in the IBM Institute for Business Value Education Survey (Zaharchuk *et al.*, 2015), identified "creativity and innovation problem solving capabilities of students", alongside "contribution of students to social enlightenment and cultural development" (p. 7) among the top three measures of the effectiveness of higher education institutions (job placement rates being number one).

We argue that preparation like this better equips students for the range of challenges they will face in the world of work. They begin with opportunities rooted in their own living experience, facilitated within academia, rather than reliance on the lived experience of corporate strangers in more traditional case studies.

The opening words from the course handbook clearly state the challenge being posed:

> Your first year at university gives you opportunities to explore who you are, and review what you already know, while at the same time providing new personal and academic challenges that ask you to step outside your comfort zone (Model 1—Being).

> This module provides a breadth and depth of challenge that may surprise some of you; but has been crafted to enable you to start to make connections across business, the humanities, social sciences, and even the natural sciences (Model 1—Knowing).

> We hope you will embrace the challenge of this module, and enjoy using your creativity and imagination as part of your exciting personal learning journey (Model 1—Doing) (internal intranet document).

Format of the course

While formal learning outcomes are outlined in the course handbook, students are advised these will be met through a variety of different weekly creative, playful and innovative formative activities, with a final reflective summative assessment. The course lists what appear to be normative learning outcomes, but these resonate with different elements of the Learning Self Model, and are subject to innovative and distinctive professional interpretation, influenced by the underpinning teaching philosophy that requires students to move out of their comfort zone (see Table 3.1). The explicit aim of this course is to equip and empower students to move from instrumental to more personally engaged learning within a traditional academic structure.

Table 3.1 **Links between learning objectives and the learning self**

Learning objectives: what the course requires students to do	Learning self: what students can do/want to do as a result of engaging with the course
Review and assess progress in relation to personal, academic and professional development	Develop a personal narrative/self-understanding in terms of who I am/becoming, what I know and what I do
Analyse key arguments and theory in research articles	Evidence formal knowing and doing
Demonstrate ability to communicate coherent ideas orally and in writing, and build skills of reflective practice	Demonstrate being, knowing and doing in relationship to others
Assess factors that contribute to the development of effective time management	Consider externalities that influence self-management in terms of being and doing

From the outset, students are introduced to a model of learning (Blakeley, 2007) that highlights the need to move out of their comfort zone in order to construct new ways of being, knowing and doing that will help them better cope with complexity and change.

Although the course is programmed as a weekly one-hour lecture for all students and two-hour seminar in groups of approximately 25, there are no formal lectures. The lecture space has been renamed "9 to 10" as each session starts at 9 a.m. and there is a different topic and delivery style each week. Some weeks require more than one course tutor to orchestrate the session, and usually students are invited to participate. Tutors are responsible for lectures and individual classroom sessions—four academic tutors were involved in this course.

Weekly two-hour seminars are very interactive, and require students to actively engage in a range of activities. Given the non-traditional teaching format and content of this course, tutors are given three pieces of guidance:

- Classrooms can generate learning energy that needs to be harnessed, rather than artificially restricted and directed towards predetermined outcomes.

- There are many emergent learning pathways to the same outcomes.

- Use your professional discernment and "go with the flow" when a creative learning spirit is evidenced.

Participants

There were 184 undergraduates on this first year course in spring 2015, with students working in nine seminar groups; led by four different academic staff.

Summative assessment

- 90% of marks awarded for completion of a reflective portfolio
- 10% of marks awarded for active participation and contribution to learning (1% evidenced each week)

The requirement for active participation is not just turning up for class, but engagement with learning materials, tutors and other students. Students therefore make personal decisions about their commitment to their learning and that of others. Authorized absences are allowed, but generally feeling a little unwell or sleeping through the alarm clock are not sufficient reasons for non-attendance. However tutors take into account any learning support issues that might affect a student's ability to contribute to class activities.

Course activities

Over the 12 weeks of the course students undertake five core activities: creative group work, peer-to-peer coaching, personal reading, civic engagement and academic research as vehicles for helping movement away from instrumental learning to a more foundational responsible learning mind-set. The academic research activity involves more standard independent study that provides some academic security for students at the outset.

Each of these elements is recorded and reflected upon in the final summative portfolio. These different exercises are explicitly designed to delegate control and encourage a more trusting learning environment in which individuals take increasing responsibility for their progress. They ask students to think about who they are/becoming (as in Model 1), and how they can turn innovative learning experiences into new patterns of personal behaviour as part of their developing learning narratives.

Student reflections on four of these five core elements are offered in the next sections, alongside general comments about the course.

1. Creative group task, weeks 1–3 (focus on being and doing— elements of Model 1)

Learning objectives: personal development, communication skills
A deliberately abstract creative group work task was undertaken and completed in the first three weeks, in order to challenge ongoing dependence on detailed instructions and to encourage students to take risks with their learning. In small groups of three or four, students demonstrated, through the use of an allocated resource, their group's interpretation of learning. Students were free to interpret the task in any way they chose, but they had to justify their interpretation and each demonstration needed to illustrate creativity, innovation and serious playfulness. The explicit invitation to playfulness reflects one of the core ideas behind Lego®

Serious Play® which encourages "creativity, exuberance and inspiration to play to the serious concerns of adults in the business world" (Trivium, 2013, p. 7).

How the task was undertaken

By the end of the first two-hour seminar, each group was required to submit a creative bid to use one of the following resources over the next two weeks, as the basis for a group task of their interpretation of learning. Given the time limitations on this bid process, they used any resources they could find on the day: for example, paper, mobile phones, cardboard boxes, themselves. The six resources for which students were bidding comprised:

- Lego bricks
- Technology—video, blog, etc.
- Textiles and bric-a-brac
- Modelling clay
- Books
- Role play

They also had to offer a contingency choice in case of an unsuccessful bid. Group bids included short films, a reading box and creative use of origami.

The results of these bids were announced in week 2, and students then allowed class time, with their chosen or contingency resource, to prepare for their group demonstration that took place in week 3. Each individual resource was only available to one group in each class. Demonstrations on their interpretations of learning ranged from short films, puppetry and textured models, to book sculpture and classroom dramas.

Student responses

This introductory task was greeted with anxiety and disbelief for some at the outset, with students questioning its relevance to business management, echoing research by Reynolds *et al.* (2013) and clearly linked to a fear of failure. One student commented, "creative freedom is not usually given during education, therefore when we are given freedom we tend to be apprehensive". This highlights the tension between new academic freedom and the difficulty of transitioning out of an instrumental learning space.

Some students remained risk averse, perhaps modelling their own learning experience, and chose to use technology to present their ideas, rather than using the actual physical resource. For others, after some initial hesitation, they embraced the opportunity to explore creativity and playfulness: "I didn't really think university wanted us to think creatively...so this was a refreshing week to be told that actually they want us to think outside the box". One student recognized the affective nature of learning when she commented, "At first I was somewhat sceptical about the benefits of creative learning, however, after seeing, or more accurately, feeling connections and applying my learning...I am no longer sceptical".

This task reflected the emotional discomfort (being) of trying to understand a new approach to learning (knowing) and responding to a new challenge (doing). In terms of the Learning-Engagement Model, students were trusted to engage in an independently interpreted task—key elements in developing a foundational responsible learning mind-set. Despite the initial discomfort of this first creative task, it provided opportunity for students to make new connections between ideas and action, which is echoed in the demands of responsible management that requires constant adaptation and strategic innovation. IBM's report on higher education stresses the need for today's academic model to adapt and evolve to meet the changing needs of a global workforce (Zaharchuk *et al.*, 2015).

2. Peer-to-peer coaching, weeks 2, 4, 6 and 8 (focus on being, knowing and doing—elements of Model 1)

Learning objectives: personal, professional and academic development, reflective practice, time management, communication skills

Another element of encouraging students to take responsibility for their own learning, and that of others, was to introduce peer-to-peer coaching (P2P) in class. Students worked in self-selected pairs or triads and coached each other on issues emerging from seven dimensions of learning: planning, processing, embracing change, perspective, self-disclosure, trust of self and trust of others (Walker, 2015). As preparation for this exercise, students read about coaching, watched coaching skills being demonstrated in a "9to10" space, and used exemplar coaching questions to begin each session.

Initially this exercise was met with reluctance, discomfort and some amusement, but as the weeks progressed, several students, many of whom lacked self-confidence, discovered the merits of this approach to self-development. Not only did coaching impact on learning in the course, but influenced wider learning:

> The P2P coaching was something I was not overly keen on as I am not very confident and struggle to share my ideas...after reflecting on my actions I am able to see a large improvement as I moved out of my comfort zone, and made sure my ideas were put forward.

> P2P coaching in semester 2 has been the highlight of my first year...I am now looking forward to the second year hoping I can transfer the skills I have learnt with international students who might find the transition hard.

Opportunities to self-reflect and work outside expected patterns of learning are key to helping students move from instrumental learning to a more foundational responsible learning mind-set. We suggest, based on research, classroom experience and work observation, that reflection is a precursor to being able to demonstrate courage in embracing change and uncertainty in the workplace; it also helps develop self-understanding that is central to the Learning Self.

3. Civic engagement (focus on being and doing—elements of Model 1)

Learning objectives: personal and professional development, communication skills, time management

In the UK context of this task, students were required to choose an activity in which they could either be a spectator (e.g. visiting an historic place, local homeless shelter) or become an actor in society (e.g. volunteering to help out at community events; Freire, 1996). The impetus to require students to undertake some form of civic engagement as part of academic study was informed by two factors:

- Responsible business takes regard of the social, cultural, political, economic and environmental context in which it operates. IBM's 2015 report argues that civic engagement is an element of creating and nurturing effective ecosystems of enterprises, institutions and individuals (Zaharchuk *et al.*, 2015).

- Earlier research with first year students highlighted the limited environment in which some students choose to live; echoed in student comments such as:

   I think being at university makes you be less part of the world in a sense because being on campus you always encounter the same people, and so you see the world a different way. You're not a part of it.

   I think we all still live in a bubble...I live here, things are here, lectures are here and I don't go down to town that much because we get shopping in. So literally this is my life.

Students were therefore required to take part in some self-selected activity—either individually, or in groups of no more than three. Activities were confined to the environs of the university or city in order to encourage an experiential understanding of social and cultural capital. The city offers many free events in the cathedral, library, military museums, local charities and community events. Attendance at university sports clubs was not admissible to ensure as many students as possible worked out of their comfort zones.

They were required to complete an observation form, which included a "selfie", as evidence of participation. Photos of all the different forms of civic engagement were included in a student showcase in a "9to10" session, and students were invited to share their experiences. " I decided to take a risk and volunteer to go up and speak in front" (international student).

During the "9to10" session students were introduced to Freire's concepts of being actors or spectators in society (1996). Together they concluded most had chosen to be spectators, but some evidenced real participation in university or community events. For a few, their chosen experience proved to be truly transformative:

> Freire spoke about becoming an actor in society as opposed to a spectator which, accordingly, is what I became. I felt honoured and rewarded in actually being part of an organization that I will continue to work with, as a result of the opportunity offered through the civic engagement task.

Once again, this task provided students with choices that allowed them to demonstrate different levels of curiosity and engagement. Peer review of these experiences led some to later reflect on their own lack of real engagement, in choosing to spectate rather than actively taking part in community. Increased curiosity and understanding of wider society is an important element of stakeholder management and at the core of the essential dynamic that animates the Learning Self.

4. Personal reading choices (focus on being and knowing — elements of Model 1)

Learning objectives: personal and academic development, reflective practice, communication skills, analysis of academic articles

We need to help students develop critical reading skills, yet we know that as mobile devices take centre stage in the lives of young adults, with computer games, video streaming and social media competing for time and attention, students are beginning to show increasing reluctance to read (Brabazon, 2007; Turkle, 2011; Atlas, 2015). Brabazon suggests that while recommended textbooks, reading lists and hard copy resources are still offered, online sources are preferred, with the result "clicking replaces thinking" (p. 16). To counter this seeming pedagogical impasse, the course required everyone to choose two books to read during the 12 weeks. No limits were put on the selections (i.e. classic fiction, autobiography, motorbike maintenance manuals, etc.) and there were two class opportunities to share choices and learning from this activity, plus the chance to debate their views about the actual requirement for wider reading.

Once again, many responded to this task with initial unwillingness and resentment, arguing they did they have time for, or see the relevance of, additional reading. Many suggested compulsory reading in secondary education had extinguished any personal pleasure in books. However this simple exercise proved to be one of the most transformative activities for many, as readers became connected with themselves and their learning, reflecting Michael's earlier observation of the benefits of engaging in a task for its own sake, rather than for some extrinsic reward.

> I found myself thinking more broadly about my own life. After putting the book down, it had refocused me on my own journey at university.

> I now recognize that the challenge is not reading during the semester, but conversely it is my flawed perception of when books are to be read, and my inability to effectively manage time and self.

This exercise provided many students with an opportunity to re-evaluate their view on reading, and reinforced for some the importance of their own values that were reflected in their choices. Asking students to take personal responsibility for their own reading selections made it more difficult for them to "give up" on the task; and their later reflections illustrate the tension between reading and other competing demands on their time. This task connected all the elements of the Learning Self Model in that, for some students, their personal narrative was revised in the light of how they felt (being), what they learned from their selections (knowing) and how it changed their behaviour (doing). In terms of the Learning-Engagement Model, this task was based on trust and demanded high student engagement—both key factors in developing a foundational responsible learning mind-set.

Student experiences

End of course student feedback was obtained in three formats:

- An online course evaluation (university requirement)
- In-class self-evaluations (optional)
- Summative reflections (assessment)

Online evaluation

The format and content of this course met with initial opposition from many students who did not understand its immediate relevance to their short-term educational demands and needs that were still rooted in instrumental learning. Barnet's "ontological discomfort" was reflected at the end of 12 weeks as some students remained unconvinced with online comments including: "didn't see the relevance to my course", "unrelated to business management course" and "unable to see how the course is academic and will benefit my future career".

Self-evaluations

In contrast, those who completed end of course self-evaluations in class, illustrate how positive learning outcomes can still be achieved "out of the comfort zone". Of these 71% agreed they were now able to identify and overcome barriers to success in their academic work that they were previously unaware of; 74% agreed they were now able to identify and work on barriers to success in their future career. In terms of the development of new skills leading to changes in behaviour, self-management and better use of time were mentioned as key learning outcomes for many. This evidences progress against the learning objective relating to more effective time management.

Summative reflections

However wider learning outcomes can be very personal experiences as illustrated by the following comments from students' reflective work, which evidence progress towards a foundational responsible learning mind-set:

although I was quite sceptical and confused...the module has helped me transform from a school student into a university student, and has given me the confidence to push myself...to become an all-round better learner [improved metacognition as part of a responsible learning mind-set].

I liked...the opportunity to manage and organize our own learning during this module [self-efficacy is a key element of a responsible learning mind-set].

I discovered you can learn from everything around you, and since then I have taken much more time to learn about my surroundings [self-equipped and empowered to recognize wider learning opportunities as part of a responsible learning mind-set].

The tyranny of end of course evaluations can sometimes blind deeper insights into real learning outcomes. Hindsight suggests that student discomfort is paradoxically evidence of impact and success, as if students remained passive about their learning experiences, this would argue for little movement out of the comfort zone. Having no opinion would itself suggest they did not care, or had not engaged with their learning, but triangulated feedback illustrates students recognize learning has often taken place, even through discomfort: "after reflecting on my actions I am able to see a large improvement as I moved out of my comfort zone". In Box 3.4 we turn to Michael Coleman's perspectives on professional learning.

Box 3.4 **Preparation for complex learning environments**

Relevance

The world of learning is changing as MOOCs (massive open online courses), blogs, video sharing sites, etc. all provide new, rich sources of learning. Successful learners need to develop the ability to select and engage with diverse educational sources. Providing students with the learning experience detailed here will better equip them to thrive in this increasingly complex learning environment.

Rigour

Moving students beyond the instrumental learning style with which they are familiar can make them unsettled and most likely less satisfied, at least in the short term, with their learning. Student evaluations may offer negative feedback as their preconceptions about learning have been challenged. Any organization introducing change in their own professional learning needs to acknowledge that happiness scores can temporarily go down, and this is not necessarily a bad thing.

Life preparation

With the increasing use of online content and ever more sophisticated personalization there is a significant risk that we will live our lives in "echo chambers" forever being fed content that meets our own preconceptions and prejudices. "You liked this so you'll probably like that" can be very helpful, but it does nothing to promote a breadth of insight, awareness or understanding. In an age where I can leap directly to the article I want to read, no longer having to flick past other content, there is less chance that I might alight on something different. In this context, nurturing a broad perspective will increasingly need to be a conscious act, and one that a responsible learning mind-set supports.

Broader implications

Introducing any new course into an already overcrowded curriculum requires an encouraging school ethos, departmental negotiation and individual determination. The experience of devising and implementing this new course was not without its own particular challenges. Although researching and devising different elements took 12 months, collection and division of resources such as Lego and textiles for nine different teaching groups took additional time and energy, as did regular updates with my fellow tutors as the course began to unfold.

However, the greatest challenge was implementing these new ideas with colleagues and students, and facilitating learning "out of the comfort zone" that required competences in managing ambiguity, emotional intelligence and embracing uncertainty. Teaching staff must be ready to embrace the same challenges as students, but not everyone likes "teaching on the edge", particularly when students are reacting against a changing learning environment.

Implications for educational practice

In this section we discuss implications for practice arising from our learning from this experience using the key models framing the approach. Ultimately it has been a very rewarding, often inspirational, experience, but the following factors need consideration.

Content

A common pedagogical vision of the value of a "responsible learning mind-set" needs to be shared among all teachers (i.e. *relevance*). In contrast to more traditional courses, the content is less about specific knowledge and "knowing" and more focused on elements of "being" and "doing" that together make up the *Learning Self.*

Students need a clear explanation of the objectives and methods used on this course, and the educational rationale behind each activity to minimize their fear of failure and any "defensive disassociation" discussed earlier (i.e. *relevance* and *rigour*).

Delivery

As learning is specifically designed to take students out of their comfort zones, this includes deliberately changing the teaching space from high control to a more facilitative environment. Teachers need to be prepared for negative emotions and behaviours arising from change and uncertainty (i.e. *life preparation*). This requires a supportive teaching team with a commitment to the course.

Assessment

Understanding that the learning journey is as important as the final summative assessment is key to this approach. This journey encompasses both students and teachers, and can be difficult. Emergent learning outcomes need to be appreciated and celebrated as much as predetermined ones (i.e. *relevance of learning*) that requires teachers to value their professional judgement as well as metrics. The unexpected value and relevance that students assigned to participating in the reading exercise demonstrates the additional learning that can emerge in a trusting learning space.

End of term student evaluations may be mixed, but what matters is students evidencing personal change in being, knowing and doing as a springboard for learning for life (i.e. *relevance, rigour* and *life preparation*).

Wider application

We believe encouraging students to develop a fusion of responsible learning within a subject discipline can be integrated into other degree courses. Notions of relevance, rigour and life preparation are an essential element of any learning in higher education and therefore part of a student's personal narrative and learning self. Developing a responsible learning mind-set empowers learners across all disciplines to become more engaged with their learning and themselves.

Growing interdependence in society means that every discipline impacts on our world, and therefore Principle 3 of PRME about effective learning experiences for responsible leadership embraces all sectors and organizations. Learning that taking personal responsibility is not an "add on" to content, but works from the "inside out", meaning we need responsible mind-sets regardless of subject area.

Challenges

The challenge is to move faculty members beyond the narrower confines of traditional subject knowledge to embrace a more holistic approach to learning and teaching in the 21st century. We acknowledge this is difficult in a culture that favours and rewards measurable research output and impact over more intangible student learning.

However we need to model that which we ask of our students, be willing to take risks, step outside our own comfort zones and above all remain curious about how we keep our teaching relevant in a changing world.

In this chapter we have argued that responsible management education needs to be underpinned by a responsible learning mind-set that embraces the "learning self" of the student. The learning journey to this mind-set is not without challenge and discomfort, but pedagogy that engages and empowers students to take responsibility for their own learning better equips them as responsible managers of the future. They are prepared, with relevant skills and life preparation, to address the complexities of our dynamic world.

References

American Academy of Arts and Sciences (2013). *The Heart of the Matter: The Humanities and Social Sciences for a Vibrant, Competitive and Secure Nation.* Cambridge, MA: American Academy of Arts and Sciences.

Atlas, J.L. (2015). The need to read. In G.M. Hardy & D. L. Everett (Eds.), *Shaping the Future of Business Education.* London: Palgrave Macmillan.

Barak, M. (2009). Idea focusing versus idea generating: A course for teachers on inventive problem solving. *Innovation in Education and Teaching International*, 46(4), 345-356.

Barnet, R. (2007). *A Will to Learn: Being a Student in an Age of Uncertainty.* Maidenhead: Open University Press.

Barnet, R. & Coate, K. (2005). *Engaging the Curriculum in Higher Education.* Maidenhead: Open University Press.

Blakeley, K. (2007). *Leadership Blind Spots, and What to do About Them.* Chichester: Jossey Bass.

Brabazon, T. (2007). *The University of Google.* Aldershot: Ashgate Publishing Ltd.

Buckley, A., Soilemetzidis, I. & Hillman, N. (2015). *HEPI-HEA Student Academic Experience Survey.* York: Higher Education Academy & Higher Education Policy Institute.

Colby, A., Ehrlich, T., Sullivan, W. M. & Dolle, J.R. (2011). *Rethinking Undergraduate Business Education: Liberal Learning for the Profession.* San Francisco: Jossey Bass.

Cowden, S. & Singh, G. (2013). *Acts of Knowing: Critical Pedagogy, In, Against and Beyond the University.* London: Bloomsbury Academic.

Everett, D.L. & Page, M.J. (2013). The crucial educational fusion: Relevance, rigor and life preparation in a changing world. In G.M. Hardy & D.L. Everett (Eds.), *Shaping the Future of Business Education: Relevance, Rigor and Life Preparation.* New York: Palgrave Macmillan.

Felman, J. L. (2001). *Never a Dull Moment: Teaching and the Art of Performance.* Routledge: London.

Freire, P. (1996). *Pedagogy of the Oppressed.* London: Penguin Books.

Gibbs, G. & Coffey, M. (2004). The impact of training of university teachers on their teaching skills, their approach to teaching and the approach to learning of their students. *Active Learning in Higher Education,* 5(1), 87-100.

Hardy, G. M. & Everett, D.L. (2013). *Shaping the Future of Business Education: Relevance, Rigor and Life Preparation.* New York: Palgrave Macmillan.

Mansell, W., James, M. & the Assessment Reform Group (2009). *Assessment in Schools. Fit for Purpose? A Commentary by the Teaching and Learning Research Programme.* London: Economic and Social Research Council, Teaching and Learning Research Programme.

Muff, K. (2012). Are business schools doing their job? *Journal of Management Development,* 32(7), 642-662.

Palmer, P. (1998). *The Courage to Teach.* New York: Jossey Bass.

Palmer, P. J. & Zajonc, A. (2010). *The Heart of Higher Education: A Call to Renewal – Transforming the Academy through Collegial Conversations.* San Francisco: Jossey Bass.

Pixton, P., Gibson, P. & Nickolaisen, N. (2014). *The Agile Culture.* New Jersey: Pearson Educational, Inc.

Polanyi, M. (1983). *The Tacit Dimension.* Gloucester, MA: Doubleday & Co, Inc.

Reynolds, C., Stevens, D.D. & West, E. (2013). "I'm in a professional school! Why are you making me do this?" A cross-disciplinary study of the use of creative classroom projects on student learning. *College Teaching,* 61, 51-59.

Robinson, K. (2011). *Out of Our Minds: Learning to be Creative.* Chichester: Capstone Publishing Ltd.

Sunley, R. (2005). Realising the spiritual dimension in secondary education: Listening to the voice of secondary teachers. Unpublished PhD thesis, University of Bristol.

Trivium (2013). *Facilitator's Manual: Designing and Facilitating Workshops with the Lego® Serious Play® Method.* Copenhagen: Trivium.

Turkle, S. (2011). *Alone Together.* New York: Perseus Book Group.

Walker, S. (2015). Navigating the world by heuristic bias, in submission. Retrieved from http://simonpwalker.com/research-publications/4587873262

Zaharchuk, D., Marshall, A. & King, M. (2015). *Pursuit of Relevance: How Higher Education Remains Viable in Today's Dynamic World,* IBM Institute. Retrieved from http://www-935.ibm.com/services/us/gbs/thoughtleadership/pursuitofrelevance/

Zajonc, A. (2010). Attending to interconnection, living the lesson. In P.J Palmer & A. Zajonc (Eds.), *The Heart of Education: A Call to Renewal.* San Francisco: Jossey Bass.

4
Choosing food yet consuming plastic
Learning to notice the difference in management education

Maria Humphries, Anna Casey-Cox and Kahu Dey
Waikato Management School, University of Waikato, New Zealand

Introduction

In *Management Education for the World,* Muff *et al.* (2013) posit that many societies are stretched to the point of fracture and that management education is out of
step with the scale and nature of the challenges humanity must face (p. xxiii). Their
book is generated from a coming together in the 50+20 initiative of the Globally
Responsible Leadership Initiative (GRLI) and the World Business School Council
for Sustainable Business (WBSCSB). The Principles for Responsible Management
Education (PRME) was seen to be "a natural third partner" (p. xvii) to develop new
ways and opportunities to recast management education into a form that "does
not aim to be the best in the world, but the best *for* the world" (p. xxii). They call for
nothing less than the "metamorphosis of business organizations from maximis-
ing short-term profit to becoming servants of society" (p. xvii) and for an education that prepares a leadership for this mandate. Drawing on a US National Survey
of Student Engagement, Muff *et al.* (2013) report that business majors "display a
lower capacity for caring about a world beyond themselves, and are less likely to
contribute to the greater good of society" (p. 47). Accordingly they call for a radical
transformation of management and leadership education that entails the development of reflective awareness that is "defined by an evolved level of consciousness and personal awareness, clarity, focus and commitment on a personal and

organizational level, deep values and ethics, humility and humanity, empathy and resonance with others…" (p. 35).

In their call for a re-visioned management education, Muff *et al.* (2013) are mindful of the risk of inappropriate imposition of Western values through this aspiration for greater global influence. They propose to bridge an embedded East–West divide in thinking and call for attentiveness to the universal common good. They urge a move away from narrow functionalist theories and amoral reasoning still typical in much management education towards a respect for complexity in considerations of production and consumption with an ethics of responsibility as guidance. They insist on a greater awareness and respect for distinctive cultural values and press for nothing less than a re-visioning of our identities as individuals and communities. They call for a reframing of the human relationship with Earth.

We respond to the call by Muff *et al.* (2013) for a reframing of the human relationship with Earth by paying greater attention to indigenous ways of being and the subtle ways this attention enriches our work. Our example comes from Aotearoa, a country also known as New Zealand, where Maaori are the indigenous peoples. Maaori have been staunch in their resistance to European colonization and today take leadership in the United Nations with regard to the Declaration of the Rights of Indigenous Peoples (United Nations, 2007) and the implications of this on all aspects of the UN's mandate. We include these implications in our response to Muff *et al.* to make ourselves more visible in our writing as "whole people". As authors of this chapter, each of us engages to some extent in the work of endorsing indigenous sovereignty. We do so, however, as women not brought up under the watchful eye of specific indigenous elders—though Kahu has strong biological ties and social awareness of being Maaori. Anna has placed herself under the guidance of a widely respected Maaori leader. Maria has 30 years of experience in working locally in community organizations and in management education to raise an alert to the system-preserving consequences of "diversity management" under the imposition of a Western value-laden regime (Humphries and Grice, 1995). She is drawn to the potential of greater indigenous influence to change this form of structural racism (Verbos and Humphries, 2012, 2014, 2015 a, b; Came and Humphries, 2014). We offer our voices as academics, as practitioners and as people connected in a living relationship with Earth. We do this in three ways. We:

- Make ourselves visible as mothers, teachers and daughters of Mother Earth, as authors attentive to the calls of indigenous peoples, and as teachers invigorated by the scope of the Principles for Responsible Management Education (PRME)

- Demonstrate our response to calls by indigenous people to see ourselves more holistically and as integrally woven into the web of life and in so doing, to accept a responsibility for our human relationship with Mother Earth

- Apply our concerns with universal human and planetary wellbeing to an embodied, experiential and co-learning exercise that connects management education to everyday life.

We seek to illustrate aspects of the call by Muff *et al.* (2013) to more self-reflection, a noticing of the possibilities for humanization of relationships in organizational formats, attention to spiritual matters, a reanimation of Earth, and a commitment to forms of relational ethics that are encouraged in practitioners committed to PRME. With Dyer *et al.* (2014) we are concerned about traditions and systems often mired in an industrial model of dehumanized production and consumption directed to serve economic or organizational growth above all else. We draw on Judi Marshall's (1999, 2001) notion of "living life as enquiry" and her rejection of the artificial boundaries we are often asked to uphold in our professional identities (as scholars and as practitioners) and in our wider life responsibilities and commitments. We are exploring in our personal practices the ways we might inspire our students to join us. We start where we are: teachers, parents and consumers.

Following Freire (1992) and Marshall (2011) we seek to contribute to calls to enhance human consciousness and conscience through our expression of a holistic andragogy. We are actively looking for organizational understandings that underpin the flourishing of life. We advocate for a broadened palate of theoretical orientations and we introduce Radical Human Ecology as one such orientation. We encourage what critical theorists call praxis. In our teaching we use everyday examples that allow us to confluence our various commitments into one exercise. For example, for this chapter we take as our starting point the complex connection of oil extraction to the lives of many indigenous people. As oil is a critical ingredient in the production of plastic, we invite a deep reflection beyond a simple cost–benefit analysis of the specific exploitation of indigenous land in the search for oil, to a focus on their leadership as caretakers of Earth.

Our introductions below demonstrate an accessible way to include ideas from indigenous peoples that call us to an integrated sense of self and other. In this simple enhancement of how we present ourselves to and through others, the indigenous theme of connectedness is subtly embodied. We then outline our chosen focus on PRME, particularly Principle 3. We give close consideration to the call by Muff *et al.* (2013) for the PRME to be an opportunity to *create educational frameworks, materials, processes and environments that enable effective learning experiences for responsible leadership* for "a world worth living in" (p. 3). We respond to this call as a practitioner guide to our profession as teachers for a "world worth working for". We present an exercise to invite noticing and countering the excessive use of plastic in the wrapping of produce on sale in supermarkets. The exercise can be adapted for an "in class" activity by inviting students to list all examples of plastics in "eyes-reach" that could be replaced by more environmentally sustainable alternatives. In reflecting on the normalization of plastic in wrappings and elsewhere, we invite a deep reflection on the supply chain all the way from the extraction of oil to the disposal of the ships and containers that carry the plastics and the consequences for the vitality of Mother Earth.

Ngaa Mihi: Being Anna, Kahu and Maria

Our introduction of ourselves as authors of this chapter is a greeting of sorts. It is a type of greeting which in Aotearoa is called a *mihi*. It is a greeting that expresses a cultural value of Maaori where priority is given to inform a gathering "from whence we hail". For those who know their lineage, this "from whence" includes the naming of ancestors. Some of these ancestors may be named as mountains, rivers and oceans. Such a *mihi* can be a thought-provoking reminder of the human relationship with the ancients, those yet to be born and with Mother Earth. These relationships entail responsibilities that cannot be deflected. In contexts where Maaori protocols prevail, such identification comes prior to a disclosure of "what we do"—the more typical identifier in Western introductions. In our adaptation of such *mihi* we situate ourselves as authors and as teachers in the context of our wider lives.

Mihi: Anna

> Ko Maungatautari te maunga, Ko Maungakawa te maunga.
> Ko Waikato te awa.
> Ko Paakehaa me te Karaitiana ngaa iwi.
> E ahau Airihi, Kotimana, me te reo Ingarihi tupuna.
> Ko Anna Mary Casey-Cox ahau.

I introduce myself through the mountains (maunga) that were close to me in childhood and the river (awa) water that flows through the land that nourishes me. I introduce myself as a Paakehaa New Zealander, an identity that is also inspired and guided by the teachings and life of Jesus. I acknowledge Te Tiriti o Waitangi, a treaty signed in 1840 between Maaori leadership and the British Crown. Te Tiriti sets forth a path for co-inhabitation of Aotearoa by the incoming settlers now generally referred to as Tauiwi or Paakehaa. I take my responsibility to live in accordance with the guidance and principles of this living document. I remember my ancestors who came from Ireland, England and Scotland, and in particular my Irish grandmother who I knew well.

God as creator and caller of justice and peace, love of Earth and people, and my awareness of human and planetary suffering inspire me to advocate for policies and practices that support the flourishing of life. Inspired by writers who value reflective practice, I work to notice the ways that I am human in all the places and spaces that I live—including the grocery store. At the Waikato Environment Centre, "Plastic Free July" is a commitment that I have recently invited myself and others to because it can encourage more thoughtfulness in our consumption. The care of Earth and the care of people are deeply interconnected in my mind, heart and action.

Mihi: Kahu

> Ko Mataatua te waka.
> Ko Kopukairua te maunga, ko Mauao te maunga.
> Ko Tauranga te moana.
> Ko Waitao te awa.
> Ko Ngaati Puukenga te iwi, ko Ngai Te Rangi te iwi.
> Ko Whetuu-o-te-rangi te marae, ko Tahuwhakatiki te marae, ko
> Tamapahore te marae.
> Ko Kahurangi Jean Dey ahau.

Through the *mihi* above I introduce myself and place myself with my Maaori ancestors, the Mataatua waka (canoe), the maunga (mountain) Kopukairua, and Mauao, the Tauranga moana (harbour), the Waitao awa (river), the iwi (people) Ngaati Puukenga and Ngai Te Rangi, and the marae (places we organize our lives) Whetuu-o-te-rangi, Tahuwhakatiki and Tamapahore. Growing up in a comfortable New Zealand home, the interdependence and relationships of these entities were among many things I often took for granted. As I have aged I have come to appreciate this way of looking forward and looking back. My mother was the connection for my sisters and I to this world; my sisters and I are that connection for our children, and they will be for theirs.

Food charities, food banks, food insecurity and food poverty have all become features of a neoliberal New Zealand landscape. I am saddened by the hunger that now persists in the daily lives of many people in our land of plenty. As a critical researcher I ponder the impact of food systems dominated by global corporations. As a critical mother I see my children influenced by advertising and attractive packaging, while I ache for safe, nutritious, affordable food, provided for in sustainable ways that will be healthy for the planet and us all.

Mihi: Maria

> Holland is the land of my birth.
> My family migrated to New Zealand when I was eight years old.
> I feel that Aotearoa is my home.
> It is the home of my daughters and my grandchildren.
> My name is Maria Theresia Humphries-Kil.

My parents were greengrocers in Holland—one of the few occupations open to them as post-WWII young adults deprived of an education by the war. By the late 1950s, supermarkets were pressing small business people out of existence. Life looked bleak to my parents. They looked for somewhere better to call home. We migrated to New Zealand in 1961. My father hoped to work on a farm. He could find work only in a factory. Many migrants and increasing numbers of rural New Zealanders in the 1950–1960s were being channelled into jobs supporting an industrial economy. My father was among them.

I now call Aotearoa home. I am an Associate Professor in a School of Management Studies. The impact of the industrialization of food is close to my heart. Through its espoused efficiency goals, my father lost his business. His is just one example of the shaping and assimilation of populations to serve a form of globalization that does not serve all people well. I think of myself as a daughter of Mother Earth, daughter to my mother, mother to my daughters, and grandmother to grandchildren whose futures stand before me as the futures of all children must. I think deeply about the ways in which our humanity is organized and managed and where I find my professional footing as a teacher in a business school.

Teachers, researchers and practitioners as activists

We three authors of this chapter have a passion to contribute to the critical consideration of the colonizing dynamics of contemporary economic globalization. With Deetz (1992) we see this form of globalization as a form of colonization of the life world—a world in which the positing of the values of production, consumption and economic growth as a necessity are so normalized they seem like a necessary or natural way of being. It is a way of being drawn into our very identities. It is a way of being we seek to challenge in our elaborated greetings, in our relationship with our students and in our practices in our homes. It requires deep attention to the ways we embody our humanity.

In this chapter we give attention to the way we introduce ourselves, the way we teach and the way we shop. Our focus is on Principle 3 of the PRME. Our engagement with this principle has drawn us towards greater attention to the work undertaken by Radical Human Ecologists. Their work invites a commitment to actively contribute to the shaping of identities, responsibilities and actions that can transform our very sense of self and our relationship with Mother Earth. Our focus is on the many things we can learn from the resistance to colonization by indigenous people, to expand our understanding of contemporary processes of colonization of the life world globally. This focus fuels the anger we feel when we think about the implications of oil extraction on the lives of people all over the world—oil extraction often undertaken on lands retained by or allocated to indigenous peoples of a region. Invigorated by this anger, we find our way to hope through the work of those seeking to alert us not only to the dangers of oil extraction and the proliferation of plastics, but also to a reflection of their wider implication into the colonization of our life world. Our anger turns to a reflection on our responsibility to transform ourselves and our practices. In this chapter this reflection on noticing anger and hope in ourselves is expressed in our response to Principle 3 of PRME.

Learning from ancient wisdom by integrating being and doing

Chief Arvol Looking Horse (2015) refers to the 2010 Gulf of Mexico oil spill as a desecration of the Sacred Earth. He speaks of other such violations of The Sacred. He is one of many indigenous people and their allies around the world who are calling us to account for the exploitative practices now associated with globalization (Amnesty International, 2015). Management educators, particularly those committed to the PRME are among such leaders who are responding to this call to account. Examples of issues and concerns generated from a closer encounter with indigenous ways of being are indeed being brought into management education. The *Journal of Management Education* special issue "Enhancing the Circle of Life" (Fitzgibbons and Humphries, 2011) is one example, and a caucus led by indigenous people has now found voice in the Academy of Management (2015).

Learning from Radical Human Ecology

Williams *et al.* (2012) are among those Radical Human Ecologists who present a way of thinking about indigeneity that does not seek to conflate or diminish the unique effects of intrusion and conquest by colonizing powers on formally recognized indigenous groups. Rather, descendants of colonizers are invited to examine their part in bringing justice to this history. This is a radical call. It is a call that acknowledges the disruption to ancient wisdom that depicts Mother Earth as a living entity. It is a reassertion that from Mother Earth flow all sustaining energies or life-forces. It is an awareness that we degrade Mother Earth at our peril. Williams *et al.* (2012, p. xv) acknowledge the evidence that suggests the path of humanity "points increasingly towards a future of peril". They intend to inspire radical reorientation of our humanity "through a deeply reflective and revitalized human ecological perspective" (*ibid*). This perspective has its roots in storytelling: "Oral communication was a world changing palette for binding human experience, memory, and imagination" (*ibid*). And it remains so. Western mechanistic science and related organizational theories are stories about our way of being (Capra and Luisi, 2014). These stories depict life as divisible into parts of a whole. The parts work together like clockwork. These scientific stories separate the human observer from the storytelling. These stories differ from those of indigenous peoples. The stories of indigenous peoples reverberate more closely with the stories emerging from the Radical Human Ecologists.

In his introduction to Williams *et al.*'s (2012) *Radical Human Ecology: Intercultural and Indigenous Approaches*, Richard Borden finds in the revitalization of human ecology an unconventional and timely andragogy of hope—an andragogical orientation we have long engaged with through the work of Paulo Freire and like-minded educators. It is in the deeply felt relational ethic assumed necessary for a hopeful future that we are drawn. In exploring this ethic we notice rich threads of connection to ideas about the potential of the PRME expressed by Muff *et al.* (2013) as a need to accelerate an uplifting of consciousness in management educators and students. We find calls from thought-leaders well versed in the tradition of Western economic logic that add substance to this call by Muff *et al.* Each calls for different ways of knowing for a different way of being. According to Korten (2015), we are "in the midst of a deep shift in human consciousness. The elements of its framing story are emerging but they have yet to find coherent, unifying expression" (p. 34). Capra and Luisi (2014) provide an insight into aspects of this perceived shift in human consciousness. They introduce the notion of the eco-ethical: the consideration of the self and nature "as one". Logic alone will not make the connection between this idea and related ways to behave. We suggest experience can be our guide. We demonstrate a way of bringing our own experiences to our classes in our response to calls by indigenous people to see ourselves more holistically and as integrally woven into the web of life. By doing, we demonstrate a responsibility for our human relationship with Mother Earth. It follows that "if we have the deep ecological experience of being part of the web of life, then we will…be inclined to care for all of living nature (Capra and Luisi, 2014, p.15).

Such a change in consciousness will not come about automatically in a context where mechanistic thinking prevails as the dominant form of learning and certification (Capra and Luisi, 2014; Korten, 2015). Our contribution in this chapter is to urge the creation of opportunities to rethink the human relationship with all life, to respond to its degradation and to change behaviours. The small changes we can encourage alone will not change the destructive impact of our ways of life but they will be part of the consciousness raising so necessary to shift human thinking from "command and control" to "empathetic cohabitation" as suggested in work such as Capra and Luisi (2014), sung into being by the Council of Grandmothers,[1] and demonstrated in the andragogical approach telling of human relationships with Earth, as is done for example at Schumacher College and many indigenous houses of learning.

The degradation of life reported in *To the Last Drop* (McGuire, 2014) and the vast array of information about the destructive effects of the use of plastic and the human dependence on oil are just two dynamics in a complex web of life that we have chosen to weave together for this chapter.

Learning to notice

Much of our part in social and environmental degradation is embedded in the everyday life that Berger and Luckmann (1996) refer to as the taken for granted. Like many of our peers and the students we teach, we too are deeply embedded in a

---

1 http://www.grandmotherscouncil.org/

way of life likely to exacerbate the social and environmental degradation we are called to transform. Much of our contribution to this degradation is unconscious. Paulo Freire (1970, 1992) is an educator who insists that consciousness raising is a crucial element of education for a just society and that educating with and for *hope* is vital. Such education often requires a disruption to our taken-for-granted way of being to draw our attention to an anomaly between the way we live and the values we uphold. As teachers can we create opportunities to bring such anomalies into the light of discussion and to encourage a closer scrutiny of everyday behaviour? We name this call to scrutiny the practice of *noticing* (Casey Cox, 2014). We draw on Seo and Creed (2002) who show that the noticing of paradox and contradiction is a positive step in the transformation of injustices embedded in a taken-for-granted way of being because in doing so we can locate the place for action.

To notice and begin to act on anomalies between our taken-for-granted ways of being is a necessary aspect of the development of what Bauman and Donskis (2013) call an ethical gaze. It takes commitment and courage to hold our attention on matters that unsettle what we and our community have always taken for granted. In our personal life, this simple understanding is rather difficult to put into practice. How do we find ways to live-for-change when we take so much for granted? And how is this desire to live-for-change linked to our interest in indigenous influence on the shaping of the future? We begin all our teaching with a notion that social justice and environmental integrity is or should be of value to all our students—no matter what their specialism in their management education. We have found the documentary *To the Last Drop* (McGuire, 2014) to be very effective.

The documentary demonstrates the impact of the tar sands operations on the lives of the indigenous people of Alberta. Their ill health, the pressure to move away from the lands they feel mandated to protect, and the undermining of the credibility of their advocates are all brought into view. Such manifestations of corporate exploitation are inconsistent with the many values our students assume to be part of their image of themselves as a "just people". The valiant struggles by indigenous peoples to survive the conditions created by overt and covert processes of historic and contemporary colonization are instigated by resource grabs and fuelled now by our addiction to plastic. Our addiction intensifies a need for ever more oil. Noticing that our taken-for-granted ways of being should be bought at such a hefty cost to a specific group of people and to the land they love, is an example of the kind of paradox and contradiction Seo and Creed (2002) invite us to notice and Bauman and Donskis (2013) suggest we do not deflect our attention from.

The justification of the extraction of oil at the cost of wellbeing and displacement of indigenous people may fuel a form of constructive or righteous anger that we believe ought to be expressed by all people aspiring to be a just people. Following Freire, it is an anger we urge to be more often expressed in our classes where drinking from plastic water bottles may or may not be a norm, where lunches wrapped in plastic, and sitting on furniture that might never decompose may go unnoticed. Freire writes that the kind of education "that does not recognize the right [or duty] to express appropriate anger against injustice, against disloyalty against the negation of love, against exploitation, and against violence fails to see the educational role implicit in the expressions of these feelings" (Freire as cited in Darder, 2015, p. 53).

Freire is not alone in calling us to notice and express anger as an impetus to a commitment to change. Diminishing our reliance on plastic is a small example of a much wider challenge to our ways of being human.

We share the view of Muff *et al.* (2013), of Capra and Luisi (2014), Klein (2014), Korten (2015), Stiglitz (2015) and many more authors and activists, that the trajectory of the prevailing market-driven global development exacerbates inequality and insecurity within and across nations. As mothers and as teachers we fear this story not only for the future of our own children—but for all the children of Mother Earth. The model of development being amplified the world over is on a path to pain for many who are increasingly excluded from the means to existence and self-determination (United Nations, 2013). It entails a degradation of Mother Earth she will not tolerate forever (Pope Francis, 2015). Our focus on the downsides of "global development" or "globalization" is fuelled by our passion as mothers and as teachers and by what we know about development, love, sharing, compassion, greed and power—threads of our identities formed in relation with family and community, students and teachers that cannot be segregated.

What is the story of global development we seek to question? In jurisdictions exemplified as the epitome of development, indicators of social and environmental decline are being drawn to our attention in a myriad of ways. Examples of decline in wellbeing are plentiful (World Watch Institute, 2015). In "clean green" New Zealand, a nation espousing environmentalism and egalitarianism as core values, the gap between the rich and poor has burgeoned (Rashbrooke, 2013). Our waterways have never been so dirty (Proffitt, 2010). It is not a condition for life-bearing that we envisage for our children or theirs. We know that the impact of systemic exploitation could beset any of us at any time. These circumstances are just some among many more tickets to poverty—experienced not only by indigenous peoples in many places in the world, but also by many people marginalized by the processes of ongoing colonization in which the selective participation of indigenous peoples add complexity and paradox (Williams *et al.*, 2012).

Practitioners and praxis: our call to action— holistic thinking and being in management education

We began the chapter by demonstrating that our identities as mothers and as teachers are deeply entwined. It is not common for teachers to be so personal. It is even less common to have mothers as teachers identify themselves as daughters of Mother Earth—and to call for a greater respect for our common Mother. The PRME initiative has given a mandate to create teaching agendas with a transformational intent.

Noticing: Maria

I was disturbed on seeing a documentary showing explicit footage of plastic sea debris found in the gullets of pelicans. Recognizing the anger I felt generated the energy needed to investigate this claim to plastic addiction and what it implies. This led to an invitation to an immediate circle of friends and family, to also "notice" plastic in their lives and to do something about it.

I invited them to a two phase exercise in noticing followed by action:

- Week One: Please record everything bought or *noticed* in food-related activities—particularly food shopping—where plastic is involved in some way.

- Week Two: Write down the ways such plastic may be reduced/eliminated from food-related activities.

The response to my call was immediate and passionate:

> I don't know if I have time, commitment and motivation to carry out the supermarket challenge you sent us last week. I feel guilty about this as I know what an important challenge this is but here are a few examples that are now on my mind

> Fruit and veggies: I mostly use the plastic bags provided. There are 3 reasons for this

> 1. We reuse the bags as dog-waste (what would be a good alternative?)
> 2. The veggies stay fresh for longer in the bags
> 3. Putting the fruit loose into the supermarket trolley would not be an option.

> Like the link you posted with the invite, I notice a lot of unnecessary packaging with plastic fruit and veggie specials. I resist these.

> I often get a dog-bone from the butcher's counter at the supermarket. It is always wrapped in meters of plastic wrap. I know a bone is a blood product, and they must be very careful but it does seem a little "overkill".

Anna's response to noticing was soon turned to action—which brought its own challenges to act upon.

Noticing and action: Anna

Having made the decision to notice and avoid plastics, a trip to the supermarket became a field trip for the family. A number of possibilities, constraints and confusions related to "no plastic" choices were noticed:

> The necessity to remember to bring smaller cloth shopping bags to avoid using plastic for produce

> We could not purchase any meat or cheese in this supermarket. It was all covered in plastic

My intention was, as advocated by proponents of rubbish free living to find a friendly butcher who might put meat into a reusable container I provided. I have not succeeded so far!

We could only buy bread from the bakery using our own bags. Our regular plastic covered bread was no longer an option. Interestingly, prior to choosing some rolls from the bakery, I noticed that the baker emptied a bag of plastic wrapped rolls into the bin, from where I then selected my "plastic free" buns...the buns were not as plastic free as I would have thought.

It was impossible to tell if boxed items contained plastic. Very often they do. On the outside packaging, the manufacturer may proclaim a commitment to recycling and all things "natural" while the plastic is hidden from view.

I noticed at the "Binn Inn" the puzzlement of the staff that I would be using my own reused plastic bags and not new ones that they kindly and repeatedly, offered me. I could have talked about this with them, but with four children investigating bins and knocking one over, I was quite in a hurry to get my shopping done.

The contents of the knocked over bin were swept into a plastic bag and thrown in the rubbish...

The practice of "noticing" plastic and avoiding took some concentration—but alternatives could be found—often in the same supermarket.

The exercise had some interesting ripple effects:

My partner has joined in on the experience. He had a very interesting conversation at the delicatessen section, similar to the one I had at the cheese shop, when asking if he could please use his own container rather than having his "lunch meat" plastic wrapped. Both our conversations resulted in confusion and grumpy compliance with our "no plastic" requests.

Value conflicts and contradictions are more identifiable in the *conscious* navigation of a supermarket:

I noticed how the woman at the supermarket checkout offered to wrap our meat in more plastic because the packages were "terribly leaky". I noticed her desire to care for us and to save our car from drips of blood. My "no thank you" may have seemed like brushing off her kindness, but in the hurried place of a supermarket checkout there is no time for a deeper conversation.

The "noticing-action-noticing" cycle turns to reflection:

I think about the delicatessen workers, the bakers, the care takers, the bin attendants, the check-out operators, and the constraints and pressures that they are under and the unsettling conversation that we may bring to them in our individual calls for "no plastic" as we shop. They are the often overworked and underpaid faces of an organization, but are not the ones responsible for the decisions, including the extensive use of plastic, that seems to constrain our moral choices.

Our taken-for-granted ways of life, as shoppers and as employees who serve us, are based on a form of market-driven model for global development that Deetz (1992) invites us to be cautious about. In taking our starting point from such concerns and holding our gaze on its paradoxes and contradictions, we are compelled to take reflective action in our personal lives and in our leadership responsibilities as teachers. Reflection on experiences and how they link to models of learning and action are well established in management education and can be brought into the discussion. The significance of a commitment to such reflections is exemplified in the work of David Kolb (1984) whose work on experiential learning is well known in management education. Our starting point, however, is not on action, as is the work of Kolb, but on noticing (the intuition that something is awry in the world, to look about oneself (close to home) to notice the things and the activities in the light of an aroused intuition. Our contribution is to pay close attention to the move from an initial intuition and its follow up observations of the world of everyday taken-for-grantedness, to "something must be done about this" and to "what can I do in my time and place, with my resources and my circumstances?"

Maria's intuitive response to witnessing the plastic in the gullets of pelicans led to a shared inquiry among friends about the prevalence of plastic in our lives. This became the genesis of classroom application and an invitation to grow towards an eco-ethical way of being in our own lives and with our students—finding more actions to galvanize a commitment to change. In the thinking and doing, Maria thought much about the indigenous ways of being where the pelican is our beloved relation and the Earth our common home, and how an extended introduction of herself in class might evoke interest in seeing the world through relational dynamics. Kolb (1984), Freire (1970, 1972), Seo and Creed (2002), Bauman and Donskis (2013) could come into the conversation; but much later, well after establishing the invitation to "notice" ourselves, our complexity, our everyday lives, ourselves in a world of complex relationships where entitlement must bring response-ability. But how? It is a good opportunity to draw attention to the predominance of structural functional theories in management education depicting the world in mechanistic ways. People and planet are reified as resources. Resources are at the disposal of the corporation, the investor, the consumer. To *notice* this opens an opportunity to contrast this way of thinking with the work emerging from the Radical Human Ecologists impacting organizational studies such as Capra and Luisi (2014), Boje (2014) and the work being undertaken at Schumacher College and elsewhere. Their orientation to the world is more closely aligned to that generated from the dualistic and instrumental orientations of Western organizational studies. The accessibility for non-indigenous people to indigenous ways of knowing and being in the world is increasingly accessible to teachers and students through selective exposure on the internet.

Below we provide an example of how the exercise generated from the initial observation may focus our attention on "noticing"—and that such noticing can and does lead to a change in behaviour as it did and continues to do for us as mothers, shoppers and teachers deeply entwined in the life of Mother Earth. The exercise can be readily adapted to reflect the makeup of a class, the subject orientations of the students or a particular social, organizational or environmental concern they may be willing to voice. Food was our starting point. For others it may be transport, wildlife, water governance, identity formation and ever more creative examples.

We provide below an approach we as mothers and teachers, scholars and practitioners have found enlightening and energizing in our own attempts to move towards a more eco-ethical way of being. We now offer some activities that can be adapted to other unsustainable or unjust practices in ways that reflect different issues and geographic locations.

An experiential exercise: choosing food— consuming plastic

Given the diverse population in our classes, choosing a topic of common interest for an application of theory is our priority. A focus on the universal need for healthy food, the cultural dynamics of food in community, commerce and health is a way to explore universal needs and rights, and to distinguish common and unique values expressed through food. This discussion makes an easy transition to the aspects of a management education by drawing attention to the various forms of production, transport, consumption and disposal of food. Most will have experienced education designed to impact efficiency and profitability.

Below we restructure our activities into usable teaching and learning exercises where students are encouraged to move from being (*mihi*), to noticing (supermarket), to reflecting (class) and to changing behaviour as individuals, consumers and family members.

Being: Adapt and adopt the practice of *mihi* to situate yourself

As we demonstrate early in this chapter, an extended introduction of selves or others can be imagined in a number of ways. We have done so by adapting our understanding of the way Maaori prefer to do this in Aotearoa. There may be parallel examples in the experience of a particular group of students who are informed by other cultural practices and protocols. Researching and preparing a *mihi* which demonstrate values of connectedness can be a wholly creative project a group of students can be asked to do and to reflect on. Asking individuals to express who they are, and consider the people and places they are from and connected to is an accessible way for students to consider their deeper sense of self and their cultural origins.

The opportunity to prepare and the time given to this exercise can be adjusted to the situation. Explain how in an indigenous context, this protocol may take a very long time. It is a time of relating one to the other, of building trust, of placing that which is significant into the conversation to be had. In "clock-time" this may seem very "time-consuming". In "efficiency" considerations, any corporate or governmental representatives engaged with indigenous peoples over the co-management of land, water or intellectual property will know its significance. If time is short, the teacher could prepare their own and lead by example. Be thoughtful, relational and personal. Add something fun, sad and controversial to encourage them to do so also. It is about "making visible", "making relationships"—expressed in Te Ao Maori as whakawhanaungatanga (making family)—in which the mountains and the rivers are introduced *as* relations—to all of us through our common Mother Earth. If time is more elastic—some preparation could precede or follow—use audio visuals, guest speakers—whatever is feasible to shift from head to heart—to awaken the consciousness of relationality in some way. If classes are very large, the process could be done in small groups. If time allows, each group could "perform" a greeting, a composite in a formal or even fun way.

The *mihi* situating could be placed just ahead of the noticing exercise or alternatively, serve as an orientation to a new class. Situating themselves could begin with sharing their sense of "being" and thus quite a personalized orientation to the course as a whole. Regardless of where it is placed, the *mihi* situating can then lead into some reflections on the importance of "noticing" self, others, world—diversely. This then could lead into the exercise about plastics—or some variation of it—to serve as an experiential opportunity to "notice" how they choose to behave and to associate "noticing" with "doing" and their doing with its wider impact on society—in all its diverse ways of thinking about this. This can bring the class nicely full circle.

Noticing: Initiate the practice of seeing

A great class can be built on the telling stories of plastics—from production to its eventual presence in the nigh invisible micro-particles to be found in fish causing cancer in humans (Andrews, 2012). There is more in this story than any teacher can tell in the time constraints of a class. Plastic is everywhere—and the price of its use goes well beyond the wrapping of our food. Prepare a class for an activity by showing some thought-provoking media about plastics. We recommend *To the Last Drop*. Do not be afraid to generate some strong feelings. But make time to process such feelings. Work with anger and fear to generate conversations of hope, creativity and courage. Maria's 8-year-old granddaughter did a project on climate change. She is a thoughtful child and she explained that her project had made her feel scared. Feelings of fear are "appropriate"—but must be (and were) nurtured to action. She has made a list of actions she can do now and ask her friends to do. She knows she can learn more and become part of the solution. What might a teacher, with little or a little more time, do in a management class in a school committed to advance PRME?

- Invite a group discussion about a chosen media item such as *To the Last Drop* and ask students to reflect how significant they think the issue is. Set an investigative assignment that will draw out the significance of the concern in terms of students' areas of professional or community located expertise: environmental damage, economic issues, employment concerns and marketing or public relations contributions.

- Invite students to observe/notice the plastic in the world around them.

- Craft an exercise in which students are given a finite amount of time to "notice" a consumer-related matter they may not have paid much attention to. Two examples are the number of gadgets in their line of sight that require "rare earth" components, or the volume of goods in their line of sight that require significant transport.

- If group work is valued, invite them to share their lists. Then discuss the sustainability issues of production of consumer products from source to disposal. It is a great opportunity to introduce "cradle to cradle" design (McDonough, 2005). The orientation of the class can be on supply chain management, human resources management, accounting, finance and marketing—but preferably not as isolated specialisms—with an opportunity to both draw on and integrate disciplinary specialisms. Assignments can be framed to include searches for active responses to tackle these matters by corporations, consumers, activists and individuals.

Reflecting: Action in the classroom and beyond

An invitation to self-reflective journalling can deepen the exercise into a wider consciousness of each person's capacity to notice, to contribute to change—as managers, parents, citizens.

- Invite students to consider how the cost of extracting oil and transportation and disposal of the plastic products are calculated into the price of the plastic wrap around a cucumber or a plastic bottle of water.

- Invite them to imagine and include the real cost of attaining the source of the plastic to the eventual de-commissioning of the vehicles that transport the oil and the products.

- Invite them to consider the net effect of the growing noise pollution in seas and the skies that are disrupting the flight paths of many species, adding to their distress and perhaps extinction.

These questions allow for an introduction to the insights of Radical Human Ecologists. Our focus on plastic is just one of many examples of consumer engagement that may span from home to classroom for an authentic module that any student, any family, any teacher and executive could initiate. The ripples will flow. Together we would be contributing to what Muff *et al.* (2013) call a world worth living in— and what we call a world worth working for.

Conclusion

"Noticing" the human addiction to plastic and the subsequent encouragement to examine the impact of this addiction on the web of life can bring to our attention some of the paradoxes and contradictions we seem to agree to live with. We need not! The exercises we propose above will have ripple effects into communities beyond the classroom, particularly if the demarcations between "school and life" are made more porous and students and teachers learn to value personal experiences and nurture a deep sense of integrity in all aspects of our lives together with and on this planet. For this we recommend the notion of a *mihi* as an orientation to such a class. Borden (as cited in Williams *et al.*, 2012, p. xvi) suggests that "mixing personal anecdotes and self-reflection with scholarly content can be risky" but that doing so can also be a "most effective mode of teaching". We have offered some ideas about how closer attention to the aspirations of indigenous people can enrich our sense of self, invite a more personal relationship with our students and contribute in a practical way to the call by Muff *et al.* (2013) for "a world worth living in".

Showing how our greetings are influenced by our interests in indigenous ways of being positions us in relation to Earth and all life and makes room for a more critical reflection on the past and current circumstances of indigenous people. This is so particularly where these circumstances interface with interests in natural resources such as oil and the pollutants associated with the production, use and disposal of plastic. A focus on the web of life connects our addiction to plastic, which threatens the health and wellbeing of particular indigenous peoples and undermines the responsibility they feel for the wellbeing of Earth and all her creatures, to our own everyday lives. Our focus on the proliferation of plastics and their production costs to Mother Earth is a practical example most readers will be able to relate to. Our students certainly do. One student writes in her journal:

> *To the Last Drop* explains how Canada's livelihood is dependent on the tar sands to provide paid employment and economic prosperity for Canada... Indigenous people are pressured to move away from their home because of extreme poisoning of the land and the wildlife, depleting any ability to live sustainably. Individuals in the community are developing life threatening illnesses at an increased rate, including various types of cancer (McGuire, 2014). As consumers continue to be addicted to plastic, corporate exploitation of indigenous people and the environment continues... Corporations are able to exploit the need of paid employment. Happiness is sold to us as products, brands, lifestyles, and image etc. Our thinking becomes colonized. As we compete for work, we spend more money to meet our desires, yet we feel unsatisfied. We buy more. Our consumerism puts more pressure on the demand for oil. While some people are meeting their economic needs in paid employment, the environment is being exploited. Indigenous people are losing their livelihoods and health, all to provide for consumer items that further destroy the earth. We are effectively buying our way to unsustainable lifestyles... Personal leadership would include taking a confident stand

in breaking the "colonized" ways of thinking of consumerism and status "dogma". Rather than following trends or falling into dominant ways of thinking, education through a deep ecology lens encourages a holistic approach to work and life.

The managers we are educating now are a vital part of that web. The PRME as infused in its aspirations allows for infinite ways to develop such an expanded consciousness and hope for a sustainable future and a vision of a world worth working for.

References

Academy of Management (2015). Native and Indigenous Caucus. *75th Annual Meeting of the Academy of Management Program 2015 Opening Governance Conference.* Retrieved from http://my.aom.org/ProgramDocs/2015/pdf/AOM_2015_Annual_Meeting_Program.pdf

Amnesty International (2015). *Amnesty International Report 2014/15: The State of the World's Human Rights.* Retrieved from https://www.amnesty.org/en/documents/pol10/0001/2015/en/

Andrews, G. (2012). *Plastics in the Ocean Affecting Human Health.* On the Cutting Edge. National Association of Geoscience Teachers. Retrieved from http://serc.carleton.edu/NAGTWorkshops/health/case_studies/plastics.html

Bauman, Z., & Donskis, L. (2013). *Moral Blindness: The Loss of Sensitivity in Liquid Modernity.* Oxford, UK: Polity Press.

Berger, P. L. & T. Luckmann (1966). *The Social Construction of Reality: A Treatise in the Sociology of Knowledge.* Garden City NY: Anchor Books.

Boje, D. (2014). *Storytelling Organizational Practices.* London and New York, NY: Routledge.

Came, H. & Humphries, M.T. (2014). Mopping up institutional racism: Activism on a napkin. *Journal of Corporate Citizenship,* 54, 95-108.

Capra, F. & Luisi, P.L. (2014). *The Systems View of Life: A Unifying Vision.* Cambridge, UK: Cambridge University Press.

Casey-Cox, A. (2014). *The Transformative Possibilities of "Noticing" in Community Gardens and my Life.* PhD thesis, University of Waikato, Hamilton, New Zealand. Retrieved from http://hdl.handle.net/10289/8837

Chief Arvol Looking Horse (2015, April 26). *Featured Speaker: Chief Arvol Looking Horse— 2015 Nobel Peace Prize Forum* [video file]. Retrieved from https://www.youtube.com/watch?v=bIbjYzHmM94

Deetz, S. (1992). *Democracy in an Age of Corporate Colonization: Developments in Communication and the Politics of Everyday Life.* New York, NY: State University of New York Press.

Darder, A. (2015). *Freire and Education.* New York, NY: Routledge.

Dyer, S., Humphries, M.T., Fitzgibbons, D. & Hurd, F. (2014). *Understanding Management Critically: A Student Text.* London, UK: Sage.

Fitzgibbons, D.E & Humphries, M.T. (Guest Co-Editor) (2011). Enhancing the circle of life: Management education and indigenous knowledge. *Journal of Management Education,* 35(1), 3-7.

Freire, P. (1970). *Pedagogy of the Oppressed.* New York, NY: Seabury.

Freire, P. (1992). *Pedagogy of Hope.* London: Continuum International Publishing Group.

Humphries, M. T. & Grice, S. (1995). Equal employment opportunity and the management of diversity: A global discourse of assimilation? *Journal of Organizational Change Management*, 8(5), 17-33.

Klein, N. (2014). *This Changes Everything: Capitalism vs the Climate*. New York, NY: Simon & Schuster.

Kolb, D. (1984). *Experiential Learning: Experience as the Source of Learning and Development*. Englewood Cliffs, NJ: Prentice Hall.

Korten, D. C. (2015). *Change the Story, Change the Future: A Living Economy for a Living Earth*. Oakland, CA: Berrett-Koehler.

McDonough, W. (2005). *Cradle to Cradle Design* [video file]. Retrieved from https://www.ted.com/talks/william_mcdonough_on_cradle_to_cradle_design?language=en

McGuire, B. (2014). *To the Last Drop* [video file]. Retrieved from http://topdocumentaryfilms.com/last-drop/

Marshall, J. (1999). Living life as enquiry. *Systemic Practice and Action Research*, 12(2), 155-171.

Marshall, J. (2001). Self-reflective inquiry practices. In P. Reason & H. Bradbury (Eds.), *Handbook of Action Research: Participative Inquiry and Practice* (pp. 433-439). London, UK: Sage.

Marshall, J. (2011). Images of changing practice through reflective action research. *Journal of Organisation Change Management*, 24(2), 244-256.

Muff, K., Dyllick, T., Drewell, M., North, J., Shrivastava, P. & Haertle, J. (2013). *Management Education for the World*. Cheltenham, UK: Edward Elgar Publishing Limited.

Pope Francis (2015, May 24). Laudato si *On Care for Our Common Home*. Retrieved from http://www.news.va/en/news/laudato-si-the-integral-text-of-pope-francis-encyc

Proffitt, F. (2010). *How Clean Are Our Rivers?* National Institute of Water and Atmospheric Research (NIWA). Retrieved from https://www.niwa.co.nz/publications/wa/water-atmosphere-1-july-2010/how-clean-are-our-rivers

Rashbrooke, M. (2013). *Inequality: A New Zealand Crisis*. Wellington, NZ: Bridget Williams Books.

Seo, M-G., & Creed, W.E.D. (2002). Institutional contradictions, praxis, and institutional change: A dialectical perspective. *The Academy of Management Review*, 27(2), 222-247.

Stiglitz, J. (2015). *The Great Divide: Unequal Societies and What We Can Do About It*. New York, NY: W.W. Norton and Co.

United Nations (2007). *Declaration on the Rights of Indigenous Peoples*. Retrieved from http://www.un.org/esa/socdev/unpfii/documents/DRIPS_en.pdf

United Nations (2013). *Business Guide on Rights of Indigenous Peoples*. Retrieved from https://www.unglobalcompact.org/docs/issues_doc/human_rights/IndigenousPeoples/BusinessGuide.pdf

Verbos, A.K., & Humphries, M.T. (2012). Decoupling equality, diversity, and inclusion from liberal projects: Hailing indigenous contributions to institutional change. *Equality, Diversity and Inclusion: An International Journal*, 31(5/6), 506-525.

Verbos, A.K., & Humphries, M.T. (2014). A Native American relational ethic: An indigenous perspective on teaching human responsibility. *Journal of Business Ethics*, 123(1), 1-9.

Verbos, A.K., & Humphries, M.T. (2015a). Indigenous wisdom and the PRME: Inclusion or illusion? *Journal of Management Development*, 34 (1), 90-100.

Verbos, A.K., & Humphries, M.T. (2015b). Amplifying a relational ethics: A contribution to PRME praxis. *Business and Society Review*, 120(1), 23-56.

Williams, L., Roberts, R., & McIntosh, A. (2012). *Radical Human Ecology. Intercultural and Indigenous Approaches*. Aldershot, UK: Ashgate Publishing Limited.

World Watch Institute (2015). *State of the World 2015: Confronting Hidden Threats to Sustainability*. Retrieved from http://www.worldwatch.org/state-world-2015-confronting-hidden-threats-sustainability-0

5

Experiential learning through shared responsibility and risk

Alan Wagenberg
Fundación Capital, Colombia

Roberto Gutiérrez
School of Management, Universidad de los Andes, Colombia

An invitation

Entrepreneurship begets the innovations that reshape industries. According to a study about the lifespan of firms among the S&P 500 Index, the average tenure has decreased from 61 to 18 years since 1958 and at the current turnover rate, 75% of the S&P 500 will be replaced by 2027 (Innosight, 2012). Twenty-first century leaders require an entrepreneurial mind-set.

As teachers, how can we ensure that future leaders create value rather than just capture it? We believe that teaching entrepreneurship is the act of shaping leaders to develop solutions in a way that creates value for all stakeholders. Can this be taught? We have learned that we must challenge students to learn from hands-on experiences and encourage them to be responsible for their own learning. To do so, we changed the way questions about their entrepreneurial projects were posed: rather than phrasing questions in conditional tense (e.g. what would happen? Or how would you avoid failure?), students had to answer for past events (e.g. what happened? Or what did you learn from your failure?). Students had to take action, engage with society and be accountable. For teachers, it meant no longer discussing whether or not entrepreneurship can be taught. The relevant question to be addressed by students was: Do you have what it takes to be an entrepreneur? This chapter is an account of how we increased student engagement in an entrepreneurship course and discusses how instructors can use these methods in other courses so students are better prepared to become responsible management leaders.

Since 2001, a triple-crown university[1] has been offering a course on entrepreneurship in its undergraduate programme. Roberto Gutiérrez, as an Associate Professor, started teaching this course in 2011. In 2014, Alan Wagenberg joined as a co-teacher and brought his experience as a social entrepreneur. In particular, Alan's experience in helping small artisans to earn better prices for their products provided insights about how businesses create value for suppliers, employees, clients and investors. Since then, both teachers have been experimenting with adapting entrepreneurial education to today's context. The collective voice in this chapter is the result of an intense collaboration for more than a year. Our individual voices only appear when a particular issue is of concern to either one of us.

Back in 2007, Roberto was part of the international task force that developed the Principles for Responsible Management Education (PRME). Since then, he has been exploring how these principles transform business education offered by the School of Management where he works. Since Principle 1 aims to "develop capabilities of students to be future generators of sustainable value for business and society", he used the initial entrepreneurship course at the school to test some ideas of how to abide by these principles. Entrepreneurship is an area where value creation is paramount. Also, could an entrepreneurship course "enable effective learning experiences for responsible leadership" (Principle 3)?

In exploring three contemporary meanings of responsibility, we followed Harmon's ideas (1995). First, responsibility as agency (i.e. freedom of will makes people authors of their actions) supported the notion of students being responsible for taking action and for their own learning. Second, responsibility as accountability (i.e. people answer for their actions) refers to students responding for their decisions and actions within a world-view that considers issues beyond shareholder value maximization. Third, responsibility as obligation (i.e. action corresponding to external principles and standards) alludes to students' contributions to their teams and the course.

Valuing responsibility all along the course set the stage for our interactions. Our working hypothesis was that this experiential course would: (a) encourage students to take greater responsibility for their own learning (i.e. agency); and (b) help develop students as more responsible leaders, initially accountable and obliged to course standards (i.e. obligation and accountability)[2] and to society.

As teachers, we also had corresponding notions: as agents we acted to create the needed frameworks, materials, processes and environments; we were responsible for ensuring students are motivated and engaged, and were obliged to uphold the principles and quality standards set by the School of Management.

More importantly, our responsibility as teachers is not only to make sure students learn but also to help them apply their skills and knowledge towards the

---

1 A triple-crown university is one whose programmes have been accredited by the Association to Advance Collegiate Schools of Business (AACSB), EFMD Quality Improvement System (EQUIS) and the Association of MBAs (AMBA).

2 Thanks to the anonymous reviewers who helped us frame this issue with greater clarity.

benefit of society. Greenberg and her co-authors (2011) highlight social, economic and environmental responsibility and sustainability as one of three characteristics of entrepreneurial leaders. This is not only a moral argument but also a profitable one. Companies taking actions towards sustainability outperform the market, have lower cost of debt and equity, are more efficient at using resources and have better financial performance (Fulton, 2012; Carbon Disclosure Project, 2013; Eccles *et al.*, 2011).

This is because society demands greater accountability from companies and their leaders. In 2013, for example, three-quarters of the top leading companies globally reported on their social and environmental impact (KPMG, 2013). At the same time, only one in two people trusted companies worldwide (Edelman, 2015), and one in three consumers globally desired products or services that were good for the environment and society (BBMG and GlobeScan, 2014). This means businesses are under greater pressure to be sustainable and to perform responsibly than ever before.

Another shift in businesses thinking is related to an understanding of failure. Historically, business leaders were trained to avoid failure at any cost. Entrepreneurs minimized risk by developing comprehensive business plans prior to starting their ventures. New frontiers in entrepreneurship education recognize the need for students to "begin to experience success and failure as well as practice methods for navigating unknown territories" (Neck and Greene, 2011, p. 63). And, business schools and incubators promote methodologies such as the "Business Model Canvas" (Osterwalder *et al.*, 2009) and "Lean Start-Up" (Ries, 2011; Blank, 2013), which encourage failing fast, often and cheaply as a way to validate business ideas and models.

Although some successful businesses have been created without much need for testing and planning, most businesses have been the result of trial and error. For example, Amazon.com was first started as an online bookstore, but has found that it is more profitable to offer its infrastructure to other markets. Similarly, PayPal initially developed security software for handheld devices but then transformed into an electronic money transfer service. Many cases show that successful businesses are not the result of careful planning, but rather the result of learning by doing.

However, since one cannot afford to leave success to luck, one must systematically create a method to control and accelerate trial and error in order to validate hypotheses. We believe that anyone who is committed to practising this method and embracing failure can be an entrepreneur. As such, we argue that entrepreneurship is a method that can be learned. But, it requires students to have the right state of mind, including taking responsibility for their actions and learning.

It was in this setting that we decided to change our approach to the entrepreneurship course which we describe here. First, we describe the characteristics of our past approaches and then explain what changes were implemented and the outcomes that ensued. Finally, we highlight some lessons related to the whole process and consider, under the Principles for Responsible Management Education, what we learned about entrepreneurship education and what we could contribute to other areas of management education.

Past approaches

Students took this entrepreneurship course in the middle of their undergraduate programmes. On average, this course has 32 students. The course required groups of four students to create a venture using two tools: (1) design thinking to propose a solution to a problem they identified; and (2) prototypes that used the business model canvas to test venture proposals. In Neck and Greene's (2011) typology, the first half of the course, centred on design thinking, was close to a process approach. We understand design thinking as a systematic approach to solving problems. The second half of the course pushed students to work with business models to bring solutions to fruition. Selected readings were assigned to help students better understand entrepreneurial ideas and models. Two exams required students to use those ideas and models in specific situations.

The groups were formed using an online tool, CATME (Comprehensive Assessment of Team Member Effectiveness), that collects information from students (e.g. discipline, gender, interests, expertise) through a survey and then assigns them to teams according to previously specified criteria (e.g. maximize diversity in disciplinary background).[3] However, we accepted changes to group membership if all students involved agreed.

As for the outputs, it was exceptional that any of the created ventures materialized at all or that they had any sales. A common occurrence was to see ventures that were not ambitious enough. Even more frustrating was the fact that most students were not interested in the ventures they decided to create. In other words, few students were engaged in the entrepreneurial process despite our efforts to create a favourable environment for their initiatives. It is true that not every individual dreams of becoming an entrepreneur and this course was mandatory for management students. However, our course was also offered as an elective for students who were not management majors and who had a clear interest in the subject matter.[4] Specifically, 50% of students (out of a total of 32 students, on average) were management majors while the other half came from a wide array of disciplines (e.g. biology, art, design, geoscience and engineering). Most were starting their junior

---

3 See http://info.catme.org/

4 In our university, a mandatory course in one school is open to students from another school as an elective. In those cases, the mix between students who have a keen interest in a subject matter with those with no interest in it poses some problems, especially for teamwork.

year, and were between 20 and 22 years old; only two students were seniors and the rest sophomores (in the second year at college).

When we assigned a task, students provided all kinds of justifications for not completing it. Except in subjects like maths, where questions and exercises have a specific answer, tough situations dissuade students from giving straight answers. In previous entrepreneurship courses we taught, students searched for ways to do the least amount of work possible while believing or trying to convince us they had done enough. For example, we asked students to create prototypes in order to test their products or services. Most of them designed fancy presentations that detail how they planned to do their prototypes, but never actually did any testing. For those who went beyond presentations, the typical prototype consisted of asking their closest friends, not potential clients, to complete a short survey. Undoubtedly, we witnessed much more storytelling than action.

In our role as facilitators, we tried to be aware of where students stood emotionally and devised methods to engage each one. In our past experience with this course, students were attending class, yet their level of engagement with the subject matter and their projects was poor. In their own words, they were just "complying with assignments"; instead of a deep approach to learning, they were taking a strategic approach (Biggs, 1999). No matter how creatively constructed our exercises were, their efforts never surpassed our expectations and it felt as if they were "going through the motions". One possible explanation is that we were trying to change the way students were taught: they were conditioned by course requirements, questions had only one right answer, feedback was provided on results rather than on progress, and rigid syllabuses or impersonal lessons did not allow for idiosyncrasies. It is difficult to change students' attitudes towards learning in this context. Rather than thinking of learning as a process, they chose to invest their time studying for a time-bound result.

Additionally, when asked to develop business ideas, they tended to focus on their own circumstances in which they have a limited view of the world and which are characterized by abundance rather than unmet basic needs. This prevented them from identifying pressing problems with higher scale potential.

Roberto, therefore, could not avoid asking himself: how can students take more responsibility for their education without the need for teachers to rely on limited assessments (e.g. quizzes) and threats? If they could not take responsibility for their own education, how can they be responsible leaders? When Alan joined the course, he wondered how one could challenge students to go beyond their comfort zones in order to experience other realities and find bigger opportunities. He also wanted to discover new methods for teaching and engaging students since he found that conventional methods no longer worked because students today have shorter attention spans, deal with rapidly changing environments and use the internet to learn. Can creating learning experiences be a better way to teach? John Dewey's (2015) voice resonated with both of us: "We never educate directly, but indirectly by means of the environment. Whether we permit chance environments to do the work, or whether we design environments for the purpose makes a great difference."

A new approach

According to Mockus (1999), there are mainly three ways in which one can influence behaviour: namely, legal, moral and cultural norms. Usually, universities try to influence behaviour through a legal perspective—grades as a proxy to compliance. However Mockus argues that moral self-gratification and cultural approval are by far more powerful motivators. To address the lack of engagement and poor results in our course, we redesigned it to favour moral norms (satisfaction from succeeding or even trying) and cultural norms (recognition) over threats or punishment (low grades).

According to Krueger (2009), entrepreneurship education is inherently constructivist. In the constructivist framework, teachers are facilitators: someone who provides guidelines, creates a favourable environment and avoids a focus on transferring content knowledge (Pizarro, 2014). In this regard, we hoped to help students discover their own lessons as opposed to being the medium by which they learn.

In our approach to experiential learning, we heeded Fiet's advice about how to teach entrepreneurship: "If our students leave talking about being entrepreneurs instead of about us, we have probably figured out how to involve them in activities that help them to develop personal competencies" (Fiet, 2001, p. 101). Our overall approach to the course did not change: it started with the identification of a problem and a possible solution using design thinking, and then proceeded with the search for a business model using multiple prototypes and the canvas model. By the end of the semester, students had gone through several iterations of the entrepreneurial process, developed evidence-based business models and could examine if they enjoyed it and had the will to face its challenges.

In general, we favoured practice over theory and their personal experience over case studies. "Rather than ask whether a sustainable solution to a particular challenge is possible, entrepreneurial leaders need to learn how to develop, implement, and measure the effects of responsible and sustainable solutions" (Greenberg *et al.*, 2011, p. 17).

Our efforts pushed the limits of the constructivist framework in some of its dimensions. A way in which "the teacher-student distinction is thus blurred mindfully; both are learners, both are teachers" (Krueger, 2009, p. 38) has been by sharing risk with students. One way that we tried to align our interests and those of students was to offer our salary as seed capital. If we failed to engage them and teach them properly, we would lose our money. We mentioned this decision to the Undergraduate Programme Director and updated him on the results of our experiment. At one point, he offered to use programme funds as the seed capital for ventures in this course. Although this would have secured institutional resources, we felt it would take away some pressure from students who needed to assume a personal commitment with a couple of teachers who believed in them. To avoid ethical dilemmas, students were made aware of the consequence of partaking in our course on the first day and were able to register in sections with other instructors, their grade was tied to their own learning reflections rather than making money, and they were not required to repay the money or any interest.

We also tried to "corner" students by increasing our expectations and making it more difficult for them to justify their inaction. The changes had to do with the following:

- Provide them with seed capital so that they could invest in their start-up as they deemed appropriate (incentivized their agency and made them accountable to us)

- Streamline the syllabus so that each course activity and grade was aligned with their venture creation process (stated their obligations)

- Use an automated tool (i.e. CATME) to create heterogeneous groups and monitor their performance (created an obligation towards their team members)

From the first class, we asked students to go out into the world and create a venture that attempted to solve a problem. Our role was to support them and address any need they could have: knowledge, coaching, inspiration, methodologies, financing, etc. But, at the same time, we wanted them to take responsibility for their actions or for their passivity.

We had already tried this in our previous course, but this time we decided to provide our salaries to students in the form of an interest-free loan so they could invest in their own start-ups. We emphasized that we believed in them and were committed to doing everything in our reach to support their learning process as long as they made a best effort. Yet, we expected them to generate revenues from their ventures. Also, we warned students that they would need to fail many times in their pursuit of a solid business model. We rewarded failure, as long as it was well documented.

To ensure they understood our proposal and their share of responsibility, we asked students to sign an agreement which stated the terms and conditions of our offer, and included the following:

- Acknowledgement that they received a set sum from us

- Their commitment to make their best effort during the semester

- Their pledge to use the money exclusively for their ventures

- An agreement to return the loan at the end of the semester or, in case their venture failed, to recover the initial investment, to provide a report detailing their failures, what they learned from the experience and what they could have done differently

- Our commitment to provide guidance, timely feedback and tools throughout their process

Our signed agreement strived to align student and teacher interests, and to level the playing field by sharing risks. It was also a clear signal to students that we expected them to develop a real venture. Volkema points out that although real money "increase[s] students' attention or focus as a result of the additional sense of realism that it fosters, there is no guarantee that there will be increased learning (i.e. acquired knowledge put into action)" (2007, p. 484). However, the task of creating a venture went beyond playing a role, as in the negotiations described by Volkema. It was meant to be a meaningful experience where we expected attention to occur and learning to follow (Beck and Kosnik, 2006).

The aforementioned changes were a move to make the entrepreneurial experience more real, simplify the syllabus so that students could identify the most important milestones of their learning process and, at the same time, to diminish excuses and distractions. All in all, our aim was to encourage failure and push students out of their comfort zone. According to one student, "although I appreciate the trust provided by our teachers in us and in our ventures, the idea of receiving seed capital had many implications. Particularly, it meant feeling under greater pressure and knowing that more was demanded from us." Another one said, "I honestly thought of changing to another class section because I feared playing with other people's money and I did not want to leave my comfort zone". These reactions allowed us to verify that the new course design was better at promoting agency, accountability and obligation. It also demonstrated to us that our new course design was better at engaging students by placing more emphasis on cultural and moral norms than grading (legal norms).

Outcomes

Student engagement and more prototyping were some outcomes of the changes we introduced. The following accounts come from our observations, self-evaluations by students and external evaluations at an Innovation Fair.

The idea of being accountable for real money created a greater sense of responsibility towards us, pressured students to take action and allowed us to highlight that the process was more important than the end result. Providing seed money to students was a way of forcing them to answer concrete questions such as: how much have you invested until now or how much have you sold? By posing these questions to students, they had to demonstrate real progress (or failure) as opposed to plans and ideas on paper. As the quotes that closed the previous section state, students noticed this from the beginning.

At the beginning, we asked students to visit public libraries and identify problems they could address with their ventures. During previous semesters we had asked students to identify problems in other locations. Framing their observations helped them because observing without boundaries resulted in students developing a business based on their personal interest rather than on a real problem. As Ebben and Johnson (2014) have experienced, "student creativity is inhibited when facing a blank white board with no constraints…a single, rather loose constraint would provide a springboard to launch the students' creativity and engage their entrepreneurial spirit".

Students were surprised during their fieldwork. For example, someone was appalled to find out that some students attending public universities are not able to afford photocopies. Interacting with other socioeconomic strata led some students out of their comfort zone. And, by the end of the course, there were several reports of the advantages of exchanges with a variety of people.

In the end, they identified problems that were close to their lives: a friend finder, student tutorials or mobile chargers. The prototypes that students devised and the solutions they proposed were limited to the university environment. We were unable to veer them towards problems of a larger scope, such as the ones Krippendorff (2013) describes:

> Great companies are those that dedicate themselves to a problem that matters. When they solve the problem, they exit the stage triumphant. And companies that survive do so because the problem they exist to solve (their purpose or mission) is so big that there is still work to do. Longevity is not a goal in itself; it is a bi-product (*sic*) of taking on a big problem.

Throughout the semester, we encouraged students to invest the seed capital and generate sales. Weeks went by without consulting demands from students. But they sought help as soon as they felt pressure from harsh feedback, low grades or an impending deadline, not necessarily due to failures with their ventures. Despite different ways in which we tried to get students to embrace failure, they were overly cautious. It seemed that their financial obligation towards us constrained their agency. An increase in obligations to the authority in the classroom paralysed some students. Ironically, many of them avoided spending our money without realizing that they were not required to repay our loan as long as they documented their journey and learning. In other words, they failed to realize we were assuming most of the financial risk.

Although the changes to the course increased student engagement considerably, there were class sessions when commitment waivered. In one particular occasion, students had not prepared the assigned reading, so we decided to first express disappointment and then walk out. As we put it then, we were not willing to waste time and effort if they were not going to honour their commitments. This was a collective shock that caused students to place more effort in subsequent classes. But, exactly how much pressure to exert is a question that has to be answered considering the characteristics of each particular case (e.g. a student's level of tolerance to failure).

We also tried to use social pressure and recognition as a substitute to punishment (grades). We invited entrepreneurs to hear student presentations and provide them with further guidance and feedback. Students came better prepared for these sessions since they feared losing face. In one of these sessions, an entrepreneur was very critical about some of the proposed ventures. Some students were shocked, but eventually realized that the feedback was useful and consequently they made adaptations to their business models. This type of feedback gave students a glimpse of how demanding investors can be, and made them reflect about whether they had the stomach to be entrepreneurs. Unlike students and teachers who tend to avoid conflict, particularly when it impacts motivation (Sava, 2002), external guests can be more open about the way they provide advice.

One main activity for students was to examine each one of their hypotheses about the elements of their business models. In this endeavour our suggestion was to follow a free MOOC (massive open online course) taught by Steve Blank about "How to Build a Startup". In the words of one student, "I learned that the only way to be certain if something works or not is by testing the market with a small pilot". These pilots are models or prototypes of the product or service to be offered.

At three different points during the semester we asked students to present these prototypes. The exercises showed their advances with design thinking and with the search for a profitable, replicable and scalable business model. Several students recognized that they could have done more with their prototypes, and that one shortcoming of not having done so was a lack of confidence in their venture.

The final external validation came at the end-of-the-year Innovation Fair where all the ventures had a stand, along with projects from other university departments. Peer pressure was a crucial element in the Fair. No need, then, to have it as part of the grading system. The lack of confidence, expressed by "we weren't sure about our idea and we didn't believe in ourselves", was shot down by enthusiastic responses from attendees at the fair. As we had told several teams when examining their insights and business models, our opinions paled in comparison to the reactions they got from the market segment they aimed at.

Compared to previous years in which grading included in-class participation, an interview write-up and progress reports, the new system better aligned performance to our objectives of developing evidence-based business models. As we dropped assignments and grades not connected to outputs and outcomes, we placed less emphasis on assessments and highlighted the importance of attempting, experimenting, documenting and reflecting. Our feedback privileged actions (e.g. identifying a problem, prototyping, selling) and embraced failure (see Table 5.1).

Table 5.1 **Comparison of grading structures**

Task	2014 (%)	2015 (%)
Entrepreneur interview write-up	5	
Speaker write-ups	10	
Weekly progress reports (posted on a Wiki)	15	20
Presentations of prototypes	15	15
Midterm exam	15	10
Elevator pitch	5	*Extra credit*
Innovation Fair	5	
Final presentation of their business models	5	
Written business plan	10	
Group accountability report		30
Individual accountability report		15
Final exam	15	10
Total	100	100

As evidenced by Table 5.1, the new course design reduced the amount of grading and favoured agency and accountability over obligations. Assignments like speaker write-ups and entrepreneur interviews ensured class participation and exams were also a way to check if students read and understood theoretical frameworks. These assignments attempted to guide their learning, but did not promote agency or provide students with a chance to be accountable for decisions beyond their decision to study or not.

We kept a midterm and final exam as indicators of students' understanding of an entrepreneurial process. Traditional exams can get in the way of shifting responsibility for learning from teachers to students, and shifting from legal to cultural and moral norms. Our exams, as an exercise in applying knowledge, were different. For example, the final exam provided an opportunity to put to good use all the ideas and experiences of the course to understand another entrepreneur's journey. Students were asked to analyse the characteristics and evolution of the business model used by a seasoned entrepreneur who told his or her experience to the group during the first hour of the exam.

Reflective practice

One way of encouraging students to reflect about their own experiences was to invite successful entrepreneurs to present their ventures. Students could compare their efforts to those of five entrepreneurs throughout the semester. Particularly, two speakers made a lasting impression. The first was a 21-year-old student who started a food delivery business. The fact that he was just a high school graduate, and that he had been running his business for more than four years, spurred in students feelings of not taking advantage of their education. One student added, "something I would have done differently was to take more advantage of the seed capital; reflecting back on our progress, I could have learned more if I had taken more risks in this course."

The second speaker described how her efforts to solve her sister's disability resulted in a successful social enterprise that addresses communication disability. This entrepreneur has been recognized by MIT Technology Review as one of the world's most promising innovators under the age of 35. She inspired students to consider businesses as a force for good and that anyone with enough will power can contribute enormously to society.

We followed Neck and Greene's focus "on doing, then learning, rather than learn then do. As a result a reflective practice component is incredibly important to learning" (2011, p. 62). Therefore, our grading system rewarded self-reflection. Each group was responsible for posting their findings and lessons from each prototype in a wiki. In turn, we provided feedback and guidance outside the classroom using this online tool, and also kept track of how their thinking evolved throughout the semester.

On occasion, we felt the need to intervene at a particular juncture and we asked students to reflect on an issue. For example, there was a group whose initial proposal was a venture for communicating bits of information among acquaintances. Using "Yik Yak" (an app that allows anonymous postings and to "check out what everyone's saying around you") as a model, and fearing the deleterious consequences of gossip, we sent them an article titled "Who Spewed That Abuse? Anonymous Yik Yak App Isn't Telling" that appeared on the front page of the *New York Times* (NYT) local edition (Mahler, 2015). A week later, when the group proposed a different venture, we asked them about the reasoning behind their change. It did not have to do with possible consequences of their app; it had to do with the time it would take them to sell and reap the benefits of network effects for a new app. Here, sales arguments took precedence over ethical arguments. This demonstrated to us that although we discussed their personal responsibility in learning, we failed to explore with students their responsibility in taking into account the negative impacts of their ideas.

As the semester progressed, a group veered to a new business idea. We pointed out that they were proposing something very similar to what another group was already working on for weeks. Some thought this was just a coincidence, while others felt they had copied their idea. Without judgement on our part, we allowed them to reflect on these competitive developments. Interestingly, the group that had the idea first did not complain, but rather used the coincidence as evidence to support that their insights and findings were heading in the right direction. The other team ended up working harder to demonstrate that their solution was different and superior.

In these and other instances, students had opportunities for real-time learning about responsible management. In the first case, we wanted the group of students to understand the possible consequences of the venture they were considering. The NYT article did not speak to them and there seemed to be no questioning among them on ethical grounds about possible consequences, nor did we notice any self-awareness of their participation in initiatives that could be hurtful. In the second case, both groups had a mature response by acknowledging competition, its advantages and drawbacks, and we did not have to intervene.

Midway through and at the end of the semester, we asked students to reflect on their experiences as they tried to spark their start-up. Two accountability reports, one by groups and an individual exercise, were a large component of final grades. Groups provided a profit and loss statement, a timeline that detailed the evolution of their process (including changes in their market segmentation, insights, solutions and business model) and a document that explained their failures. Individuals could submit a video or schedule a face-to-face interview in which they were asked to discuss key lessons, analyse what could have been done differently and make a personal assessment of their character as an entrepreneur. Individual reflections, as well as group analyses, allowed us to examine what some students learned. For example, one student wrote in her final report:

> I understood the difficulties, which are not few, along the road for an entrepreneur; constant failures, being lost and confused when deciding which route to take. But, I also understood that those failures are necessary to shape goals, and arrive strongly and surely to a destination. In this course I became convinced that whoever loses actually wins, learns and grows through experience.

Reflections became justifications too, as students ignored their agency. One student explained his poor performance: "This semester I felt that, despite my best efforts, it was a bit difficult to spend time on Entrepreneurship since I was taking two courses in Chemical Engineering that demanded a lot of my time." Another one wrote:

> Unfortunately, I took this course along with others that required much time and effort, and that were equally important for my goals as a design professional. Therefore, I could not give it enough attention and commitment, those characteristics that identify a real entrepreneur.

Another dimension of students' experience in the course was related to teamwork. Although research on group dynamics demonstrates that diversity within teams can improve their performance (Phillips, 2014), some students complained that different ideas among team members in terms of choosing an idea, distributing the workload and what to prototype made tasks harder and advocated for teams to be organized around common interests. After compromising about the venture to pursue, one student admitted that "I never identified with our business idea and perhaps this explains why I was not motivated enough". Another student stated, "I completed the course being satisfied with what I learned, but would have liked to take more advantage of the seed capital and a different team might have worked better".

In the second use of the CATME tool, students responded to a peer evaluation instrument. Beyond their self-evaluation, students could compare their appraisals with ratings from teammates and average ratings for the whole team. Among their challenges, students stated that they had to deal with free-riders within their teams. All three dimensions of responsibility were at play here: agency, obligation and accountability. At the end of the semester, many students reported not giving their best efforts in terms of leadership and individual contributions. As one student declared, "I did not lead like I usually do; my teammates were not putting any effort into our project and I lost my motivation because of this".

A more responsible education?

> We are living at a time when we have more resources and knowledge than ever before to solve these problems, if only we take responsibility (Denise Restauri, 2015).

One can ask many questions about privileges and responsibilities when working at an elite university in an economically developing nation. A basic one is whether education is transforming the lives and world-views of the students we interact with. In accordance with Principle 1 of the Principles for Responsible Management Education, are we developing "the capabilities of students to be future generators of sustainable value for business and society at large and to work for an inclusive and sustainable global economy"? And, related to our teaching methods, are we creating the "processes and environments that enable effective learning experiences for responsible leadership"?

Not only were we unhappy with our answers to these questions in previous courses, but we also feared self-deception about having impactful teaching and learning. Lack of student interest in their own ventures and poor results were just symptoms. In discussing what these symptoms could reveal, we decided our first responsibility was to engage students. In a move to do so, we changed some of our teaching practices in the entrepreneurship course described above.

Attempting to avoid deceit, we sought to confront students with reality. The idea was to connect students' experience with entrepreneurship concepts and theories. We believe advances in that direction existed. One student recognized, at least, the need to integrate that underlies our approach: "I believe more courses should be like this one, where students have to integrate their previous knowledge about marketing, finance and economics to develop a product". The demands he detected were real and he had to muster all his knowledge to respond adequately.

Real demands have the effect of "cornering" students. It is, thus, more difficult to invent or deceive. Since the first day of class we made it clear to students that our course design would not provide them with much learning unless they accepted the challenge of developing a business idea, testing it, failing, trying again and learning from this process. In other words, they had responsibility for their own learning. They had the possibility of taking the same course at the same time with another professor with a more traditional approach. As we mentioned before, our aim was to shape leaders who are responsible for their actions.

Another change we observed from previous semesters was that although some students still failed to give their best effort, they now acknowledged such failure rather than denying it to themselves or to us. This was an accomplishment because those students were able to place their performance in a larger context and gain insights. They were responsible for their decisions and actions.

However, getting students to engage responsibly was not an easy task. The way we "cornered" students in the course (i.e. providing seed capital and demanding sales) was coherent with entrepreneurial endeavours, but it also had disadvantages. One of the disadvantages we identified was that the type of preferred start-ups could be heavily influenced by their sales potential. One team, for example, deliberately chose to resell an existing product in order to demonstrate a quick turnaround. Other teams tried, as in previous semesters, to develop ventures that had no apparent connection to real problems and that offered limited value to society. For example, one group proposed a company that organized events targeted at students. Although there might be a need for entertainment, our class emphasized solving problems rather than attempting to fulfil general needs. In such cases, the promise of students as generators of sustainable value was not fulfilled, at least within the context of the course.

Other conditions, like having many other obligations, distractions or group conflicts, were not new to them. We suggested using a small amount of the seed money to ease dialogues (e.g. go out together) and alter difficult group dynamics, but there were no takers for this type of option. It is possible that our suggestions came too late in the semester. We did use the CATME tool to allow students to compare their appraisals of teamwork with those of their teammates. Overall, however, we failed to provide appropriate tools to deal with conflict and diversity within teams. We encouraged diversity to obtain more innovative proposals but, in the absence of experience by undergraduate students, diversity became an obstacle and caused frustration. As organizational behaviour research suggests, the types of group conflict and how teams handle them determines whether diversity is effective in increasing or reducing performance (Brett *et al.*, 2006; Neale *et al.*, 1999).

At the end of the semester, students turned in a self-evaluation of their own entrepreneurial process (i.e. observe, identify real problems, find and prototype creative solutions, learn, develop a business model and continue prototyping until the model creates value to society). These reports answered questions about what students took away, what they would do differently and their appraisals about themselves as entrepreneurs. Regarding their thoughts about whether they consider themselves entrepreneurs after trying it throughout the semester, most students identified with some character traits such as leadership, persistence, doers, openness to failure and empathy (required to identify problems). However, the vast majority had difficulty being flexible and incorporating new information into their business after each prototype or feedback round. Others claimed that they were not creative, despite our efforts to promote different techniques to promote creativity in devising alternative solutions.

Did we act as responsible teachers? Most of our efforts focused on creating nurturing yet demanding environments. As a result, we observed ventures that were tested and had potential. Also, some students expressed that they were interested in continuing to develop their business models.

A distinguishing feature of the course was an environment that decreased the probabilities of delusion among teachers and students, and forced the latter to act in response to certain worldly demands. As with transformative experiences, students left their comfort zone and came up with some alternatives to solve the problems that they had identified.

We also increased our commitment to students. By offering them our salaries we created a greater incentive for ourselves to provide adequate guidance. If we failed in our duties, it was less likely that teams would be able to recover our investment. In the end, we recovered 70% of the seed capital given to students (about US$1,000 in total). In most cases, sales were the source of the repayment funds; but there were a couple of groups of students who decided to pay from their own pockets what they had spent in their ventures.

After each class we asked ourselves: what can students discover and learn today? Every session was a challenge, and we kept distancing ourselves from the known realms of teaching entrepreneurship and getting closer to the new frontiers that offer a world of value creation (Neck and Greene, 2011). As we approached entrepreneurship as method, we also honoured the first Principle for Responsible Management. Within extreme approaches, rooted in the differences between causation and effectuation logics, our course was consciously situated closer to the latter. In Sarasvathy's words (2001, p. 245):

> Causation processes take a particular effect as given and focus on selecting between means to create that effect. Effectuation processes take a set of means as given and focus on selecting between possible effects that can be created with that set of means.

We departed from traditional approaches in which students were instructed to research market opportunities, and where the main source of lessons was case studies. Instead of attempting to transfer knowledge about entrepreneurship to passive students, we sought every chance to engage them in entrepreneurial action. Table 5.2 summarizes our approach.

Table 5.2 **Course activities corresponding to an effectuation logic**

Effectuation	Logic	Examples
Entrepreneurial mind-set	Embrace failure	From day 1, doing is privileged over "doing it right"; and we point out that to err is fine, but to not learn from mistakes is a problem. At the end of the semester each student must reflect on whether or not they have an entrepreneurial spirit.
Main source of ideas	Problems and unsatisfied needs	First half of the semester is spent defining which problem students will attempt to solve during the second half. During eight weeks they gather observations and try to make sense of them. Although we require them to make observations in a specific space (e.g. farmers markets), every group identified a different problem.
Planning philosophy	Plans considering uncertainty	Since it is uncertain when groups are ready to advance to the next stage in their projects, our syllabus does not impose topics on specific dates. The only deadline is the end of the semester. Additionally, they design and prepare prototypes but do not control how their prototypes will be received by the market. Usually, after receiving feedback from potential clients, they have to change their plans and start all over.
Preparation	Participatory-action research	Students start their fieldwork during the second week and remain in the field until the end of the semester. They learn various research methods traditionally used in sociology and anthropology. Their entrepreneurial projects span across very diverse industries (e.g. food, tourism, culture, educational technology, garments).
Source of lessons	Directly from own experience	We teach two theories that can basically be taught in two days. The rest of the semester, students are required to put theory into practice and learn by doing. In class, we discuss their learnings. A final report consists of those lessons from these experiences.
Teacher's role	Facilitates learning by coaching and sharing risks with students	Besides our intrinsic motivation to contribute to students' education, we are risking the money that funds their entrepreneurial initiatives. In our first experiment, we recovered 76% of the seed capital.
Student's role	Co-creators of learning experiences	As we progressed along different stages in the entrepreneurial process, students provided feedback about their learning process and are consulted in order to identify their needs at specific stages in the entrepreneurial process

The first course we taught together in 2014 did not get as close to an effectuation logic as the second one in 2015. The elements of the entrepreneurial process were the given means used by students during the semester. From day one we encouraged trial and error, provided examples of our own failures and rewarded experimentation through prototypes. The more they tried different paths to developing their ventures, the more they learned.

There are several limitations in the approach we took to our responsibilities as teachers in this course. On the one hand, several changes we implemented followed more intuition than theory. As we reflected on the newly created conditions, we did contrast them with different theoretical approaches to learning. In many respects, our approach is similar to the new frontiers Neck and Greene (2011) describe as teaching entrepreneurship as a method.

On the other hand, we ignored many students' reactions to the changes we implemented in the course. For example, students prefer to have greater freedom to choose their business, and abolish midterms or final exams. Although we designed specific tasks to collect student data and kept detailed field notes, there were many reactions that we barely glimpsed. End-of-the-semester formal evaluations done by the university did not provide any pattern. Comparing the two courses Alan and Roberto have taught together since 2014, there was a slight increase in the average points awarded to a question about engagement (i.e. "The course promotes my engagement (effort and commitment) with the study of this subject matter"); but there was a lower average for a question about evaluations (i.e. "Evaluations are adequate and consistent with the objectives of this course"). Our systematic examination of the contrasts between different teaching approaches can be improved.

In the end, we found a way to push students beyond their comfort zone, an alternative that is different from creating disequilibrium and working with Vygotsky's zones of proximal development (Blake and Tambra, 2008). "Cornering" students so that they face what they did, and what they avoided, brought honesty to the whole entrepreneurial process. It became a true test of themselves as entrepreneurs, and this was no easy accomplishment. Achieving honesty in teacher–student relations is a challenge in any subject area.

Individual perspectives and suggestions for other educators

The need for responsible leaders is acute in economically developing countries. Efforts to promote teaching that honour the PRME are welcome. As for developed economies, most if not all implications of what has been discussed in this chapter are applicable. Entrepreneurial ecosystems are more nurturing in developed economies, so conditions are less stringent and students have more support to develop their ventures (e.g. it is easier to access venture capital). Nevertheless, students in developing economies can hone their skills to confront the tougher conditions. However, disappointment with student engagement during several semesters led us to devise seed capital as an instrument to move students towards less discourse and more action.

Each of us had particular interpretations of what happened in the course. For Roberto, the new approach reduced the amount of deception and increased worthy efforts. Finding mechanisms that increased student engagement and improved their performance was a highlight during the semester. Even the beliefs and practices of "strategic learners" (Biggs, 1999) were shaken. An unfavourable context for alternative approaches (e.g. heavy academic loads, extrinsic motivators) could explain why more was not accomplished. Still, the question of what keeps students from engaging more profoundly remains.

For Alan, the new approach was fulfilling because it framed an experience close to the business world; one in which entrepreneurs are required to present and defend their ideas clearly and succinctly, justify their decisions and mistakes, execute and show results, and be open to criticism. However, the course still failed to transfer responsibility for learning to some students who continued to respond to grades and assignments rather than to their own motivations. In other words, those students did not realize that entrepreneurship is a way for them to achieve their personal goals as opposed to an end in itself.

An entrepreneurship course, where students are "cornered" and they reflect about their practice, can "enable effective learning experiences for responsible leadership" as the third principle in the PRME states. As with the first principle related to generating sustainable value, the changes we introduced increased their responsibility, but there still is room for improvement. Our recommendations for those who would like to try a similar approach to teaching responsible management, not just entrepreneurship would be:

1. **Entrepreneurial mind-set**: Design a learning environment that forces students to examine reality and pushes them out of their comfort zone. Reward those who try, fail and learn, over those who play it safe. Even in classes about accounting or economics, students who take risks, ask unorthodox questions and challenge themselves are more likely to be better at solving problems. The lever to push out of comfort zones need not be seed capital, but if money is chosen it does not need to come from the instructors' salaries. Although offering one's salary sends a powerful message of commitment to increase students' performance, money can come from the university or from a sponsor. Seed capital can be an enabler of actions, but be aware that accountability and obligation can paralyse students.

2. **Course preparation**: Devise mechanisms in which your interests and those of students are aligned so that both share risks and rewards. Common mechanisms for most courses could include fewer assignments for those who try harder and additional support for those students that are willing to implement ideas.

3. **Source of lessons**: Demand reflective practice at the same time you reduce the number of assignments to those that reward doing and reflecting about actions.

4. **Teacher's role**: Team up with an entrepreneur to take advantage of both theory and practice. Students notice an additional advantage; namely, they have an extra pair of ears and eyes for their trials and tribulations. However, make sure the entrepreneur has time to prepare classes, allows the students to learn from their own experience rather than speaking only of his or her own experience, and brings in new ideas to class. Take advantage of different styles and experiences when co-teaching to provide valuable feedback and to generate more discussions than lectures. For example, teachers can contradict each other in order to demonstrate that there are no right or wrong answers.

5. **Student's role**: Place high expectations and make sure students understand what success in class looks like from day one. Also, create activities for smaller groups during class in order to increase student engagement and to personalize their learning.

Final thoughts

Teaching entrepreneurship requires greater emphasis on cultural and moral norms than on legal norms. Entrepreneurship requires a person to take responsibility for their actions, but most importantly it demands character traits that go beyond compliance and defy the status quo. For us, responsible management education allows students to understand that they need to create value for society not because it is expected from them, but rather because they can achieve self-fulfilment by doing so.

References

BBMG & GlobeScan (2014). *The 2014 Aspirational Consumer Index*. Retrieved from http://bbmg.com/wp-content/uploads/2014/07/BBMG_GlobeScan_TheAspirationals.pdf

Beck, C. & Kosnik, C.M. (2006). *Innovations in Teacher Education: A Social Constructionist Approach*. Albany, NY: State University of New York Press.

Biggs, J. (1999). *Teaching for Quality Learning at University*. Buckingham: Society for Research into Higher Education and Open University Press.

Blake, B. & Tambra P. (2008). Developmental psychology: Incorporating Piaget's and Vygotsky's theories in classrooms. *Journal of Cross-Disciplinary Perspectives in Education*, 1(1), 59-67.

Blank, S. (2013). Why the lean start-up changes everything. *Harvard Business Review*, May, 63-72.

Brett, J., Behfar, K. & Kern, M. (2006). Managing multicultural teams. *Harvard Business Review*, November 2006, 84-91.

Carbon Disclosure Project (2013). *Sector Insights: What is Driving Climate Change Action in the World's Largest Companies—Global 500 Climate Change Report*. Retrieved from https://www.cdp.net/cdpresults/cdp-global-500-climate-change-report-2013.pdf

Dewey, J. (2015). *Democracy and Education*. New York: Sheba Blake Publishing. (Original work published 1916)

Ebben, J. & Johnson, A. (2014). "The Lemonade Stand Project": A refreshing approach to teaching undergrads. Entrepreneurship & Innovation Exchange. Retrieved from https://eiexchange.com/content/70-the-lemonade-stand-project-a-refreshing-approach-to-teaching-undergrads

Eccles, R., Ioannou, I. & Serafeim, G. (2011). The impact of a corporate culture of sustainability on corporate behavior and performance. Harvard Business School working paper, HBS Working Knowledge, Number 12-035.

Edelman (2015). Edelman Trust Barometer 2015. Retrieved from http://www.edelman.com/insights/intellectual-property/2015-edelman-trust-barometer/

Fiet, J.O. (2001). The pedagogical side of teaching entrepreneurship. *Journal of Business Venturing*, 16(2), 101-117.

Fulton, M., Kahn, B. & Sharples, C. (2012). *Sustainable Investing: Establishing Long Term Value and Performance*. Deutsche Bank Group.

Greenberg, D., McKone-Sweet, K. & Wilson, J. (2011). *The New Entrepreneurial Leader: Developing Leaders Who Shape Social and Economic Opportunity*. San Francisco: Berrett-Koehler Publishers.

Harmon, M.F. (1995). *Responsibility as Paradox*. Thousand Oaks, CA: Sage.

Innosight (2012). *Creative Destruction Whips through Corporate America*. Retrieved from http://www.innosight.com/innovation-resources/strategy-innovation/upload/creative-destruction-whips-through-corporate-america_final2015.pdf

KPMG (2013). *The KPMG Survey of Corporate Responsibility Reporting 2013*. Retrieved from http://www.kpmg.com/Global/en/IssuesAndInsights/ArticlesPublications/corporate-responsibility/Documents/corporate-responsibility-reporting-survey-2013-exec-summary.pdf

Krippendorff, K. (2013). Great companies solve problems that matter. *Fast Company Magazine*. Retrieved from http://www.fastcompany.com/3023216/leadership-now/great-companies-solve-problems-that-matter

Krueger, N.F. (2009). The microfoundations of entrepreneurial learning and...education: The experiential essence of entrepreneurial education. In G.I. Page, L. Gatewood, and G. Shaver (eds.), *University-wide Entrepreneurship Education* (pp. 35-59). Cheltenham, UK: Edward Elgar.

Mahler, J. (2015, March 8). Who spewed that abuse? Anonymous Yik Yak App isn't telling. *New York Times*, A1.

Mockus, A. (1999). *Harmonizing Law, Morality and Culture*. Inter-American Development Bank.

Neale, M. A., Northcraft, G. B. & Jehn, K. A. (1999). Exploring Pandora's Box: The impact of diversity and conflict on work group performance. *Performance Improvement Quarterly*, 12, 113-126.

Neck, H. & Greene, P. (2011). Entrepreneurship education: Known worlds and new frontiers. *Journal of Small Business Management*, 49(1), 55-70.

Osterwalder, A., Pigneur, Y, & Clark, T. (2009). *Business Model Generation: A Handbook for Visionaries, Game Changers, and Challengers*. Amsterdam: self-published.

Phillips, K.W. (2014). How diversity makes us smarter. *Scientific American*, 311(4), 43-47.

Pizarro, N. (2014). An institutional and pedagogical model that fosters entrepreneurial mindset among college students. *Journal of Entrepreneurship Education*, 17(2), 143-162.

Restauri, D. (2015, March). Move over summers in France, this woman is changing the face of study abroad. *Forbes.* Retrieved from http://www.forbes.com/sites/deniserestauri/2015/03/09/move-over-summers-in-france-this-woman-is-changing-the-face-of-study-abroad/3/

Ries, E. (2011). *The Lean Startup: How Today's Entrepreneurs Use Continuous Innovation to Create Radically Successful Businesses.* New York: Crown Business.

Sarasvathy, S. (2001). Causation and effectuation: Towards a theoretical shift from economic inevitability to entrepreneurial contingency. *Academy of Management Review* 26(2), 243-263.

Sava, F. (2002). Causes and effects of teacher conflict-inducing attitudes towards pupils: A path analysis mode. *Teaching and Teacher Education,* 18(8), 1007-1021.

Volkema, R.J. (2007). Negotiation for money: Adding a dose of reality to classroom negotiations. *Negotiation Journal,* 23(4), 473-485.

6

Walking the talk
Empowering undergraduate business students to act on their values

Melissa Manwaring, Danna Greenberg and James Hunt
Babson College, USA

With commentary from Lee Augsburger and Megan Houlker*

> [B]usiness schools have a more critical role than ever in instilling a sense of right and wrong in their students (Association to Advance Collegiate Schools of Business, 2009, p. 1).

> Nobody is ever going to invent an ethics class that makes people behave ethically after they step out of the classroom (Jonathan Haidt, 2012, p. 90).[1]

---

* The academic co-authors are deeply appreciative of the practitioners' generosity and thoughtfulness in contributing commentary to this piece.

1 Thomas Cooley Professor of Ethical Leadership at the Stern School of Business, New York University.

Introduction

The problem: Teaching ethical competences that managers actually use

When it comes to bridging academia and practice, there may be no realm more challenging than business ethics. To be sure, there are widespread efforts to teach business ethics. Most business schools incorporate ethics and social responsibility into their curricula and the number of business ethics courses is on the rise (Rasche *et al.*, 2013). Major accrediting institutions such as the Association to Advance Collegiate Schools of Business (AACSB) and the EFMD Quality Improvement System (EQUIS) explicitly call for business schools to include ethics in their curricula (AACSB International, 2015; EQUIS, 2015). Despite these efforts, there is little evidence that ethics education in the classroom translates into ethically responsible action in the workplace (Rasche *et al.*, 2013). Indeed, some still question the wisdom of providing any academic instruction in business ethics (Bisoux, 2015). Meanwhile, vivid examples of corporate ethical failures abound worldwide—from the Deutsche Bank spying debacle and the BP Gulf oil spill to more recent scandals over Libor fixing, systematic bribery of doctors in China by GlaxoSmithKline (Plumridge and Burkitt, 2014), corporate corruption at Olympus (Office of the Inspector General, 2016), and emissions test "defeat devices" at Volkswagen. Critics continue to partially blame business schools for these ethical missteps, claiming that business school graduates lack the skills to effectively address real ethical issues in the workplace (Ghoshal, 2005; Zingales, 2012). The gap between academia and practice continues to loom large.

This challenge of teaching ethics is paramount to the Principles for Responsible Management Education (PRME). The first Principle commits institutes of higher education to "develop the capabilities of students to be future generators of sustainable value for business and society at large and to work for an inclusive and sustainable global economy". Effectively responding to values-based conflicts is paramount to inclusive leadership and sustained value generation. Principle 3 requires signatories to "create educational frameworks, materials, processes and environments that enable effective learning experiences for responsible leadership". Thus, to support the development of responsible leadership, higher education institutions must continue to search for new paradigms for educating students to respond to ethical challenges. What might institutes of higher education start teaching—or teach more effectively—if they are to cultivate more responsible business leaders?

Chapter overview

This chapter introduces an action-oriented approach to responsible management education that focuses on developing students' ability to both *recognize* and *act on* values-based conflicts. The primary voices are those of Melissa Manwaring, Danna

Greenberg and James Hunt, all management faculty at Babson College in the United States. These academic co-authors discuss the premise, development, implementation and implications of Babson College's approach to developing responsible business leaders. Two practitioners familiar with this approach—Megan Houlker and Lee Augsburger—provide commentary on its relevance in the real world of business. Formerly the Director of Babson College's Undergraduate Center for Career Development and now a Senior Manager for Talent Acquisition at Staples Inc., Megan is attuned to the behavioural competences required of responsible managers and to the increasing significance companies place on these competences as they hire, train and promote managers. Lee Augsburger is Senior Vice-President and Chief Ethics and Compliance Officer at Prudential Financial, Inc. Lee has a strong commitment to action-oriented approaches to teaching ethics in both higher education and business organizations.

In the next section we outline three challenges that both students and managers face when responding to values-based conflicts: recognizing the conflict, assessing where they stand on the conflict, and taking appropriate action. These challenges highlight corresponding competences that responsible managers must have and that we believe business schools must teach. We go on to introduce Giving Voice to Values (GVV), a curricular framework designed to support the development of the competences and self-efficacy needed to proactively address values-based conflicts. In the subsequent section, we provide a detailed case study of how Babson College incorporates the GVV framework into an experiential first-year undergraduate course on management and entrepreneurship. This is followed by a discussion of the challenges and limitations of this pedagogical approach along with ideas for addressing those challenges. Finally, the chapter concludes with suggestions for adapting this approach to other educational contexts, along with its broader implications for responsible management education.

The challenges of responding to values-based conflicts

Business students, like managers, face three key challenges as they respond to ethical issues: recognizing that the issue exists, determining what they believe is right in that situation, and taking appropriate action. We discuss each challenge below.

Recognizing the issue

Recognizing that an ethical issue exists is, of course, a prerequisite to deciding what is right and taking action, but this may not be as easy as it seems. Putting aside the deliberate dismissal or suppression of ethical dilemmas, institutional pressures and cognitive biases can lead to "ethical fading", or the tendency to ignore ethical dimensions of a decision in favour of economic, legal or other factors. As a result, even the best-intentioned professionals sometimes engage in ethically question-able behaviour because they do not notice ethical issues in the first place (Bazerman and Tenbrunsel, 2011). Unfortunately, teaching ethics as a stand-alone course (or even on "ethics day" in some other course) does little to help students learn to recognize ethical issues in natural, complex, real-world situations (Rasche *et al.*, 2013). Lee Augsburger sees the issue as follows,

> The only way to teach students the skill of effectively giving voice to values is in an integrated context. Ethical problems have to be addressed in the larger context of business. In a standalone course, it is too easy for individuals to assume that ethics and compliance issues are "someone else's responsibility".

Deciding what is "right"

Once a business leader (or student) recognizes that an ethical issue exists, the next challenge is to determine—whether through introspection, values clarification or intellectual analysis—the "right" thing to do. Of course, stakeholders often disagree on which values should take priority in a conflict and which course of action best aligns with those values. For instance, despite commitments they may have to social and environmental value creation, business leaders often prioritize economic value creation over those commitments. In the face-off between the individual and the organization, the organization—or particular sources of organizational power—will often have more influence over the "the right thing to do" in a conflict. While certain values such as honesty, respect, fairness and compassion tend to be fairly universal, individuals from different cultural backgrounds may prioritize values differently depending on the context. Self-serving biases can fuel rationalizations, leading well-intentioned individuals to make decisions that seem glaringly unethical in retrospect but which may have seemed justifiable in the moment (Bazerman and Tenbrunsel, 2011). Traditional business ethics courses can help managers address some of these challenges, as they often focus on ethical analysis and decision-making.

Taking appropriate action

Finally, after a manager (or business student) recognizes a values-based dilemma and determines what she feels is right, she is left with the challenge of deciding what to do about it. Should she speak up? If so, to whom, when, and how? The reality is that many students and organizational actors simply do not give voice to their values because they do not know how (Gentile, 2012). They lack what some scholars would describe as a sense of self-efficacy in the face of an ethical challenge (Nelson *et al.*, 2012). As Megan Houlker of Staples observes,

Even in situations where they know they need to speak up, recent college graduates often do not know how to do so effectively. Too often, these new hires lack the vocabulary and maturity to respond to these conflicts when they enter the workplace. They may lack the initiative for raising the issue or they lack the skills to dialogue and advocate effectively for their beliefs. As such, when they encounter value based conflicts, rather than taking effective action recent college graduates may just complain about what they witness. In other instances, these new hires may want to do something but they don't know where to start, who to go to, or what to say. They struggle with where and how to have these conversations.

Such challenges draw our attention to the importance of experiential, situated education for teaching students business ethics. In order to prepare students to behave ethically in real-world business contexts, ethical instruction must include authentic, integrated contexts in which students will actually experience the pressures associated with recognizing and acting upon ethical issues in the workplace.

The *Giving Voice to Values* framework

A cornerstone of our interdisciplinary approach to this teaching challenge is **Giving Voice to Values** (GVV; Gentile, 2012), an award-winning, interdisciplinary, global curriculum designed to help people recognize, articulate and act on their values in situations that appear to conflict with those values.[2] Developed by Mary Gentile, PhD and implemented in more than 400 educational and business institutions around the world, GVV focuses not on ethical analysis (deciding what's right) but on implementation (taking action after deciding what's right)—what some have called "performative ethics", as distinct from descriptive and normative ethics (Edwards *et al.*, 2015). Deciding which action to take is contextual and personal: one manager might raise concerns about questionable accounting practices through cooperative inquiry, while another might prefer to assert her objections more directly, and yet another might bring the issue to senior management. GVV therefore offers a framework for voicing values in a way that is tailored to each individual's strengths and circumstances.

The GVV curriculum is based on a framework encompassing seven "pillars", or core guidelines for action in a values-based conflict (Gentile, 2010a, "The To-Do List", pp. 1-2; see Table 6.1).

2 See www.givingvoicetovalues.org

Table 6.1 **Giving Voice to Values pillars**

Values	Know and appeal to a short list of widely shared values: e.g. honesty, respect, responsibilities, fairness and compassion
Choice	Believe you have a choice about voicing values by examining your own track record … and recognize, respect and appeal to the capacity for choice in others
Normality	Expect values conflicts so that you approach them calmly and competently
Purpose	Define your personal and professional purpose explicitly and broadly before conflicts arise… Similarly, appeal to a sense of purpose in others
Self-knowledge, self-image and alignment	Generate a "self-story" about voicing and acting on your values that is consistent with who you are and that builds on your strengths
Voice	Practise voicing your values in front of respected peers, using the style of expression with which you are most skilful and which is most appropriate to the situation, and invite coaching and feedback
Reasons and rationalizations	Anticipate the typical rationalizations given for ethically questionable behaviour and identify counter-arguments

Drawing on these seven "pillars", the GVV curriculum centres on a series of customizable short cases, with complementary readings, teaching plans and annotated bibliographies.[3] The cases—drawn from actual experience, and many of which are co-written by faculty and practitioners from across North America, Europe and Asia—describe a protagonist who is confronted with a values-based conflict. Case contexts range from academic to corporate to non-profit, with protagonists at all levels of the organizational hierarchies and settings across the globe.[4] As an example, a university student intern receives a request from a client to share his university identification number and password, which would allow the client to access the university's electronic databases in contravention of the database licences ("Student Privileges with Strings Attached"). Another involves a business consultant hired by the state to conduct a financial evaluation of a community organization that assists severely disabled clients, who learns that the organization has exaggerated some disability reports in order to secure maximum state funding for its clients ("Doing Bad to Do Good"). And in "This Whole System Seems Wrong", a purchasing director for a Spanish electronics company visits the Chinese factory

3 GVV material, including free curricular materials for educators, can be found at www.givingvoicetovalues.org or at the PRME website http://www.unprme.org/resources/display-resources-sub.php?scid=40.
4 In collaboration with PRME, GVV also offers an India-specific case collection, with materials written by Indian faculty and professionals and dealing with interpretations of anti-corruption in an Indian context (see Gentile, 2010b).

that supplies most of its components and is concerned about the unhealthy working conditions for its employees—most of whom are girls in their early teens.

Using the GVV cases, participants develop a script for addressing the values-based conflict. This process involves identifying values-driven positions, analysing key parties affected by the conflict and then considering whom to engage and how. To develop their script, GVV students consider four key questions:

1. What is at stake for the key parties?

2. What are the reasons and rationalizations the protagonist will need to address?

3. What levers/arguments can the protagonist use to influence those with whom he or she disagrees?

4. What is the protagonist's most powerful and persuasive response to the reasons and rationalizations he or she needs to address?

Through the process of scripting responses, students learn how to plan out where, when, how and with whom they might begin a conversation about a values-based conflict, anticipate likely justifications for the questionable behaviour (such as "everyone does it" or "it is not hurting anyone") and prepare responses.

These exercises are *not* based on the assumption that a real values-based conflict in the workplace can be addressed in an entirely predictable fashion. A key component of scripting is helping students learn to respond in their own voice based on who they are, how they work most effectively and what would be appropriate in the context. One student working in a family business might feel perfectly comfortable scripting a conversation with her father—the founder and CEO—about a change in her roles and responsibilities. Another student might find such an approach inappropriate, perhaps because of personal preferences or cultural expectations—and might script a conversation with his mother, in which he asks his mother to advocate on his behalf with his father. Scripts might also vary depending on the organizational culture and context. As Lee Augsburger observes:

> Company cultures vary and what works in one organization will not necessarily work in another. Prudential, for instance, has a supportive culture. This can sometimes make it challenging to hold difficult conversations for fear of offending others. In this context, one has to develop broad interpersonal skills in order to voice one's values. When new employees join the company they need to be able to diagnose the context and adapt their approach to the context. Having the skills and mind-set to hold those conversations and adapt to the context is one of the critical competences we look for when hiring new graduates.

Scripting is also important because it builds "muscle memory". Having responded to values-based conflict previously, one will be able to recall and adapt these scripts to future values-based conflicts. Individuals who have given voice to their values in the past are more likely to do so in the future—and be more confident and effective in doing so (Gentile, 2012).

Students learn to *recognize* and *act on* values-based conflicts

In this section we explain in detail how one educational institution, Babson College, has integrated the GVV framework into an interdisciplinary undergraduate course on management and entrepreneurship. The goal of this approach is to cultivate students' competences in *recognizing* and *acting on* real values-based conflicts— skills that tend to be difficult to learn and teach in a typical classroom setting.

The context: An interdisciplinary business immersion course at ·Babson College

Overview of Babson College

Babson College, located near Boston, Massachusetts in the United States, is a speciality business college recognized for its expertise in entrepreneurial leadership, though its alumni are represented in nearly all fields of business. Babson was one of the 25 founding colleges that launched the Principles for Responsible Management Education, and it includes both ethics and social, environmental and economic responsibility and sustainability in its college-wide learning goals. The college curriculum stresses building of competences and the ability to make use of knowledge in practice, as well as more traditional analytical capabilities. As such, Babson has a deep commitment to using experiential pedagogies to give students an opportunity to experiment with knowledge in practice, reflect on their efforts and receive feedback to help them improve their skills as well as their knowledge.

Overview of the Foundations of Management and Entrepreneurship (FME) course

Our flagship undergraduate course, Foundations of Management and Entrepreneurship (FME), was selected to provide an authentic context for developing students' capacities for addressing ethical challenges. FME is a required, interdisciplinary, year-long, team-based course in which students develop, launch, run and close down a real business utilizing the resources available to them, including a loan from the College of up to US$3,000. The creation of both social and economic value for all the stakeholders involved is stressed throughout. All profits, if any, are donated to a not-for-profit partner organization. Concurrently with this business project, students receive more traditional instruction in organizational behaviour and entrepreneurship, with lessons from the disciplinary coursework integrated into the business experience and vice versa.

FME business teams of 10–25 students experience uncertainty and competition, not unlike actual businesses. The acceptance of a business proposal is not automatic. Students must first "rocket pitch" a business idea for consideration by faculty and fellow students. Acceptable business ideas then undergo a feasibility study to determine the viability and impact of the potential business, and faculty and students vote on whether or not the actual business itself should be funded. Each class ends up with two or three actual *businesses*. Past FME businesses have included the retail sale of existing consumer products (clothing, electronics, accessories) and the creation of new products (mobile applications, customized headboards for residence hall beds, fertilizer supplement created from used coffee grounds collected on campus, student-harvested and packaged honey) and services (on-campus delivery of fresh fruit or late-night snacks, event production such as film screenings and speaker series, and a bullying/suicide awareness campaign). As they run their businesses, student teams face disagreements (some of which are values based), sort out leadership issues, work with a diverse population, address communication barriers, deal with frequent setbacks and grapple with thorny conflicts—again, much like in the real business world.

Authentic ethical conflicts within the course

The rich experiential challenges of the FME business project provide an incubator for students to develop their competences in recognizing, analysing and acting on values-based conflicts. Situated learning theory posits that students cannot fully develop these competences out of context (Brown *et al.*, 1989). Values-based conflicts take a variety of forms in FME. Conflicts can occur as the business faces a variety of ethical dilemmas that emerge over time as well as over the broader ethical stance the business should take. Such dilemmas are, of course, opportunities for teachable moments, reflection and practical skill-building through action. We looked to the Giving Voice to Values framework to provide students with the knowledge and skills to more effectively address these challenges.

Integrating the Giving Voice to Values framework into the FME course

Integrating the GVV framework into FME involved the development of curricular materials to best support students' learning in the unique context of the FME business project. While Gentile has used a crowd source model to develop a wide array of GVV cases, many such cases are not relevant to first-year undergraduate students. Cases that centre on protagonists who are managing corporate divisions or setting global strategy can be difficult for undergraduate students to relate to and learn from. We decided, therefore, to create customized cases to be used in conjunction with the GVV framework.

Creating relevant cases for classroom-based practice in the GVV methodology

In order to identify relatable topics for the customized GVV cases, two FME faculty convened focus groups in which 10–12 students shared situations they had experienced, seen or heard about in FME that had challenged their values. Based on these discussions, the faculty identified categories of typical values-based challenges in FME. Examples include:

- **Questionable sales techniques**. As they strive to meet their self-imposed sales goals, FME students sometimes approach sales in a way that violates FME guidelines. For example, students are not allowed to engage in a business-to-business sale with a parent without signing a conflict of interest form. They are also discouraged from buying their own businesses' products for the sole purpose of meeting sales targets. These guidelines were created to ensure that students experience the authentic challenges of selling. While students understand the purpose of these guidelines, they still sometimes choose to circumvent them.

- **Quality control**. In product-based businesses, students sometimes find that a product does not meet their quality expectations and in rare instances does not even work. This might happen for a number of reasons, such as students failing to check a sample before placing an order or failing to perform a thorough quality check when the product arrives. Students may be tempted to sell a product in spite of these issues.

- **Intra-team conflict**. One of the most troubling areas of conflict is how students work with one another. We found instances where students were marginalized, ignored, or unfairly criticized—sometimes because of personality clashes and sometimes for more insidious reasons such as racial, gender or ethnic bias. Approximately one-quarter of Babson undergraduates come from outside the United States (more than 50 countries are represented in the Class of 2019), which can lead to cross-cultural conflicts as well.

For each theme that emerged, we aggregated the stories we had heard and built GVV cases customized for the FME context.[5] While the cases were fictitious, the student reviewers found them realistic, as each conflict was set in a plausible FME business and involved students wrestling with the very issues our students regularly face.

Once we developed the customized cases, we then developed a pedagogy for teaching GVV in FME and connecting it to students' businesses. We now elaborate on this pedagogy.

---

5 Copies of these cases can be obtained from the first author.

First semester: Classroom-based GVV theory and practice

In the first semester of FME, the organizational behaviour curriculum focuses on the individual and the theme of self-understanding, including topics such as identity, emotional intelligence and behavioural style. The GVV framework aligns closely with this theme as it focuses on understanding what your values are and learning to act on your values in a way that is authentic to who you are.

Figure 6.1 **Overview of integration of GVV framework into FME curriculum**

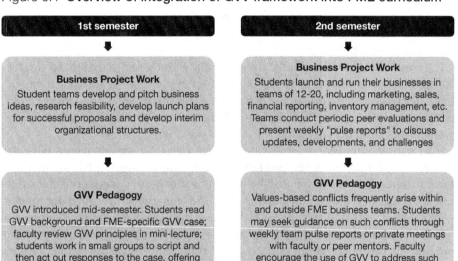

Our learning objectives for the GVV session are: (1) that the students understand and learn how to use the GVV framework to analyse values-based conflicts; and (2) that students begin to develop their ability to respond to these conflicts using the GVV approach. In preparation for the introductory GVV session, students read GVV background material and prepare a GVV case by developing scripts for addressing the conflict. Students then break into small groups to share and revise their scripts. Several groups are then invited to role play their scripts for the class. Following Gentile's suggestions, we ask the role players what is going well and where they are feeling stuck. We encourage other class members to provide suggestions for how to get "unstuck" and then invite a new class member to assume the protagonist role and continue the role play. In this way, the class works as a team to explore and practise scripts for responding to values-based conflicts.

Students are very engaged with this unit. Most first year students have already experienced values-based conflicts in high school, so they recognize their own discomfort and shortcomings in responding effectively to these situations. Moreover, students appreciate that these are the types of conflicts they will likely encounter both in their FME business and in the real world.

Second semester: Opportunities to recognize and act on authentic values-based conflicts

As the first semester of FME closes and the second semester begins, the student teams prepare to launch their businesses. As described above, these are real businesses, real products or services, suppliers, customers and money at stake, along with equally real intangibles such as reputations, emotions and relationships. Students quickly find themselves facing conflicts both within and outside their teams, often over values-based issues such as those described above. While specific conflicts may be difficult to predict and impossible to schedule, their existence *is* predictable. Such conflicts offer multiple experiential opportunities to apply and reinforce the GVV framework.

The course design allows for the time and space for these discussions to emerge. During the second semester, the first 30 minutes of each class is set aside for an in-depth discussion about one of the businesses. This discussion period gives faculty an opportunity to review and engage GVV as it relates to authentic values-based conflicts that students are facing.

For example, one FME business had a customer who experienced a personal injury due to faulty use of the product. While the injury was not life threatening, this customer did visit a doctor. The customer was quite upset about the situation and suggested they might sue the team. The team quickly reached out to their teaching assistants and faculty. Some of the team members wanted to stop selling the product immediately. Other team members felt the customer was at fault and that the business did not need to do anything. After speaking to the College's legal department, the faculty determined that the team was not legally responsible because the product had a warning label. That of course did not mitigate the underlying values issue. The faculty used the in-class discussion time to reinforce the GVV framework, focusing on the rationalizations for continuing to sell as well as scripting responses to these rationalizations. After reflection and a number of developmental role plays, the team decided to continue selling the product, but they changed their marketing materials to provide a stronger warning to customers, including putting a large, yellow caution label on their product. This caution label served as a catalyst for a new, creative marketing campaign. This is the hallmark of engaging GVV successfully as it leads to innovative responses to values-based conflicts.

Another business team struggled with internal power and leadership dynamics. As the team was preparing to launch its business, two students were nominated to serve as co-CEOs and confirmed by a majority vote of team members. A third student ("Jacob"), who had unsuccessfully sought the CEO position, then nominated himself President, with little opposition. As the team began operating its business and holding team meetings, Jacob asserted himself as the final authority on all decisions. Team members began to complain—at first in private to each other, then to peer mentors and faculty and finally directly to Jacob. The team felt Jacob's leadership style was too authoritarian and team motivation was declining.

The co-CEOs were on friendly terms with Jacob outside of class and didn't want to hurt his feelings, but were also concerned about the direction of their business and the overall experience for the other team members. An internal peer survey documented widespread dissatisfaction with the leadership dynamics. After several discussions, the co-CEOs decided to take action by asking Jacob to move to an individual contributor position in the financial department. They met privately with the other team members to confirm their support for this move, used the GVV scripting approach to prepare and then proposed the transition to Jacob during an all-team meeting, using the survey results to legitimize their proposal. Jacob ultimately decided to move to a different business team altogether, as he felt that it would be difficult to ignore the established dynamics within his original team. Following Jacob's departure, team morale and motivation improved considerably and Jacob found a useful niche within the other business team. In subsequent private meetings between the faculty and Jacob, the co-CEOs and other team members, it became clear that the entire experience—though emotionally difficult—generated meaningful lessons for all involved, and everyone, including Jacob, ultimately acknowledged the benefits in the way the co-CEOs voiced their (and their team's) values.

While these examples show how the faculty can coach students in applying the GVV framework to their business conflicts, the ultimate goal is for students to voluntarily engage the framework without prompting—just as they will have to do as managers. Much of the work for the FME businesses happens out of the faculty's sight. It is outside of class, in formal and informal interactions related to business crises and interpersonal conflicts, where students are likely to have the greatest opportunity for engaging GVV.

Examples of student responses to authentic values-based conflicts

One way faculty learn about students' unprompted use of GVV is through an open-ended writing prompt. Near the end of the course, students write a reflective essay about an interpersonal conflict they experienced in their business and analyse that experience using organizational behaviour concepts. In some essays, students analyse how they tried to use GVV to respond to a values-based conflict and why their approach was or was not successful. For example, Alison[6] analysed a values-based conflict she had with a team member. Alison wrote:

> I followed the action framework outlined in Mary C. Gentile's book, *Giving Voice to Values*... By maintaining my values and voicing them during and after the events, I was able to maintain my personal and professional relationships. Prior to this conflict, I had established a set of core *values* that included honesty, fairness, respect and responsibility. Lisa's actions were in clear violation of these core values. I had also realized that I had

---

6 All students gave permission that their work be used in this chapter. All students' names were changed.

a *choice* as to whether or not I should voice my values; I could keep my silence in the meeting and in the future or I could be honest with my peers and my faculty... Regarding the situation aftermath, I made my *purpose* clear to all parties. I made it clear that my profession *[sic]* purpose was to do what was best for the business which meant separating my friendship from the situation. This helped me express my values and opinions to Lisa and others after the situation had unfolded. I then anticipated the *reasons and rationalizations* that could be given by Lisa to explain her viewpoint and actions (Gentile, 2012). I was aware of her perspective and how she felt justified based on the work and energy she had contributed. I then discussed the events and my feelings with my class mentor and another teammate so I could practice *voicing* my values (Gentile, 2012).

As Alison's story illustrates, she drew on her GVV knowledge to respond to this difficult situation—entirely without faculty prompting.

Not all students are as successful as Alison in their use of GVV. Sometimes they find they are unable to influence their teammates to see a values-based conflict from a different perspective. Sometimes students can help a teammate see the conflict but the students do not know how to change the course of action. Students learn as much from these failed attempts as they do from successful attempts. As Maya wrote,

I could have voiced my values more effectively had I thought of a stronger, powerful and appealing argument to propose my marketing idea. I should have thought of the costs to both affected parties (i.e. company and customers), should have properly scripted my action planning and thought of the situation in terms of the wider purpose for the company, rather than on an immediate basis. In ETA [Entrepreneurial Thought and Action], taking action is the key and through GVV, I can commit to taking action and learning from the action. I am glad that I gathered confidence to take action by speaking up in the meeting, even though I could not communicate well to my team members and influence them to implement the marketing strategy that I suggested.

Students also write about conflicts in which they did not use GVV, but recognize in retrospect that GVV would have been helpful. In these papers, students analyse how they could have handled the situation differently if they had used GVV. For example, Cole wrote,

I personally would be afraid of saying to a group of 20 people, in a way that does not seem self-righteous. Going back to finding allies to help voice concerns, I should have at least tried to get Luisa as an ally because I know that she would not have hesitated to talk to the group.

Students are not required to use or write about GVV when they encounter a values-based conflict. Such examples demonstrate that students can both understand the GVV framework conceptually and integrate it into their actual practice. Through such experiences, students learn that there is more complexity to engaging GVV compared with the in-class cases that were taught in the first semester. As they work through this complexity, students adjust and adapt GVV and create their own scripting approach. In so doing, students transform GVV from a framework they learn in class to a set of behavioural skills they will carry forward beyond FME.

Challenges and limitations

Because the GVV framework is an experiential approach that moves from recognizing a values conflict to taking a course of action, we believe it provides a strong methodology for teaching practical ethics in an academic context. At the same time, we continue to evolve our own efforts to fully integrate this framework into our curriculum.

Building the skills to address values-based conflicts requires practise and feedback. The wide breadth and rapid pace of the FME course means that in-class practice time competes with other curricular demands. Because the opportunity to apply the GVV framework naturally arises in the context of the FME businesses, not all students experience these reinforcing situations. Moreover, because business operations take place almost entirely outside of class, it can be challenging for faculty to identify opportunities to coach students as they encounter real-world dilemmas regarding responsible management. Despite these challenges, the final reflection paper indicates many students do indeed recognize values-based conflicts without faculty intervention and feel empowered to address them in ways that they might not have prior to the course.

A limitation of the GVV curriculum more generally, though entirely intentional, is that it does not help guide ethical decision-making. GVV starts from the assumption that in many cases, managers (or in our case, students) already know what they believe is right and simply need to decide whether and how to act on that conviction. This in no way diminishes the importance of pedagogical efforts to help students recognize, analyse and make decisions regarding ethical dilemmas. It is intended as a complement to standard ethical analysis, not as a replacement (e.g. Gonzalez-Padron *et al.*, 2012).

A less obvious limitation is that students might apply the GVV approach too quickly or too broadly, without first analysing the ethical issues and determining whether voicing their values is appropriate or even relevant. Though GVV is designed to help people *challenge* assumptions about what is right or fair or acceptable, if misinterpreted it could actually be used to *reinforce* one's own assumptions, potentially contributing to the entrenchment of competing positions (Manwaring, 2013). In other words, there can be a dark side to the GVV framework which involves engaging this approach to reinforce an inaccurate position. As Megan Houlker states,

> The first challenge with helping recent college graduates learn how to effectively respond to values-based conflicts in the workplace lies with

helping them differentiate which values-based conflicts need to be addressed. Recent college graduates often have a black and white view of these conflicts and will respond with the same intensity and judgement when a friend leaves work early and doesn't tell the manager as they do to observing workplace theft. They also struggle to understand that when they are told information by a manager that might be relevant to a friend in another division their ethical responsibility is to keep the confidence of their manager, not protect their friend. Recent college graduates also struggle to recognize that in the workplace individuals are motivated for different reasons and may choose to contribute in different ways and that these differences can and should be accepted. They may quickly judge others rather than learn to accept differences. As such, college graduates often struggle to differentiate between real situations where they need to speak up about a values-based conflict and those where they don't.

Moreover, persuasively voicing values requires emotional intelligence (Goleman, 2000). Individuals may find their concerns ignored or dismissed if they are not able to manage their emotions or to read the emotions and cues of those around them. In FME, we introduce the concept of emotional intelligence very early in the course, and reinforce it throughout the year with readings, discussions and exercises. Based on the reflection papers, at least some students connect emotional intelligence with GVV and, whether deliberately or subconsciously, use self-awareness, empathy and social skills in developing their action plans for addressing values-based conflicts. As Lee Augsburger comments:

> Being able to effectively give voice to values begins with social awareness and empathy. The only way to teach students the skills of social awareness and empathy and effectively giving voice to values is by teaching these skills in an integrated classroom context.

If individuals are lacking in emotional intelligence or have not been introduced to this framework, they may not have the baseline skills to successfully engage the GVV methodology. Furthermore, undergraduate business students face an additional challenge in this regard (Baxter and Rarick, 1987). The typical adolescent first-year college student is at Kohlberg's "conventional level" of moral development, driven by the need to avoid disapproval (Kohlberg and Lickona, 1976). For most undergraduates, speaking up about a values-based conflict in the face of rationalizations or even opposition from their peers and managers is a developmental leap. Our theoretical introduction of the GVV framework followed by in-class practise with hypothetical situations and then opportunities for authentic practice is intended to provide scaffolding for these undergraduates as they develop not only their behavioural competences but also their ethical meaning-making.

Broader implications for responsible management education

While the FME course is unique to Babson College, the same approach to teaching ethics could be incorporated into other applied management courses in which students engage real-world problems. The GVV curriculum has already been used in a wide variety of business courses, including economics, sustainable business, accounting, human resource management, entrepreneurship, leadership and marketing, among others (see Gentile, 2013). We have leveraged GVV's skill-building focus by incorporating it into a course with a substantial experiential component, in which students can recognize and address organically arising values-based conflicts in an authentic organizational context. The key to this approach is combining frameworks for voicing values with opportunities to practise—not just in simulations, but in real contexts involving real conflicts. Other courses with an authentic experiential component could offer a similar opportunity, as could clinical programmes, student consulting projects, internships and the like. In the context of such a course or programme, faculty could adopt the four basic principles of our approach, which include:

- **Theoretical framework**. Introducing students to a framework for taking action in response to a values-based conflict, such as the *Giving Voice to Values* curriculum. This introduction might include readings, lectures, demonstrations or videos, for instance.

- **Practice**. Running classroom exercises in which students practise acting on their values in a hypothetical situation. GVV offers dozens of cases free of charge to educators. Faculty may also adapt these cases—or develop new ones as described above—to ensure their relevance to their particular students.

- **Recognizing and responding to authentic conflict real-time**. This may be the biggest challenge for educators, because authentic conflict by definition cannot be scheduled or predicted. Educators can, however, create an environment in which authentic conflict is likely to arise. In any course, an applied project that requires students to work in teams for a period of time provides the context for explicit or implicit values conflicts to arise.

- **Reflection and discussion of responses to authentic conflict**. Finally, we suggest that educators be flexible in course delivery so that they can respond to values conflicts as they arise and provide opportunity for students to ask questions or share stories about voicing their values. Written assignments, student presentations or private conversations with faculty can provide students the opportunity for individual reflection on the values-based conflicts they experienced.

Courses that involve consulting projects, service-learning programmes, entrepreneurship practicums and the like all afford the opportunity for values-based conflicts to arise in an authentic manner. Such courses could easily be adapted to engage GVV. Faculty must be willing to be responsive to conflicts as they arise rather than always following a structured curriculum. Furthermore, faculty will need to move beyond the traditional role of teaching conceptual material to coach students as they deal with emergent values conflicts. In so doing, faculty can help their students build the competences required of responsible managers.

The Principles for Responsible Management Education are not simply about improving business schools. Their core purpose—as stated in Principle 1—is to "develop the capabilities of students to be future generators of sustainable value for business and society at large and to work for an inclusive and sustainable global economy". When it comes to equipping students to address values-based conflicts, business schools must take seriously Principle 3 (Method) to "create educational frameworks, materials, processes and environments that enable effective learning experiences for responsible leadership". To be truly effective, such experiences cannot limit students to analysing ethical dilemmas and deciding what is right; they must also help students learn to recognize such dilemmas *in situ* and to develop the skills and confidence to take appropriate action. Our practitioner commentators speak to the value of these skill sets:

> **Lee Augsburger**: Prudential Financial actively manages to our core focus on trust. Customers have to trust the company in order to participate in long-term investments and insurance coverage. The foundation behind building customer's trust is maintaining a culture of integrity. Employee surveys have shown that transparency around discipline and compliance is essential to building this culture of integrity. Employees need to know the company is fair and that disciplinary issues are dealt with at the line level the same way they are dealt with at the leadership levels. Furthermore, we work with employees to build their skills at proactively responding to values-based and ethics conflicts. We have clear, high expectations for behaviour and we follow through and reinforce these in order to build this culture of integrity.

> **Megan Houlker**: Recent college graduates need more support from both their educational institutions and their new employers to learn to appropriately identify and effectively take action in these situations. They need to be taught an analytic framework that helps them understand when a values-based conflict needs to be confronted, how to confront a situation, and how to develop the language and behaviours to effectively resolve these conflicts. They need to learn how to identify a problem so that others can hear their perspective and then how to work collaboratively with others to solve the problem. When they enter the workplace, the employer can continue to help these younger employees effectively respond to values-based conflicts by clarifying to new employees what are the company's core values, particularly around ethics, and how those values are lived and guide employees in the organization and when

confronting these situations. In this way, new college graduates develop the analytics and advocacy for more effectively responding to values-based conflicts at work.

Business schools cannot by themselves cultivate responsible managers with the inclination and skills to voice their values in the face of a conflict, yet they have a critical role to play. The gap between theory and practice in the realm of business ethics remains wide. We propose that by integrating theoretical ethics instruction with behavioural skill building and opportunities to apply those skills in an authentic context, schools can contribute to the bridging of that gap.

References

AACSB (Association to Advance Collegiate Schools of Business) (2009–2010, Dec–Jan). Ethics: More important now than ever. *eNEWSLINE, Management Education News from AACSB International*, 1.

AACSB International (2015). *Eligibility Procedures and Accreditation Standards for Business Accreditation*. Tampa, FL: AACSB), 31.

Baxter, G.D. & Rarick, C.A. (1987). Education for the moral development of managers: Kohlberg's stages of moral development and integrative education. *Journal of Business Ethics*, 6(3), 243-248.

Bazerman, M.H., & Tenbrunsel, A.E. (2011). *Blind Spots: Why We Fail To Do What's Right and What To Do About It*. Princeton, NJ: Princeton University Press.

Bisoux, T. (2015, February 9). B-Schools: Stop teaching ethics? BizEd, AACSB International.

Brown, J.S., Collins, A., & Duguid, P. (1989, Jan–Feb). Situated cognition and the culture of learning. *Educational Researcher*, 18(1), 32-42.

Edwards, M., D. Webb, S. Chappell, N.K., & Gentile, M. (2015). Voicing possibilities: A performative approach to the theory and practise of ethics in a globalised world. In Daniel E. Palmer (ed.), *Handbook of Research on Business Ethics and Corporate Responsibilities* (pp. 249-275). Hershey, PA: IGI Global.

EQUIS (2015). *2015 EQUIS Standards and Criteria*. Retrieved from https://www.efmd.org/images/stories/efmd/EQUIS/2015/EQUIS_Standards_and_Criteria.pdf

Gentile, M.C. (2010a). An Action Framework for *Giving Voice to Values*: Giving Voice to Values Curriculum Collection. Babson Park, MA: Babson College. Retrieved from www.GivingVoiceToValues.org

Gentile, M.C. (2010b). Giving Voice To Values INDIA Collection: Supported by United Nations Global Compact PRME. Babson College. Retrieved from http://www.unprme.org/resource-docs/GVV.IndiaCollectionOnePageOverview.2.2014.pdf

Gentile, M.C. (2012). *Giving Voice to Values: How to Speak Your Mind When You Know What's Right*. New Haven, CT: Yale University Press.

Gentile, M. (2013). *Educating for Values-Driven Leadership: Giving Voice to Values across the Curriculum*. New York, NY: Business Expert Press.

Ghoshal, S. (2005). Bad management practices are destroying good management theory. *Academy of Management Learning and Education*, 4, 75-91.

Goleman, D. (2000). Leadership that gets results. *Harvard Business Review*.

Gonzales-Padron, T., Ferrell, O.C., Ferrell, L., & Smith, I. (2012). A critique of Giving Voice to Values approach to business ethics education. *Journal of Academic Ethics*, 10, 251-269.

Haidt, J. (2012). *The Righteous Mind: Why Good People are Divided by Politics and Religion.* New York, NY: Pantheon Books.

Kohlberg, L. & Lickona, T. (1976). *Moral Development and Behavior: Theory, Research and Social Issues.* Holt, NY: Rinehart and Winston.

Manwaring, M. (2013). Developing negotiation skills through the Giving Voice to Values scripting approach. In M. Gentile (ed.), *Educating for Values-Driven Leadership across the Curriculum: Giving Voice to Values.* New York: Business Expert Press.

Nelson, J., Poms, L., & Wolfe, P. (2012). Developing efficacy beliefs for ethics and diversity management. *Academy of Management Learning and Education,* 11(1), 49-68.

Office of the Inspector General (2016). Settlement of $646 million reached against Olympus Corporation in kick-back case. Washington, DC: Office of the Inspector General. Retrieved from http://oig.dc.gov/release/settlement-646-million-reached-against-olympus-corporation-kick-back-case

Plumridge, H. & Burkitt, L. (2014, September 19). GlaxoSmithKline found guilty of bribery in China. *Wall Street Journal.* Retrieved from http://www.wsj.com/articles/glaxosmithkline-found-guilty-of-bribery-in-china-1411114817

Rasche, A., Gilbert, D., & Schedel, I., (2013). Cross disciplinary ethics education in MBA Programs: Rhetoric or reality? *Academy of Management Learning and Education,* 1, 71-85.

Zingales, L. (2012, July 12). Do business schools incubate criminals? Bloomberg Business. Retrieved from http://www.bloomberg.com/news/articles/2012-07-16/do-business-schools-incubate-criminals-

7

Thinking Conversational Intelligence® for sustainable business relationships in an age of digital media

Judith E. Glaser
Benchmark Communications Inc., USA

Roz Sunley
Winchester Business School, UK

Introduction

Based on the premise that responsible management begins with individuals who resolve to approach the complex challenges of global business using head, heart and spirit, this chapter redefines the importance of conversation—as a "meeting of minds" (Zeldin, 1998, p. 14). This is still an essential skill in an age of hyper-connectivity and technological innovation. While business schools are beginning to increasingly value softer skills such as communication, networking, creativity and relationship building (Hobsbawn, 2014; Palmer, 2010), this chapter suggests the ability to establish and sustain these relationships needs greater attention in order to prepare global managers for the complex challenges they will face. Lengthening supply chains and subcontracted customer service providers are redefining relationships with global goods and services, increasing the challenges of risk management, so that leveraging collaborative partnerships has become a vital element of global business success (Jones, 2011).

As stakeholder relationships become an increasingly important element of responsible business, it cannot be assumed that 21st century communication skills are being adequately taught in existing management education programmes to meet the multitude of constituencies and their varying cultures and styles. We offer that a growing priority for business education should be to equip the next generation of responsible managers with conversational skills that meet the needs of a new global "relational economy" (Mulgan, 2013). Our model for this responds to Principle 3 of the Principles for Responsible Management Education by describing an educational framework that enables "effective learning experiences for responsible leadership"—in this case conversation and dialogue.

We argue conversational skills, as an element of social cognition, are part of the fabric of sustainable business, and therefore essential in responsible management education.

In this chapter we provide a synthesis of academic and practitioner voices. Judith E. Glaser offers her model of Conversational Intelligence® (C-IQ) as the cornerstone of an academic discussion with Roz Sunley about how conversational skills can be integrated into responsible management education. She illustrates how C-IQ has the power to elevate conversation from Level I, which is a transactional level, where information and facts are exchanged on the basis of individual need, to Level II,—which is positional or where we advocate and inquire to defend what we believe, to transformational or Level III conversations where we are sharing and discovering things we did not know before and are co-creating together. Level III can lead to the co-creation of new ideas, energies and trusting relationships. Judith believes Level III conversations activate a network of neural connections that rewrite the capacity to think with new and fresh perspectives. Our brain becomes patterned with the capability to think in new ways when we feel we can trust others. This defines innovation as more than "an idea", but as new ways of thinking about ideas.

We begin by highlighting the power of Conversational Intelligence, and its role in the authors' first conversation with each other, and then together unpack key elements of Conversational Intelligence, and why these skills are important in responsible management education. Next we explore the different contexts for conversation in an age of technology before Judith shines a spotlight on the work of Angela Ahrendts, previous CEO of Burberry, who gave voice to the younger generation of "digital natives" as part of her transformation of a 150-year-old traditional British company to one of the world's most innovative global retailers. The chapter concludes with practical ways in which Conversational Intelligence can be embraced and embedded as part of responsible management education, and suggestions for how a "Conversational Dashboard" can be used to help students prepare for some of the difficult conversations they will undertake throughout their personal and professional lives.

Background and context

Foundational conversation

Judith and I first met at a social event preceding a management education conference in Philadelphia, Pennsylvania. We each reflect on that evening, and the impact of our initial conversation, to demonstrate how it transformed a chance social encounter into a trusting professional and personal relationship.

Roz: Judith, reflecting on our first unforgettable and serendipitous conversation in Philadelphia, it epitomized many of the elements of what I have come to understand as your notion of Conversational Intelligence. The surprising alchemy of our conversation was very unexpected and inspirational, and my journal testifies to how energized I felt afterwards, but at the same time physically and emotionally relaxed. Although I had no knowledge of your "Conversational Dashboard" until we spoke, you navigated many of its features as we co-created our reality, and discovered mutual narratives and ideas that sparked off our conversation into what you call "Level 3 or transformational conversations". We established a powerful connection and valuable relationship in those moments, and the impact of that conversation has stayed with me, resulting in this writing collaboration.

I can still recall the conversational space we created, which has reinforced for me the value of good conversational skills in all aspects of our lives, even when conversations prove difficult. I now have a commitment to helping my students develop Conversational Intelligence as an essential skill in their management education. My final thought that day was sometimes we find ourselves sitting next to the person we need to meet on our learning journey.

Judith: Roz, walking into that evening reception, I wondered if I was going to find a "conversational partner". Everyone seemed to be with someone, chatting away as though they knew the person well—and as I later found out—most of them did. While I'm not an introvert, I wasn't sure the academic spirit was in my blood that night and I was working out where I might stay long enough in a conversation to find a point of connection.

Our immediate connect opened the door to an outpouring of amazing ideas. We seemed to do a quick scan of each other's interests, and then didn't stop talking for hours. We needed no validation that our ideas were in sync—they just were. One idea after another about radical education sent my brain into a joyous neurochemical cascade. It was an oxytocin high, coupled with a jolt of dopamine, that made all of the room disappear, and our conversation become centre stage.

What we were experiencing was a "Co-creating Conversation®". It was as if we were "writing on each other's brains", having an impact not just by creating something outside of ourselves, but also through a deeper sensation of inner writing; with a new set of pathways being created in each other's mind because of the quality of our conversation. I just wanted more.

What is Conversational Intelligence?

Judith now outlines the nature of Conversational Intelligence® and how it can contribute to better conversations in business environments.

In working with hundreds of companies and tens of thousands of employees in many of America's largest organizations over the last 30 years, I've discovered that a lack of Conversational Intelligence® (C-IQ) is at the root of breakdowns in many relationships. Simply put, Conversational Intelligence is essential to an organization's ability to create shared meaning about what needs to be accomplished and why, so that employees get excited and are clear about the future they are helping to create together.

Conversational Intelligence enables us to discern the types of conversations that are suited for different situations.

- At one end of the conversational continuum are transactional conversations that allow us to transact business and share information with one another, which I call **Level I**.

- As we move across the continuum we engage in "positional" conversations— i.e. those in which we have a strong voice and point of view, and work to influence others to understand or accept our view of the world; these are **Level II** conversations.

- And as we reach the highest level, which I call **Level III**, we are communicating with others to transform and shape reality together, a powerful type I refer to as Co-creating Conversations®. Co-creating Conversations are the highest form of conversation; they not only let us advance our conversations with others, but I believe they are actually writing new "DNA" that can be passed along to the next generation. Co-creation is a set of skills and a complementary mind-set that enables us to have extraordinary, transformational conversations with others.

Although human beings are built for Level III conversations and hard wired for social cognition or "making sense of other people and ourselves" (Lieberman, 2013, p. 19), most environments do not activate this capability, and in fact deactivate it. Knowing we all have this capacity and are designed for it, means that understanding how to activate this hard-wired skill through our conversations is vital to our success. See Box 7.1 for a summary of these three levels of conversation.

As a starting place, it is important to know that Conversational Intelligence is a competence that can be cultivated. It allows us to connect, navigate and grow with others, and it is the single most important intelligence that gets better when "WE" do it. This means that by practising what we are talking about in this chapter, and by experimenting with the conversational rituals and frameworks, we can actually build the muscle for elevating Conversational Intelligence in our everyday lives.

While the other intelligences are more "I-centric" in nature—meaning they are intelligences we develop individually, such as mathematical intelligence or linguistic intelligence (acquiring knowledge)—Conversational Intelligence exists as a collaborative effort, and when we practise it together we raise the C-IQ of relationships, as well as teams and organizations. I suggest that because C-IQ leverages all other kinds of individual intelligences, there is no more powerful skill, nor a more necessary one, to master.

Box 7.1 **Summary: three levels of conversation**

Conversational Intelligence provides a framework and practices for the way individuals, teams and organizations listen, engage, architect and influence the moment and shape the future, in all situations. When we use our C-IQ in business we strengthen the organization's culture in order to achieve greater business results. Conversational Intelligence talks about three levels of conversation:

Level I is transactional and is designed to confirm what we know. It involves "telling and asking" as the key interaction dynamics.
Level II is positional, and is designed to defend what we know. It involves "advocating and inquiring" as the key interaction dynamics.
Level III is transformational and it focuses on co-creating with others. It involves "sharing and discovering" as the key interaction dynamics.
Understanding how to "level set" our conversations—i.e. use the right level for each situation—gives us the power to work together in harmony to transform reality.

Importance of conversation in responsible management

Our first meeting demonstrated how a meaningful conversation can be more than a transactional exchange of information and facts, and become transformational in terms of energizing participants, stimulating ideas, nurturing human relationships and encouraging productivity. The world's first professor of networking, Julia Hobsbawm, argues, "Despite all the stories of friendships formed through social media conversations and support groups, nothing can replace the human connection that comes from meeting in person" (2014, p. 8). While acknowledging the value of professional networks, she contends that face-to-face communication is still superior for "relationship building, and observing and managing the development of relationships". She is supported in the value of personal connection by social psychologist Matthew Lieberman who argues "our entire lives are motivated by social connection" (2013, p. 5) and by the discovery of mirror neurons in the human brain that "demonstrate the profoundly social nature of our brains" (Siegel, 2007, p. 166).

This has important implications for responsible management education where conversation to understand and evaluate the various perspectives of different stakeholder groups, including colleagues, employees, clients, shareholders, contractors and NGOs, is a precursor to responsible decision-making. In our new "relational economy" (Mulgan, 2013) the ability to have conversations with different individuals and interest groups has become increasingly important in public, non-profit and private organizations, yet writers suggest that many leaders still have difficulty with the softer social skills of listening, communicating and empathizing (Peltier, 2010; Lieberman, 2013; Swart *et al.*, 2015). We argue that conversational skills are an essential element of responsible management education, as social cognition underpins the relationships that sustain global business practice.

What Judith calls "transactional conversations" (Level I) may still form the bedrock of many individual business exchanges, but being able to express a point of view and working to influence others to understand or accept our view of the world (Level II) is becoming an increasingly important skill in a stakeholder world. In the face of constant global change and innovation, understanding how to shape an organization's culture and future, and engaging employees to meet these challenges, requires the highest level of communication (Level III)—what are called "Co-creating Conversations". We contend learning how to reframe conversational skills for sustainable business practice needs greater attention in a digital age.

The advent of technology changed expectations about how we communicate, so that previous reliance on face-to-face conversation has been supplemented with use of the telephone, internet and more recently "cyberinfrastructure" or "Web 2.0 technologies" (Sharpe *et al.*, 2010, p. 17) allowing greater participation and interaction. Social media is changing the landscape of business, social conversations and personal and professional relationships (Lenhart *et al.*, 2010; Boyd, 2014) with the result that conversational skills are being modified by what Turkle (2011, p. 11) calls "machine-mediated relationships on networked devices". In her latest book, *Reclaiming Conversation*, Turkle (2015) suggests that graduating students are increasingly reluctant to engage in face-to-face conversation, evidencing "flight from conversation" and preferring to communicate via social media where listening, empathy and responding to others is less spontaneous or immediately challenging. However, her discussions with business people around the world reveal that face-to-face conversation is still essential in building trusting relationships that lead to sales, contracts and competitive advantage.

Turkle cites studies undertaken by researchers at MIT Media Lab (Waber, 2013) that demonstrate that people are more productive at work when they spend time in face-to-face interactions. While it may seem counterintuitive that taking time out for conversation actually makes people more productive and creative, we agree with the German writer von Kleist (translated by Constantine, 2004, p. 405) when he suggests we get "a gradual completion of thoughts while speaking"; and argue that synergies of concepts and ideas can be powerfully made with other people "in the moment", as demonstrated in our opening conversation.

We now discuss some of the different types of conversation that new technology facilitates, and the implications for business communication.

The new reality of social connection and conversation

In an age of exponential virtual space, rather than shared physical geography (Boyd, 2014), there are now many different types of social connection available in our personal and professional lives. In her book about young people's engagement in social media, Boyd suggests young people using public social networks are today's "digital flaneurs" (p. 203), reflecting Baudelaire's 19th century *flâneurs* who strolled the Parisian streets in order to be part of visible society.

Some writers suggest the digital age "emphasizes the more participatory and communicative capabilities of new technological applications" (Sharpe *et al.*, 2010, p. 17) allowing people to engage in the world in new ways. These participatory modes offer asynchronous and synchronous opportunities that require different levels of conversational agility and spontaneity, and are premised on different conversational mind-sets. Table 7.1 highlights different levels of conversation that each can encourage.

Table 7.1 **Digital conversation and the three levels of conversation**

Conversation type	Conversational level	Conversational mind-set	Focus
Twitter Facebook WhatsApp Instagram *(asynchronous)*	Level I	Telling in a public space	Confirming what I/we know
Text *(asynchronous)*	Level I & II	Telling and asking Advocating and inquiring	Concern for the other
Email *(asynchronous)*	Level I, II, III	Advocating and inquiring Sharing and discovering	Open to exploration and new ideas
Telephone *(synchronous)*	Level I, II, III	Telling and asking Advocating and inquiring Sharing and discovering	*Any of these:* Confirming what I/we know
Skype *(synchronous)*	Level I, II, III	Telling and asking Advocating and inquiring Sharing and discovering	Concern for the other
Face to face *(synchronous)*	Level I, II, III	Telling and asking Advocating and inquiring Sharing and discovering	Open to exploration/new ideas

We highlighted earlier that conversational skills are being modified by "relationships on networked devices" (Turkle, 2011, p. 11), yet while people are connecting to each other in wider social networks, they are not necessarily learning, or being equipped with, the professional skills to listen and respond to others "in the moment". Neuroscientist Daniel Levitin (2014) argues that considerable use of social media has actually undermined empathy in college students as they spend more time alone, but seemingly connected. These online relationships lack depth and substance so that "the cost of all our electronic connectedness appears to be that it limits our biological capacity to connect with other people" (p. 127). Understanding the changing nature of our conversations, and having a language in which to discuss it, is becoming an essential, but often overlooked, skill in a relational economy (Mulgan, 2013). The following case study told by Judith illustrates the importance of harnessing and maximizing contemporary conversations in meaningful relationships that encourage participation in sustainable business success.

Case study: Burberry and the value of good conversational relationships

Judith now demonstrates the relevance of Level III conversations in business today, and how trusting relationships can be pivotal to corporate success. In the example shown in Box 7.2 she illustrates the importance of internal stakeholder conversations, which are a key ingredient of responsible management.

Box 7.2 **How Millennials transform a culture**

Consider the challenges Angela Ahrendts faced when she became CEO of Burberry in 2006. This 150-plus-year-old, tradition-rich British company was languishing. She knew it was her mission both to protect a legacy company and to help it launch an exciting and growth-oriented future. She and her team asked, "How can we sustain our company for another 150 years?"

Angela, with whom I worked for 20 years, saw "digital" as the future strategy for Burberry's growth. She did something many leaders would fear to do. She hired a new team of "digital natives" and put them to work to solve the company's core challenge—reinventing the brand. Focusing on using social media and digital technology, she and her team set out to reach millions of new young customers around the globe, and to build a social community to embrace and be part of the company's transformation "as it was happening".

Ahrendts knew she had to nurture unconventional relationships so people could learn to work together in unconventional ways. Merging technology and creative aspects and promoting their runway shows globally on the Web not only created a conversation, but an external conversation with the customer.

She decided that she would hire people with two really important facets of their personalities. First she would hire for trust, meaning she had to really trust someone before she would hire them, no matter how good they were. She had a "gut feel" about what she needed. And she also hired Millennials because she felt they were "digital natives", and could help identify new ways to innovate at Burberry that she had never thought of before. With Millennials on board, she created the Innovation Council made up of her new "digital native" hires, and also created the Strategic Council (senior executives) to help figure out ways to fund these ideas. The Millennials came up with innovations that can now, looking back, be seen as the impetus for many of the major transformations at Burberry. The conversations between Millennials and senior executives represented Level III conversations at their best.

The difference at Burberry is that Ahrendts made a strategic decision to create a conversational forum that included everyone in the company. In the same way she used technology to connect with customers, she created a platform that encouraged people inside the company to communicate directly with her and with others on the senior team, moving employees into a "share and co-create" mode. By creating a culture where everyone is empowered to share what's on their minds, she avoided the pitfalls of leaders who lose the benefit of valuable employees' ideas by not encouraging young, forward-looking managers to propose radical new ways of thinking about the business. Ahrendts suggests, "we involved the ideas from the next generation so they could have a voice. It was a revolutionary idea".

The results were stunning—turning Burberry into one of the fastest growing fashion companies in the world.

Most fascinating is that Angela is now at Apple as the Global Head of Retail where she is leveraging her fascination with integrating technology into our everyday life in powerful and highly effective ways.

Reprinted or adapted with permission from Conversational Intelligence: How Great Leaders Build Trust and Get Extraordinary Results by Judith E. Glaser (Bibliomotion, 2014).

This example of employee empowerment demonstrates responsible management at its best; valuing and responding to the voice of internal stakeholders regardless of hierarchy or years of employee experience.

Judith now introduces her Conversational Dashboard as an innovative visual tool to help improve conversational skills, before outlining conversational blind spots that can cause conversations to go off track.

Conversational Dashboard

The Conversational Dashboard is like a gauge with distinguishing markers (see Fig. 7.1). We believe the visual dashboard model of Conversational Intelligence provides a valuable tool for building conversational alignment and tracking outcomes. In a larger sense, dashboards help us identify gaps where conversations can help bring reality more in line with expectations, increasing our chances to partner with others in a healthy and innovative way.

Figure 7.1 **Conversational Dashboard™**

Reprinted or adapted with permission from Conversational Intelligence: How Great Leaders Build Trust and Get Extraordinary Results by Judith E. Glaser (Bibliomotion, 2014, p. 69).

The Conversational Dashboard has three different levels (summarized above) and five different types of conversationalists.

- **Resistors** are focused on their perspective and point of view and spend more time confirming what they know than finding out what others are thinking.

- **Sceptics** are more open; however they question a lot, or are not sure they can trust your opinion over theirs. Resistors and Sceptics are often using more "telling and asking" as their interaction dynamics—with less curiosity about others' points of view: **Level I**

- **Wait and see** are wanting to be more open; however they realize that there is peer pressure about "whose opinion is right", and they are trying to gauge the tides in a conversation and see what position they want to take: **uncertainty in levels**

- **Experimentors** are open to take risks—they are in a "share and discover" mind-set: discovering conversational agility: **experiment with Level II and III**

- **Co-creators** are willing and open to influence, and want to see what can be discovered that they did not know before: **Level III**

The purpose of using the Conversational Dashboard is to give us a visual language for discussing how we are feeling inside about others' sense of fair play, and how we translate this into all of our conversations. Through Conversational Dashboards, we are able to put words to the feelings we have inside about others being unfair with us, or others taking advantage of us, or others taking up too much airtime—all the exchanges that get us worried about how much we can trust and open up to others. Our opening conversation illustrates the value of using the dashboard as a diagnostic tool in encouraging greater trust and connection.

Even with the benefits of a Conversational Dashboard, when we are entrenched in our own point of view, resistant to changing our viewpoint and "Addicted to Being Right" (Glaser 2013), we see the world through our own eyes, and what makes us blind is that we think others see the same things we see—which is not true. We become blind to the perspectives of others, we stop listening to them, we push our ideas and opinions on others, and are more often in monologues expressing our "wisdom" with little attention to the engagement of others.

Reality gaps cause blind spots

Based on my own extensive work and research into the nature of conversation, I suggest there are five blind spots that cause us to not see the impact we have on others, and also disable our ability to step into each other's shoes and appreciate the world from another's perspective; all symptoms of Level I conversations.

Blind spot #1

Assumption that others see what we see, feel what we feel and think what we think.

- **Rationale:** When we are engrossed and attached to our point of view, we are unable to connect with others' perspectives. If we did, we would realize how differently they see the world. Yet our bodies pick up the lack of connectivity and switch on a stronger need to persuade others we are right. Human beings actually have a high addiction to being right. When we persuade others we are right (i.e. a desired outcome), the level of dopamine goes up (Swart *et al.*, 2015). It's like a natural high—it is part of the brain's reward centre and we want to do more.

- **Example:** Winning a point makes us feel good while it makes others feel bad; but we often don't know it because we assume they feel what we feel.

Blind spot #2

Failure to realize that fear, trust and distrust changes how we see and how we interpret reality—therefore how we talk about it.

- **Rationale:** When in a state of fear, we release cortisol, which closes down the prefrontal cortex or "executive brain" and prepares us for flight or fight (Swart *et al.*, 2015). We feel threatened, move into protective behaviours and often don't realize we are doing it.

- **Example:** A leader has responsibility for launching a new product and the pressure for success is high. One employee responsible for the customer-facing programme is new to the project and company. The leader is worried about this person's ability because they are new and the stakes are high. The leader is in a state of fear and starts to watch the employee with distrust—and finds things the employee is doing "wrong". The more he looks the more he finds wrong, creating a spirit of distrust and causing repercussions of higher levels of mistakes—validating his judgement about the employee.

Blind spot #3

Inability to stand in each other's shoes when we are fearful or upset.

- **Rationale:** Researchers at the University of Parma in Italy discovered (through research on monkeys) that our brains have unique neurons called mirror neurons (Rizzolatti and Craighero, 2004). These act like mirrors to give us a view into what others are feeling, thinking and meaning. When we listen deeply, turn off our judgement mechanisms and allow ourselves to connect with others, we are activating the mirror neuron system, now thought of as "having empathy for others".

- **Example:** Two executives are arguing about how they want to use the budget to accomplish their goals. Each of them has a lot at stake—they will be evaluated on the success of achieving their own goals. Both fall into Level II—persuasion—and fail to listen to each other, or explore the other person's fears, hopes and aspirations. If they were able to stop, listen and "share and discover" (Level III) they would find ways to join forces in support of each other's goals.

Blind spot #4

Assumption that we remember what others say, when we remember what we think about what others say.

- **Rationale:** My research with 350 executives in a large accounting firm mapping how they dropped out of listening externally and went into processing internally, suggests we drop out of conversations every 12–18 seconds to process what people are saying. In 2015 when presenting at the Society of Actuaries, I was able to help executives gain self-awareness about occasions when they "drop out" of listening, and to understand how to notice it. We often remember what we think about what they are saying because it's a stronger internal process and chemical signal. In my experience with companies over the years, our internal listening and dialogue trumps their speaking.

- **Example:** We are in a conversation with someone and while we are talking about some important things with them, the conversation triggers other things in our head about the implications of our conversation. A day later we are reflecting on the conversation and all we can remember are the implications that we thought about—not what they said.

Blind spot #5

Assumption that *meaning* resides in the speaker, when in fact it resides in the listener.

- **Rationale:** For me to make meaning I need to draw out what I think you are saying from my vault of experiences. My brain will pull meaning from my experiences and I *bring them into the conversation* to make sense of what I hear. That's why in my mind's eye I can see a totally different picture of what you are saying from what your mind sees. Meaning resides in the listener until the speaker takes the time to validate and link back to make sure both have the same picture and shared meaning.

- **Example:** A leader is talking with an employee, telling them what they need to do on a project. The employee listens to ensure they understand, they even take notes and they look like they are getting the message. They don't ask many questions; just nod their head as if all is clear. A week later the leader checks in to see if the project has been completed as he anticipated, and is really surprised to find the work is very different. The leader assumed the employee's understanding and meaning matched his own view, when it was now clear that they both saw a completely different outcome in their mind's eye.

(This section is adapted with permission from Conversational Intelligence: How Great Leaders Build Trust and Get Extraordinary Results by Judith E. Glaser (Bibliomotion, 2014).)

These conversational blind spots highlight the reality of interpersonal challenges such as the desire to be right, flight or fight, fear, internal processing priority and meaning-making challenges. Inversely, we highlight human capabilities such as empathy, trust and listening to others, which are all key ingredients of responsible management. If business education is to reflect the ever-changing nature of global economic, social and political environments (Escudero, 2011), then conversational skills for sustainable business relationships and sustainable practice need to be at the core of the academic curriculum. Visser (2015) contends that two of the essential characteristics of future leaders are emotional intelligence with its "humility to listen and be aware", alongside the ability "to see interconnections" (p. 20) and understand the context of the business. Sustainable business relationships need managers who can understand their potential blind spots in stakeholder conversations, and combine internal emotional intelligence with external Conversational Intelligence.

Conversational Intelligence as an element of responsible management education

Responsible management education provides space in which to explore questions about the nature of contemporary business, and the wider consequences of personal, corporate and global business decisions. It therefore requires students to find their voice, both literally and metaphorically, when dealing with difficult decisions. Experimenting with conversational frameworks can help students understand that responsible management is not just about subject content, but how people respond and behave in complex situations.

Dillard and Murray (2013) argue that to act responsibly is to accept an "ethic of accountability" (p. 14) which requires "an ongoing conversation among all affected parties" and "communal dialogue whereby rights and responsibilities of all community members are recognised" (p. 15). At the core of responsible management is society's expectation that business respects and embraces divergent stakeholder perspectives, and minimizes any negative impacts on people, planet and profit; but this can only be achieved through genuine human interaction which involves open and trusting conversations between different actors.

While discourse ethics and renowned programmes such as *Giving Voice to Values* (Gentile, 2014) offer pathways to developing some of the necessary competences required of a responsible manager, we suggest the foundational skills of listening and conversation are still deficient in many managers (Rogers, 2008; Swart *et al.*, 2015). Active listening is not an easy skill, but is fundamental to good conversation as it helps build rapport and trust (Rogers, 2008). It involves more than merely paying attention, but also being physically attentive, and actively "being in the moment", devoid of any other distractions. In an age of social media, this is becoming an increasingly elusive skill, as the demands of technology lure us into the illusion of multi-tasking in our efforts to be seemingly more productive and efficient (Levitin, 2014).

We agree with Peltier when he contends "Humans will allow themselves to be influenced *after* they decide they have been heard and understood" (Peltier, 2010, p. 109). Listening without judgement, engaging, influencing the moment and shaping the future are the cornerstones of Level III conversations in the C-IQ model. Students need opportunities to practise these skills to help them navigate different conversational situations and the responsibilities they will face in their future careers. It might be assumed that higher education is premised on good discussion and conversation, and yet a curriculum regime of predetermined learning outcomes often precludes time and space in which to rehearse the very conversational skills that lie at the heart of discovery and co-creative possibility.

Having discussed the relevance of Conversational Intelligence in a digital age, we now present some practical ways in which conversational skills can be practised in the classroom. These approaches are from activities that have been used by Roz Sunley and are recognized as examples of teaching excellence.

Putting theory into practice

Despite the pressures of formal evidenced learning outcomes, it is possible to value conversation as a way of helping students literally and metaphorically "find their voice" as part of critical thinking skills. Although classroom layouts are not always conducive to class conversation, with students confined to rigid rows or hidden behind computer screens, here is one relatively simple way to instigate a new approach.

Socratic dialogue with the Question Box

The use of Socratic dialogue encourages students to develop their own thinking through the collaborative use of questions. This approach not only encourages critical thinking, but quickly changes the classroom conversational levels from Level I (i.e. waiting for the teacher to give the necessary information), to Level II as students work to influence and convince others of their viewpoint, and occasionally to Level III where new ideas and discoveries are created in the learning space. Conversation moves from point scoring (Blind spot 1) to shared meaning making and understanding (countering Blind spot 5) in an inclusive questioning dialogic space.

This simple approach starts with advising students that at the beginning of class they will be required to post a written question into the group's Question Box (a shoe box covered in question mark paper provides a good visual resource). Students can choose any question arising from the week's preparatory reading, or lecture, independent study, or even the news, as long as the question posed cannot easily be answered by a quick web search. A question is then randomly selected from the box for quick discussion in pairs or small groups for a couple of minutes before a class conversation on the topic. Students are encouraged to listen to each other, query and debate different perspectives on the question raised, and contribute their thinking and understanding "in the moment". This counters the rising tendency of "flight from conversation" and fear of not speaking without having first rehearsed what they are thinking for fear of being wrong.

This process is repeated four or five times, within a limited predetermined time slot of 23–30 minutes. Although this exercise can initially be quite intimidating for many students, as they become more accustomed to this weekly practice, the standard of questions being posed improves and, with good facilitation, the classroom becomes a conversational space in which opinions are exchanged, challenged and justified, and new ideas generated and shared. These are all key elements of critical thinking as well as the cornerstone of potentially transformational conversations (Level III).

I have successfully used Socratic dialogue in discussions on global issues and diversity, but the methodology could also be useful in business ethics and social entrepreneurship.

Peer-to-peer coaching

Peer-to-peer coaching is a more formalized approach that provides opportunities for listening to connect as partners, which lies at the core of Level III conversations. Sometimes known as reciprocal coaching, it is based on coaching and mentoring skills that are increasingly being valued in the workplace (Rogers, 2008; Jarvis *et al.*, 2006). While this approach can seem formal and stylized, and is not an activity exclusive to responsible management education, it provides a sound skill base for this and other disciplines, and offers a valuable addition to learning in the classroom. The specific importance of peer-to-peer coaching for responsible management education is that it encourages self-reflection and action-on-reflection which underpin reflective leadership in all sectors of society.

Skills and learning objectives:

Coaching requires particular skills that include:

- **L**istening to connect—uncovering new ideas based on deep listening without judgement

- **A**sking questions for which we have no answers. Using verbal communication with high levels of discovery questions

- **P**riming for trust—this is about building trusting relationships

- **S**ustaining conversational agility—staying alert and in the moment

These are the core conversational skills; we call them the Conversational Essentials (LAPS)[1] that provide a framework within which students can help each other become more confident, independent learners by encouraging greater meta-cognition and self-regulation.

Structure and roles:

This activity can be undertaken in classes of 20 students by dividing them into pairs or triads. Each person takes turns in the role of coach or coachee (person being coached.) The aim is to allow each person time to think aloud and reflect on any key issues or learning biases (e.g. relying on others rather than using own initiative,

---

1 LAPS is short-hand for the Essential Conversational Skills that are the foundational skills we all need to use and develop.

getting easily distracted and lacking self-discipline) that are affecting their academic life. Working as a peer coach demands listening to connect to the other person, and using appropriate questions "in the moment" to help the coachee recognize any learning biases that are getting in the way of their progress. Coachees are then encouraged to think about, identify and take responsibility for one or two achievable learning strategies they commit to implementing in the next few weeks.

Instructional materials

Having a series of pre-prepared open coaching questions provides a valuable starting point for the first session—particularly for students who are new to this form of listening conversation (see Appendix 1). It is also useful if students can observe coaching in action before they are asked to undertake it themselves, so they can see for themselves that coaching is not about giving advice, but listening to and guiding the other person towards self-recognition of what they wish to change in their life. This can be done as a demonstration between two teaching staff in a lecture space or similar teaching environment.

Students then need to be encouraged to remember the core elements of coaching on every occasion they engage in peer-to-peer activity:

- Listening, without judgement, to what is being said, with the purpose of connecting with their coachee, rather than thinking about what they want to say about their experience or giving advice on whatever is being discussed

- Asking questions for which they have no answers which require high levels of discovery questions: for example, how would you like your behaviour to change in this situation?

- Building trusting relationships that respect the confidentiality of what is being shared

- Staying "in the moment"; not checking their mobile phones or drifting into general conversation, but focusing exclusively on the person being coached, and alert to the possibility of Level III conversation in which new insights and observations could arise.

Suggested timeline

This process and opportunity needs to be repeated at regular intervals (e.g. every two weeks) over several weeks to allow students to build up their coaching skills and for them to begin to experience the benefits of committing to changes in behaviour—that they really can make a difference to their own learning and lives. Follow-on coaching provides opportunity to reflect on the impact and challenges of realizing these new approaches in practice.

Common challenges and suggestions:

Initially there can be some discomfort about this exercise as students are generally being asked to work out of their comfort zone. They do not always believe they have the requisite skills for this type of activity and can quickly lose focus, leading to general chat or reversal to Level I conversations in which students attempt to "fix" problems for each other. Lack of trust or less effective interpersonal communication skills can inhibit the benefits of peer-to-peer coaching (Ladyshewsky, 2006), and therefore students need to be prepared for and develop peer coaching skills over time.

Benefits of peer-to-peer coaching

Despite the challenges, peer-to-peer coaching provides valuable space in which students can discover for themselves the challenges of listening to connect that highlight many of the conversational blind spots discussed above. Coaches have to seek clarification of the other person's meaning during the conversation, rather than assuming understanding from their own perspective (Blind spot 1). Trust is essential as it can feel threatening for the coachee to share personal perspectives (Blind spot 2), and coaches have to really focus on what is being said, and not lose attention (Blind spot 4). They have to be able to put their own concerns to one side and be able to accurately summarize what the other person has been saying. This evidences keen attention and focus, builds trust and is a very useful generic skill in meetings and teamwork.

Students also benefit from learning how it feels to take responsibility for their own decisions which they have verbally agreed with their coach/es. This public goal setting is far stronger than any private good intention as it promotes confidence, determination and resilience (Jarvis et al., 2006). Taking responsible decisions and putting them into practice at a personal level is a good preparation for responsible decision-making that affects others.

One of the essential preconditions for coaching and responsible management is the establishment of healthy trusting relationships. This can only take place when genuine interest and empathy have been established. Covey suggests that empathic listening is about "listening with intent to understand" so as to "understand the other person's world" (2004, p. 240). This is a useful skill in the arena of responsible management when attempting to understand different stakeholder perspectives.

Application to different conversations

As a classroom exercise, students could reflect on difficult conversations they need to have, and rehearse them with a peer using Level III conversational skills: for example, talking with a team mate who has not delivered his or her contribution to a team project. This is similar to a coaching situation where the coachee rehearses a difficult conversation with their coach in preparation for a discussion with a colleague, manager or head of department. These scenarios mirror responsible management conversations that take place in real organizations where team dynamics and success are influenced by a variety of factors (see Appendix 2).

Broader implications for responsible management education

This chapter has highlighted the importance of conversation in an age of digital media, with its many facets of social and professional connection. The theory/practice dialogue discussed here illustrates how transformational conversation can lead to new knowledge providing original ideas for both classroom and business. Judith and I both value the deepening of our individual and shared understanding that reinforces what we do in our different professional spheres.

We contend that Conversational Intelligence needs to be included across all management courses to encourage healthy, resilient and productive personal and professional relationships. As part of "effective learning experiences for responsible leadership" (PRME Principle 3), students need opportunities to practise their conversational skills. By experimenting with conversational frameworks such as the Conversational Dashboard, students can actually build their competence for elevating Conversational Intelligence in their professional lives as responsible managers every day—at work and at home.

References

Boyd, D. (2014). *It's Complicated: The Social Lives of Networked Teens*. New Haven, CT: Yale University Press

Constantine, D. (ed. and trans.) (2004). *On the Gradual Production of Thoughts Whilst Speaking*. Indianapolis, IN: Hackett Publishing.

Covey, S. (2004). *The 7 Habits of Highly Effective People*. London: Simon & Schuster.

Dillard, J. & Murray, A. (2013). Deciphering the domain of corporate social responsibility. In K. Haynes, A. Murray & J. Dillard (Eds.), *Corporate Social Responsibility: A Research Handbook*. London: Routledge.

Escudero, M. (2011). PRME and four theses on the future of management education. In M. Morsing & A. Sauquet Rovira (Eds.), *Business Schools and their Contribution to Society*. London: Sage.

Gentile, M. (2014). (ed.) *Educating for Values-driven Leadership across the Curriculum: Giving Voice to Values*. New York: Business Expert Press.

Glaser, J.E. (2013, February 28). Your brain is hooked on being right. *Harvard Business Review*. Retrieved from https://hbr.org/2013/02/break-your-addiction-to-being/

Glaser, J.E. (2014). *Conversational Intelligence*. Brookline, MA: Bibliomotion Inc.

Hobsbawm, J. (2014). *Fully Connected: A Look Ahead to Working and Networking in 2020*. London: Ernst & Young. Retrieved from http://www.criticaleye.com/insights-servfile.cfm?id=3909

Jarvis, J., Lane, D.A. & Fillery-Travis, A. (2006). *The Case for Coaching*. London: Chartered Institute of Personnel & Development.

Jones, D. (2011). *Who Cares Wins: Why Good Business is Better Business*. Harlow, UK: Pearson Education Ltd.

Ladyshewsky, R. (2006). Building cooperation in peer coaching relationships: Understanding the relationships between reward structure, learner preparedness, coaching skill and learner engagement. *Physiotherapy*, 92, 4-10.

Lenhart, A., Purcell, K., Smith, A. & Zickuhr, K. (2010). *Social Media and Mobile Internet Use among Teens and Young Adults*. Washington, DC: Pew Research Center.

Levitin, D. (2014). *The Organised Mind*. London: Penguin Books.

Lieberman, M. D. (2013). *Social: Why Our Brains are Wired to Connect*. New York: Crown Publishing.

Mulgan, G. (2013). *The Locust and the Bee: Predators and Creators in Capitalism's Future*. Woodstock: Princeton University Press.

Palmer, P. (2010). *The Heart of Higher Education: A Call to Renewal, Transforming the Academy through Collegial Conversations*. San Francisco: Jossey Bass.

Rizzolatti, G. & Craighero, L. (2004). *Annual Review of Neuroscience*, 27(1), 169-192.

Rogers, J. (2008). *Coaching Skills: A Handbook*. Maidenhead: McGraw Hill & Open University Press.

Peltier, B. (2010). *The Psychology of Executive Coaching*. New York: Routledge.

Sharpe, R., Beetham, H. & De Freitas, S. (2010). *Rethinking Learning for a Digital Age: How Learners are Shaping their own Experiences*. London: Routledge.

Siegel, D.J. (2007). *The Mindful Brain: Reflection and Attunement in the Cultivation of Well-Being*. New York: W.W. Norton & Co.

Swart, T., Chisholm, K. & Brown, P. (2015). *Neuroscience for Leadership: Harnessing the Brain Gain Advantage*. Basingstoke: Palgrave Macmillan.

Turkle, S. (2011). *Alone Together: Why We Expect More from Technology and Less from Each Other*. New York: Perseus Book Group.

Turkle, S. (2015). *Reclaiming Conversation: The Power of Talk in a Digital Age*. New York: Penguin Press.

Visser, W. (2015). *Sustainable Frontiers: Unlocking Change through Business, Leadership and Innovation*. Sheffield: Greenleaf Publishing.

Waber, B. N. (2013). *People Analytics*. New Jersey: FT Press/Prentice Hall.

Zeldin, T. (1998). *Conversation: How Talk Can Change Your Life*. London: Harvill Press.

Appendix 1

Coaching questions

Types of open questions to help start peer-to-peer coaching. Similar questions can be applied to different topics: for example, time management, confidence, planning.

These questions were used in a demonstration to students of a coaching session between two academic staff.

Topic: processing information

The faculty member being coached shared they had a preference for focusing on big picture tasks and losing interest in detail which resulted in poor record-keeping and administrative competence, which often led to time wasting searching for missing paperwork.

Q: Can you tell me why you chose how you process tasks (or other topic) for your coaching session today?

Q: How would you like your approach to processing tasks to change? (*future orientation*)

Q: Can you recall a time when not being into detail (from poor processing—or other relevant result from not addressing the issue) had a negative impact on you? (*the past*)

Q: How did you feel?

Q: What would you like to have happened instead?

Q: *Bringing you back to the present*, what would be the benefit to you of being more into detail/organized? (*processing*)

Q: How do you think that could happen? What changes do you think you could *realistically* make? (*future orientation*)

Q: And how would you do that?

Q: So, what is the first step to which you will commit?

Appendix 2

Scenario 1: talking with a tutor after missing several classes

In this situation a student (John) has been asked to a meeting with a tutor to discuss his repeated absence from class. He does not currently have a good working relationship with this tutor.

John is a dedicated student, but he has difficulty with time management and often leaves work until the last minute. He has been absent due to some family health issues and felt too embarrassed to say anything, thinking he could make up any missing work. However, he does not really understand the assignment set in his absence and every time he thinks about it, he finds himself anxious about failing and unable to concentrate on his work.

Initial approach:

John thinks about blaming his absence on his family problems and not sharing the real challenges with his work. He mentally starts to prepare his story—and even finds himself exaggerating the details to avoid telling the truth. He fears his tutor will judge him as a poor student, incapable of completing the work.

When we are frightened about how people will think about us, we often behave differently. We go into a protect mode, and become afraid to share what's on our minds, afraid to share the truth, and try to look good (Level I). We may fabricate stories, blame others, or just avoid the conversation when we feel we may say things that make us look like we can't handle our life effectively.

Second approach:

John decides to put his Conversational Intelligence into practice.

- He reminds himself that Level III conversations are important.

- He primes his mind for the need to be open, honest, transparent and willing to take the risk to communicate the truth of what is really happening.

- He imagines his tutor being caring and committed to his success. He decides to discuss his real difficulty, his reticence about asking for help, rather than an inability to complete the work.

- He starts the conversation asking his tutor to understand that he tried to do the work on his own, but found it challenging, and shares why.

- He takes the risk to voice what is really on his mind, and even shares his fear about being perceived as incapable.

- He asks for support and help, and his tutor provides it. His honesty opens up a stronger relationship of trust for the future.

This simple reframing of a difficult conversation can make all the difference to the outcome. As a result of John's open, sharing attitude, the tutor also learns that she can unknowingly appear intimidating, and that she needs to check student understanding more often, and remind them of her ready support.

Scenario 2: talking to a peer working in a team project about his or her failure to deliver work according to an agreed timeframe

In this situation the student team leader for a project (Louise) has been delegated responsibility for discussing a colleague's failure to deliver his or her contribution on time.

This is Louise's first experience as a team leader, and she is both excited and nervous. She is one of the youngest in the team, and the newest, and has some worries about being able to assert herself with her peers. As the team leader she is responsible for ensuring the team gets the project completed on time and presented in class within two weeks—a timeframe she knows requires everyone to deliver what they promise. George is one of the students in her group and she is having trouble with his level of productivity on the project, most of all his failure to deliver his part of the project on time.

First approach:

Louise uses Level I—transactional—conversation, telling George what to do. On three occasions, she tries to nudge him to finish his part of the project; however she gets little change in his behaviour from her efforts. On reflection, she realizes she has been using Level I conversational dynamics—telling him to do it. His response is to avoid her and not make progress.

Second approach:

Shifting into discovery (Level III), she decides to go into a wait and see mode, and observe him rather than tell him what to do, noticing what she has not noticed before. By moving herself to a Level III state of mind (open, non-judgemental, aware, listening to connect) she also starts to see things she has never noticed before—about how he interacts with two of the other students. She notices that he is having trouble getting time with one of the students he needs to work with. Her awareness expands and she sees things she has missed when she was focused on the student being wrong and failing to produce his work on time. She notices the other two students are strong willed and opinionated, and they close George out of conversations, so he is unable to get clarity on his part of the project.

After staying in wait and see mode for a day, Louise learns what she needs to do.

- Level III leads to higher levels of "discovery and sharing—rather than judging". She realizes she needs to elevate her role as team leader and to call upon her Level II and Level III conversational skills. Being the youngest on the team and seeing how strong some of her colleagues are, she has shied away from taking charge.

- She calls her team together and sets the rules of engagement for a productive team discussion about the project and progress. She gets them to agree how they can work together collectively.

- Louise encourages the team to "share and discover" their insights—and work out how to speed up their work—encouraging them to pair up with the mindset of "supporting shared success".

8

Integrating the six Principles of PRME in practice through Pragmatic Inquiry®
A sustainable management case study

Scott Kelley and Ron Nahser
DePaul University, USA

We are all familiar with the six Principles for Responsible Management Education (PRME)—Purpose, Values, Method, Research, Partnership and Dialogue—and their impact on business education at the institutional level. But how do students experience their impact in practice? This chapter will argue, using the case method, that the educational experience in a capstone course for the MBA concentration in Sustainable Management at DePaul University, titled *Developing Sustainable Strategies: Capstone Practicum*, highlights the challenges and opportunities of integrating the PRME Principles into management education from the student perspective. It explains how one student engaged in an arc of Pragmatic Inquiry® (an example of Principle 3: Method) to develop a sustainable strategy (an example of Principle 1: Purpose), but Pragmatic Inquiry touches on each of the PRME principles. In this case we introduce Steve Lu and Garfield Produce, the sustainable value he created, and then we explain how Steve's educational experience using Pragmatic Inquiry helped him create sustainable value using illustrations from his coursework to show his arc of inquiry from idea to reality. The chapter includes a number of specific Pragmatic Inquiry exercises to facilitate the creation of sustainable value, and concludes with a summary of how classroom endeavours, at any level of higher education, can benefit from it.

An introduction to Steve Lu, Garfield Produce and Pragmatic Inquiry

When Steve Lu decided to leave his job at Weber Grill in autumn 2012 to develop the idea of an urban, indoor, hydroponic farm, he took a significant risk. There was no guarantee that his venture would succeed, and he had enough life experience and wisdom to know that many entrepreneurial ventures fail. On top of the usual business challenges facing his venture, Steve also faced an additional set: he wanted to generate sustainable value by breaking into a new market, by developing a production facility in an abandoned part of Chicago, and by providing a handful of new jobs to people in the area looking for stable work. If his management education did not prepare him to succeed in *this* venture, then its value to live up to the Principles for Responsible Management Education would be dubious. It is one thing to prepare for advancement in a well-established company such as Weber Grill, it is another to generate the kind of sustainable value that disrupts decades of neglect and serves new labour markets in a troubled area of a large metropolis like Chicago. In what ways did his educational experience inform his entrepreneurial experience? Did it prepare him to create sustainable value in an underdeveloped urban environment?

The result: Garfield Produce Company

Garfield Produce Company is an urban hydroponic farm located in Chicago's west side that seeks to empower the community through wealth creation. Since it opened in 2014 it has received significant recognition and was featured on Good-WorkChicago, an initiative that brings together non-profit leaders, social entrepreneurs, government officials, philanthropists and civically minded business people to share best practices and exchange ideas (see Fig. 8.1). Garfield Produce was also asked to cater for On The Table, hosted by Breakthrough Urban Ministries, a non-profit that focuses on social services, housing and education in the Garfield Park neighbourhood of Chicago that has high rates of unemployment, homelessness and a host of other social challenges.

Garfield Produce Company did not pop up overnight; it was not a rushed business plan that caught the eye of an angel investor or venture capitalist. Rather, it was an idea that developed gradually and methodically over two years through an arc of inquiry that moved from a general idea through critical analysis to reflective interpretation to a robust business plan, all of which eventually culminated in the business itself. As he developed the concept of Garfield Produce Company, Steve's educational experience became much more than the acquisition of a set of skills or an accumulation of business theory or technical terms. It was, at its most basic, a process of formation and discovery—the cultivation of a dynamic, innovative, learning mind-set equipped to generate sustainable value. The produce on display at the 61st Street Farmers Market stand (Fig. 8.2) reflects technological, entrepreneurial and social innovation that also took time and care to cultivate.

Figure 8.1 **Steve being recognized at GoodWorkChicago**

Figure 8.2 **Produce sold at the 61st Street Farmers Market**

Source: https://www.facebook.com/GarfieldProduce/photos/pb.651863228215632.-2207520000.1434391809./758742890860998/?type=3&theater

The process: Pragmatic Inquiry

In many ways, Steve's experience in the classroom has been a kind of litmus test for PRME. The purpose of PRME described in Principle 1 is to help students become "generators of sustainable value", to create "an inclusive and sustainable global economy". Steve's educational experience illustrates how the method of Pragmatic Inquiry enables students to be generators of sustainable value moving through five distinct phases and their corresponding mind-sets: Begin *attentively*, Explore *openly*, Interpret *imaginatively*, Decide *responsibly*, Act *courageously* (see Fig. 8.3). In each phase students are challenged to observe the movement of their own thought over time and to adopt a certain stance towards the insights they discover in each phase. In the Begin phase, students are encouraged to be attentive to the concern, doubt, challenge or opportunity that initiates the inquiry. In the Explore phase, students are encouraged to be open to new data and new facts, especially when they challenge or contradict assumptions. In the Interpret phase, students are encouraged to imagine new possibilities and drivers of value. In the Decide phase, students are encouraged to identify responsible courses of action. In the Act phase, students are encouraged to communicate and take action with the kind of courage that comes from clarity and conviction.

Figure 8.3 **Visual representation of the phases and activities of Pragmatic Inquiry (note the cyclical and dynamic nature of the diagram)**

Source: Created by Corporantes Inc. Copyright 2015 and used with permission

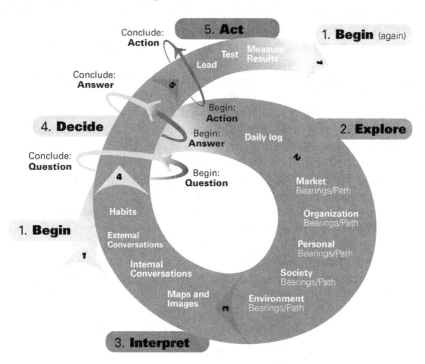

Pragmatic Inquiry and the reflective mind-set

Pragmatic Inquiry differs from a traditional case study because of its explicit focus on the reflective mind-set throughout the five phases, but especially in the Interpret phase. In the traditional case study, students are asked to analyse a given set of data, largely outside the realm of their own experience, and to arrive at a decision through careful analysis. The mind-set is analytical, not reflective, and the control of meaning is logic. There is little, if any, room for intuition, or wisdom that transcends logic. In a traditional case study, the student *presumes* that the data is worthwhile, that the circumstances constitute a problem that is worth paying attention to, and that the solution can be found through a "scientistic" analytical process. Pragmatic Inquiry, in contrast, asks students to evaluate their own experience as a source of value: to identify a challenge that matters to *them*, to analyse the challenge with the same rigour as the case approach, but to also reflect on the pre-scientific acts that uncover sources of meaning that are driving the inquiry. Unlike the traditional case study, students are asked to do something about it—to develop a strategy and act on it. Through the Pragmatic Inquiry process students discover that they are originators of value themselves, that they are responsible in the fullest sense of the self and not just machines for analysing data.

While beginning with corporate engagements over 30 years ago, Pragmatic Inquiry was early on deployed in a variety of educational contexts, engaging business executives and students in programmes such as undergraduate, graduate and executive education at DePaul University, the Presidio School of Management, Stanford Graduate School of Business, Kellogg EMBA, Beta Gamma Sigma business honours society, executive education at the Notre Dame Mendoza College of Business, and most recently at the 2015 Global Forum for Responsible Management Education—6th PRME Assembly in New York.

Educating for responsible management is a big promise. While the principles of responsible management education are both noble and needed, it is a very big challenge to develop the capabilities of students to be future generators of sustainable value for business and society at large, especially when contrasted with the dominant belief that "the social responsibility of business is to increase its profits", as Milton Friedman (1970) and his many followers have professed for over four decades. Management education cannot develop the capacity of students like Steve Lu to become the generators of sustainable value that the PRME envisions if it narrowly frames the role of business in society in the way that Milton Friedman did. Management education as a whole must unlearn some of its most deeply held assumptions about business, about society and about knowledge itself. Pragmatic Inquiry helps students become generators of sustainable value because it operates from five basic principles concerning the nature of knowledge, value and responsibility that challenge many of the assumptions of traditional management education:

- All learning begins from doubt

- Insights emerge within an arc of inquiry

- Social responsibility emerges from systems thinking
- Generating value requires that students become sources of value
- Sustainable strategies must be driven by personal and organizational values

We will analyse each of these foundational claims in relation to Steve's arc of inquiry, following the five phases of Pragmatic Inquiry: Begin, Explore, Interpret, Decide and Act.

All learning begins from doubt

Fostering the capacity for ongoing critical inquiry is a very different approach to learning from the transmission of an "already out there" set of insights aggregated over many years by a community of experts in a particular discipline. In *Managers Not MBAs: A Hard Look at the Soft Practice of Managing and Management Development*, Henry Mintzberg (2004) criticizes the way that management developed into a "coalition of functional interests" (p. 31) that ceased to have an organizing or integrating framework. The evolution of specialized sub-disciplines had the net effect of conflating management to decision-making, decision-making to analysis and analysis to technique (pp. 36-39). As a result, inquiry and discovery have not been a significant part of the overall management educational experience. Even innovations in management pedagogy, like case studies and game simulations, often reflect the ongoing specialization that can take faculty and students further away from the very foundations of learning that are necessary to generate sustainable value. Responsible management education is more than the mastery of settled management wisdom.

When Steve Lu began a course titled "Developing Sustainable Strategies" for the Sustainable Management Concentration offered through the Kellstadt Graduate School of Business at DePaul University in the spring quarter of 2012, he began an approach to learning called Pragmatic Inquiry that is a foundation, method and pedagogy for developing sustainable strategies (Kelley and Nahser, 2014). In the Begin phase of Pragmatic Inquiry, Steve identified a baseline challenge question, or **Cq** in the shorthand of Pragmatic Inquiry, and created a digital ePortfolio that would capture his own arc of inquiry as it unfolded. The premise of Pragmatic Inquiry is a simple one: putting into practice the philosophy on which it is based, learners at all levels discover the experience of inquiry and values-driven decisions when they seek to solve a problem.

The baseline **Cq** exercise at the start of the Begin phase is a set of five basic questions that identify a baseline for the overarching question, answer and action:

Baseline questions:

1. As you move forward, what market need, problem, issue or opportunity do you see which you or your organization might address? Why is it important to you and the organization?

2. What challenge or question (symbolized as **Cq**) do you face in meeting this need? Who else is your challenge/question important to, and why? (**Cq** can also be described as a barrier, concern, problem or issue)

Baseline answer:

3. What is your preliminary answer now?

4. What are the values (organizational and personal) impacting your answer?

Baseline action:

5. What actions are you planning to take or are taking now?

Starting the course with the baseline **Cq** exercise serves a variety of purposes. It immediately engages the students with questions important to *them* and to *their* career aspirations. It positions learning in the context of problem-solving. It establishes a starting point that will be revisited numerous times. Most significantly, the baseline **Cq** exercise of Pragmatic Inquiry changes the student–instructor relationship by putting students in the driver's seat of their own learning. In this way, it differs from a traditional case study approach because the case is the student's own, not a hypothetical situation often outside the realm of a student's experience. The role of the instructor, then, is also changed at the very beginning to a kind of gadfly or midwife, as Socrates used to call himself. Students are not often prepared for this kind of personal investment in their own learning process, and can respond to the baseline **Cq** hastily without much thought. They soon discover, however, that if *they* do not truly care about their own **Cq** then the instructor certainly will not and the inquiry falls apart. It may take students some time to awaken the desire to know that underlies all inquiry, and so the instructor can push students by constantly asking, "who cares about this" or "what difference does this make" or "why do you care about this"? Students quickly discover that it is a waste of everybody's time to work on a **Cq** they are not committed to. This does not mean the **Cq** cannot change; in fact, students often do change their **Cq** as they feel the pull and tension of the challenge inquiry and their attention is drawn deeper and wider.

Looking back at Steve Lu's baseline **Cq** from his electronic portfolio in 2012, two full years before the launch of Garfield Produce Company, it is easy to see the seeds of a profound idea:[1]

> As more people are moving back to cities, the cost of transporting food to cities is also increasing. There is, and always will, be a need to feed people delicious and nutritious food at an affordable price. The farming industry needs to evolve in order to meet the rising demand of healthy food in a sustainable way. Resources should be used to add value to the crop growing and distribution chain, and not wasted on transportation and wasteful practices.

---

1 The following excerpts come from Steve Lu's Digication ePortfolio, which documents his learning throughout the course and the programme. All excerpts are used with permission and are available at https://depaul.digication.com/eco798_lu/About_me/published

He continued to refine the **Cq** in his response to the second question:

> For the industry, the biggest challenge is in educating consumers on the food distribution value stream. Consumers need to be more aware of how their food is grown, and where it's coming from. Change has to start from the consumers. Only then will the market respond to changing consumer demand. This problem impacts everyone, but has an especially large impact on impoverished areas, or food deserts. It is also our responsibility to teach future generations on the value of creating sustainable food sources.

In these basic responses, Steve had identified a social challenge and a basic value proposition from the start: to create an urban farm (with strawberries as the primary crop) that would: (1) demonstrate the feasibility of urban farming to consumers; and (2) provide a complete business plan for a commercially viable urban farm. Steve was also aware of the values that were driving his question and hypothesis:

- Emphasis on educating consumers
- Must build and cultivate community
- Business model must be profitable, and subject to the laws of supply and demand
- Use of industrial engineering background and experience with lean manufacturing, the operational model must be systemically efficient

At the outset of his project, Steve had already identified a way to test his assumptions: "in order to supplement my lack of agriculture knowledge, I've invested $600 in an ebb & flow hydroponics setup to be done right in my living room". Consistent with his engineering background, Steve wanted to better understand the inputs necessary to grow produce hydroponically, so he built a hydroponic lab in his apartment with materials he bought from a local hardware store.

Steve also took full advantage of the learning opportunities a university has to offer. After deciding to leave his job at Weber Grill and to develop the concept of Garfield Produce full time, he took a series of part-time jobs over the course of two years that contributed significantly to his discovery process. Learning is a process that integrates experiences from many dimensions of life, not just what happens in the classroom. Steve managed a rooftop greenhouse to learn more about the cost of energy inputs required to grow produce hydroponically. He managed an urban garden on campus to learn more about agricultural processes and techniques. Through these additional learning opportunities, Steve quickly developed the knowledge and relationships to launch Garfield Produce Company. The structured arc of inquiry that he experienced through Pragmatic Inquiry integrated insights from his own experience and oriented his learning towards action.

Insights emerge within an arc of inquiry

At its very core the PRME aspiration for students to be generators of sustainable value is about learning, discovery, innovation and disruption. As *Dealing with Disruption: Clearing Pathways for Entrepreneurial Innovation*, a 2014 report from the World Economic Forum argued, disruptive, transformative innovation is by definition uncharted. Established businesses rarely act as radical disruptors or innovators in their core business, according to the World Economic Forum report, because they often predict the future by extrapolating from the past more than inventing the future they want, one that is non-linear and full of new possibility. Disruptive entrepreneurs who are able to generate sustainable value for business and society will necessarily be masters of discovery, masters of innovation. PRME educators, therefore, must help students to become experts at discovery and innovation; they must rediscover in their own experience the arc of inquiry that includes questioning, answering, defining and testing. Educating for responsible management is less about the transmission of existing knowledge, the mastery of big data, or the development of a set of functional skills. It is about discovery. Unfortunately, management education has not given adequate attention to the centuries of philosophical debates over learning, inquiry, cognition or epistemology. As the Jesuit Philosopher Bernard Lonergan observed, "in all one's questions, in all one's efforts to know, one is presupposing some ideal of knowledge, more or less unconsciously perhaps" (as quoted in Morelli and Morelli, 1997, p. 351). When assumptions of knowledge are not made explicit, they often go unchallenged and are absorbed uncritically into one's pattern of thought. As Charles Sanders Peirce argues, "in order to learn you must desire to learn, and in so desiring not be satisfied with what you already incline to think" (Peirce, 1932, p. 56). Pragmatic Inquiry operates as an integrated arc, moving from initial doubt through analysis to interpretation and finally through decision to action. Prior insights yield entirely new questions and new assumptions that will also be tested and will subsequently lead to new courses of action.

A dramatic example: Archimedes' eureka experience

The desire to know that initiates the discovery process can easily be dismissed, overlooked or underdeveloped in any educational endeavour if the teachers assume that learning is merely the transmission of knowledge from an experienced expert to a novice. Answers often eclipse the very questions they address. One of the most important experiences a student can have, at any level, is to experience what it is like to be gripped by "intellectual desire, an eros of the mind" that is not satisfied with half-truths, ideologies or mistaken concepts (Lonergan, 1992, p. 372). When students experience the tension of a question, of wanting to find some insight they do not yet have, they begin a process that reconnects the open seeking of inquiry with the temporary satisfaction of answer, which is in turn expressed through action.

The story of Archimedes provides a dramatic illustration of the experience of insight. Having sought a way to differentiate real gold from fool's gold, Archimedes rushed naked from the baths of Syracuse shouting "Eureka!" or "I have discovered!" after he realized that measuring the different volumes of displaced water would be a viable way to accomplish his goal. His dramatic experience provides a number of clues about the nature of insight, as one moment in a longer experience. As Lonergan (1992, p. 27) describes:

- It comes as a release to the tension of inquiry that often lasts for a period of time
- It comes suddenly and unexpectedly
- It is a function of inner conditions, not outer circumstances
- It pivots between the concrete and the abstract
- And it passes into the habitual texture of mind

Like Archimedes, students must be prepared to recognize the arc of their own thinking that leads to insight. When students notice, in their own experience, that the tension of inquiry precedes insight, they become aware of the dynamic relationship between relevant questions, answers that address them, and the ongoing pull from what is yet to be discovered. In an era of big data especially, it is easy to privilege fact over inquiry, data over learning. Archimedes' experience was not a mastery of what had already been discovered; it was the profound experience of connecting the dots, of finding a pattern, of solving a problem. It is not easy to turn the fundamental orientation of a management classroom from the accumulation of data to an arc of inquiry. The focus on inquiry does not excuse students from mastering *content* in any given field, but it does mean students must locate their *own arc of inquiry* in the larger trends of a given field, in a given body of content.

Disruptive pedagogy

Pragmatic Inquiry can be viewed as a disruptive pedagogical innovation considering the significant critiques of management education over the last decade. In "Bad management theories are destroying good management practices", Sumantra Ghoshal (2005) argues that business schools have adopted and propagated amoral theories severed from the realm of human intentionality and, therefore, from any moral or ethical consideration. Business schools have increasingly adopted an approach that seeks to discover patterns and laws that function as causal determinants of corporate performance (Ghoshal, 2005, p. 77). Ghoshal refers to the economist Friedrich Hayek's critique in "The pretense of knowledge" (Hayek, 1975) to describe this mind-set. Hayek was highly critical of what he calls the "scientistic" attitude that has contributed to the propensity in economics to imitate the physical sciences. The scientistic attitude mechanically and uncritically applies habits of thought from the physical sciences to fields different from those in which they have been formed, a problem Bennis and O'Toole (2005, p. 98) call "physics envy". Hayek has a more humble view about the acquisition of knowledge:

> if man is not to do more harm than good in his efforts to improve the social order, he will have to learn … he cannot acquire full knowledge which would make mastery of events possible… [h]e will therefore have to use what knowledge he can achieve … to cultivate a growth by providing the appropriate environment, in the manner in which the gardener does this for his plants (Hayek, 1975, p. 442).

Gardening is a fitting metaphor to describe the way insights emerge in the Pragmatic Inquiry process. By being attentive to the dynamic, and often subtle signs and indicators of the larger ecosystem, the gardener constantly adapts, adjusts and responds to the needs of the seedling at any given point in time, creating the conditions that encourage growth. In Steve's particular case, there were numerous insights that emerged because he was attentive, open, imaginative, responsible and courageous.

Social responsibility emerges from systems thinking

When Steve was interviewed for *Distinctions*, an internal DePaul University publication, he explained that the sustainable management programme "puts two skill sets together—business and sciences—so that students are prepared to tackle real-world issues". He continued to explain that:

> Sustainability is a "big picture" problem: It's not about changing light bulbs or driving electric cars; it's about our whole economic and social system. That's why the program is so good and so important: It takes students beyond a conventional, narrow framework (*Distinctions*, 2015).

Helping students get beyond a "conventional, narrow framework" that focuses exclusively on profits, as Steve alludes to, is precisely what PRME expects of the management classroom. The PRME aspirations require students to think in systems because a conventional, narrow framework focusing exclusively on profitability is not equipped to see the ways in which business ventures are embedded in larger socio-cultural and environmental systems. Through the Explore phase, Steve began to see that his **Cq** was embedded in an overlapping network of social, cultural, economic and ecological systems. Such an expansive vision requires an exploratory mind-set that seeks patterns of connection, which is increasingly difficult in an educational environment that Henry Mintzberg describes as a "coalition of functional interests" (2004, p. 31). In the Explore phase of Pragmatic Inquiry, students examine their **Cq** from multiple stakeholder perspectives, which significantly broadens Milton Friedman's notion of responsibility, and becomes a necessary perspective for the development of sustainable strategy.

Systems thinking: analysis and synthesis

The capacity to engage in systems thinking, which includes the mind-sets of analysis and synthesis, is a critical dimension of Pragmatic Inquiry and an important foundation for PRME. Pragmatic Inquiry aims to help students identify leverage points, the points where actions and changes in structures can lead to significant, enduring improvements (Senge, 1994, p. 114). When students are able to see the ways in which their **Cq** is embedded in a network of overlapping systems, they are better equipped to discover a specific leverage point for systems intervention.

In the Explore phase of Pragmatic Inquiry, students are asked to examine their **Cq** in the context of a network of overlapping systems (see Fig. 8.4):

- **Market** as a distinct system of needs being met (efficiently or inefficiently) by a number of organizations and sectors that operate competitively or cooperatively

Figure 8.4 **Visual representation of how multiple systems overlap**

Source: from Figure 9.5: Strategic Relationships, in Nahser (2009, p. 189). Copyright 2009. Image used with Permission.

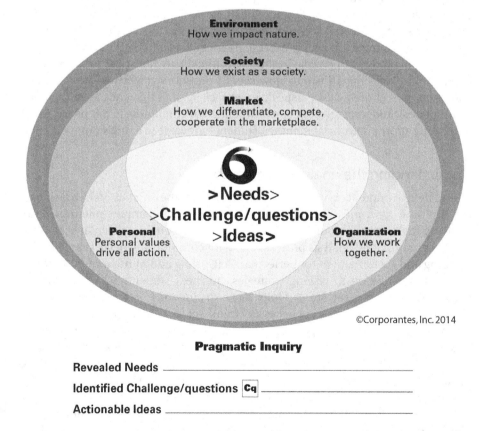

- **Organization** as a singular, discrete system that aims to serve market needs in ways that assemble and utilize natural, financial and social capital

- **Personal** as a set of ethical, intellectual and emotional systems comprising assumptions, values, inherited viewpoints, needs and desires that shape one's world-view

- **Society** as a distinct network of complex social systems including the political, legal, religious, economic and cultural, where each system operates on different levels of scale including the micro, local, regional, domestic, international and global

- **Environment** as a finite set of ecosystems that create the conditions for all human activity, including energy, water, soil and climate that also operate on different levels of scale including the micro, meso and macro

In order to facilitate such a comprehensive stakeholder systems analysis and for students to become more aware of their own habits of mind, Developing Sustainable Strategies requires students to address particular questions about each of the stakeholder perspectives in an ongoing reflection log in their ePortfolios (see Fig. 8.5). Students are also required to develop an annotated bibliography (see Fig. 8.6) of resources that sufficiently capture the various systems perspectives being considered, and the sources that will constitute their evidence. In the Explore phase students are encouraged to engage in divergent thinking, where data from their own research and reflections inspires new sets of questions, challenges assumptions and introduces entirely new perspectives, especially ones that contradict their own assumptions. Students can often be overwhelmed by complexity in this phase, which is perfectly appropriate. In later phases, students converge to a single point of action.

Understanding the analytical mind-set

The analytical mind-set is what discovers facts. From the original Greek *ana* meaning "up" and *lyein* meaning "loosen", analysis loosens complex phenomena by breaking them into component parts. It is a foundational intellectual skill of the business mind. Good analysis provides a tool for common language, shared understanding and measurement for performance (Gosling and Mintzberg, 2003). From market segmentation to pricing strategies, business students must develop the analytical skills necessary to carefully make distinctions between elements of a larger whole. While analysis is a necessary mind-set for clue gathering, it is not sufficient to yield understanding of complex systems or the explanatory narrative that binds clues together. Analysis alone can, in fact, lead to significant distortions if not balanced with the mind-set of synthesis, as Donella Meadows argues in *Thinking in Systems: A Primer* (2011). Since the Industrial Revolution, she argues, "Western society has benefited from science, logic, and reductionism over intuition and holism" (p. 4). On one hand, she continues, we are taught to analyse using rational ability—tracing paths from cause to effect, looking at things in small pieces, solving

Figure 8.5 **View of Steve's Pragmatic Inquiry digital ePortfolio (note the tabs correspond to the five phases of Pragmatic Inquiry)**

Source: used with permission and available at https://depaul.digication.com/eco798_lu/About_me/published

problems by controlling the world around us. On the other hand, however, we all deal with complex systems, including our own bodies, long before we were educated in rational analysis (p. 3). Insight, then, necessarily involves both mind-sets, the analytical to gather data and the synthetic to put things into a larger context:

> You can see some things through the lens of the human eye, other things through the lens of a microscope, others through the lens of a telescope, and still others through the lens of systems theory. Everything seen through each kind of lens is actually there (Meadows, 2011, p. 6).

Understanding the systems mind-set

While analysis is necessary for understanding component parts of a system, it is not sufficient for understanding the behaviour of the system as a whole. Bernard

Figure 8.6 **Steve's annotated bibliography**

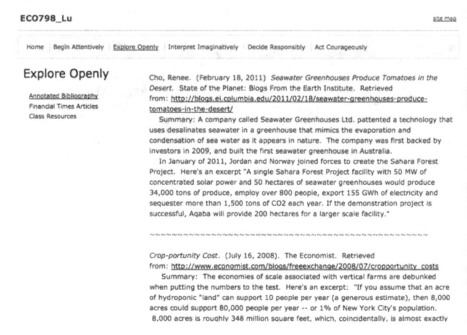

Lonergan's detective analogy is helpful for seeing the relationship between analysis and synthesis:

> In the ideal detective story the reader is given all the clues yet fails to spot the criminal. He may advert to each clue as it arises. He needs no further clues to solve the mystery. Yet he can remain in the dark for the simple reason that reaching the solution is not the mere apprehension of any clue, not the mere memory of all, but quite distinct activity of organizing intelligence that places the full set of clues in a unique explanatory perspective (Lonergan, 1992, p. 3).

To continue with the detective metaphor of learning and discovery, the detective is a person who is able to connect the dots, to piece together a coherent explanation from a set of given facts. A fact or data point only becomes a *clue* when its relationship to a larger story emerges. The detective does not merely accumulate new facts or new data through analysis, she also discerns possible connections and patterns until she arrives at a coherent, explanatory narrative. Arrival at an explanatory narrative is experienced as a release to the tension of inquiry, where one may shout "Eureka!" as Archimedes did. Insight, then, is "not any act of attention or advertence or memory but the supervening act of understanding" (Lonergan, 1992, p. 3).

Clues disclose a larger explanatory narrative about an event in the way that facts can disclose a larger system as "an interconnected set of elements that is coherently organized in a way that achieves something" (Meadows, 2011, p. 11). Systems thinking, then, provides a way to piece together diffuse clues, disjointed bits of data and an array of facts into a coherent, explanatory narrative. While such a narrative may be tentative and evolving, it is essential for discovering broader patterns of relationship and potential responses.

Some clues Steve pieced together

On 16 April , Steve discovered a clue while listening to a story on National Public Radio that examined the spread of Salmonella in some Dole brand salads. He began to think about food safety as another potential point of differentiation for his crop:

> When food is brought to these huge processing centers, the entire stock of food is then exposed to any infections, like salmonella. So the origins of the poisoning may have started in 1 farm, or maybe even introduced to the processing center from another source outside the farm. But by the time the infection is caught, thousands of pounds of food may have been infected... if food is purchased locally ... the source can be more easily traced. The counter argument for that maybe that it's easier to regulate food safety if it were done aggregately... I need to think about that one.

The natural unfolding of Steve's desire to know had discovered that the larger story of food safety could be a significant reason for consumers to consider local, hydroponically grown produce:

> Last year, the Center for Science in the Public Interest compiled a list of the 10 foods that had been recalled most often by the FDA since 1990. Of all the foods in the country, leafy greens topped the list, with 363 reported outbreaks resulting in more than 13,000 illnesses ... "It comes down to concentration and centralization of the food supply", said Marion Nestle, author of *Food Politics* and a food studies professor at New York University. "If something goes wrong at a place that produces hundreds of thousands of eggs, they all have to be recalled. If it's just a local farmer, it's just a few dozen".

In the Explore phase of Pragmatic Inquiry, Steve was able to analyse and synthesize different data points to see how urban hydroponics could be a disruptive innovation in a food system that is highly centralized, highly commoditized and vulnerable. Steve was also able to challenge some of his own assumptions:

> When I was talking to farmers at the Good Food Fest, I noticed that some of the farmers really loved their crop, almost as if they were their children. I can understand that now. I found myself showing pictures of my strawberries to co-workers and friends this past weekend as if they were my own kids.

But two days later, he discovered a challenging clue:

> ... during class on Monday ... [The professor] had mentioned to be careful not to fall in love with the product, but fall in love with the market ... so many of the farmers there were really in love with their crops. And I really

> admire that ... So maybe to amend [the Professor's] comment, maybe it's my job as the visionary to *fall in love with the market, so that I can help create opportunities for others to fall in love with the product* ... I must remember this. Otherwise I will become too disconnected from the people that I'm trying to serve.

Learning how to fall in love with the customer, not the product, was a subtle insight that inspired Steve to pivot from growing strawberries to focus more on leafy greens, like bok choi and basil. Seeing that his venture was embedded in a larger market system allowed Steve to find other market opportunities, because the primary insight was not about strawberries, but about urban hydroponics.

Learning to become a source of value

Systems thinking is a foundational requirement for pursuing the lofty aspirations of PRME, but it is not sufficient for generating sustainable value. Managers must also understand meaning: "[t]hese days, what managers desperately need is to stop and think, to step back and reflect thoughtfully on their experiences" because "[u]nless the meaning is understood, managing is mindless" (Gosling and Mintzberg, 2003, p. 57). The reflective mind-set demands that attention be turned *inward* so that the turn *outward* is likely to see something familiar through a new lens.

The reflective mind-set in practice

Steve's ongoing reflection log reveals the importance of a reflective mind-set. He wondered if produce really was a commodity or if there could be meaningful product differentiation:

> How can one have a competitive advantage when it comes to commodities? Commodities are defined as not having any qualitative differentiation across the market, no matter who produces it ... are crop (*sic*) really commodities? I believe the answer is no ... Even for low quality differentiated crops like wheat or rice, the real/perceived qualitative difference can be linked to ethical factors, such as the following:
>
> 1. Method of production (hydroponics? traditional? permaculture?)
> 2. Place or origin (local produce? or imported from 2000 miles away)
> 3. Distribution method (farmer's market produce vs. mass retail)

Steve questioned whether the explanatory framework of "commodity" accurately described how he or others view produce because he found at least three elements that could be meaningfully differentiated. Had he continued to believe that produce necessarily functions as a commodity, he may not have had the insight that his crop could be meaningfully differentiated by the method of production, the place of production and the distribution method.

Steve found another very important clue when researching urban farming in Detroit. After reading an article in the *Detroit Free Press* about Michigan State University's proposal to create a 100-acre urban-farming research centre in Detroit, Michigan, Steve discovered the importance of having representation from the neighbourhoods themselves: "If the people aren't ready to go, the good ideas get scrapped". The article triggered a reflective, self-critical mind-set:

> I'm reminded to be proactive in engaging the community. This is one of my weakest points right now. And if I were to really invest in this project, I also need to consider partnering with someone with a strong connection with the community.

Although the article added another data point that reaffirmed Steve's general commitment to urban farming, it also provided an insight into the importance of community support. Through reflection, Steve realized that he did not yet have community support.

By exploring other companies working in the same space, Steve found another important clue about his own system of value. GreenUrbanPonics is a for-profit social enterprise that seeks to provide a year-round supply of fresh, wholesome, locally grown produce to urban communities. Steve discovered that "they are a for-profit organization that works closely with the North Lawndale Employment Network to provide not only produce, but jobs for the local community. YES". He discovered that GreenUrbanPonics valued community support so much that they had a dedicated person to manage community development relations.

Sustainable strategies must be driven by personal and organizational values

Pragmatism holds that we know our values by looking at the evidence of experience. Values are what ultimately drive us, as we see in Steve's experience. As Ghoshal's critique points out, there really are no such things as amoral theories.

Vision, intuition and the pre-scientific act

In "The scientific process: Vision and rules of procedure" at the beginning of his classic work *History of Economic Analysis*, the economist Joseph Schumpeter (1949) argued the act of analysis is impossible without a "prescientific act" where sensory data is recognized as having some meaning or relevance that justifies further inquiry. Schumpeter used the terms "vision" and "intuition" to refer to the mixture of perceptions and prescientific analysis that are not entirely our own. Vision and intuition are shaped by the work of predecessors, contemporaries or by ideas that float around in the public mind. For this reason, critical self-reflection is imperative and cannot be dismissed as soft skills. Rather, it is foundational if one heeds the arguments of management scholars like Mintzberg and Ghoshal or economists like Hayek and Schumpeter.

For Lonergan, who himself was a philosopher and an economist, self-aware-ness describes the evolving understanding that one's conceptual categories, one's interpretive filters, are not absolute and immutable but are shaped, coloured and nuanced by the emotional life, culture and social location. The responsible man-ager is a person who skilfully navigates a complex realm of emotion, commitment, aversion, fear, passions, culture and meaning.

The scissor movement of insight

The relationship between data, analysis and intuition is like a pair of scissors where the upward movement of the lower blade (the accumulation of data) meets the downward movement of the upper blade (mental categories) (Lonergan, 1990, p. 293). These two different dimensions of insight are captured in the Explore and Interpret phases, where data is collected through stakeholder analysis and where accumulated data is interpreted relative to one's values, world-view and concep-tual framework. Insight involves the "cutting" intersection between the two blades, one accumulating data, the other interpreting it. As a narrow focus on the lower blade of the scissors alone, the scientist attitude fails to grasp that the categories framing, directing and explaining the data are themselves historically conditioned, emergent, open to revision and animated by values. The framing categories are expressive of human values and merit attention on their own terms. Values select which questions are asked, which facts are judged to be relevant and which cat-egories are most useful for analysis. Values, therefore, must be viewed as a *driver* of strategy and not just an afterthought. In the Interpret phase exercises students discover within themselves a source of originating value, the values that are driving their inquiry (see Fig. 8.7).

In one journal entry, Steve discovered a very important clue about his values:

> I'm at a very interesting intersection of my life, where my values, ambition, and creativity are all juxtaposing on each other ... at 28 years old I think I have enough under my belt to know not to squander an opportunity like this. I know now more than ever that I'm heading down the right path.

Not long after, Steve discovered even more:

> I've been thinking a lot about my values ... beneath all of the passions and ambition and techiness, I value efficiency more than anything ... social justice is just another form of efficiency. Social justice is simply expressing the desire for human beings to live up to their fullest potential ... As a social entrepreneur, it's my responsibility to create platforms for people to find opportunities to live their lives to the fullest potential.

Having identified and clarified his own values, Steve not only found a source of meaning to sustain his ongoing inquiry, he also found a source of courage to act.

Figure 8.7 **Image of the Interpret exercises**

Source: Created by Corporantes Inc., used with permission

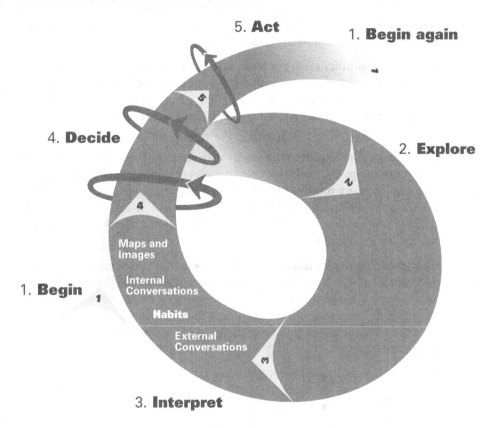

Pragmatic Inquiry in higher education

Steve Lu's learning experience is one of many that demonstrate Pragmatic Inquiry is a powerful pedagogical method for creating the kind of sustainable value envisioned by PRME.

Educating for responsible management is less about the transmission of existing knowledge, the mastery of big data, or the development of a set of functional skills, and we argue that the principles of Pragmatic Inquiry make a valuable addition to responsible management education and encourage students to become generators of sustainable value. PRME educators can adapt these principles in their own contexts:

- **All learning begins from doubt**. The baseline **Cq** is a set of questions that begin from a doubt, a challenge, an opportunity. This locates the entire learning process within the context of the student's experience, not a hypothetical case.

- **Insights emerge within an arc of inquiry.** At the heart of Pragmatic Inquiry is an ongoing dynamic of question-answer-action that unfolds in an arc that moves from problem to understanding to interpretation to decision and eventually to an action. Through each phase students constantly reconstruct their own experience based on new evidence.

- **Social responsibility emerges from systems thinking.** Systems thinking is one foundation of social responsibility, so students begin to think in systems when they examine their **Cq** from a variety of stakeholder perspectives. As they gather data relative to each perspective, students are constantly evaluating the credibility and sufficiency of the evidence they discover.

- **Generating value requires that students become sources of value.** Through a reflective mind-set, students begin to understand that their own values are operative in every phase of Pragmatic Inquiry, shaping the questions they ask, the answers they find and judge to be adequate or insufficient, and the actions they envision. The reflective logs help students understand what values are driving their inquiry.

- **Sustainable strategies must be driven by personal and organizational values.** Values are the dynamic source of sustainable strategy as the capacity to account for social and environmental impacts. By considering multiple stakeholder perspectives in their systems analysis papers, students uncover the extent to which their questions do or do not account for social and environmental impacts.

Additional Pragmatic Inquiry resources are listed in the Appendix.

The PRME aspirations are much bigger than management education, however, and point to a deeper commitment common to any higher educational endeavour: a desire to build the future we want. Pragmatic Inquiry is more than a pedagogical technique for the management classroom, and has been used at all levels of higher education, ranging from undergraduate courses focused on sustainability, ecology and business ethics all the way to executive education for professionals. Because Pragmatic Inquiry participants take ownership of their own inquiry, the learning environment is adaptive and responsive; the role of the instructor is not to transmit knowledge, but to facilitate ongoing inquiry. Naturally students discover and present their findings in different ways and with differing levels of complexity, but the underlying arc of inquiry is the same. As students proceed through the five phases—Begin *attentively*, Explore *openly*, Interpret *imaginatively*, Decide *responsibly*, Act *courageously*—their own habits of mind and their own values become transparent in response to a challenge they wish to address.

Considering various criticisms from scholars like Sumantra Ghoshal, there appears to be a significant disconnect between the aspirations of PRME and management education. As a result, it is reasonable to wonder how management education in its current form can develop the capabilities of students to be future generators of sustainable value for business and society at large and to work for an inclusive and sustainable global economy. How can the values of global social responsibility as portrayed in international initiatives such as the United Nations Global Compact become drivers of business strategy?

This chapter has demonstrated that the PRME aspirations can indeed be a driver of business strategy, but only when PRME educators recognize that students themselves generate sustainable value through arcs of inquiry—Pragmatic Inquiry being one such arc—that lead to discovery and innovation. With Steve Lu's educational experience as an example, which culminated in the entrepreneurial venture of Garfield Produce Company, it is not difficult to see how the management classroom can put PRME into practice and help students become generators of sustainable value. Steve's arc of inquiry is one illustration of the power of Pragmatic Inquiry, which is why Georg Kell, former Executive Director of the United Nations Global Compact, has been so supportive: "we have begun to incorporate Pragmatic Inquiry in our work to further sustainable development—'The Future We Want'—the most pressing task facing us today" (as quoted in Nahser, 2012, p. ix).

References

Bennis, W. G., & O'Toole, J. (2005). How business schools lost their way. *Harvard Business Review*, 83(5), 96-104.

Distinctions (2015, January 23). Beyond the bottom line. *Distinctions*. DePaul University. Retrieved from https://resources.depaul.edu/distinctions/featured-stories/Pages/sustainable-business.aspx

Friedman, M. (1970, September 13). The social responsibility of business is to increase its profits. *New York Times Magazine*, 32-33, 122, 124, 126.

Ghoshal, S. (2005). Bad management theories are destroying good management practices. *Academy of Management Learning & Education*, 4(1), 75-91.

Gosling, J., & Mintzberg, H. (2003). The five minds of a manager. *Harvard Business Review*, 81(11), 54-63.

Hayek, F. (1975). The pretense of knowledge. *Swedish Journal of Economics*, 77(1), 433.

Kelley, S.P. & Nahser, F.B. (2014). Developing sustainable strategies: Foundations, method, and pedagogy. *Journal of Business Ethics*, 123(4), 631-644.

Lonergan, B. (1990). Method in Theology. Toronto: University of Toronto Press.

Lonergan, B. (1992). Insight: A Study of Human Understanding (5th ed., Vol. 3). F. E. Crowe & R. M. Doran (Eds.). Toronto: University of Toronto Press Scholarly Publishing Division.

Meadows, D. (2011). *Thinking in Systems: A Primer* (Kindle ed.). Hartford: Chelsea Green Publishing.

Mintzberg, H. (2004). *Managers not MBAs: A Hard Look at the Soft Practice of Managing and Management Development* (1st ed.). San Francisco, CA: Berrett-Koehler.

Morelli, E. A. & Morelli, M.D. (eds.) (1997). *The Lonergan Reader.* 1st ed. Toronto: University of Toronto Press.

Nahser, F. B. (2009). *Journeys to Oxford: Nine Pragmatic Inquiries into the Practice of Values in Business and Education* (1st ed.). New York: Global Scholarly Publications.

Nahser, F. B. (2012). *Learning to Read the Signs: Reclaiming Pragmatism for the Practice of Sustainable Management* (2nd ed.). Sheffield, UK: Greenleaf Publishing.

Peirce, C. S. (1932). *Collected Papers of Charles Sanders Peirce*. Cambridge, MA: Harvard University Press.

Schumpeter, J.A. (1949). Science and ideology. *American Economic Review*, 39(2), 345-359.

Senge, P.M. (1994). *The Fifth Discipline: The Art and Practice of the Learning Organization* (1st ed.). New York: Doubleday Business.

World Economic Forum Report (2014). *Dealing with Disruption: Clearing Pathways for Entrepreneurial Innovation*. Retrieved from http://reports.weforum.org/dealing-with-disruption-clearing-pathways-for-entrepreneurial-innovation/?code=OR004

Appendix: Resources for educators

For a more complete overview of Pragmatic Inquiry, see the following list of resources:

Pragmatic Inquiry website http://pragmaticinquiry.org/

Nahser, F.B. (2009). *Journeys to Oxford: Nine Pragmatic Inquiries into the Practice of Values in Business and Education* (1st ed.). Global Scholarly Publications.

Nahser, F.B. (2013). *Learning to Read the Signs* (2nd ed.). Sheffield: Greenleaf Publishing. Appendix III includes a full copy of the Pragmatic Inquiry Field Notebook that explains the five phases (Begin, Explore, Interpret, Decide, Act) and the related activities, available at http://www.greenleaf-publishing.com/productdetail.kmod?productid=3793

Kelley, S. & Nahser, F.B. (2014). Developing sustainable strategies: Foundations, method, and pedagogy. *Journal of Business Ethics*, 123, 631-644. Retrieved from http://works.bepress.com/scott_kelley/16/

Steve Lu's Digication ePortfolio, which is used in this chapter with permission and is available at https://depaul.digication.com/eco798_lu/About_me/published

9

A holistic learning approach for responsible management education

Isabel Rimanoczy
Nova Southeastern University, USA

with practitioner commentary by Roger Saillant and Craig Teal

Introduction

What are the learning methodologies most appropriate to develop responsible managers? This is the question proposed by Principle 3 of the Principles for Responsible Management Education (PRME). This question has however assumed that a previous one has already been addressed: What are the skills, competences, habits of mind or knowledge ("capabilities") that educators need to focus on to develop responsible managers?

This chapter addresses these two questions. To do so, it starts by first briefly exploring the definitions of responsible management in the literature, its origins and evolutions to present times. This is followed by the findings of a qualitative research that looked precisely at the same two questions: What do we need to teach in order to develop a generation of responsible leaders, and how should we do it? From these inquiries, the exploratory study identified what made leaders ready and prepared to champion in their organizations initiatives with a positive impact on the environment and the community, and presents the elements identified, which corresponded to a particular way of thinking and being, termed the "sustainability mind-set".

The real purpose of understanding what the sustainability mind-set or responsible management means, is to be able to intentionally develop a new generation of managers. The elements of the sustainability mind-set have therefore been converted into learning objectives, which are presented in the third section of this chapter, applying the learning process found among the leaders studied. This learning approach followed a sequence of receiving information, making personal meaning out of it, connecting it with the personal values and purpose, and getting into action to lead change. This sequence has been observed in other studies as knowing-being-doing, or engaging head, heart and hands (Sipos *et al.*, 2008).

After this, information is presented about the content areas covered in the programme to best meet those learning objectives, which include ecoliteracy, systems thinking, aspects of emotional and spiritual intelligence and collaborative, innovative action. The holistic development proposed calls for different learning methods, and blended pedagogical approaches are best suited. Activities for each of the learning objectives are shared in the Appendix.

Although empirical research measuring the transformational impact of this programme is still being developed, the holistic learning approach has been piloted in the US, and adapted or integrated into courses on five continents.

The final section of this chapter presents two practitioner perspectives. One corresponds to a seasoned corporate leader, Roger Saillant, who has lived intuitively within a "sustainability mind-set", validating from his experience the learning objectives presented here, and the other corresponds to a graduate student, Craig Teal, who participated in the programme and reflects on the impact the holistic and blended learning methodology had on him.

Defining responsible management

It is natural and essential for educators to ponder periodically what may be the best ways to convey their teachings. This concern historically inspired research and a variety of instructional design models (Burke and Hutchins, 2007; Reigeluth, 2013; Reiser and Dempsey, 2011; Tennyson and Park, 1980; Tomlinson *et al.*, 2003). Whether concentrated on the best pedagogy (how to teach) or andragogy (how adults best learn), every approach starts with analysing a situation in order to identify what needs to be developed, in view of the particular context. Stating the learning objectives for a specific audience becomes the foundation on which materials, sequence, approaches and techniques will be then selected or developed.

In this perspective, before identifying the learning objectives for developing responsible managers, we need to answer: What makes "responsible managers" anyway? How do we recognize them?

Early writings about the social responsibility of managers date from the 1930s and 1940s (Carroll, 2008). A poll conducted by *Fortune* in 1946 asked businessmen whether they were responsible for their actions in matters going beyond profit and loss statements. The question specifically asked: Do you think businessmen should recognize such responsibilities and do their best to fulfil them? To which 93.5% answered, *yes*. Asked about what percentage of the businessmen they knew would rate as having a social consciousness of this sort, the largest number of answers were in the "about a half" or "three quarters" sectors (*Fortune*, 1946, pp. 197-198, cited in Bowen, 1953, p. 44). Despite these responses, before the 1950s responsible management was mostly connected to philanthropy; in the next decades it became connected to increasing awareness of the overall responsibility and involvement in community affairs; later came the concern with "issues", such as racial discrimination or pollution; and in the 1970s the trend became to examine corporate ethics (Murphy, 1978). In the following decades corporate scandals gave rise to themes of governance, and social accountability accelerated by increasing exposure of activities to the public (WikiLeaks, consumer protection organizations, investigative journalism and local or global grass-roots activism). More recently, responsible management expanded to encompass the design and manufacturing of socially responsible products, corporate processes (Carroll, 2008, p. 41), including responsibility for the practices of vendors and suppliers across the globe, and employee relations.

With such an expansion of the expectations towards corporations, and their leaders, responsible management is addressed from a number of angles: developing corporate social responsibility (Matten and Moon, 2004; Orlitzky and Moon, 2010), ethics (Murphy *et al.*, 2012), corporate responsibility, corporate governance, social accountability and sustainability. An important moment in the history of education towards responsible management occurred in 2005 when the UN established 2005–2014 as the Decade of Education for Sustainable Development (ESD). Educating for responsible management thus became a synonym of developing a sustainability mind-set, a construct that refers to a way of thinking and being that will be explained in detail in the "Findings" section below.

A few years later, the Principles for Responsible Management Education were defined, inviting business schools from around the world to adopt the principles and report on their progress. Extracurricular student-led organizations began to attract members to lead initiatives reshaping the thinking about responsibility. These initiatives include Net Impact, with over 60,000 members on six continents, and Oikos International, the student-led sustainability organization with over 40 chapters around the world as of 2015.

In addition there is pressure on accrediting bodies such as the Association to Advance Collegiate Schools of Business (AACSB) to include stand-alone ethics curricula as part of the criteria for accreditation, and more recently to include sustainability (Nicholls *et al.*, 2013; Sharma and Hart, 2014).

These all point to the need to develop responsible managers, although it is still unclear what specific "knowledge, skills, perspectives and values" (in UNESCO's ESD words, 2006) have to be developed.

Exploratory research

Howard R. Bowen, in his book *Social Responsibilities of the Businessman*, observed that hundreds of large businesses were centres of power and decision-making that touched the lives of citizens. He wondered what responsibility we would expect these business people to assume. These reflections were published in 1953, and some argue Bowen should be called the Father of CSR for this reason (Carroll, 2008, p. 5).

Five decades later, a similar question occurred to me as I wondered if business leaders were aware of the impact of their daily decisions on the lives of people across the globe. I identified some who had unusual behaviours—they championed initiatives that transformed their organizations into more socially or environmentally responsible institutions—or at least launched them down that path. Why were they doing it? What motivated or inspired them? What led them to take this action, and what had shaped their thinking? The assumption was that if we were able to understand their learning process, we would have greater insight into how to intentionally develop a new generation of responsible leaders (Rimanoczy, 2010). What I initially thought of as "responsible management", became indistinctly connected with a "global call for sustainability" (Alcaraz and Thiruvattal, 2010).

I conducted a qualitative exploratory research project, studying 16 business leaders who had championed initiatives that had a positive impact on the environment or the community. The US-based group belonged to different sectors: food, retail, technology, restaurant business, pharmaceutical, household products, apparel and NGOs. Their positions were high in the institutional hierarchy: from CEOs, to founders, vice presidents (VPs), chairman, director, global senior VP. A selection criterion was that they had not been hired to initiate any sustainability related changes; on the contrary it was an uphill battle for them to launch and implement their evolving ideas.

Findings

The results shone a light on a number of aspects that had played a major role in these people becoming leaders championing sustainability initiatives; yet several of these aspects cannot be replicated, such as their upbringing, personality traits, meaningful mentors and traumatic experiences. But there were other elements found across the disciplines and industries where participants worked that could be developed intentionally. These were classified into the categories derived from the research: Thinking (here Knowing) and Being (Adams, 2008). Since all the leaders engaged in collaborative action, the Doing category was added (see Table 9.1).

Table 9.1 **Elements of the sustainability mind-set**

The Knowing		
Ecoliteracy		
Systemic	Both–And logic	
	Interconnectedness	
	Cyclical flow	
	Long-term perspective	
Innovative	Right brain perspective (holistic, intuitive)	
	Creative, imaginative, versatile, flexible	
The Being		
Oneness with nature		
Introspective, self-awareness		
Mindfulness, consciousness		
Reflective		
Larger purpose		
The Doing		
Collaborative action		

Within Knowing, there were three distinct sub-categories: Ecoliteracy, Systemic thinking and Innovative thinking. Ecoliteracy relates to the understanding of the state of the planet, particularly how natural resources, social issues, climate change, contamination and waste are impacted by our behaviours. Systemic thinking relates to how the individuals address information, what logic they use. For example: they could entertain paradoxes, feeling comfortable with a "both–and" logic as opposed to the usual "either/or" thinking; they understand that everything is interconnected, that there are cyclical flows rather than one-directional, linear relationships; they incorporate a long-term perspective when analysing situations or data.

Innovative thinking, the last sub-category, relates to engaging in creative thinking or production, feeling comfortable using imagination, and showing versatility and flexibility in considering different perspectives at the same time; listening and incorporating their voice of intuition as another source of information or guidance, not limiting themselves to rational and logical thinking, but also accepting unclear perceptions, vague impressions, gut feelings or imaginative, irrational considerations.

Within the Being dimension, elements were included that touched the deeper self of the person: introspective practices that enhanced their self-awareness; mindfulness in their day-to-day life, and increased consciousness of themselves within a larger system; a sense of oneness with nature or with all that is; and a comfort with reflection, considerations about their role or life purpose and collaborative attitudes (Rimanoczy, 2013).

Finally the Doing dimension relates to initiatives that demanded collaboration and changed the way the corporation was operating, and in some cases also made a positive difference in the community.

These elements were grouped into a construct called "sustainability mind-set". I define sustainability mind-set as a way of thinking and being that results from a broad understanding of the ecosystem's manifestations and from an introspective focus on the personal values and the higher self. The mind-set finds its expression in actions for the greater good of the whole. The mind-set can be seen as a platform, a world-view that creates an interpretative frame for any kind of sustainability initiatives, since it shapes a new way of looking at the world, making meaning of data, analysing problems and exploring possible solutions.

From elements to learning objectives

The findings that comprise the sustainability mind-set seem to be at the foundation of behaviours that correspond with responsible management. Thus they can become learning or developmental objectives for programmes that seek to develop responsible managers. Instructional design principles indicate that to create a programme we have to start by identifying the outcomes. What do we want the participants to know, to do, to be, as a result of this programme? This relates to the traditional Knowledge-Skills-Attitudes taxonomy (Bloom *et al.*, 1964; Krathwohl, 2002). Table 9.2 presents the elements converted into learning objectives.

Now that the question of *what* to develop has been addressed, we can focus on the *how*.

Learning process

The study sought to understand what these atypical leaders knew, how they thought, what they felt and why they acted, but also *how they learned* their way through the maze. Taking a closer look at their stories, it was clear that the leaders had developed these elements over time and through a variety of ways, yet there was one evident pattern with three steps. In most of the cases it started with an understanding of the state of the planet, which brought with it not so much depth

Table 9.2 **Learning objectives in the Knowing, the Being and the Doing**

The Knowing

*If these are elements of the sustainability mind-set, **learning objectives** become that the students:*	Learn about energy, water, soil, depletion of natural resources, contamination, pollution and waste, urban sprawl, social issues and climate change, connecting the dots and identifying the reinforcing feedback loops.
(a) Become "Ecoliterate"	Understand paradox and complexity, and use a both–and logic to develop solutions.
(b) Use a systemic framework to interpret data and to develop solutions	Identify the interconnections and develop multi-stakeholder perspectives in their solutions.
	Look beyond linear cause–effect relationships, seeking feedback loops and cyclical flow, anticipating such in the solutions they develop.
(c) Use the creative potential and the inner wisdom to develop innovative solutions	Develop scenarios that contemplate the long-term impact of their solutions to problems.
	Develop personal ways to access the right brain hemisphere perspective, to enrich their understanding through a holistic and intuitive view of reality.
	Develop confidence generating creative, imaginative, out-of-the-box ideas. Practise mental flexibility to develop versatility to better respond to the unexpected.

The Being

See themselves as part of a larger ecosystem, recognizing the laws of Nature that govern all that is. Analyse problems and develop solutions from within the framework of oneness with Nature.

Develop introspective habits, to understand self, practising revision of the personal motives, values (both espoused and in action), as well as anchors of their own identity.

Learn to slow down, incorporate practices to quieten the mind, achieve moments of inner peace, connect with the higher self, experience higher alertness and consciousness.

Develop habits of reflection to pause and ponder situations without jumping to quick answers.

Include the dimension of the personal larger purpose into their decisions, life plans and choices. Weigh options with the criteria in mind, what brings meaning to their life, what difference they want to make.

The Doing

Connect with their community/place to discover unseen aspects of their real context

Uncover and review mental maps and models by exposure to unfamiliar situations or relationships.

Develop social sensitivity.

Practise and develop team working skills.

Develop comfort collaborating with others to address challenges.

Practise innovation.

but *breadth* in the understanding of the ecosystem's circumstance, and a perspective of its complexity. This was followed by a second step with emotional reactions as they connected data to themselves, to their life, to their daily decisions, lifestyle or context, with many introspective moments as they reflected on their personal values. This was accompanied by a wide spectrum of feelings: guilt, despair, anxiety, confusion, anger, uncertainty, sense of responsibility, regret, hope, empathy, care and compassion. The third distinctive moment in the pattern was the need to act: to share with others, not to be the only one knowing or seeing this picture, the desire to make a difference, the urge to act immediately.

The sequence was not linear or a one-time-cycle. It happened several times, reinforcing or building upon the previous insights, and while it seemed to start in a sequence of head (knowing, thinking), heart (being, feelings) and hands (doing) (Sipos *et al.*, 2008) (see Fig. 9.1), it soon evolved into cycles where the action created new feelings or fed new knowledge; deeper insights (being) launched more actions, that led to new rationales, etc. (see Fig 9.2).

Figure 9.1 **First pattern of knowing, being, doing**

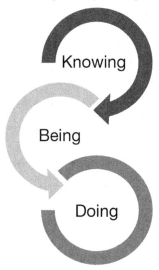

The "action" aspect was essential, as it provided the leaders with a way to transform their feelings into something tangible and useful. This is something frequently observed: when we are confronted with a disturbing reality that makes us feel sad, angry or frustrated, we can try to ignore or deny it, accept it with resignation or do something about it. Learning from this, the author assembled a blended learning approach to develop the sustainability mind-set, which specifically uses the three learning platforms of knowing, being and doing throughout the course. The course has been taught for five years in this format, in different institutions.

Figure 9.2 **Mixed sequences of being-doing-knowing, doing-knowing-being, being-knowing-doing, etc.**

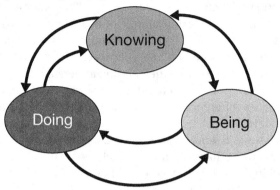

Blended learning is defined here as the combination of instructional methods (Graham, 2012; Rossett, 2002), face-to-face sessions and online self-directed activity (Rooney, 2003; Young, 2002). The holistic learning outcomes identified for developing a sustainability mind-set for responsible managers include personal development aspects that have not traditionally been considered in business schools (with some exceptions, such as the Schumacher College in the UK or Pinchot University in the USA). Yet aspects like systems thinking, social impact and ecoliteracy are increasingly being included in the most forward thinking institutions these days: for example, Antioch University in New England, the University of Vermont's Master's in Sustainability, Presidio Graduate School in California and many others listed in the Net Impact (2014) Guide to Graduate Studies.

The majority of business schools focus on cognitive aspects such as acquisition of conceptual or technical knowledge and on skills related mostly to analysis of problems, decision-making, planning, writing and reporting, logical reasoning and rational thinking. Even the inclusion of cases, projects and ethical dilemmas which allow for discussion and different perspectives still mostly avoid getting into more personal, psychological, emotional or spiritual dimensions.

Yet the need to consider the whole person (not only the cognitive dimension) when developing responsible managers has been a growing field of research, also within the context of work environments (Edwards, 2004; Murray, 2006). Emotional intelligence was incorporated into leadership development programmes (Langley, 2000); spirituality and the workplace became a topic of research (Lewis and Geroy, 2000; Mitroff and Denton, 1999) promoted by the Academy of Management division of Management, Spirituality and Religion. Shifting away from the rational, objective approach of management education, other lines of research explored personal values in the business schools classrooms, such as the Giving Voice to Values programme (Cote *et al.*, 2011), in parallel with emerging corporate practices that also sought to develop more holistic employees—offering meditation or mindfulness practice to the workforce, as is the case at Aetna, Google, Target and General Mills (Gelles, 2012).

Several authors have observed that when it comes to developing sustainability or responsible leadership, the goal is not just a cognitive enrichment, but a transformational learning experience (Lange, 2004; Moore, 2005; Sipos *et al.*, 2008; Sterling, 2011; Svanström *et al.*, 2008). As an example of how blended learning approaches are being tried out to aim at more holistic development, we can point to a successful MOOC (massive online open course) that reached over 35,000 participants. It was launched in 2015 by Otto Scharmer, aiming at personal, business and society transformation by incorporating ecoliteracy, exploration of personal values and real projects to make a difference (Massachusetts Institute of Technology, 2015).

The course to develop the sustainability mind-set has been taught since 2010 in different graduate and undergraduate courses in New Jersey, New York and Florida, and practitioners have incorporated elements into their existing courses in Indonesia, Philippines, India, Argentina, France, Australia and the USA. The different versions address the "Knowing" through ecoliteracy and systems intelligence, the "Being" through aspects of emotional and spiritual intelligence, and the "Doing" through collaborative projects where students are invited to make a difference, using innovative thinking and real community or environmental needs (see Fig. 9.3).

Figure 9.3 **Instructional framework to develop a sustainability mind-set**

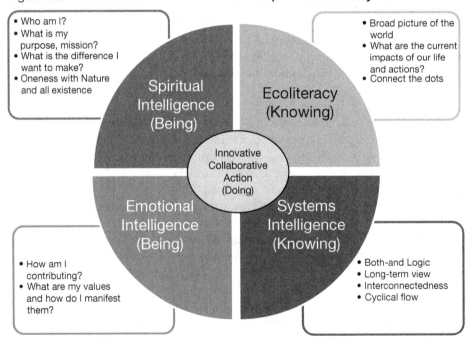

The first aspect, ecoliteracy, relates to the ecopedagogy movement, which has been addressing ways to incorporate environmental and social impact information into curricula (McBride *et al.*, 2013; Goleman *et al.*, 2012; Kahn and Kahn, 2010;

Semetsky, 2010; Rowe, 2002). Ecoliteracy is developed through exposure to information about the current state of the planet and its resources. This can be done via readings, self-directed research (e.g. "Explore sea-level rise"), lectures, movies, etc. Students are invited to explore their feelings and connect information with their own life and habits. Feelings of being overwhelmed are common, especially since the purpose of ecoliteracy is to help students "connect the dots" and get a fuller picture of our reality. The second aspect, systems intelligence, is developed by highlighting the interconnections, the long-term impacts of decisions, multistakeholder perspectives, etc. (Nguyen *et al.*, 2012; Wiek *et al.*, 2011; Smith, 2011; Porter and Cordoba, 2009). The third aspect, emotional intelligence (Chopra and Kanji, 2010; Shrivastava, 2010; Goleman, 2006; Weinberger, 2009), is addressed by helping students identify their feelings and the role they play in their everyday life, what are the anchors of their identity, identify their espoused values and the values in action, etc. The emotions are also used as fuel to engage in action, and participants are invited to identify an area they feel passionate about and where they would like to make a difference during the term of the course. This is an important component of the course, and students' testimonials refer to it as the highlight of their experience, referring to it as their "passion project". The fourth content area, addressing aspects of spiritual intelligence (Stead and Stead, 2014; Borland and Lindgreen, 2013; Collins, 2010; Heuer, 2010; Venkatesh, 2010), opens up dialogues and personal reflections on topics such as purpose, sense of calling or life mission, or aspects of their higher self, which pave the way for students to find a project that is personally significant and fulfilling for them. This project becomes the catalyst to engage in collaborative teamwork, to experiment with innovative thinking and to experience aspects of the reality that they may otherwise be unaware of: for example poverty in their city, pollution, soil erosion, waste in their community, food or health related issues or social issues. The projects also become a new source of information (knowing), awakening new feelings or deeper insights (being). In addition, they develop a sense of empowerment, as students realize that they actually can make a difference.

The feedback from the immediate beneficiaries of their projects is critical as it reinforces their learning and their sense of satisfaction and hope. At the end of the semester they have proved to themselves what they can do:

> This journey has certainly impacted my life in a positive way. I'm now more interested in making a difference than making money. I'm more conscious of my role in life (Student A).

> There are a number of educational truisms related to the rationale for this type of learning, [...] such as I hear, and I forget; I see, and I remember; I do, and I understand . I love that in this class, we did! Sure we heard, saw, spoke, read, wrote, and that inspired learning, but the power of this experience was in the doing—and that every day we live, we do, we act, and we impact. With great influence comes great responsibility, and I see that better now, and will aim to aspire to this promise (Student B).

The learning outcomes to develop the sustainable mind-set that makes for responsible managers pertain to the cognitive, attitudinal and experiential areas (McDonald, 2013). Responsible management education calls therefore for a holistic approach that addresses the thinking, being and doing. To attend to the different learning styles of the students and their personal developmental journey (Kegan, 1994; Schein, 2014; Torbert and Herdman-Barker, 2008; Visser and Crane, 2010), different instructional methods and settings need to be used. This means that independently of the subject, when educators are aiming at developing responsible managers, the learning methods need to engage more than the intellect: they need to be suited to engage aspects of the being and the doing. The learning objectives, a description of them and examples of activities used to meet those learning goals are presented in the Appendix.

Implications for practice

Instructors interested in exploring a blended approach to developing responsible managers through a sustainability mind-set can find here two different conceptual frameworks to guide them. One is the conceptual framework centred on content areas: ecoliteracy, systems intelligence, emotional intelligence, spiritual intelligence and collaborative innovative action (Fig. 9.3). The model helps as a checklist, to see if and how questions related to the different content areas are or could be included into their lesson plan. For example, in the area of ecoliteracy, do the students have sufficient information about the current challenges related to our planetary resources? In the area of systems intelligence, are opportunities sought to highlight the impact of either/or thinking versus a both–and perspective? (or any of the other systems thinking lenses) In the area of emotional intelligence, does the instructor invite the students to develop self-awareness, to connect with their feelings and notice their emotional reactions when discussing sustainability issues? In the area of spiritual intelligence, are sufficient opportunities created to explore personal purpose, or what brings meaning to their life? Finally, what conditions are created to promote participants working together, engaging in real actions or projects to make a difference, and exploring creative, innovative solutions to their challenges?

The second conceptual framework looks at the learning goals as they relate to the knowing, the being and the doing. For example, a learning goal related to the knowing is to understand paradox and complexity, and to use a both–and logic to develop solutions. A possible activity for this learning goal could be to distribute newspaper pages, and invite the participants to circle "both–and" and "either/or" stories. Either/or stories polarize positions, describe mutually excluding choices, like in a win–lose situation. Both–and stories are characterized by inclusion of differences, by integration of diverse needs or perspectives in a way that meets the needs of all stakeholders. For example, news about Israeli military bulldozers that demolished 23 houses in two impoverished southern West Bank villages, including structures that were home to more than 100 people is an either/or story. Another example such as "Insurance firm turns to planting trees in South Africa to combat drought risk" illustrates both–and thinking. The instructor can then facilitate a dialogue about the implications and consequences of both. Some questions could be: If you were an Israeli military person, would you also see this as an either/or logic? How is this news different from the second one? Could the second one also be seen as an either/or? This activity can be done both face-to-face and virtually, as an assignment where students find examples of those stories and comment on them.

Related to the being, the learning goal of seeing themselves as part of a larger ecosystem, recognizing the laws of Nature that govern all can be triggered by inviting the group to meet outside the classroom, in a park or a garden. Such a session certainly would have other contents, and individual silent reflection time while sitting or walking in nature, can be a powerful exercise to develop awareness. This should be followed by an exchange in pairs, and in the larger group. The instructor will play a facilitation role to set up a dialogue, guiding with some questions such as: What did you experience? How was it? What impacted you most? What did you learn about Nature and about our place in Nature? How would you react if you were a frequent visitor of this park and a developer wanted to build a mall on the property? This type of questions will help participants in analysing problems and developing solutions from within the framework of oneness with Nature.

The Appendix presents a guide for instructors that links each learning goal (i.e. **Develop social sensitivity**) with a number of concrete activities and exercises for students (i.e. Invite the students to interview a person belonging to a demographic sector they feel most estranged and distant from in terms of age, gender, social class, ethnicity, religion, profession, race or nationality). These examples can also serve educators as inspiration to create other exercises (see Arevalo and Mitchell, forthcoming).

In the next section the reader will find two practitioner commentaries: from a corporate leader and from a student who participated in the sustainability mindset course.

Voices from the field

Learning as a life mission

By Roger Saillant

Dr Roger Saillant is the Executive Director of the Fowler Center for Business as an Agent of World Benefit. He has over 35 years' experience in business, where he was VP at Ford Motors, President and CEO at Plug Power and Chairman of the board at Worldwide Energy, and serves on several non-profit boards. He has been a lifelong advocate for the environment.

Living should be a learning experience. Learning should continue even when we step outside of the formal boundaries of an educational institution of any type. Businesses leaders have a remarkable opportunity to support the personal growth of each of their employees. After all, people work at least 3040 hours per week for probably more than the 40 years of their careers and many beyond that. Those career hours are rich opportunities for personal growth which, when blended with professional growth, can yield tremendous benefits to both the employees and the business.

I have always cared about the personal growth of each member of my organizations and have observed that when the people have grown the corporate cultures flourish which in turn enables the creation of high performing organizations. What seems to happen is that personal growth leads to an ability to handle ambiguity better and *"either/or" thinking declines and both-and logic and systems thinking increases*. This leads to an *awareness of a deeper self and one's larger purpose* which frequently opens the person to *mindfulness practice* and, ultimately, to a *sense of oneness and deep connection to all that is*. This all creates a positive reinforcing loop whose benefits often extend to the community.

I am reminded of an instance when I was the CEO of a publicly traded fuel cell company. When I arrived the company was struggling to find its way and each individual I spoke to seemed to be struggling as well. Many had come to the company with hopes of making a lot of money quickly since it was a start-up in a very "hot" area at a time when Wall Street money was flowing, only to experience disappointment as the realities of the technical challenges dampened the Street's enthusiasm. What seemed to be needed was to *have everyone slow down and think about what they were doing and why they were doing it.*

Fuel cells are one of the most energy efficient conversion devices known and are a natural for people who are interested in lowering their carbon footprint. Yet, very few of the employees had a truly deep commitment to sustainability or as discussed in the chapter the sustainable mind-set. The transition to a deeper understanding of *how we are all connected* to and *dependent upon a healthy natural world* began by engaging the help of outside consultants from the Society of Organizational Learning network. All employees went through several days of learning about *personal mastery, systems thinking* and other principles taught by the consultant team. This created situational awareness about each person's role in the company and the potential of the company to influence the way people thought about energy conversion and its impact on the planet.

The employees with few exceptions began to undergo *personal transformations* which led to a new mission statement for the company which was inspiring on both emotional and intellectual levels. They completed a cradle-to-cradle profile of the environmental impact of each component in the fuel cell systems. And they initiated *community involvement projects* like painting and repairing a foster care centre as well as a centre for abused women and children. In addition, they set up a *meditation centre*. They began to see themselves as *part of a greater whole*.

Probably the single greatest impact of the *transformative learning* and growth was that the managers who were part of the process took their knowledge with them to other organizations and have continued their work. The ideas they embraced in their home company have been carried by them like the seeds from a healthy tree riding the wind and coming to rest in fresh soil to sprout and flourish. Managers will learn to see themselves as gardeners.

The reflections of this corporate leader present an interesting correlation with the aspects of the sustainability mind-set in action described in this chapter. Furthermore, the importance of a holistic approach is noted by this practitioner, as he describes how the company sought to develop a sensitivity towards sustainability by engaging the mind, the emotions and the soul of the employees.

The following commentary is from an MBA student who participated in the Sustainability Mind-set course, who shares his insights about the learning methodology he experienced in the course, and the unique contents. He also reflects on the lasting impact the course has had on his professional and personal life, including his wife.

What blended learning meant to me

By Craig Teal

Craig Teal graduated from the Gabelli School of Business at Fordham University in 2014 with a Master's in Business Administration in Finance and Management. Presently, he is a Financial Analyst for USI Insurance Services and resides in Seattle, WA. Outside of work, he volunteers with Seattle Works and enjoys the outdoors.

I was first exposed to a blended approach course as a graduate business school student in Professor Isabel Rimanoczy's "Developing a Sustainability Mind-set" course in the fall of 2014. To this day the course has stayed with me because of its methodology and content. My memory of specific sessions and discussions are strikingly vivid. In no other course can I recall the emotion, depth and feeling of the course and the people in it as this one.

At the heart of this blended approach course were two characteristics that were in stark contrast to 99% of the other courses available. They allow me to recall the main tenets of the course to this day. In fact, this contrast with other courses only further reinforced the content because it's the outlier among your typical lecture-centric courses.

The first characteristic was apparent upon entering the classroom for the initial session. The chairs were facing each other in a circle versus in rows behind a desk. There are a few courses and professors that attempt this as part of this course, but to have your course begin and end like this provides a strong evidence of the commitment to student engagement and peer teaching. Each component, whether it was an activity or thought-provoking question, was designed for us to interact with fellow students and our professors at a level that was new to many of us. That connection strengthened what we learned. Together our learning process was a complex journey, not a series of linear lectures. And better yet, by stoking participation, we learned from each other as colleagues, utilizing the talent in the room that is often wasted when only the professor and a select few students speak.

The second characteristic that impacted me in this experience was its focus on the world outside the classroom. Each question posed or activity given required students to confront the challenge of taking knowledge and theory and integrating it into our professional and personal lives. At the end of a "normal" course you are always left with the same question: What now? How can I integrate this knowledge into my everyday life? Often the answer is messy, so we fail to act. We compartmentalize that knowledge to that course only and it loses its power to effect change. By provoking the "What now?" question in the midst of learning, together as a group we brainstormed how to move forward. In no component of this course was this more evident than in our "passion project". At the start of the semester, we were asked to find a real world project to make a difference, but something that we would be passionate about. Before the last class we had to take active steps toward achieving it. With the support of our classmates and professors, we struggled with implementing this new knowledge, but because we struggled and supported each other together, we accomplished more. It provided us a guide on how to take theory and make it reality.

This course has set me on a complex journey, started but not yet complete. It altered my mind-set to internally and externally challenge the way business is conducted. Business is no longer just about maximizing shareholder value in the name of ROI (return on investment). It is consciously building an organization that's aware of its impact both positive and negative, and actively seeks a net positive influence. It changed my personal and professional lives in a multitude of ways, from what I eat, to where I live, to the people I surround myself with. One of the reasons my wife and I moved out to Seattle last year was because we wanted to surround ourselves with individuals and organizations that were socially and environmentally aware. I currently work at USI Kibble and Prentice, an insurance brokerage in the city. With its roots dating back to the 1970s, I was drawn to its belief that a company's role is more than just doing business, but being a part of the community. As a member and chair of the volunteer committee, we encouraged management to reaffirm this commitment. In August 2015 we organized a Day of Service where over 120 associates volunteered at service organizations in Greater Seattle. As I continue to find new and challenging ways to integrate what I learned the journey will continue, sometimes in a sprint and other times in a gentle walk.

Conclusion

When we see the importance of a holistic management education, is it possible to separate the contents from the learning methods? Addressing students from a holistic perspective may be not new as a goal: Dewey in the 1900s was suggesting that the purpose of all education should be developing self-awareness, and he placed reflection and learning by doing as the best methods to do it. Yet it has been given scarce attention in educational institutions, particularly in technical and business schools, as if technical or business formation could isolate intellect from the whole person.

Fortunately, the challenges are speaking to us so loudly that many are starting to look for what has to change. Scholars are writing about it; corporate visionaries are bringing more holistic development options into their organizations; social entrepreneurs are shaping their organizations using a "business as an agent of world benefit" approach (BAWB);[1] grass-roots activists are acting with social sensitivity and care; religious leaders are calling for profit for good (Cardinal Peter Turkson, 2015); and students across the world are realizing that responsible management education is not just a matter of developing knowledge and skills.

Responsible management education (RME) is a term that is increasingly present in academic research, publications and forums. This chapter started with the origin and evolution of the term, and followed by presenting the findings of an exploratory research that sought to understand what and how we could intentionally develop "responsible managers". The elements found in this study were characterized as components of a "sustainability mind-set", a particular way of thinking, being and acting that represents the highest level of responsible management. The elements, converted into learning objectives, became part of a course, which called for a blended teaching/learning approach, engaging head, heart and hands. This chapter offered the reader two conceptual frameworks: one focuses on content areas (ecoliteracy, systems, emotional and spiritual intelligence, and collaborative innovative action) and provides a checklist for lessons plans; the other focuses on learning objectives from the perspective of knowing, being and doing, and offers examples of activities and exercises for the practitioner.

In this chapter we explored ways to educate managers so they become (more) responsible, the core of Principle 3 of the PRME, and found a way to it via developing their sustainability mind-set. But responsible management education can also have another meaning: How are *we as educators* conscious of our responsibility when educating the future managers? That is perhaps where the motivation for educators starts: in the vision of the difference we can make, by shaping a world that works for all. The time to act is now.

---

1 The Fowler Center for Business as an Agent of World Benefit. Retrieved from https://weatherhead.case.edu/centers/fowler/

References

Adams, J. D. (2008). Six dimensions of mental models. In J. Wirtenberg, W.G. Russell & D, Lipsky (Eds.). *The Sustainable Enterprise Field Book: When It All Comes Together.* Sheffield, UK: Greenleaf Publishing, 66-70.

Alcaraz, J. M., & Thiruvattal, E. (2010). An interview with Manuel Escudero. The United Nations' principles for responsible management education: A global call for sustainability. *Academy of Management Learning & Education,* 9(3), 542-550.

Arevalo, J. & Mitchell, S. (Eds.) (forthcoming). *Handbook of Sustainability in Management Education: In Search of a Multidisciplinary, Innovative and Integrated Approach.* Cheltenham, UK; Northampton, MA: Edward Elgar Publishing.

Bloom, B.S., Masia, B.B. & Krathwohl, D.R. (1964). *Taxonomy of Educational Objectives* (Two Volumes: The Affective Domain & The Cognitive Domain). New York, NY: David McKay & Co.

Borland, H., & Lindgreen, A. (2013). Sustainability, epistemology, ecocentric business, and marketing strategy: Ideology, reality, and vision. *Journal of Business Ethics,* 117(1), 173-187.

Bowen, H.R. (1953). *Social Responsibility of the Businessman.* New York: Harper.

Burke, L. A., & Hutchins, H. M. (2007). Training transfer: An integrative literature review. *Human Resource Development Review,* 6(3), 263-296.

Carroll, A.B. (2008). A history of corporate social responsibility: Concepts and practices. In: A. Crane (Ed.), *The Oxford Handbook of Corporate Social Responsibility.* Oxford: Oxford University Press.

Chopra, P. K., & Kanji, G. K. (2010). Emotional intelligence: A catalyst for inspirational leadership and management excellence. *Total Quality Management,* 21(10), 971-1004.

Collins, M. (2010). Spiritual intelligence: Evolving transpersonal potential toward ecological actualization for a sustainable future. *World Futures,* 66(5), 320-334.

Cote, J., Goodstein, J., & Latham, C. K. (2011). Giving voice to values. *Journal of Business Ethics Education,* 8(1), 370-375.

Edwards, M. (2004). Good for business: An integral theory perspective on spirituality in organizations. *Journal of Spirituality Leadership and Management,* 3, 2-11.

Gelles, D. (2012, August 24). The mind business. *FT Magazine.* Retrieved from http://www.ft.com/cms/s/2/d9cb7940-ebea-11e1-985a-00144feab49a.html#axzz24gGdUpNS.

Goleman, D. (2006). *Emotional Intelligence.* New York: Bantam Books.

Goleman, D., Bennett, L., & Barlow, Z. (2012). *Ecoliterate: How Educators are Cultivating Emotional, Social, and Ecological Intelligence.* Hoboken, NJ: John Wiley & Sons.

Graham, C. R. (2012). Blended learning systems. In: C.J. Bonk & C.R. Graham (Eds.). *The Handbook of Blended Learning: Global Perspectives, Local Designs.* Hoboken, NJ: John Wiley & Sons.

Heuer, M. (2010). Defining stewardship: Towards an organisational culture of sustainability. *The Journal of Corporate Citizenship,* 40, 31.

Kahn, R., & Kahn, R.V. (2010). Critical pedagogy, ecoliteracy, and planetary crisis: The ecopedagogy movement (Volume 359). New York: Peter Lang Publishing.

Kegan, R. (1994). *In Over Our Heads: The Mental Demands of Modern Life.* Boston, MA: Harvard University Press.

Krathwohl, D. R. (2002). A revision of Bloom's taxonomy: An overview. *Theory into Practice,* 41(4), 212-218.

Lange, E. A. (2004). Transformative and restorative learning: A vital dialectic for sustainable societies. *Adult Education Quarterly,* 54(2), 121-139.

Langley, A. (2000). Emotional intelligence: A new evaluation for management development? *Career Development International,* 5(3), 177-183.

Lewis, J. S., & Geroy, G. D. (2000). Employee spirituality in the workplace: A cross-cultural view for the management of spiritual employees. *Journal of Management Education*, 24(5), 682-694.

McBride, B. B., Brewer, C. A., Berkowitz, A. R., & Borrie, W. T. (2013). Environmental literacy, ecological literacy, ecoliteracy: What do we mean and how did we get here? *Ecosphere*, 4(5), 67.

McDonald, R. (2013). *A Practical Guide to Educating for Responsibility in Management and Business*. New York: Business Expert Press.

Massachusetts Institute of Technology (Producer) (2015). *Transforming Business, Society, and Self with U. Lab*. [MOOC]. Retrieved from https://www.edx.org/course/transforming-business-society-self-u-lab-mitx-15-671x#!

Matten, D., & Moon, J. (2004). Corporate social responsibility education in Europe. *Journal of Business Ethics*, 54(4), 323-337.

Mitroff, I.I., & Denton, E.A. (1999). A study of spirituality in the workplace. *Sloan Management Review*, Summer 1999. Retrieved from http://sloanreview.mit.edu/article/a-study-of-spirituality-in-the-workplace/

Moore, J. (2005). Is higher education ready for transformative learning? A question explored in the study of sustainability. *Journal of Transformative Education*, 3(1), 76-91.

Murphy, P.E. (1978). An evolution: Corporate social responsiveness. *University of Michigan Business Review*, November, 20-22.

Murphy, R., Sharma, N., & Moon, J. (2012). Empowering students to engage with responsible business thinking and practices. *Business and Professional Ethics Journal*, 31(2), 313-330.

Murray, T. (2006). Collaborative knowledge building and integral theory: On perspectives, uncertainty, and mutual regard. *Integral Review*, 2(1), 210-268.

Net Impact (2014). *2014 Business as Unusual: The Social & Environmental Impact Guide to Graduate Programs—For Students By Students*. San Francisco: Net Impact. Retrieved from https://netimpact.org/sites/default/files/documents/business-as-unusual-2014.pdf

Nguyen, N. C., Graham, D., Ross, H., Maani, K., & Bosch, O. (2012). Educating systems thinking for sustainability: Experience with a developing country. *Systems Research and Behavioral Science*, 29(1), 14-29.

Nicholls, J., Hair, J. F., Ragland, C. B., & Schimmel, K. E. (2013). Ethics, corporate social responsibility, and sustainability education in AACSB undergraduate and graduate marketing curricula: A benchmark study. *Journal of Marketing Education*, 35(2), 129-140.

Orlitzky, M., & Moon, J. (2010). Assessing corporate social responsibility education in Europe. *Toward Assessing Business Ethics Education*, 143.

Porter, T., & Córdoba, J. (2009). Three views of systems theories and their implications for sustainability education. *Journal of Management Education*, 33(3), 323-347.

Reigeluth, C. M. (Ed.). (2013). *Instructional Design Theories and Models: An Overview of their Current Status*. New York: Routledge.

Reiser, R. A., & Dempsey, J. V. (2011). *Trends and Issues in Instructional Design and Technology*. Chicago: Pearson Merrill Prentice Hall.

Rimanoczy, I. B. (2010). *Business Leaders Committing to and Fostering Sustainability Initiatives*. ProQuest LLC.

Rimanoczy, I.B. (2013). *Big Bang Being: Developing the Sustainability Mindset*. Sheffield, UK: Greenleaf Publishing.

Rooney, J. E. (2003). Blending learning opportunities to enhance educational programming and meetings. *Association Management*, 55(5), 26-32.

Rossett, A. (2002). *The ASTD e-learning handbook*: New York: McGraw-Hill.

Rowe, D. (2002). Environmental literacy and sustainability as core requirements: Success stories and models. In: W. Leal Filho (Ed.). *Teaching Sustainability at Universities*. Frankfurt: Peter Lang.

Schein, S. (2014). *The Ecological World Views and Post-Conventional Action Logics of Global Sustainability Leaders*. Doctoral dissertation, Fielding Graduate University.

Semetsky, I. (2010). Ecoliteracy and Dewey's educational philosophy: Implications for future leaders. *Foresight*, 12(1), 31-44.

Sharma, S., & Hart, S. L. (2014). Beyond "saddle bag" sustainability for business education. *Organization & Environment*, 27(1), 10-15.

Shrivastava, P. (2010). Pedagogy of passion for sustainability. *Academy of Management Learning & Education*, 9(3), 443-455.

Sipos, Y., Battisti, B., & Grimm, K. (2008). Achieving transformative sustainability learning: Engaging head, hands and heart. *International Journal of Sustainability in Higher Education*, 9(1), 68-86.

Smith, T. (2011). Using critical systems thinking to foster an integrated approach to sustainability: A proposal for development practitioners. *Environment, Development and Sustainability*, 13(1), 1-17.

Stead, J. G., & Stead, W. E. (2014). Building spiritual capabilities to sustain sustainability-based competitive advantages. *Journal of Management, Spirituality & Religion*, 11(2), 143-158.

Sterling, S. (2011). Transformative learning and sustainability: Sketching the conceptual ground. *Learning and Teaching in Higher Education*, 5, 17-33.

Svanström, M., Lozano-García, F. J., & Rowe, D. (2008). Learning outcomes for sustainable development in higher education. *International Journal of Sustainability in Higher Education*, 9(3), 339-351.

Tennyson, R. D., & Park, O. C. (1980). The teaching of concepts: A review of instructional design research literature. *Review of Educational Research*, 50(1), 55-70.

Tomlinson, C. A., Brighton, C., Hertberg, H., Callahan, C. M., Moon, T. R., Brimijoin, K. … & Reynolds, T. (2003). Differentiating instruction in response to student readiness, interest, and learning profile in academically diverse classrooms: A review of literature. *Journal for the Education of the Gifted*, 27(2-3), 119-145.

Torbert, W. R., & Herdman-Barker, E. (2008). Generating and measuring practical differences in leadership performance at postconventional action-logics: Developing the Harthill Leadership Development Profile. In A. Coombs, A. Pfaffenberger, & P. Marko (Eds.), *The Postconventional Personality: Perspectives on Higher Development* (pp. 39-56). New York: SUNY Academic Press.

Turkson, P. (2015, May 22). Pope's climate change aide urges business to favor planet over profit. Planeta Azul. Retrieved from http://www.planetaazul.com.mx/site/?p=111924&upm_export=print

UNESCO (2006). United Nations Decade of Education for Sustainable Development: The First Two Years. Paris: UNESCO. Retrieved from http://unesdoc.unesco.org/images/0015/001540/154093e.pdf

Venkatesh, G. (2010). Triple bottom line approach to individual and global sustainability. *Problems of Sustainable Development*, 5(2), 29-37.

Visser, W. & Crane, A. (2010). Corporate sustainability and the individual: Understanding what drives sustainability professionals as change agents. SSRN Working Paper Series.

Weinberger, L. A. (2009). Emotional intelligence, leadership style, and perceived leadership effectiveness. *Advances in Developing Human Resources*, 11(6), 747-772.

Wiek, A., Withycombe, L., & Redman, C. L. (2011). Key competencies in sustainability: A reference framework for academic program development. *Sustainability Science*, 6(2), 203-218.

Young, J. R. (2002, March 22). "Hybrid" teaching seeks to end the divide between traditional and online instruction. *Chronicle of Higher Education*, A33.

Appendix: Learning objectives and examples of activities

Learning objective	Examples of activities
Learning objectives about the Knowing	
Overarching goal: develop ecoliteracy	Use videos, readings, blogs, newspapers to get updated information about the planetary challenges. Discuss, invite to post, write essays and commentaries. Invite guest speakers
Overarching goal: use a systemic framework to interpret data and to develop solutions	Set up a debate holding opposite positions and ask the class to develop a both–and solution. Write a "Both–and" sign on the board and give credit to who finds an either/or situation that needs to be converted into "Both–and". Highlight (or invite them to find) when paradoxes appear in readings or dialogues. Use a newspaper to circle "Both–and" and "either/or" stories and have a dialogue about the implications and consequences of both.
Understand Paradox and complexity, and use a both–and logic to develop solutions.	Generalize the findings, to show how the both–and logic can be used in other situations, and the benefits or necessity of it. Explore exceptions. Connect some challenges of our planet to the either/or logic and invent "Both–and" solutions. Invite them to identify some "Both–and" solutions they have personally created and were successful. You can use readings, videos, a walk around the block, a question to post reflections on Blackboard as scenarios for the above.
Identify the Interconnections and develop multi-stakeholder perspectives in their solutions.	Using one news item from the day, have them draw arrows of impact, then share and discuss interconnections. How would the exercise be with another piece of news? Use expanding circles: me, my circle, my neighbours, my region, my country, my continent, my planet. Also future generations. Identify the impact on different stakeholders of a recent purchase or decision. Discuss what interconnections should be considered in their own context/business, and when do interconnections not apply Explore consequences of ignoring interconnections, and of considering them. Invite them to identify one area where they would like to include multi-stakeholder perspectives and report on the result. Create a skit where different students represent a different stakeholder. How many different ones can they suggest? You can use readings, videos, a visit to a supermarket, an interview with a relative, their "passion project" or direct questions to post reflections as scenarios for the above.

Look beyond linear cause–effect relationships, seeking for feedback loops and cyclical flow, anticipating such in solutions they develop.	Create a map with challenges to our planet and identify feedback loops which show the connections between the challenges. Identify a non-sustainable habit and depict the feedback loops we are supporting through that Identify feedback looks in current decisions they are taking, and invite them to explore alternatives Discuss the purpose of identifying feedback loops and how it can help to have a better life/planet/future? Invite them to identify a feedback loop that resulted in a problem in their life that they hadn't noticed until now. What would they do differently? Incorporate that lens into their own "passion project". You can use readings, videos, journalling, data from their "passion project", a dialogue face-to-face or direct questions to post reflections as scenarios for the above.
Develop scenarios that contemplate the long term impact of their solutions to problems.	Use a current decision from the newspaper of the day to explore short-term/long-term impact. How do we incorporate the long term into our decisions? What are the benefits and the problems of focusing on short or on long term? Incorporate that lens into their own "passion project". You can use learning partners, newspapers, journalling, data from their "passion project", introducing this lens at work as scenarios for the above.
Overarching goal: use the creative potential and inner wisdom to develop innovative solutions.	
Develop personal ways to access the right brain hemisphere perspective, to enrich their understanding through a holistic and intuitive view of reality.	Always start with an exercise to access the right brain information, and follow with a cognitive processing of it (debrief, dialogue, posting, journalling) White flipcharts and markers: Draw your world (no words) Think of a current problem/dilemma. Walk in a park and find the answer that is hidden there. Create a list of what you perceived when you walked in (atmosphere) What is intuitive wisdom and how have they experienced/ accessed it in the past? Trust or distrust that information? How do animals receive and process non-verbal information? What information may be lost if we stay only with the rational input? Explore fragmentation (analysis) versus holistic understanding You can use journalling, creative productions (i.e. drawing, communicating with subtle body language, skits), observing art, the Little Wise Person inside, as settings to trigger the dialogue around the above-mentioned questions. Individual work, combined with work in duos is a good technique for unusual and personal assignments.

Learning objective	Examples of activities

Learning objectives about the Knowing

| Develop confidence generating imaginative, out-of-the-box ideas. Practise mental flexibility to develop versatility to better respond to the unexpected. | Set a stage going back in their mind when they were five to lower self-critique and censorship around creativity. Use music, Nature, interaction with children, children's books, jokes, collage, brainstorming, Lego, colours, clay, to experiment representing ideas through symbols, shapes, and also finding shapes and symbols in objects. Debrief, explore feelings and why they felt good (or bad), examples when creative thinking made their life easier. Explore versatility in their life and how it can make their life easier, and ways to keep that present. |

Learning objectives about the Being

| See themselves as part of a larger ecosystem, recognizing the laws of Nature that govern all that is. Analyse problems and develop solutions from within the framework of oneness with Nature. | *Start with an activity to experience Nature.* Walk in Nature, alone, to observe. Then write down the thoughts. Distribute seeds and invite students to plant and grow them. Meet for class outside—in a garden, park, Japanese garden. Visit a zoo. How is Nature present in this classroom? Explore Nature's services that we take for granted. How are we part of Nature? What is our relationship with Nature: Control, domination, stewardship, users, protectors, restorers? Discuss how Nature is integrated into their decisions, in their workplace or in their profession, in the different subjects they are taking at school. *Offer prompt questions, such as what did I learn about myself in Nature? What did I learn about Nature that relates to my life? Combine experiential activities with videos, readings (i.e. Biomimicry)* |
| Develop introspective habits, to understand self, practising revision of the personal motives, values (espoused and in action), as well as anchors of the own identity. Develop self-awareness. | Flipcharts and colours to draw "Who am I" (no words) MBTI—Learning styles inventory, other instruments. What makes me me? What could I give up and still be me? Values of our culture: Explore growth, wealth, independence, achievement, speed, comfort, control, knowledge and competition as Anchors of the un-sustainability. Exercise "In your shoes": Identifying their personally most unacceptable person, enact a skit "walking in his/her shoes". Work in duos, debrief. Explore my contribution: Identify an unacceptable circumstance (planet, society, news) and explore what is our personal, individual contribution to the problem. Then work in duos, identifying an unacceptable circumstance at work or home, and identify the personal (unintentional) contribution to the problem. Debrief and explore how this connects with the challenges we have as individuals and as society, and what we can do as an individual. *Use silent reflection, journalling, questions posted in Blackboard, sharing in duos, debrief, dialogue face-to-face* |

→

Learn to slow down, incorporate practice to quiet the mind, achieve moments of inner peace, connect with the higher self, experience higher alertness and consciousness.	*Always go from an experience to the debrief. Don't start talking about slowing down—have them experience it first.* Start the classes with 3–4 min meditation walk or sit in Nature. Use music in the room. Invite them to notice their body posture, the internal bodily sensations, their breathing Invite them to go to a coffee shop with no phone or device, stay 45 minutes just being there, as an assignment. Then they write down about the experience. Debrief. *Use individual experiences, sharing impressions in duos or trios, dialogues in the group. Debrief and make connections with how they felt, and how this is different from their everyday. Consequences of speed and slowing down. What would they like to try out/change themselves? Use journalling, questions to post reflections.* *As the facilitator, control your own pace and rhythm, explain to the students that it will be slower sometimes than they are used to, and explain the purpose. Introduce segments with different pace.*
Develop habits of reflection to pause and ponder situations without jumping to quick answers.	Use "Stop-Reflect" minutes for individual reflection before starting a dialogue or sharing thoughts in a group. Debrief how it felt to sit in silence, writing down thoughts before talking. Explore implications of not doing it in the day-to-day life, benefits of pausing. How would this make our life easier, better, more gratifying?
Include the dimension of the personal larger purpose into their decisions, life plans and choices. Weigh options with the criteria in mind, what brings meaning to their life, what difference they want to make.	Amazing Achievement Award: Write an acceptance speech for an award for an amazing achievement you did, that you will receive in 7 years. Describe what you did, what obstacles you had and who helped you. Drawing: Me and what is missing to be fully me. Share, debrief, extract meaning. What are my values and how are they manifested in what I do? If I could do anything, what would I do? *Use inspirational readings, videos, poetry, interviews with the homeless, or the elderly. Use questions to post reflections, journalling, work with learning partners, dialogues.*

Learning objectives about the Doing

Connect with their community/ place to discover unseen aspects of their real context	Encourage them to identify a project to make a difference serving a real need of their current community, their neighbourhood, their city.

Learning objective	Examples of activities
Learning objectives about the Doing	
Uncover and review their mental maps and models by exposure to unfamiliar situations or relationships	Encourage projects that require interaction with unfamiliar contexts, with demographic characteristics that are unfamiliar to the team (age, gender, social class, ethnicity, religion, profession, race, nationality, etc.). Invite them to write about the impact on them individually of the interaction with the target group, and what they are learning about themselves, about their own assumptions, values, prejudices. Debrief how this connects with the challenges our society has, and what could be different. Debrief how this connects with other subjects they are taking.
Develop social sensitivity	Complementing the above, invite them to interview a person belonging to a demographic sector they feel most estranged and distant from (age, gender, social class, ethnicity, religion, profession, race, nationality, etc.). Invite them to reflect and write about what they learned about themselves.
Practise and develop team-working skills	Encourage team projects, rather than individual ones. Provide templates for practising and keeping records of shared leadership, decision-making, feedback, meeting management, time management, appreciation, contracting expectations. Encourage debrief: What is working, what do we need to do differently?
Develop comfort collaborating with others to address challenges.	Encourage extracting individual lessons: What am I learning about myself in a team? Explore what makes for positive collaboration versus competition and rivalry, and how this connects with the challenges we as a society are living with, and what we can do.
Practise innovation	Encourage out-of-the box thinking in identifying the project, in finding solutions and in presenting the results. Encourage playfulness
Develop self-confidence and hope	Encourage projects that can start and finish within the term, that have a real impact, that are meaningful for them. Even small goals are valuable, as opposed to large ambitious projects that will not be achieved in the term.

10

The Daniels Compass
Global business education for management professionals

Don Mayer and Bruce Hutton
Daniels College of Business, University of Denver, USA

Introduction

In "Becoming a real person", David Brooks (2014) argues that universities have historically been assigned three purposes: the commercial purpose (starting a career), a cognitive purpose (acquiring information and learning how to think), and a moral purpose (building an integrated self). Brooks contends that leaders in academia no longer try to promote moral purposes in their students. This chapter describes how one business school has worked to instil the importance of ethics, values and a sense of purpose in a business career. Like any business, there are false starts, signature successes and ongoing volatility as the college and faculty debate the right balance between "hard" and "soft" skills, what content is most important, how it is delivered, and who should deliver it. Box A1 (in the Appendix) provides a timeline that charts the journey of the Daniels College of Business, a journey that continues to this day.

The Daniels journey began well before the signature development of the Principles for Responsible Management Education (PRME), yet did evolve into a programme that embraced each of PRME's six principles: Purpose, Values, Method, Research, Partnerships and Dialogue. Principle 2, **Values**, provided the foundation for our efforts. Initially, attention was focused at the local level, but faculty soon realized that the programme needed a global perspective as well, including experiences abroad. One example of students' overseas experience is with the Deutsche Bank Social Entrepreneurship Microfinance course. This course, ranked by *Forbes Magazine* in 2011 as one of the ten most innovative business school courses, is an interdisciplinary course where students do loan evaluations and performance reviews of Deutsche Bank microfinance loans. Students have travelled to seven different countries (Cambodia, Uganda, Kenya, Republic of Georgia, Philippines, India and Peru) to interview loan applicants and make their evaluations.

From the fairly basic idea of introducing ethics into the curriculum came the realization that a single course in ethics was only the beginning of the journey to responsible business education. Teaching ethical and social responsibility to students led to the understanding that subjects such as ethics inevitably cut across the traditional PhD disciplines of business education (e.g. finance, accounting, marketing, etc.). This chapter traces the expansion of ethics and values throughout the curriculum and how it was embedded in the culture of Daniels, in courses, faculty commitment, administrative support, experiential learning and community service.

We begin by introducing "The Daniels Legacy" and the creation of seven interdisciplinary focused courses created to meet the challenge given to us by Bill Daniels, a challenge to involve ethics deeply in the MBA curriculum. Our story, still in progress, ends with a review of the ongoing challenges faced by any school working to provide students with the most relevant and responsible business education. Within that story, the Daniels College of Business was recently recognized as one of the 15 most innovative MBA programmes (Rampton, 2015) in the United States for its work in ethics and social responsibility over the past two decades. This chapter includes sections on:

- The Daniels legacy: Bill Daniels's challenge to us
- The Daniels Compass: how our curriculum evolved over 20 years
- Integrating values
- Framework for broader applications

Interspersed in our story are commentaries from two University of Denver alumni, highlighting how their values-based education at Daniels has related to their own careers. Their words reaffirm the value of responsible management education, not only to themselves, but to society. We also include a commentary from John Powers, Executive Director and Founder of the Alliance for a Sustainable Colorado. His words underline society's ongoing needs for interdisciplinary studies in business that can move corporations from a singular focus on profits to business entities that embrace public environmental and social goods.

The Daniels legacy

In 1988, the University of Denver's school of business (the eighth oldest business college in the US) had been around for more than 80 years, serving a mostly local and regional student body. The university and the business school were going through hard times economically. Both were transformed economically and spiritually through an $11 million matching gift from Bill Daniels, often referred to as one of the "fathers of cable television". Daniels often said that "the best is good enough for me". But he measured "the best" not only by how much money he made, but by how he made it. To Daniels, success also meant giving back to those less fortunate and to society. Among the many firsts in his life was the creation of the Young Americans Bank, the nation's only financial institution created solely for people aged 17 years and younger so they could learn early about savings, earnings and investing (Singular, 2003). Before he died he provided funding to create the Daniels Fund to support programmes focused on ageing, substance abuse, amateur sports, disabilities, education, homelessness and youth development, as well as continuing support for ethics education.

In part as a response to the so-called "decade of greed" in the 1980s, Daniels challenged the business college at the University of Denver to redesign its core MBA curriculum to include the study of ethics, creativity and values-based leadership. The college was also charged with providing a global perspective as part of its core curriculum. At the time, such course content was rarely taught in any business school, let alone in required courses. Funds for his $11 million matching grant were raised by the college and, several years later, an additional $11 million was given to the college by Daniels for "a job well done". Subsequently the college was named the Daniels College of Business.

To guide the college's effort to build a practical, interdisciplinary, values-based global MBA programme that would meet the needs of all students, a three-point mission statement was created: "Ethical Practice. Thought Leadership. Global Impact. The Daniels College of Business is dedicated to educating ethical business leaders, advancing the theory and practice of business and making a positive global impact."

The foundational vision for the college was to create an integrated system of course content and experiential learning opportunities that reflected the way business worked and the value of ethical conduct. The primary goals were to: 1) break down the historic "silos" among the various business disciplines, a structure that had produced a largely independent series of traditional courses "owned" by the functional departments; and 2) add an interdisciplinary focus to the Master's programmes. A cross-disciplinary team of faculty, along with members of the business community, created seven unique interdisciplinary courses:

- **High Performance Management**. Focused on human skills necessary for managerial success (e.g. communication, negotiation, critical thinking, leadership, team effectiveness, power and influence). The methodology for high performance management relied primarily on experience-based learning outcomes.

- **Foundations of Business Decisions.** Focused on technical skills and how those skills are interdependent and interactive.

- **Positioning in the Competitive Environment.** Brought together strategy and core disciplines with critical foundations of law and policy.

- **Values in Action I and II.** A two-part sequenced course focused on ethics and corporate social responsibility at the individual, institutional and societal levels.

- **Managing in the Global Century.** Explored management practices, decision-making, competition and values framed in a global context.

- **Quest for Quality.** Developed managerial perspectives and the tools related to total quality management across disciplines.

- **Integrative Challenge.** Skills and competences learned in the classroom were applied to real world situations, requiring the students to understand the interdependencies of the different disciplines.

In order to provide more realistic experiences for students, a variety of off-campus activities and outside speakers were integrated into the curriculum. For example, all students were required to complete a three day outdoor adventure type of programme designed by a team of faculty and outdoor leadership experts, a two-week leadership "boot-camp" experience, and a series of workshops on subjects like cultural diversity, the role of public policy in business, business etiquette, negotiation and conflict resolution. Additionally, each student was required to complete 24 hours of community service.

Another outreach programme that increased the level of awareness of the importance of ethics in business was introduced by the statewide daily newspaper and the Daniels College. A select group of business faculty created and ran a weekly Business & Ethics column in the state's most prominent newspaper. The column answered questions from across the state regarding real world and real time business ethics dilemmas in the state.

Also in the early 1990s, all Daniels faculty (and not just those teaching the ethics courses) were provided with a variety of training opportunities in the basics of ethical theories and decision-making.

The Daniels Compass

In 2006, the faculty at Daniels took the best from the original Daniels suite of courses and created a new curriculum based on the idea that business professionals in the 21st century faced a rapidly changing and often chaotic world. The basic insight was that students needed "a compass" in order to navigate the many challenges business leaders faced from globalization, rapid changes in technology, and disruptive social and environmental factors. A faculty committee with an advisory board of business, government and non-profit professionals began developing the next iteration of an integrative educational experience.

Designating the newly created courses as the "Compass" was intentional. The compass was viewed as an appropriate metaphor for the role these courses would play in the curriculum and in the lives of our students after graduation. After all, a compass provides the ability to set our direction to arrive at a specific destination, to calculate our relative bearing to others, and to determine a back bearing so we know where we have come from. The Compass courses were designed to do the same: provide vision to a future, perspective on the world around us and a sense of history to guide us. And, the primary points on the compass remind us of key concepts necessary to consider in order to make a living and also make a difference in the world—Nature, Self, World-view and Enterprise (Hutton and Cox, 2008; see Fig. 10.1).

Figure 10.1 **The Daniels Compass**

For the functional aspects of business—what products to create, what prices to charge, how to accumulate adequate financial capital and raw materials for production, where production should take place, what labour forces are required, what kind of return is acceptable, etc.—all points on the compass should be considered, with systems thinking deployed to assess the entire set of impacts and issues. All too often, decisions in a business context are based on one point of the compass: Enterprise (profit maximization, shareholder value, etc.). Any business school will have a primary focus on Enterprise, where the issues raised would include return on investment, labour costs, market share, legal risk, etc. But many of the Enterprise issues will also require a clear reckoning with other compass directions.

For example, pricing and tax strategies will likely affect not just projected market share (Enterprise) but also Nature (creating lower prices by imposing pollution costs on others), World-view (taking advantage of cheap labour "offshore", job losses in home country, reducing public funds for needed infrastructure improvements) and Self (personal relationships with family and friends, loss of self-esteem caused by doing something you personally do not feel was ethical). For each direction, deliberate consideration. For each direction, deliberate consideration of each point on the compass is designed to create some cognitive dissonance and further reflection that a singular focus on Enterprise will not.

The Compass launch and learning outcomes

In announcing the revised programme, the Daniels College of Business website proclaimed a redesigned mission: "Our mission is to inspire students to take responsibility as citizens and professionals to make a positive difference, now and for future generations, in the workplace, the marketplace and the communities in which they live and work."

To fulfil this mission, the Compass courses embraced the following learning outcomes:

- Expose students to a world-view in which business succeeds as part of a dynamic interactive global system where economic prosperity, social equity and environmental integrity are necessary interdependent components.
- Build leadership, followership and team skills through a highly interactive and dynamic set of experiential learning activities.
- Explore the purpose of business in society and how it contributes to both quality of life and standard of living among its many stakeholders in a world characterized by extremes—in wealth, knowledge, cultural heritage, security, values and hope.
- Define what it means to be a professional and the resulting responsibilities.
- Complement and enhance core knowledge in the disciplines of business.
- Provide practical tools for achieving personal and enterprise success.
- Develop a values-based foundation for the next generation of professional global citizens.

The Compass courses described

The initial course offerings included:

- **Essence of Enterprise** (The beginning of the bottom line). "Essence" presented a global world-view and historical context for business in the 21st century

- **Leading at the Edge** (Know you. Know how). Experiential learning is the focus at the beginning of the programme, including three days of team-building and collaborative challenges in the mountains. Much of the experiential learning at "Edge weekend" was a continuation of assigned readings in leadership, teamwork and emotional intelligence. The "Edge weekend" became a rite of passage for Daniels students, not only at the MBA level, but for the Professional MBA and one year specialization programmes in finance and accounting as well.

Once back in the classroom, students engaged in a variety of Denver-based community service activities to gain an applied understanding of systems thinking in solving critical problems in an interconnected world. They were then asked to write a paper comparing the similarities, differences and inter-dependencies between environmental, economic and social systems in which they engaged.

Beyond Essence of Enterprise and Leading at the Edge, the original Compass curriculum introduced in academic year 2007/08 included these required courses:

- **Ethics for the 21st Century** (A journey to responsibility)

- **Creating Sustainable Enterprises** (What's in it for we?)

- **Global Case Challenge** (Business without boundaries)

- **Innovation Design and Execution** (The little idea that went to market)

While this new suite of courses proved popular, the need for greater flexibility for students and a lower cost of delivery required the college to again seek a different balance between content and the cost of delivery.

In 2008, the faculty initiated a final revision to the Compass, condensing the content and learning outcomes from the original suite of seven courses to three courses—The Essence of Enterprise (combining Leading at the Edge and Essence of Enterprise), Ethics for the 21st-Century Professional, and Creating Sustainable Enterprises. Global content and innovation/creativity were integrated into these three courses and became content for other discipline-oriented classes. These were positioned in the new Compass curriculum against seven guiding principles the faculty saw as necessary for a business professional to be truly ethical and effective, as shown in Table 10.1.

Table 10.1 **Guiding principles and the Compass courses: 2008–2015**

	BUS 4610 Essence of Enterprise/ Leading at the Edge	BUS 4620 Ethics for the 21st-Century Professional	BUS 4630 Creating Sustainable Enterprises
Professionalism	◆	◆	
Accountability	◆	◆	◆
Responsibility	◆	◆	◆
Social/ intergenerational equity		◆	◆
Teamwork	◆		
Self-knowledge	◆	◆	
Community and social capital	◆	◆	◆

Professionalism is emphasized at the very beginning of the programme through readings from Justice Brandeis (1914) and Nohria and Khurana (2008). The basic concept is that business management—given its primacy in contemporary society—should be considered a profession. Professionalism has long been understood to signify an occupation that is undertaken as much for social good as it is for monetary compensation. In an era when professionalism has been repeatedly misunderstood as "something you do to make money", the reminder that management can mean something much more to society is a much-needed value in business education.

Accountability underpins much of the three compass courses. In the Essence of Enterprise course all students take the Insights Discovery Profile (Insights. com), a psychological tool that helps students to know themselves better, including their working style, impact on others and how to better communicate with others, thus being able to hold themselves and their teammates to higher standards of performance. To that end, each team creates a social contract that works for them during the Edge Weekend and in other team assignments during the first quarter.

In the Ethics for the 21st-Century Professional course, students focus on their personal decision-making processes as well as the values and motivations behind them. They also move through various ethical issues confronted in modern business organizations (sales, product liability, discrimination, insider-trading, global values conflicts) to learn the difference between what is legally required and what is ethically desirable to be fully accountable to all the firm's stakeholders.

In Creating Sustainable Enterprises, the focus is on providing both perspective and tools to help students make more informed business decisions and to prepare them to meet the challenges in which success is often determined by a world-view that understands the challenges of being accountable to multiple stakeholders including shareholders, employees, customers, society and even future generations.

Responsibility is an ethical value closely aligned with accountability. In Creating Sustainable Enterprises, students see how many different kinds of companies (small to medium to large) can create not only monetary value but also social and environmental value and how these forms of value can benefit all stakeholders over time. One of the most challenging aspects of the course is accounting for future generations (intergenerational equity). This natural tension between the present and the future provides fertile ground for discussion of the appropriate role of business in society with no easily quantifiable answers. Ethical obligations take centre stage in such discussions.

Social equity and Intergenerational equity. In Creating Sustainable Enterprises, the third course in the Compass, students become practised in seeing the various ways in which businesses can serve not only economic needs but also social needs, including long-term care for the environment and future generations. In Ethics for the 21st-Century Professional, students are exposed to concepts of social justice and distributive justice, and their current applications.

Teamwork as a value is closely aligned with **self-reflection and self-analysis**. It becomes clear through the progression of all three courses that much more can be accomplished when self-aware team members work together for common purposes.

Community and social capital are critical values for the Compass courses. In its original design, students were expected to analyse critical gaps in community services, consider alternative positive outcomes and then address how creative business thinking and planning could close those gaps. Classroom assignments included readings on trust and social capital from Francis Fukuyama (1993) and Robert Putnam (2000) and others to support foundational insights from Essence of Enterprise that businesses, like individuals, do not exist in isolation from each other but rather form important parts of a larger, more complex system, and that social capital must be built and maintained in order for business to function effectively in any given society.

The importance of these seven guiding principles to the purpose and success of business and to their inclusion in business education is articulated by John Powers, the Executive Director and founder of the Alliance for a Sustainable Colorado (see Box 10.1). The Alliance is one of Colorado's most active non-profit organizations, dedicated to transforming sustainability from a vision to reality through collaborations among key civic groups, government and business. John's comments reflect a growing recognition, emphasized at Daniels, that even as our graduates must be community-minded, so must companies, as the economic engines of our communities, serve the public good. He reminds us that responsible corporate consciences are essential to an economy that works for people, communities and enterprises.

Box 10.1 **John Powers, Executive Director and Founder of the Alliance for a Sustainable Colorado**

Is "corporate conscience" relevant? Realistic? If corporations are "persons" with legal rights, what are their responsibilities? The Daniels College of Business has long considered such questions as essential for business education. Ethics, sustainability and good corporate citizenship are emphasized with students even as they learn and hone their technical skills. Daniels does that not only in courses, but with practical study outside of classrooms with companies, and especially with community service and team-building exercises. Attention to values, the Daniels way, is essential to business education today.

Historically, incorporation in the United States was granted by state legislatures to enable activities that benefited the public. Corporate charters were approved for limited periods, which expired, and the charters could be revoked for wrongdoing. But in an 1886 Supreme Court decision corporations were judged to be persons for purposes of the 14th Amendment. In creating the precedent that corporations may receive the same legal protections as people, control of corporations by public legislative bodies was weakened.

Today, statutory "Benefit Corporations" have been made legal in many states, where maximizing profits is, by statute, not the corporation's sole consideration. B Corp boards of directors consider the effects of any corporate action upon shareholders, employees, suppliers' employees, customers, the environment, and community and society. But legal changes are insufficient where the dominant paradigm assumes that corporations must maximize earnings every quarter (i.e. grow indefinitely and exponentially). Further movement towards corporate social awareness and responsibility will depend on enlightened future leaders.

Fortunately, many graduates of Daniels College of Business emerge with requisite cross-disciplinary experience and have developed an orientation towards social and environmental good. They are well poised to behave as fiduciaries of the public good. With support, these graduates can earn leadership roles that guide 21st-century business.

The true enlightenment that John Powers talks about here cannot come from classroom work alone. For this reason, Daniels has, over time, created an abundant array of experiential learning opportunities.

Experiential learning in the Compass

Over the course of developing a values-based business education, faculty came to realize that ethics is, in fact, a "contact sport" where "doing" is just as important as "knowing". Thus, Daniels faculty, over time, have created and maintained a robust set of experiential learning activities designed to complement and enhance classroom cognitive development. Four of the experiential activities are described here:

- Student-led volunteering in the community

- Pioneering an ethics award model

- Participating in case competitions

- Facilitating outdoor education opportunities

Since 1990, all MBA students have been required to engage in some form of community service. Initially, community engagement activities were identified and managed through the college. Within a couple of years, students took charge of this component of the programme and now many student service efforts are coordinated by their Net Impact chapter, a global non-profit focused on students and young professionals seeking to address some of the world's biggest social and environmental challenges.

At the local level, the Daniels College partnered with two organizations to create and launch the Colorado Ethics in Business Awards (CEBA). CEBA's yearly awards programme recognized companies, non-profits and individuals for exemplary service to the state of Colorado by their ethical conduct. A statewide nomination and selection committee of Colorado leaders in business, government and civil society provided the college with a list of finalists each year. Student teams from Daniels then undertook research and due diligence on each nominee, writing a comprehensive report of their activities and impact on the community. This research was presented to the selection committee who made the final award choices. Through this process, students gained first-hand expertise and knowledge of what a values-based ethical company could accomplish. This programme proved so successful that it was later adopted by several other business schools in different states.

The college has also embraced case competitions as a positive way to engage students in the complexities of business decision-making and their impact on society and the environment. Along with annually participating in the Aspen Institute's Business and Society Programme, including its International MBA Case Competition, Daniels College has created, and continues to sponsor, two of its own case competitions. Race & Case is a national case competition focused on ethics, sustainability and corporate responsibility. Daniels is also part of a consortium of schools in the Rocky Mountains region that has created a successful annual conference called SEE (Sustainability, Ethics and Entrepreneurship).

The most intense experiential component in the programme is associated with Leading at the Edge. The experience is the product of a partnership between the Daniels College and the Nature Place, an outdoor leadership and team-building focused nature camp in the heart of the Rocky Mountains. As team members, all students engage in a variety of outdoor activities that require collaboration and group problem solving: e.g. orienteering, rappelling and high ropes exercises. Other team challenges are provided throughout an intensive three-day retreat. When they return to class, students go through extensive debriefing about their experiences and how they are connected to situations they will ultimately find themselves in during their careers.

Integrating values: from academia to business and back again

The values taught at Daniels College of Business through traditional classroom teaching as well as through experiential learning have been described above. They are a reflection of the values that guide ethically responsible businesses, values that have been well articulated by PRME (Principles for Responsible Management Education). Daniels has built an ethics-focused culture for students through curriculum redesign and development of numerous experiential co-curricular learning activities organized by faculty and student organizations such as Net Impact. For faculty, Daniels has established research institutes and supported research in journals and books on business ethics and sustainability, as well as law and public policy that encourage responsible business activities that create social and environmental value as well as economic value.

Daniels's outreach has a variety of elements, including our Net Impact chapter, the Voices of Experience lecture series, the Institute for Enterprise Ethics (the place where professionals engaged in sustainability, ethics and compliance, and corporate social responsibility interact with Daniels's faculty and each other). These serve not only students, but the broader business community. Additionally, the Daniels Fund, a non-profit organization funded by Bill Daniels in his will, has created the Daniels Consortium comprised of selected business schools in four states (Colorado, Wyoming, Utah and New Mexico). Faculty and staff from the Daniels Fund meet quarterly to discuss ethics-related issues in business schools and to share best practices. Additionally, the Fund has created a yearly ethics focused conference to address selected topics that brings together teachers, business professionals and graduate students from the consortium schools.

An example of the value that an ethics-focused culture, integrated into traditional business education, can bring to the overall success of a business is provided by alumna Sarah Martinez, the sustainability director for Eco-Products (Box 10.2).

Box 10.2 **Sarah Martinez**

I am currently Sustainability Maven (Director) for Eco-Products, a leading brand of environmentally preferable foodservice packaging. I have also worked on the corporate sustainability teams for the global real estate firm, Prologis, and the retailer, Target. In each of these roles, understanding the "nuts and bolts" of environmental or social issues (e.g. how to calculate a carbon footprint or write a supplier code of conduct) was not the key to moving a company in a more sustainable direction. Instead, success in my role comes down to the ability to achieve buy-in across the organization. The skills to do this are not taught in conventional business classes. Fortunately for me, this was central to my experience at Daniels.

Daily, I draw upon what I learned from Daniels experiences such as the Insights Discovery Profile and the Leading at the Edge beyond-the-classroom experience. These offerings were invaluable in developing my ability to effectively engage others with different ways of thinking, communicating and motivating.

Let me give an example of how I've put this into practice. Eco-Products exclusively designs foodservice packaging with real environmental benefits. We could say "Our products have renewable resources or post-consumer content. It's enough to provide alternatives to foam and other conventional disposables". However, making "green" products and being a truly responsible company are two different things.

Shortly into my tenure with the company, I had the opportunity to share my thoughts on what Eco-Products could do better from a sustainability standpoint. Basically, I said we needed to do a better job at treating sustainability like any other important business metric: We needed to set goals, report progress and continue to challenge ourselves.

Committing to zero waste operations, phasing out legacy products that don't meet our current environmental standards, asking suppliers to sign a code of conduct, being transparent about our progress in an annual sustainability report—these are all initiatives I proposed but could not implement on my own. This required business unit leaders to commit their teams to implementing them, which in turn required that I have the ability to understand their priorities and position sustainability in a way that benefits the business and their departments.

Without the skills I learned at Daniels, I would not be able to secure this commitment. I am proud to say Eco-Products has elevated our sustainability efforts by doing the projects mentioned above and more.

By now it should be abundantly clear that the skills needed to achieve the kind of "buy-in" from various stakeholders that Sarah Martinez achieved cannot be taught to future leaders by offering a suite of courses in traditional "business disciplines".

Along with the specific Compass courses that speak to those skills, Daniels has offered complementary activities and engaged supporting organizations. These are described in the following section, which encourages business schools to make similar alignments and create similar programmes.

Framework for broader applications

This section introduces a number of specific outreach opportunities for business schools to: 1) align with existing organizations that promote PRME; 2) create their own programmes and institutions to complement the curriculum; 3) bring in outside values-exemplars for interaction with students, faculty and the community; and 4) address some predictable challenges to the kind of integration of values, programmes and curricula that Daniels has accomplished.

Outreach and alignment

Business schools have a variety of ways to reach out to the community and align themselves with specific causes and movements that show they are part of the larger community. Through various forms of community engagement, institutions can provide valuable opportunities for students to both learn from and engage with public, private and social enterprise leaders. Examples include the following:

Lecture series

Many institutions hold lecture series. Consider how you can revamp or integrate responsible management education (RME) with current practices. The Voices of Experience (VOE) lecture series is one of the many ways in which Daniels College has brought together students, alumni and the community around the Bill Daniels legacy of values-based business. In our experience, these are occasions where the entire university and college community (faculty, students, alumni and the broader community) come together to affirm and learn about ethical values in practice.

The VOE brings well-known leaders to a forum in which they can share their triumphs, mistakes and decisions as they navigated through their leadership careers. First-hand, attendees hear stories of motivation, loyalty, values-based leadership, turnaround strategies and more. For those institutions with limited resources, even traditional lecture series can benefit from adding at least one responsibility management focused speaker and having speakers address ethical issues in business.

Aligning research institutes

Many universities and colleges use research institutions as a means of highlighting their specialities as well as for faculty recruitment, development and retention.

At Daniels we established the Institute for Enterprise Ethics as a way to extend the College's expertise and resources in business ethics to the practitioner community of executives, officers and directors of commercial and social enterprises in the region. With its threefold focus on 1) enterprise ethics and compliance; 2) enterprise leadership and governance; and 3) enterprise social responsibility and sustainability, the Institute's mission is to help executives, officers and directors keep their organizations at the forefront of enterprise ethics.

The Institute's programmes are designed to be of value to businesses and service enterprises large and small. Participants have realized a variety of benefits from being a part of these events such as:

- Having access to the latest knowledge, research and practical experiences of seasoned business executives and respected scholars in the area of enterprise ethics.

- Understanding and discussing with peers new, as well as tried and true, approaches to dealing with emerging enterprise ethics issues that can be applied to actual business situations.

- Exposing young and rising executives and directors to the debate and dialogue on current ethical behaviour issues

- Networking with other practitioners who are interested in current topics in ethics, compliance, leadership, governance, social responsibility and sustainability.

We encourage others to review their current research institutes and assess how RME topics could be integrated into the current structure. Additionally, institutions should consider RME topics as top candidates when funding new research institutes.

Alignment with organizations

Business schools often align with other organizations that are consistent with their values and that create partnership opportunities for enhanced impact. For Daniels, three such organizations have been invaluable partners in our journey:

- **Business for Social Responsibility** (BSR). BSR's mission is to work with business to create and support a just and sustainable world. They believe that such a world will exist when the unique skills and resources of all three sectors of society—business, social enterprise, government—are aligned.

- **Aspen Institute Business & Society Programme**. Their stated purpose is to "help established and emerging business leaders put values at the heart of practice". The Aspen Center for Business Education runs several relevant programmes, including Academic Networks focused on best practices in teaching; Beyond Grey Pinstripes provides a premier source of data on curriculum;

CasePlace.org is a web-based collection of teaching materials; Faculty Pioneer Awards honours business educators; and an International MBA Case competition provides a forum for students to compete and connect with other students from around the world.

- **Principles for Responsible Management Education** (PRME). Launched at the 2007 UN Global Compact Leaders' Summit, the PRME initiative is the first organized relationship between the United Nations and business schools. Its stated purpose is to champion responsible management education, research and thought leadership globally.

In addition to the opportunities described above, the Daniels College of Business has also faced a variety of predictable challenges that have been continuous and sometimes vexing. These challenges parallel the struggle of establishing responsible ethical conduct in the world of business. The following section lays out the key issues the college has faced and continues to face in its quest for graduate business education that is responsible not only to traditional stakeholders, but also to communities, social institutions, governments and future generations.

Predictable challenges

Five types of challenges are discussed in detail below. These are conflicting stakeholder interests, ongoing training needs, lack of support for interdisciplinary research, revenue issues in university settings and cultural shifts.

Serving stakeholder differences

Employers, alumni, students, parents, faculty, administrators, potential donors, the community and society itself are all stakeholders in effective and responsible business education. But each set of stakeholders often assigns different levels of importance to the various values and concerns associated with any particular issue. For example, business students often place more value on technical skills believing they are the most important for gaining advantage in the job market. In contrast, employers often value communication skills, teamwork and an ability to make good decisions in the face of ambiguity. Dealing proactively with ethically marginal situations is a "soft skill" for which there is, or should be, considerable demand. For increasing numbers of employers, the technical skills from specific business disciplines are more often viewed as necessary but not sufficient. An emerging dif-ferentiator as to who gets hired lies increasingly in this second set of skills. For the business school, the challenge is how to make sure students graduate with a solid grounding in both skill sets.

But administrators at the university level may not understand these dual needs, and students may not be convinced that this second set of skills is truly in demand. Alumni must be engaged as potential employers and ongoing partners in the continued parity of "soft skills" with the more traditional technical ones, and the college must integrate its faculty hiring, training and curriculum so that all faculty are "on board" and knowledgeable in weaving principles of responsible management into the core courses. Finally, in-house assessment and third party verification of the efficacy of the curriculum (including non-course enrichment activities) must demonstrate the legitimate value of responsible management education in the minds of all stakeholders.

Training needs

Not surprisingly, faculty often have a hard time managing a curriculum that does a good job of blending technical skills with other skill sets such as ethics, corporate responsibility, sustainability and teamwork. One of the reasons for this struggle lies with the standard PhD model of training. Historically, faculty success has been dependent on a model that focuses on depth, not necessarily breadth. PhD students do not so much get a degree in business, but rather in a specialized degree within a specific discipline. So, one's degree may come from the marketing department, but the training is even narrower. For example, the marketing degree may be in consumer behaviour and within that, an even narrower specialization in something like advertising or even information processing.

Thus, investment (both buy-in and resources) for faculty training in ethics and values is a first step. The key to success is to integrate ethical theory and practice into core discipline courses, clearly showing how it can create value for stakeholders. Ethics should become part of the fabric of good business, successful business, profitable business, innovative business—business that meets the multiple needs of both consumers and society. This means that faculty must be willing, and supported by the administration, to break out of disciplinary silos and accept a more interdisciplinary focus on business decision-making. And ethics success in the classroom, whether it is the ethics class or a discipline class (e.g. marketing management, finance, accounting, etc.) will be a function of continuous learning on the part of faculty about content that is not owned by a single discipline but the whole community of business school faculty.

This kind of perspective is important to develop early, even in the content and research of one's PhD programme. Programmes today that balance in-depth training focused on traditional disciplines, such as marketing and finance, with broader interdisciplinary skills such as ethics or even sustainable development, provide students with both the breadth and depth needed to succeed in a complex interconnected world.

Research focus

The research focus, especially in schools with PhD programmes, parallels the educational model as the best journals usually require a narrow focus in traditional business subjects. Compounding the challenge of integrating courses like ethics or sustainability into a curriculum is the fact that there are few PhDs in business ethics, and even fewer departments devoted to the subject area. Consequently, in an environment 1) largely populated by traditional departments such as accounting, finance and marketing, 2) combined with economic pressures to keep costs down, and 3) the roadmap to tenure paved with publications in traditional discipline-oriented journals, it is not hard to imagine that subjects like business ethics can easily get lost.

Traditionally, academic research emphasizes theoretical and empirical studies focused on a specific discipline. Today, the research lens is widening as business realizes the value of emerging interdisciplinary topics to business success, such as sustainable development, innovation and corporate social responsibility. An increasing number of academic journals are devoted to articles with a focus on ethics and values. Interdisciplinary research is increasingly seen as valuable to understanding and operating successfully in an increasingly global economy where understanding a country's values, ethics and social fabric is as important to successful transactions as their economic situation. Doing this kind of research often requires an interdisciplinary lens. Co-authored research representing different disciplines should be valued and supported by the college. Some schools have set aside funds for faculty "hits" in target journals, and merit and promotion criteria can be adjusted to give special recognition to interdisciplinary work.

Revenue and costs

As with any industry, there comes a time when the existing business model, no matter how successful in the past, must change to meet new needs and new realities. Today's higher education system is searching for ways to better serve students by providing an affordable relevant education that takes into account and prepares students to be successful in a world characterized by globalization, new technologies and increasing concerns about the environment. Such challenges are unlikely to be met in a piecemeal kind of way (e.g. reducing credit hours, lowering costs, online courses, etc.).

Business schools and cultural shifts

The good news is that many business schools are successfully addressing these issues by changing their culture. Coffman and Sorenson (2013), in their book *Culture Eats Strategy for Lunch*, note that it is culture that connects people to purpose. Culture is the common core that creates belonging, shapes us and influences our actions. The most common barrier to an internal culture shift favouring or retaining RME is the primary organizational structure that separates disciplines (marketing, accounting, finance, management) by departments. The effects of discipline compartmentalization (often referred to as "siloing" in the United States) can easily be exacerbated within business schools based on budget models that segregate departments and programmes into "profit centres". RME can be a casualty in such processes, even where strong cultures for RME exist.

However, there are signs that significant cracks are showing in the silo culture. The importance of interdisciplinary studies, such as sustainability, are causing faculty across disciplines, both in business schools and between colleges, to start talking, to develop interdisciplinary programmes and to engage in joint interdisciplinary research.

These culture shifts are driven by both internal and external forces, and can result in significant changes over time in resources devoted to faculty training, to research priorities and to perceived revenue strategies and cost considerations.

Internally, stakeholders and their interests can shift over time, establishing, modifying or even eroding a strong level of commitment from the board of visitors, the board of trustees, the faculty, the dean and the university chancellor. Externally, forces of positive change can include major donors, media pressure for business schools to educate socially and environmentally conscious graduates, employee demand for graduates with a broader background in values-based leadership, CSR and sustainability, as well as the perceived benefits to potential students of graduate business education generally.

But external factors can also change the commitment of a business school's leadership and its subsequent moves in the education market. For example, some business school deans and other university leaders have chosen to accept endowed funds for teaching "free enterprise" principles according to Ayn Rand, or to teach supply side economics, or to fund a vaguely defined set of "entrepreneurship", "innovation", or "information technology" studies. But such funds often represent "new directions" that will move the school away from RME principles unless those gifts are well-integrated into an ongoing strategy for responsible management education. Those who lead business schools must resist the same temptations that business leaders encounter: taking what's profitable in the short term without a continuing commitment to principles of educating for responsible management.

In these times, how can any business school begin or maintain a focus on RME? There are no easy answers, but there is one common point for consideration. As with any good business, a college must be constantly attentive to multiple stakeholders. All are important, but one particularly is the reason for our being—the student. Whatever we do as a college, the true bottom line must be to provide value to the students and a healthy return on their investment. That return is a function of the set of experiences encountered in the classroom, fieldwork and interactions with faculty, students, businesses and the larger community. It will be measured not only by the job they get and the salary they earn, but also by what they accomplish both for the organization they work for and their ability to make a positive difference in their world. To the millennial generation, doing good while doing well is not an empty phrase; it is what increasing numbers of students are demanding from their jobs, and from their business education.

In Box 10.3 we turn to Kara Peck and her journey from Daniels MBA student, where she focused her educational experiences on Compass-related topics, especially sustainability, to Community Development Lead for B Lab Colorado, a non-profit organization that certifies and supports B Corporations. These are companies in the US that are certified by the non-profit B Lab to meet rigorous standards of social and environmental performance, accountability and transparency.

Box 10.3 **Kara Peck, Daniels MBA Graduate, Colorado B. Corp**

I decided to pursue an MBA to help fix what I saw as a broken system. I have long felt that as members of society, we have a duty to give back to the world by putting our unique gifts to work for the greater good. While I already had this innate passion—and even had some practical business skills—Daniels gave me an invaluable set of perspectives and tools that have furthered my ability to use business as a force for good on a daily basis.

A thorough grounding in business theory, together with an historical perspective on the evolution of business, is essential to see and meet our greatest challenges. As a sustainability professional, and now with the B Corp movement, I have seen all too often how both colleagues and clients assume that business should operate to maximize profits. For me, it was the academic inquiry into business theory that revealed this unexamined and often unconscious bias. The fact that each student at Daniels is confronted with this debate early in his or her studies is a fundamental reason that Daniels graduates are more prepared to challenge the status quo and contribute to the betterment of society in their careers.

A responsible business education programme includes the intermingling of perspectives like the ones that Daniels provides as an essential factor to the success of a comprehensive business education. While many sustainability-focused business programmes provide detailed technical topics like sustainability reporting or accounting systems, I look back and cherish the experience of passionate debates about the role of business in society.

These experiences have prepared me to navigate diverse perspectives and find common ground with those that prefer to operate from a perspective of "business as usual". This skill is one that cannot be taught; it must be learned through real life experience, and I believe the programme at Daniels helped me prepare for what would continue to be one of the greatest challenges in my career: convincing the business community that private enterprise can be a force for good, and that our organizations can help solve our social and environmental problems while still making a profit.

To help our students become "real persons", as David Brooks (2014) would have us do, the Daniels College of Business has sought to provide an array of intellectual, social and active outdoor experiences that promote the values of Principle 2 of the

Principles of Responsible Management Education. It is an ongoing effort, with singular accomplishments as well as continuing challenges. We continue to seek the best means to create future business leaders that care about themselves in the right way, extend a spirit of generosity and goodwill to others, as Bill Daniels did, and create new pathways for business as an institution that participates substantially in the stewardship of both community and planet.

References

Brandeis, L.D. (1914). *Business: A Profession*. Boston, MA: Small, Maynard & Co.

Brooks, D. (2014, September 8). Becoming a real person [op-ed]. *New York Times*. Retrieved from http://www.nytimes.com/2014/09/09/opinion/david-brooks-becoming-a-real-person.html

Coffman, C. & Sorenson, K. (2013). *Culture Eats Strategy for Lunch*. Denver, CO: The Coffman Organization, Inc.

Fukuyama, F. (1993). *Trust: The Social Virtues and the Creation of Prosperity*. New York: Simon & Schuster.

Hutton, R.B. & Cox, D. (2008). *A Compass for the Future: Curricular Innovation and Sustainable Development*. MBA Innovation. Washington, DC: MBA Round Table, pp. 6-13.

Nohria, N. & Khurana, R. (2008). It's time to make management a true profession. *Harvard Business Review*, 86(10), 70-77.

Putnam, R. (2000). *Bowling Alone: The Collapse and Revival of American Community*. New York: Simon & Schuster.

Rampton, J. (2015, September 25). 15 of the most innovative MBA programs. Inc. Retrieved from http://www.inc.com/john-rampton/15-of-the-most-innovative-mba-programs.html

Singular, S. (2003). *Relentless: Bill Daniels and the Triumph of Cable TV*. Denver, CO: James Charlton.

Appendix

Box 4A1 **History of ethics at Daniels**

This box presents a history of major developments in the course of 25 years of teaching business ethics and social responsibility to students at the Daniels College of Business. It begins with the matching grant from Bill Daniels in 1989 and ends with some singular achievements for the Daniels College over the past ten years.

1989: Cable-television pioneer presents an $11 million matching grant challenge to incorporate values-based leadership and ethics into the graduate business curriculum.

1990: The College reorganizes its curriculum to include ethics, leadership and global experiences to enhance basic learning skills. The first Integrated MBA is developed with a cross-matrix organizational structure: all departments designated faculty members to interdisciplinary areas, such as ethics, leadership, global, creativity and entrepreneurship. Courses were team taught with faculty from different disciplines.

1991: The College launches Graduates Involved in Voluntary Efforts (GIVE), a public service programme required of all graduate students and the Colorado Ethics in Business Awards (CEBA) to recognize businesses, non-profits and individuals for ethical behaviour and leadership.

1994: The matching grant $11 million is raised, and the college is renamed the Daniels College of Business. An additional $11 million is given to the college by Daniels for a new business school building.

2002: Daniels students found a Net Impact chapter with the mission to promote socially responsible, ethical and sustainable business practices. The college creates the Department of Business Ethics and Legal Studies.

2004: The college launches the Voices of Experience speaker series on ethical leadership.

2005–06: An interdisciplinary committee of faculty, business and community leaders is tasked with redesigning the Integrated MBA programme. The Daniels Compass suite of courses is created and launched in academic year 2007/08.

2006: The Bill Daniels Distinguished Chair of Business Ethics is funded by the Daniels Fund, and Dr James O'Toole is appointed to the position beginning in academic year 2007/08.

2008: The original set of six Compass courses occupying 20 credit hours in an 80 hour MBA programme is redesigned to three 4-hour courses— The Essence of Enterprise, including the experiential component, Ethics for the 21st-Century Professional, and a new course, Creating Sustainable Enterprises.

→

2009: Daniels establishes the Institute for Enterprise Ethics as the outward-facing component of the college's ethics education initiative. Daniels commits to the Principles for Responsible Management Education (PRME). Daniels joins the eight-member Daniels Fund Ethics Consortium, a partnership between the Daniels Fund and eight business schools across four western states.

2010: Daniels establishes the position of Director of Ethics Integration for the college. Dr Bruce Hutton, Dean Emeritus of Daniels College of Business, becomes the inaugural director.

2011: The Aspen Institute's Beyond Grey Pinstripes ranks Daniels No. 2 for small MBA programmes and No. 15 in the world for integration of social, ethical and environmental issues into the MBA curriculum. Bloomberg BusinessWeek ranks Daniels No. 2 for ethics.

2012: Daniels MBA students win the Aspen Institute's International Case Competition focused on social, environmental and ethical business challenges.

2015: Daniels College of Business is selected by INC. Vision 2020 as one of the 15 most innovative US business schools for its pioneering work in business ethics over the past 20 years.

Table A1 Learning outcomes and the Compass

	Self/Personal	World/Global	Nature/Ecological	Enterprise/Business
Essence/Edge	Develop a foundation of self-awareness through self-disclosure, solicitation of feedback and self-discovery. Develop the self-mastery skills required to make effective decisions under stressful conditions. Develop and improve leadership capacity as a leader and as a member of a high performance organization. Demonstrate the ability to work effectively and synergistically in teams to achieve common goals.	Articulate different models and understandings of "what business is" in the 21st century. Understand the interrelationship of government, civil society and the "private enterprise" sector in shaping the success and failure of business enterprises. How different cultures can influence our mental models of what it means to be a leader and what the purpose of a business is.	Describe current events in business as they relate to external systems, organizational systems and human systems. Discover and assess corporate business models and how they impact and take part in natural, social and political systems. Explain the difference between "take-make-waste" and "cradle to cradle". Contrast "natural capitalism" with other forms of capitalism (managerial capitalism, financial capitalism, klepto-capitalism, etc.)	Explain the meaning and value of free markets in a system of democratic capitalism. Describe "globalization" and its impacts on social, economic and natural systems. See how different styles of leadership, and of corporate culture, can influence a company's capacity to innovate and create sustainable economic and social value. Develop and improve leadership capacity as a leader and as a member of a high performance organization.

	Self/Personal	World/Global	Nature/Ecological	Enterprise/Business
Ethics for the 21st-Century Professional	Reflect on different views of "human nature" and their implications for managing and leading organizations. Assess and explore the unique responsibilities of business as a profession. Reflect on and develop a personal and professional set of standards. Examine the function and use of corporate ethics codes and credos as examples of community and organizational values to guide decision-making. Introduce students to descriptive and behavioural research in personal and organizational ethics. Explore and discuss cases of business practices to explore creative and innovative ways to fulfil ethical and professional responsibilities.	Increase awareness of the social context of business and the nature of social contract as the social basis of ethics and morality, including the tension between competition and cooperation in achieving organizational and social goals. Introduce students to normative decision-making models and frameworks. Examine ethical and professional responsibilities of business professionals, managers and leaders domestically and globally.	Explore the responsibilities of corporations and managers towards the natural environment, the social environment, and "community" generally. Understand the difference between a utilitarian ethics that is "anthropocentric" vs. "ecocentric".	Explore the ethical aspects of various issues relevant to students' interests and programmes of study, such as marketing and advertising, real estate and construction management, accounting and finance. Assess the fundamental roles and responsibilities of business and business people in their larger social context (i.e. personal, professional) and corporate organizational strategies to foster ethical climate and culture. Analyse ethical, professional, legal and public policy dimensions of selected critical areas in management: e.g. privacy in the workplace; sales responsibilities; whistle blowing; insider trading.

	Self/Personal	World/Global	Nature/Ecological	Enterprise/Business
Creating Sustainable Enterprises	Compare and contrast dimensions of sustainability as it relates to business challenges and opportunities. Explain current sustainable business reporting structures and analyse frameworks, required information, assessment criteria, and key indicators that describe the auditing process or assessment method. Detect divergent concepts and opposing points of view on the need for sustainable corporate practices. Articulate and substantiate a position that illustrates a willingness to facilitate dialogue towards common goals.	Compare and contrast the different dimensions of sustainability across cultures and nation states. Explore the interface between commerce, community and government in response to stakeholder needs across countries. Explore the concept and value of companies obtaining a "social licence to operate" in different countries. Explore the role of sustainable development as a strategy for bottom of the pyramid operations. Understand the value and risk in global supply chains and how sustainable development can be used to create value for all stakeholders.	Demonstrate awareness of the power of choice to effectuate change towards sustainability as it relates to self and the following spheres of influence: lifestyle actions and activities; community organization and civic engagement; employment options and business practice; legislation and national public policy; and the development of international protocols.	Examine the changing roles of commerce and community in response to shareholder and stakeholder interests, and distinguish key characteristics of business models that integrate the following key strategies (as it relates to sustainable development): new business innovation (startup); integration of practice and policy (response to regulation and compliance); product development (revenue to meet changing consumer interests, needs and buying trends, competition); social licence to operate (partnership development); infrastructure investment (tri-sector partnerships); and exit strategies. Critique an existing organization's sustainable operations or reporting processes, determine gaps and provide recommendations that illustrate knowledge to support organizational leadership and management decisions as they navigate and transition towards the sustainable design of products, programmes or policies.

11

Consciousness development for responsible management education

Dennis P. Heaton and Emanuel Schachinger
Maharishi University of Management, USA

with practitioner commentary by Chris Laszlo
Sustainable Value Partners, LLC, USA

Envisioning and executing sustainable value

Society today is in need of responsible managers who can create shareholder value while pursuing business in a way that conforms to the values of the UN Global Compact in the areas of human rights, labour, environment and anti-corruption. Principle 1 of the Principles for Responsible Management Education (PRME) calls for universities to commit to the purpose of developing "the capabilities of students to be future generators of sustainable value for business and society at large and to work for an inclusive and sustainable global economy" (PRME, 2015a). Sustainable value has been defined as positive value for shareholders combined with positive value for employees, customers, other stakeholders and the environment (Laszlo and Zhexembayeva, 2011).

The thesis of this chapter is that such capabilities depend, at least in part, upon a dimension of psychological differences which researchers have called consciousness development. Therefore, the incorporation of practices which cultivate consciousness development may play a critical role in actualizing the purpose of PRME. We contend that at its root, responsible management stems from a shift to a deeper level of our humanity where we realize our connectedness to our highest selves, and through that, our connectedness to others and to nature. By systematically cultivating our consciousness of connectedness, we can accelerate the evolution of management education and societal practice towards the creation of a thriving society.

To establish this point we start by describing the concept of consciousness development from the perspective of developmental psychology. We present an overview of the range of consciousness development, and we elaborate on the connections between consciousness development and the purposes of responsible management. Next we present some recent research showing how stages of consciousness development of organizational leaders can influence responsible management—through the example of a study of leaders engaged in corporate greening (Boiral *et al.*, 2014). Following that, we describe educational practices for enabling consciousness development.

Our interest in looking at the role of consciousness development in responsible management expresses our personal backgrounds. Dennis Heaton is the Director of the Management PhD programme at Maharishi University of Management (MUM) in Fairfield, Iowa, USA, which focuses on consciousness and sustainability (Maharishi University of Management, 2014); and Emanuel Schachinger is currently a student in that PhD programme. Dennis also teaches Socially and Environmentally Responsible Management in the Sustainable Business MBA programme at MUM. Emanuel is teaching conceptual maps for change-makers, covering models of human development and tools for system thinking, for the Sustainable Living Department at MUM. Dennis has explored the interface of psychological models from Western developmental psychology and Eastern models of higher states of consciousness (Alexander *et al.*, 1994; Heaton, 2011), and he is a proponent of Consciousness-Based management education, which includes the Transcendental Meditation technique (Heaton, 2016; Heaton *et al.*, 2011; Schmidt-Wilk *et al.*, 2000).

The practitioner voice for this chapter has been contributed by Chris Laszlo, who is both a consultant and an academic. As a co-founder and managing partner of Sustainable Value Partners LLC, Chris provides advisory services to help companies create competitive advantage by integrating sustainability and corporate social responsibility (CSR) into their core businesses. He has, for example, consulted to the CEO and board of a Fortune 500 consumer goods company who wanted to pursue new business ventures that explicitly take into account new stakeholder expectations for environmental, health and social solutions. His clients have included Bayer North America, L'Oréal, Tarkett and Cisco. Laszlo spent nearly 10 years as an executive at Lafarge, a world leader in building materials; he held positions as head of strategy, general manager of a manufacturing subsidiary and vice president of business development.

Chris is also Professor of Organizational Behaviour and Faculty Director for Research and Outreach, Fowler Center for Business as an Agent of World Benefit at Case Western Reserve University.[1] Chris's most recent book, *Flourishing Enterprise:*

---

1 The Fowler Center for Business as an Agent of World Benefit. Retrieved from https://weatherhead.case.edu/centers/fowler/about/

The New Spirit of Business (Laszlo *et al.*, 2014), has advocated cultivating a consciousness of connectedness to enable individuals to advance sustainability into flourishing. This book grew out of a multi-year dialogue process involving six Distinguished Fellows at the Fowler Center for Sustainable Value and four staff of the Fowler Center, to explore the role of spirituality as a key factor in helping businesses thrive in service of a prosperous and sustainable world.

What is meant by consciousness development?

What Boiral *et al.* (2014) call consciousness development is identical to the concept of self or ego development (Loevinger, 1976). Rooke and Torbert (2005) use the term "developmental action logics" for this same construct. Kegan (1994) has used the term "orders of consciousness" in his model of developmental stages.

Boiral *et al.* (2014, p. 365) point out that there are "maturational differences in the way individuals make sense, experience and act upon reality through the lens of various stages of consciousness". Other developmental psychologists (Piaget, 1969; Graves, 1974; Colby and Kohlberg, 1987) have likewise observed that as individuals develop from childhood to adulthood, there are stage-like shifts in the cognitive, interpersonal and moral structures through which they make meaning of their lives. According to Kegan and Lahey (2009, p. 21): "Each successive level of mental complexity is formally higher than the preceding one because it can perform the mental functions of the prior level as well as additional functions".

Bushe and Gibbs (1990) summarize the trajectory of psychological development: cognition moves from simple and concrete, to more abstract and systemic, yet simultaneously more specific and precise. Thinking moves from stereotypic and dogmatic towards greater openness to experience, from desire for certainty to a toleration of ambiguity, from other-directedness to self-directed. The sense of self changes from externally generated standards to self-directed standards, from an undifferentiated, contextually embedded sense of self and others, to a highly individuated perception of self and others, from a polarization of conflicts to a toleration of paradox.

The terms conventional and postconventional refer to broad tiers of development, each of which comprises a series of sequential stages. Postconventional individuals differentiate themselves from roles and expectations of authorities and define moral values in terms of self-chosen principles (Colby and Kohlberg, 1987). Other descriptors for postconventional range of development include psychological autonomy and integration, self-actualization, greater access to feelings and intuition, and wisdom (Chandler *et al.*, 2005). Most adults score in the conventional range of development (Cook-Greuter, 2002, 2004; Rooke and Torbert, 2005); only about 15% of managers have been found at postconventional levels, comprising Loevinger's Individualistic, Autonomous and Integrated stages, of which 5% are at the Autonomous (also called Strategist) level or above.

Managers at different stages of development tend to have different styles of decision-making and leadership. The ability and disposition to comprehend complex environments and engage with the variety of interests and perspectives from multiple stakeholders is enabled by postconventional development (Rooke and Torbert, 2005). Managers at later stages of development are more likely to redefine problems, and more likely to act collaboratively (Merron *et al.*, 1987). As seen in the research of Merron *et al.* (1987), postconventional managers have responded to an in-basket exercise, which simulates a manager's work day, with solutions that are more proactive, solution-oriented, participative, systemic and transformative.

Postconventional development can be seen as an underlying enabler for the three learning capabilities for sustainability which Senge *et al.* (2010) describe. These three are:

- Seeing larger systems, such as the complexity of supply chains and regions.

- Collaborating across boundaries through trust and mutuality in relationships.

- Creating futures we truly desire through vision and imagination, not just reactively solving problems.

Boiral *et al.* (2014) theorized that the skills of both environmental leadership and the upper-stages of consciousness development "include a broader and systemic perspective, long-range focus, integration of conflicting goals, collaboration with stakeholders, complexity management, collaborative learning" (p. 363). Similarly, Brown's (2011) dissertation discusses characteristics of postconventional development which may contribute to effective execution of responsible management. These include the capacity to take a systems view on reality, integrate ideas, create long-term visions with profound purposes and build truly collaborative relationships.

Our understanding about consciousness development is informed by our collaboration with Charles Alexander (Alexander *et al.*, 1990, 1994; Orme-Johnson, 2000), who constructed a model of human development connecting stage theories from modern development psychology to conceptions of higher states of consciousness in the Vedic Psychology of Maharishi Mahesh Yogi. In this understanding, higher states of consciousness are the natural continuation and dramatic extension of psychological development, culminating in "realizing the ultimate inseparability of the observer and the observed, leading to a completely unified view of self and the environment traditionally known as 'enlightenment' or 'unity consciousness'" (Hagelin, 1987, p. 59). According to Nidich *et al.* (2000), the Transcendental Meditation programme promotes moral development in the direction of the perspective of Unity Consciousness, which sees how all phenomena are connected to each other in one wholeness which is one's self. As one grows toward Unity Consciousness, one naturally integrates serving one's own interests with serving the interests of others. Thus, through the growth of higher states of consciousness we come to be naturally inclined towards those values of responsible management which are the soul of PRME.

The role of consciousness in responsible management

A recent research study explored the relationship between consciousness development and green leadership—which is one expression of responsible management. Boiral *et al.* (2014) examined cases of two kinds of manufacturing small and medium-sized enterprises (SMEs) in Canada. Six of the cases were Green SMEs, selected to participate in the study because these companies were considered environmental leaders in their respective industries. In these companies, the top managers were actively committed to promoting environmental initiatives inside their organizations. The study also included nine cases of Passive SMEs in which the top manager was not particularly concerned with environmental issues and did not provide specific information on objectives and programmes in this area. In interviews, those managers could not describe substantial environmental sustainability actions implemented by their organization.

The research focused on companies with fewer than 300 employees, because in such SMEs the green initiatives are largely discretionary and depend on the owner-manager's personal leadership, values and abilities. Thus the research design provided an opportunity to test the notion that environmentally responsible management might be strongly correlated with a measure of the consciousness development of the company's top manager.

In this study, consciousness development was measured by a standardized psychological test called the Leadership Development Profile (LDP) (Cook-Greuter, 2004). LDP is an adaptation of the Washington University Sentence Completion Test (Loevinger, 1976), which is one of the most widely used and best validated instruments in the field of developmental personality. The study examined environmental leadership through archival evidence and by interviewing leaders and their subordinates about each leader's initiatives for sustainability, environmental values and practices, and integration of complexity.

In the findings of Boiral *et al.*, differences between the Green SMEs and the Passive SMEs were clearly related to the LDP scores of the top managers of those firms. Four of the six Green companies were led by managers who tested at postconventional stages of consciousness development, and the other two Green SMEs were at the next highest stage to postconventional. On the other hand, the nine managers of Passive companies scored at a variety of development positions—all below the postconventional stages. A characteristic interview about one of the Green SME leaders described him as being very pro-environment, very proactive. Whereas, a manager of a Passive SME said in his interview that his company has environmental concerns, but environmental actions should not take priority over other important issues. Such findings do build the case that differences in psychological development, as measured by the LDP, are related to differences in environmentally responsible management.

Our thesis that transformations of consciousness are fundamental to achieving the aim of embedding responsible management builds upon a growing literature. In a special issue of *Academy of Management Review*, Gladwin *et al.* asserted that sustainability requires a new educational approach to transform "human thinking ... and ... increase the rate of people's evolutionary consciousness toward a 'new mind' appropriate for a sustainable world" (1995, p. 899). Such a 'new mind' would realize the spiritual depth of our being where we are one with nature, enabling us to live in harmony with the natural world. Likewise, Scharmer and Kaufer (2013) have identified how transformations in management and economics have their root in a transformation of consciousness, namely, "a shift from ego-system awareness that cares about the well-being of oneself to an eco-system awareness that cares about the well-being of all, including oneself" (p. 2).

The following section presents our rationale for educational programmes to develop the consciousness of future managers.

From inner development to outer responsible management

Figure 11.1 **From inner development to outer responsible management**

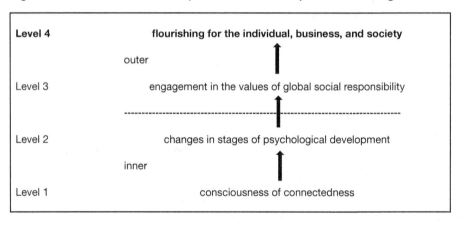

Figure 11.1 is our model of the relationship of inner development to the outer achievement of responsible impacts. The top two levels in this figure are the outer dimensions of sustainable value—enacting the values of responsible management (Level 3) through which the results of personal, organizational and societal flourishing can be achieved (Level 4). The two lower levels of the figure are the foundation for the capabilities to be generators of sustainable value—higher stages of psychological development (Level 2) and consciousness of connectedness which profoundly expands one's comprehension and concern (Level 1). Lower levels are

shown in Figure 11.1 in dimmer fonts, signifying that though they influence outer behaviour and results, they may be out of sight below the surface.

In this model, typical PRME activities, as reported in "Sharing Information on Progress" (SIP) documents of most participating business schools (PRME, 2015b), would be located at Level 3—engagement in values of global social responsibility. On this level educators construct curricula and experiences to enhance students' understanding and applying values of contributing to society, respecting the natural environment, and enhancing quality of working life. We aim for these values to then be enacted by our business school graduates so that an increasingly sustainable, just and fulfilling economy and society is realized in practice.

But the extent to which such values of responsible management actually get embedded in business institutions depends on what Chris Laszlo, in his commentary in this chapter, refers to as changing "who they are being". Our model in Figure 11.1 posits that the inner experience of consciousness of connectedness (level 1) can be a trigger that stimulates higher development (level 2) and consequently responsible practices (level 3) and positive, thriving impacts (level 4). As Laszlo *et al.* have described, a "sense of connectedness based on reflective experiences has enabled individuals to engage in qualitatively more powerful ways of thinking and acting aimed at flourishing" (2012, p. 35). Laszlo *et al.* have advocated a variety of reflective practices for "creation of a consciousness of connectedness between the world of human beings and all other forms of life and an emerging capability to tap into deeper wisdom and creative insight absent without such practices" (2012, p. 37). They wrote:

> It is only through becoming more connected to ourselves, others and the natural world that we can build the necessary foundations for caring, thinking, acting and innovating in ways that enable business organizations to operate from a platform that serves business, society and nature ... only then are we able to undertake intentional actions that habitually incorporate a sense of responsibility to others and to future generations (Laszlo *et al.*, 2012, p. 36).

Educational practices to cultivate consciousness development

The PRME movement has promoted the purpose of responsible management education (RME) "to develop the capabilities of students to be future generators of sustainable value for business and society at large and to work for an inclusive and sustainable global economy". The capabilities that come with higher consciousness development—encompassing cognitive, moral and emotional development—provide a starting point for values and practices that enhance work, contribute to society and respect the natural environment (Waddock and Rasche, 2012). What

Fisher *et al.* (1987, p. 266) argued regarding leadership education applies today to PRME Principle 1, developing the capabilities of students to be generators of sustainable value:

> Human development would seem to be a central concern of management educators, universities, management trainers in organizations, and organizational development professionals ... Given this view, organizations and schools of management would place as much emphasis on creating learning environments conducive to personal development as on teaching specific knowledge and skills.

An important question for responsible management education therefore becomes: are there educational approaches which can effectively promote post-conventional development? In the next section we report on our experience of the approach of education for consciousness development at Maharishi University of Management (MUM).[2] Then we introduce additional experiential, intellectual and environmental approaches to consciousness development that might be adapted in diverse settings.

Consciousness-Based education (CBE) at Maharishi University of Management

Maharishi University of Management (MUM) is accredited by the Higher Learning Commission[3] and is a member of the North Central Association of Colleges and Schools. At its campus in Fairfield, Iowa, USA, and through global distance education, MUM offers Bachelor, Master's and doctoral degrees in a variety of subjects. Educational methods to attain development of consciousness have been central at MUM since its founding in 1971 as Maharishi International University. Maharishi University of Management makes use of unique academic frameworks, materials, processes and environments, all of which are designed to develop the student's consciousness of unity—a sense of interconnectedness with his or her own complete self, the social environment, the physical environment and, ultimately, the entire universe.

We describe three components of the CBE system (Heaton, 2016; Dillbeck, 2011). The first component is experiential, through instruction and group practice of Transcendental Meditation and its advanced techniques. The second component is intellectual—academic disciplines are related to knowledge of the full potential of consciousness. The third component is environmental—encompassing lifestyle and living conditions.

2 Transcendental Meditation®, Consciousness-Based and Maharishi University of Management are protected trademarks and are used in the United States under licence or with permission.
3 www.hlcommission.org

The Transcendental Meditation technique

MUM features the practice of Transcendental Meditation (TM), including group meditations as part of the daily class schedule. The TM technique is a secular practice and people from all religions have learned and enjoy practising TM (Rosenthal, 2011). The TM technique is available to students and educators who are at institutions other than MUM. There are currently institutions around the world in which TM is formally recommended for students.[4] TM has been implemented in K-12 schools in the United States and elsewhere as the Quiet Time programme, supported by the David Lynch Foundation (2015).

TM is described as an effortless process through which the activity of thinking settles to a state of restful alertness in which consciousness is awake simply to itself, beyond thought, beyond the division of subject and object (Maharishi Mahesh Yogi, 1976). This Transcendental Consciousness has been described by Maharishi Mahesh Yogi (1976) as the level at which individual awareness is connected to the matrix of creative intelligence which pervades all natural systems.

The awake yet quiet state of Transcendental Consciousness is distinct from eyes-closed relaxation or sleep as evidenced by reductions in heart rate and oxygen consumption and increased brainwave (EEG) coherence (Alexander *et al.*, 1986). As reported by Travis and Shear (2010), the TM technique is fundamentally different in aim, procedure, experience and brain activity from meditation practices involving focused attention or open monitoring. The cumulative effects of TM practice have been described as a personality shift from more outer-dependent orientation to more intrinsic source of values and wisdom—from object referral to subject referral (Travis *et al.*, 2004).

In a 10-year study of alumni who had been pretested as MUM undergraduate students, Chandler *et al.* (2005) found evidence of longitudinal growth in TM practitioners in ego development, moral development and intimacy motivation. Compared with matched control groups at other universities, the MUM group grew markedly in consciousness development. The proportion of postconventional ego development scores at posttest was higher than had been seen in any previous sample using the Loevinger test; 53% (18 of 34) of the MUM subjects scored at postconventional stages; 38% scored at the Autonomous (also called Strategist) level, compared with 1% in three comparison groups. Posttest scores of the MUM graduates were significantly higher than pretest for principled moral reasoning (P% scores on the Rest's Defining Issues Test, DIT) and intimacy motivation (based on stories in response to pictures in the Thematic Apperception Test, TAT). At posttest, over 80% of the subjects scored at high levels of principled moral reasoning, as defined by Rest.

Conventional approaches to education have generally not contributed to postconventional development because "formal education emphasizes symbolic knowledge, and students and adults are continually involved in active mental processes. Development towards the higher reaches of human potential requires

---

4 https://en.wikipedia.org/wiki/Transcendental_Meditation_in_education

a means to systematically transcend thought" (Chandler *et al.*, 2005, p. 114). Chandler *et al.* (2005, p. 115) suggested "that the incorporation of the Transcendental Meditation program as an adjunct to the curriculum of any program of post-secondary education could produce adults characterized by growing values of autonomous personality, principled moral reasoning, and personal caring".

Another stream of research about the effects of TM practice on university students has looked at how this technique enhances integrated brain functioning. Studies have been conducted at MUM (Travis *et al.*, 2002) and at a university other than MUM, where subjects were randomly assigned to Transcendental Meditation practice or eyes-closed rest (Travis *et al.*, 2010). What is significant to note here is that the effects of TM have been examined not just in terms of psychological development but also in terms of brain functioning, and there is an association between brain integration and moral development (Heaton *et al.*, 2012).

Other TM results specifically relevant to the aims of RME include: a greater sense of social responsibility (Brown, 1976), a cognitive orientation towards positive values (Gelderloos *et al.*, 1987), and broadened awareness that embraces the wider interests of the community and environment (Herriott *et al.*, 2009). A comprehensive review of additional TM research on students at MUM and students at other universities has been compiled by Schmidt-Wilk *et al.* (2000).

Intellectual aspects of CBE at MUM

The experiential and intellectual aspects of CBE work together to enable learners to connect their evolving experience of development of consciousness with their understanding of the evolving business field. Two distinctive pedagogical tools of CBE which display intellectual connections between consciousness and business are Unified Field Charts and Main Point Charts (Dillbeck, 2011). In Dennis's course, Socially and Environmentally Responsible Management, the content of the course is displayed in a Unified Field chart which visually maps the content of the course in terms of a series of levels:

- **Level 1**. In CBE, the foundational level for any academic discipline is the Unified Field of All the Laws of Nature. The Unified Field Chart depicts Transcendental Meditation as a means for the conscious mind to experience this Unified Field in one's own settled awareness, which leads to enlivening natural law in conscious awareness.

- **Level 2**. Experience of the Unified Field leads to individual development of compassion, courage and comprehension, awakening the capacity for responsible management.

- **Level 3**. Developed individuals influence community standards towards accountability for principles such as those in the UN Global Compact.

- **Level 4**. Developed individuals functioning as communities influence business organizations towards more sustainable principles, practices and performance. Sustainable organizations achieve triple-bottom-line out-comes—fulfilling economic, social and environmental responsibilities.

An example of one topic in the course Socially and Environmentally Responsible Management is life-cycle assessment (LCA), which is located at level 4 on the Unified Field Chart. The course asks students to sketch a high-level LCA of one product, using guidelines from one of the course texts (Senge *et al.*, 2010) and other resources. Students identify social and environmental impacts, including labour conditions through the supply chain of the product from the sourcing of raw materials, through production, distribution, use and end of life. Students also apply concepts of the Natural Step (Bradbury and Clair, 1999) and Cradle to Cradle (McDonough and Braungart, 2013) to explore opportunities for designing the product and its industrial ecology to be more in harmony with the ecological principles of nature.

Business principles from the Natural Step and Cradle to Cradle look to the functioning of nature as a model for sustainability. CBE intellectually connects these principles to the perspective of natural law-based management from Maharishi Mahesh Yogi (1995). Maharishi identifies our own Transcendental Consciousness as the wholeness of the managing intelligence of nature. Maharishi explained that through the Transcendental Meditation technique: "our thoughts and actions spontaneously begin to be as orderly and evolutionary as all the activity of nature" (Maharishi Mahesh Yogi, 1986, p. 97). The Unified Field Chart for this course displays the logic of how we expect to see that the designs or decisions from students practising TM would spontaneously be increasingly in the direction of the natural laws at the basis of the Natural Step, Cradle to Cradle, or other truly sustainable design practices.

Another CBE tool is a Main Point Chart. The main ideas of a lesson are summarized to aid comprehension and retention by the learner. These main ideas are displayed on a poster in the classroom and provide a framework for the unfoldment of the lesson. The first part of the Main Point summarizes some discipline knowledge for the lesson. The second part of the Main Point connects the discipline knowledge to the student's own consciousness. In the following example, the connection to consciousness is presented in terms of selected research on effects of TM practice that pertain to the capacity and disposition to embrace a life-cycle perspective:

> Life Cycle Assessment (LCA) studies environmental and social impacts throughout a product's life, from raw material acquisition through production, use and disposal or reuse. The effects of TM on emotional, moral and cognitive development (Chandler *et al.*, 2005) make us more aware and more conscientious about the full range of effects of our actions (Heaton, 2015).

LCA is one tool for what Senge *et al.* (2010) describe as "seeing systems": integrative thinking which takes into account larger systems and long-term strategies, and does not simply fix isolated problems. What is specific to the intellectual approach of CBE in this example is not that we teach LCA or systems thinking, but that we teach how broad, integrative thinking is related to consciousness of the Unified Field and to documented effects of students' own TM practice.

Another unit in this course on Socially and Environmentally Responsible Management introduces integrated reporting (Eccles and Krzus, 2010) and the Global Reporting Initiative (GRI) for measuring and reporting responsible business performance. These are then examined in more detail in MBA and PhD courses at MUM on metrics for sustainability (Herriott, 2016). Integrated reporting is a system that integrates the reporting of financial, environmental, social and governance performance, with a particular focus on the ability of a company to operate in an environmentally sustainable manner. An Integrated Report presents the organization's values and governance model, and demonstrates the link between its strategy and its commitment to a sustainable global economy. The GRI framework provides reporting principles and standard indicators for a company or organization to report about the economic, environmental and social impacts caused by its everyday activities. The following Main Point summarizes the gist of integrated reporting systems and connects this emerging management practice with the concept of collective consciousness from the perspective of CBE:

> Responsible management uses measuring and reporting systems which encompass environmental, social and governance criteria as well as financial data, and aim to embed stakeholder responsibility into the strategic management of the firm. The growing use of these holistic reporting standards expresses the evolution of collective consciousness in the field of business toward more comprehensive and balanced awareness (Heaton, 2015).

Environmental aspects of CBE at MUM

In addition to these experiential and intellectual components, CBE also regards the campus environment and lifestyle as factors which contribute to cultivating wholeness and connectedness in the consciousness of campus members. At MUM, the campus dining hall features organic, vegetarian cuisine. Energy management on campus employs wind, solar and geothermal sources. Time is set aside in the daily schedule for meditation and yoga and in the yearly schedule for retreats to focus on experience and understanding of consciousness. Courses are taught on a block schedule, one course at a time, so as not to exhaust students with assignments and exams for five or more courses at once. The block system has been integral to CBE at MUM. Consciousness can focus and go deep with one course at a time. Campus buildings are constructed according to the principles of Maharishi Vastu Architecture (2015) which are said to promote mental clarity, health, harmony and good fortune.

Implications for educational practice in other settings

Experiential, intellectual and environmental aspects of CBE work synergistically in the special context of MUM, which is dedicated to higher education for higher consciousness (Schmidt-Wilk *et al.*, 2000). What are some experiential, intellectual and environmental approaches to developing consciousness that can be applied in other management education contexts?

Experiential practices for consciousness development

Transcendental Meditation, a key part of CBE at MUM, can also be learned and practised by individual students and teachers in other educational settings and may enhance their orientation towards responsible management. In addition, other reflective practices have been used to increase awareness of personal purpose and connectedness to all forms of life (Laszlo *et al.*, 2012). Three examples of such practices are journalling, Theory U and Bohm dialogue. Adding classroom exercises and homework assignments like these examples can help to engage the learner as a reflective and authentic actor and not just a passive receiver of information.

Journalling is an opportunity to listen to one's inner knowingness (Brown, 2012). One journalling practice which Emanuel uses in his teaching at MUM is a "Double-Entry Notebook" (Bean, 2011, p. 135) in which one records one's feelings and reflections in a column alongside notes about content. By giving individualized responses to students' reflections, educators can encourage students to continue to explore personal meaning and purpose.

Theory U proposes that the quality of the results that we create in any kind of social system is a function of the quality of awareness, attention or consciousness with which the participants in the system operate. Theory U teaches exercises that aim to shift one's listening from downloaded past ideas, to factual listening with an open mind, to empathetic listening with an open heart, and finally to generative listening with an open will to the future that wants to be created (Presencing Institute, 2015a). Exercises for Theory U can be found in Scharmer and Kaufer (2013) and Presencing Institute (2015b).

Bohm dialogue is a practice which favours postconventional consciousness (Baron and Cayer, 2011). Bohm dialogues (Bohm and Edwards, 1991) encourage participants to openly express opinions and judgements, as well as to inquire into the disagreements those might generate. In common with other dialogic approaches to organizational development (Bushe and Marshak, 2016), this process helps to acknowledge the individual and cultural assumptions that hinder development of common meaning. Related exercises for developing dialogue skills for working together to create a sustainable world can be found in the Toolbox sections in Senge *et al.* (2010). Such skill development exercises can be helpful in any management course concerned with community issues for which there are multiple stakeholder perspectives.

Intellectual approaches for consciousness development

Next, we identify three aspects of intellectual knowledge which can bring the dimension of consciousness development into management education in diverse institutional settings. These three are: 1) stage models of human development; 2) systems thinking; and 3) a unified view of humanity and nature.

Teaching about stage models of consciousness development can help make learners aware of postconventional possibilities. However it is unknown to what extent such intellectual approaches, in the absence of an effective experiential practice, could actually result in development transformations towards postconventional consciousness. Two articles which management educators could use to explain stages of consciousness development are Rooke and Torbert's (2005) *Harvard Business Review* article "Seven transformations of leadership" and Boiral *et al.*'s (2009) article "The action logics of environmental leadership: A developmental perspective". The former could be incorporated in courses on organizational behaviour or leadership to introduce the notion that a leader's mind-set and management style can vary as a function of his or her developmental position. We have used the latter article in classes about strategic management. Along with the reading by Boiral *et al.* (2009) we do an in-class exercise which asks students how a manager might conceive of his or her responsibilities at each of the different stages of development. This enables students to conceive that management perspectives are different at different levels of development.

As we have reviewed, the action logics of postconventional stages entail more systemic thinking, which is advantageous for responsible management. Resources for teaching systems thinking could include the *Fifth Discipline* (Senge, 1990) and *Thinking in Systems: A Primer* (Meadows and Wright, 2008). Activities such as life-cycle assessment, which asks students to analyse business impacts throughout the supply chain or industrial ecology, can broaden awareness of the interconnectedness of business, society and environment. The book *Upcycle* (McDonough and Braungart, 2013) can expand students' awareness of business in the context of nature's systems. In our introductory economics class, MUM includes John Ikerd's (2012) *The Essentials of Economic Sustainability*. In that book Ikerd depicts business and its ethical responsibilities within the bigger system of society, which in turn is part of the bigger natural system of the Earth.

RME programmes can incorporate into their business courses intellectual perspectives that are grounded in a unified view of humanity and nature. Within the context of a religiously affiliated institution this may include a theological perspective. An example is the recent papal encyclical (Holy Father Francis, 2015) which echoes St Francis of Assisi's regard for all creatures as "brothers" and "sisters". For secular educational settings, the writings of Willis Harman draw on "perennial philosophy" and new theories in science, to present the constructive role of business in transforming society (Harman and Hormann, 1990). Philosophically oriented readings for courses about sustainable business, business and society, or strategic management might include *Flourishing* (Ehrenfeld and Hoffman, 2013) and *Spirituality and Sustainability: New Horizons and Exemplary Approaches* (Dhiman *et al.*, 2016). Development of consciousness entails a direct experience of the ground of connectedness, and any intellectual conceptions about the connectedness of our being and the Being of all can be complementary to experiential approaches.

Environmental approaches for consciousness development

Finally, any institution can adopt some practices to promote holistic wellbeing. Such an approach to wellbeing could involve the coordinated efforts of all areas of the university: academic, student life, physical fitness, health services, dining and campus facilities.

In a special issue of the *Journal of Management Education* Lovelace and Parent (2012) provide practical guidance for educating students about the relationship of stress to performance and wellness, including self-assessments, case studies and activities that can be used in the management classroom. As one's physiology is freed from stress, one's consciousness can develop broader vision and increased empathy, leading to enactment of responsible management. Holistic health means not just an absence of disease, but optimal balance, vitality, happiness and mental clarity—alignment with the inner intelligence of nature which is latent in the consciousness of every individual. We encourage managers and management educators to teach that everything that nourishes (rather than pollutes) our inner environment—including diet, exercise, meditation, abstinence from drugs, life balance and the built environment—can lead towards greater flourishing in our enterprises and our societies.

Conclusion

This chapter has addressed PRME Principle 1, which calls on universities to commit to the purpose of developing "the capabilities of students to be future generators of sustainable value for business and society at large and to work for an inclusive and sustainable global economy" (PRME, 2015a). We have drawn attention to development of consciousness as the inner root from which responsible management can more fully bloom on the outer expressed level. Our chapter has presented experiential, intellectual and environmental education practices to cultivate consciousness development. Experiential practices enable students (and educators too) to draw on deeper inner capacities for awareness, creativity and caring. Intellectual aspects expose students to models of how consciousness develops towards greater capacity to encompass the wholeness of the social and environmental context. Environmental aspects promote individual wellbeing within flourishing organizations.

We have highlighted our own experience in Maharishi University of Management in which experiential, intellectual and environmental aspects are combined in an integrated system called Consciousness-Based Education. For example, our course on Socially and Environmentally Responsible Management at MUM includes the practice of the Transcendental Meditation technique and discussion of how the effects of TM on mental and emotional development support expanded management perspectives such as life-cycle assessment and integrated reporting. In our observation, there are shifts in students' values and behaviours which may be attributable to the integrated effect of the experiential, intellectual and environmental aspects of CBE. An alumni survey could help us further assess behavioural outcomes after graduation as well as students' views of how CBE contributed to their understanding and practice of responsible management.

We invite researchers in diverse university and business settings to continue to research the relationship of consciousness development to responsible management and to assess the effectiveness of RME programmes in attaining both consciousness and behavioural expressions of responsible management.

Next, we are pleased to have Chris Laszlo's commentary as part of our chapter. Chris reports below how business practitioners are finding that awakening a consciousness of connectedness is enlivening the creation of sustainable value for stakeholders and shareholders.

New consciousness for business as an agent of world benefit

Practitioner commentary by Chris Laszlo

In our recent work with business practitioners at the Fowler Center for Business as an Agent of World Benefit, we have seen two shifts in the conversation about socially and environmentally responsible management. The first is that the aspiration of companies is going beyond "doing less harm" through footprint reduction and eco-efficiency initiatives, to aim instead for "net positive" impacts—to be an agent of world benefit. This is a shift from slowing the rate of unsustainability to actively contributing to flourishing, where flourishing is defined as "to grow well, to prosper, to thrive, to live to the fullest" (Ehrenfeld and Hoffman, 2013, p. 6). Related to this is the second trend, which is recognizing that the creating of flourishing enterprises goes hand in hand with the cultivation of flourishing individuals. There is a huge gap between current sustainability practices and those that can lead to flourishing. Closing the gap will require business leaders to change who they are being, not just what they are doing. Our consulting work is now not just in terms of outer aspects of showing companies business strategies for advancing sustainable value, but also aims at awakening inner flourishing to tap into deeper wisdom and creative insight.

Our Distinguished Fellows Project of the Fowler Center concluded:

> When you peel the onion to uncover what lies behind the behaviors and actions that support sustainability—reframed here as flourishing—you find a layer of relationship-based viewpoints and experiences. Behind that layer lies the core: the journey to a greater sense of connectedness (Laszlo, *et al.*, 2012, p. 31).

A shift in consciousness from "separateness" to "connectedness" (Pavez and Kendall, 2015) is a critical factor in shifting how businesses approach social and environmental responsibility. Instead of seeing ourselves as separate from one another and separate from Nature, interested only in maximizing our own gain, we can see ourselves as deeply connected to one another and to future generations.

The big question is *how* to shift this consciousness in each of us and in our colleagues in places of work. The Consciousness-Based Education (CBE) approach described in this chapter provides one important answer, by proposing Transcendental Meditation (TM) as a means for direct experience of a consciousness of connectedness. Measurable increases in brain functioning have been found in practitioners of TM, together with subjective reports of expanded consciousness. CBE has also been found to lead to postconventional levels of self or ego development, which in turn correlates with seeing the world in systems terms and with higher environmental leadership behaviours.

I feel that the discussion in this chapter about management education for consciousness development is an important contribution towards the goal of responsible management education (RME) to develop students to be future generators of sustainable value. A flourishing world depends on business leaders who personally feel deeply connected to their life purpose, to nature, to others, to future generations. This is where compassion, mindfulness and reflective practices come in. Introducing TM and other practices to cultivate consciousness of connectedness in the workplace can help business people see themselves as deeply connected to the world, not just metaphorically, but in the sense of a physical and conscious whole. As Hagelin (1987) has suggested, pure consciousness is an experience of unity at the fine level of physical reality. Here there is no "other": the individual becomes inseparable from others and from the world.

The implications of seeing the world in these terms are critical to flourishing. It is only through such a consciousness of connectedness that it becomes customary to treat others with the same love and care we have for ourselves. Only through such a consciousness that we experience a deep sense of care for all living things. It is only then that we reflexively make lifestyle choices aimed at restoring and rehabilitating the world. Consciousness of connectedness and the practices that lead to it are our one best shot at caring enough for others and future generations to conduct business as an agent of world benefit.

References

Alexander, C.N., Cranson, R.W., Boyer, R. & Orme-Johnson, D.W. (1986). Transcendental consciousness: A fourth state of consciousness beyond sleep, dreaming and waking. In J. Gackenbach (Ed.), *Sourcebook on Sleep and Dreams* (pp. 282-315). New York: Garland.

Alexander, C.N., Davies, J.L., Dixon, C., Dillbeck, M.C., Druker, S.M., Oetzel, R., ... Orme-Johnson, D.W. (1990). Growth of higher stages of consciousness: Maharishi's Vedic psychology of human development. In C.N. Alexander & E.J. Langer (Eds.), *Higher Stages of Human Development: Perspectives on Adult Growth* (pp. 286-341). New York: Oxford University Press.

Alexander, C.N. Heaton, D. & Chandler, H.M. (1994). Advanced human development in the Vedic Psychology of Maharishi Mahesh Yogi: Theory and research. In M. Miller & S. Cook-Greuter (Eds.), *Transcendence and Mature Thought in Adulthood* (pp. 39-70). Lanham, MD: Rowman and Littlefield.

Baron, C. & Cayer, M. (2011). Fostering post-conventional consciousness: Why and how? *Journal of Management Development*, 30(4), 344-365.

Bean, J. (2011). *Engaging Ideas: The Professor's Guide to Integrating Writing, Critical Thinking, and Active Learning in the Classroom* (2nd ed.). San Francisco: Jossey-Bass.

Bohm, D. & Edwards, M. (1991). *Changing Consciousness: Exploring the Hidden Source of the Social, Political and Environmental Crisis Facing Our World.* San Francisco: HarperCollins.

Boiral, O., Cayer, M. & Baron, C.M. (2009). The action logics of environmental leadership: A developmental perspective. *Journal of Business Ethics*, 85(4), 479-499.

Boiral, O., Baron, C. & Gunnlaugson, O. (2014). Environmental leadership and consciousness development: A case study among Canadian SMEs. *Journal of Business Ethics*, 123(3), 363-383.

Bradbury, H. & Clair, J.A. (1999). Promoting sustainable organizations with Sweden's Natural Step. *Academy of Management Executive*, 13(4), 63-74.

Brown, B.C. (2011). *Conscious Leadership for Sustainability: A Study of How Leaders and Change Agents with Postconventional Consciousness Design and Engage in Complex Change Initiatives* (doctoral dissertation, Fielding Graduate University, Santa Barbara, California). Retrieved from http://integralthinkers.com/wp-content/uploads/Brown_2011_Conscious-leadership-for-sustainability_Full-dissertation_v491.pdf

Brown, J. (2012). *The Art and Science of Leadership.* Bloomington, IN: Trafford.

Brown, M. (1976). *Higher Education for Higher Consciousness: A Study of Students at Maharishi International University* (doctoral dissertation, University of California at Berkeley, California). *Dissertation Abstracts International*, 38, 649A-650A.

Bushe, G.R. & Gibbs, B.W. (1990). Predicting organization development consulting competence from the Myers-Briggs Type Indicator and stage of ego development. *Journal of Applied Behavioral Science*, 26(3), 337-357.

Bushe, G.R. & Marshak, R.J. (2016). The dialogic organization development approach to transformation and change. In W. Rothwell, J. Stravros & R. Sullivan (Eds.), *Practicing Organization Development* (4th ed.) (pp. 407-418). San Francisco, Wiley.

Chandler, H.M., Alexander, C.N. & Heaton, D.P. (2005). The Transcendental Meditation program and postconventional self-development: A 10-year longitudinal study. *Journal of Social Behavior and Personality*, 17(1), 93-121.

Colby, A. & Kohlberg, L. (1987). *The Measurement of Moral Judgement.* Cambridge, UK: Cambridge University Press.

Cook-Greuter, S.R. (2002). A detailed description of the development of nine action logics in the leadership development framework: Adapted from ego development theory. Retrieved from http://nextstepintegral.org/wp-content/uploads/2011/04/The-development-of-action-logics-Cook-Greuter.pdf

Cook-Greuter, S.R. (2004). Making the case for a developmental perspective. *Industrial and Commercial Training*, 36(6/7), 275.

David Lynch Foundation (2015). The Quiet Time Program. Retrieved from https://www.davidlynchfoundation.org/schools.html

Dhiman, S. Margues, J. & Mitroff, I (Eds.) (2016). *Spirituality and Sustainability: New Horizons and Exemplary Approaches.* New York: Springer.

Dillbeck, S.L. (2011). Consciousness-Based education and its four components. In D. Llewellyn & C. Pearson (Eds.), *Consciousness-Based Education: A Foundation for Teaching and Learning in the Academic Disciplines* (Vol. 2) (pp. 41-86). Fairfield, IA: MUM Press.

Eccles, R.G. & Krzus, M.P. (2010). *One Report: Integrated Reporting for a Sustainable Strategy.* New York: Wiley.

Ehrenfeld, J. & Hoffman, A.J. (2013). *Flourishing: A Frank Conversation about Sustainability.* Stanford, CA: Stanford University Press.

Fisher, D., Merron, K. & Torbert, W. (1987). Human development and managerial effectiveness. *Group & Organization Management*, 2, 257-273.

Gelderloos, P., Goddard III, P.H., Ahlström, H.H.B. & Jacoby, R. (1987). Cognitive orientation toward positive values in advanced participants of the TM and TM-Sidhi program. *Perceptual and Motor Skills*, 64, 1003-1012.

Gladwin, T.N., Kennelly, J.J. & Krause, T.S. (1995). Shifting paradigms for sustainable development: Implications for management theory and research. *The Academy of Management Review*, 20(4), 874-907.

Graves, C.W. (1974). Human nature prepares for a momentous leap. *The Futurist*, 8(2), 72-85.

Hagelin, J.S. (1987). Is consciousness the unified field? A field theorist's perspective. *Modern Science and Vedic Science*, 1(1), 29-88.

Harman, W. & Hormann, J. (1990). *Creative Work: The Constructive Role of Business in Transforming a Society.* Indianapolis, IN: Knowledge Systems, Inc.

Heaton, D. (2011). Transcendent experience and development of the post-representational Self. In A. Pfaffenberger, P. Marko & A. Combs (Eds.). *The Postconventional Personality: Perspectives on Higher Development* (pp. 175-188). Albany, NY: SUNY Press.

Heaton, D. (2015). *Course Syllabus: Socially and Environmentally Responsible Management.* Department of Management, Maharishi University of Management, Fairfield, IA.

Heaton, D. (2016). Toward responsible next generation leaders: Transcendental Meditation in management education. In S. Tiwari & L. Nafees (Eds.), *Innovative Management Education Pedagogies for Preparing Next-Generation Leaders* (pp.139-160). Hersey, PA: IGI Global.

Heaton, D., Schmidt-Wilk., J. & McCollum, B. (Eds.) (2011). *Consciousness-Based Education and Management.* Fairfield, IA: MUM Press.

Heaton, D., Travis, F. & Subramaniam, R. (2012). A Consciousness-Based approach to management education for integrity. In C. Wankel & A. Stachowicz-Stanusch (Eds.), *Handbook of Research on Teaching Ethics in Business and Management Education* (pp. 66-79). Hershey, PA: IGI Global.

Herriott, S. (2016). *Metrics for Sustainability.* London: Routledge.

Herriott, E.N., Schmidt-Wilk, J. & Heaton, D.P. (2009). Spiritual dimensions of entrepreneurship in Transcendental Meditation and TM-Sidhi program practitioners. *Journal of Management, Spirituality & Religion*, 6(3), 195-208.

Holy Father Francis (2015). Encyclical letter Laudato Si: On care for our common home. Retrieved from http://w2.vatican.va/content/dam/francesco/pdf/encyclicals/documents/papa-francesco_20150524_enciclica-laudato-si_en.pdf

Ikerd, J. (2012). *The Essentials of Economic Sustainability.* Sterling, VA: Kumerian Press.

Kegan, R. (1994). *In Over Our Heads: The Mental Demands of Modern Life.* Cambridge, MA: Harvard University Press.

Kegan, R. & Lahey, L.L. (2009). *Immunity to Change: How to Overcome it and Unlock Potential in Yourself and Your Organization*. Watertown, MA: Harvard Business Press.

Laszlo, C. & Zhexembayeva, N. (2011). *Embedded Sustainability: The Next Big Competitive Advantage*. Stanford, CA: Stanford University Press.

Laszlo, C., Brown, J.S., Sherman, D., Barros, I., Boland, B., Ehrenfeld, J., ... Werder, P. (2012). Flourishing: A vision for business and the world. *The Journal of Corporate Citizenship*, 46, 31-51.

Laszlo, C., Brown, J.S., Ehrenfeld, J., Gorham, Barros-Pose, I., Robson, L., Boland, B., ... Werder, P. (2014). *Flourishing Enterprise: The New Spirit of Business*. Stanford, CA: Stanford Business Books.

Loevinger, J. (1976). *Ego Development: Conceptions and Theories*. San Francisco: Jossey-Bass.

Lovelace, K.J. & Parent, J.D. (2012). The integrative nature of stress, performance, and wellness. *Journal of Management Education*, 36(2), 131-134.

Maharishi Mahesh Yogi (1976). *Creating an Ideal Society: A Global Undertaking*. West Germany: MERU Press.

Maharishi Mahesh Yogi (1986). *Life Supported by Natural Law*. Washington, DC: Age of Enlightenment Press.

Maharishi Mahesh Yogi (1995). *Maharishi University of Management: Wholeness on the Move*. India: Age of Enlightenment Publications.

Maharishi University of Management (2014). PhD in Management. Retrieved from https://www.mum.edu/academic-departments/business-administration/ph-d/phd-overview/.

Maharishi Vastu Architecture (2015). Benefits of *Maharishi Vastu* Homes. Retrieved from http://www.maharishivastu.org/benefits-of-maharishi-vastu-homes

McDonough, W. &, Braungart, M. (2013). *Upcycle: Beyond Sustainability—Designing for Abundance*. New York: North Point Press.

Meadows, D. & Wright, D. (2008). *Thinking in Systems: A Primer*. White River Junction, VT: Chelsea Green.

Merron, K., Fisher, D. & Torbert, W.R. (1987). Meaning making and management action. *Group and Organization Studies*, 12, 274-286.

Nidich, S.L., Nidich, R.J. & Alexander, C.N. (2000). Moral development and higher states of consciousness. *Journal of Adult Development*, 7(4), 217-225.

Orme-Johnson, D.W. (2000). An overview of Charles Alexander's contribution to psychology: Developing higher states of consciousness in the individual and society. *Journal of Adult Development*, 7(4), 199-216.

Pavez, I. & Kendall, L. (2015). *The Arc of Interconnectedness* [White paper]. Cleveland, OH: The Fowler Center for Business as an Agent of World Benefit.

Piaget, J. (1969). *The Psychology of the Child*. New York: Wiley.

Presencing Institute (2015a). Principles and glossary of presencing. Cambridge, MA: Presencing Institute. Retrieved from https://www.presencing.com/principles

Presencing Institute (2015b). U.Lab. Retrieved from https://uschool.presencing.com/ulab

PRME (Principles for Responsible Management Education) (2015a). About us: Six principles. Retrieved from http://www.unprme.org/about-prme/the-six-principles.php

PRME (2015b). Sharing Information on Progress. Retrieved from http://www.unprme.org/sharing-information-on-progress/index.php

Rooke, D. & Torbert, W.R. (2005). Seven transformations of leadership. *Harvard Business Review*, 83(4), 67-76, 133.

Rosenthal, N. (2011). *Transcendence: Healing and Transformation through Transcendental Meditation*. New York: Tarcher.

Scharmer, O. & Kaufer, K. (2013). *Leading from the Emerging Future*. San Francisco: Berrett-Koehler.

Schmidt-Wilk, J., Heaton, D. & Steingard, D. (2000). Higher education for higher consciousness. *Journal of Management Education*, 24(5), 580-611.

Senge, P. (1990). *The Fifth Discipline: The Art and Practice of the Learning Organization*. New York: Doubleday.

Senge, P., Smith, B., Kruschwitz, N., Laur, J. & Schley, S. (2010). *The Necessary Revolution: Working Together to Create a Sustainable World*. New York: Crown.

Travis, F. & Shear, J. (2010). Focused attention, open monitoring and automatic self-transcending: Categories to organize meditations from Vedic, Buddhist and Chinese traditions. *Consciousness and Cognition*, 19, 1110-1119.

Travis, F., Tecce, J., Arenander, A. & Wallace, R.K. (2002). Patterns of EEG coherence, power, and contingent negative variation characterize the integration of transcendental and waking states. *Biological Psychology*, 61, 293-319.

Travis, F., Arenander, A. & DuBois, D. (2004). Psychological and physiological characteristics of a proposed object-referral self-referral continuum of self-awareness. *Consciousness and Cognition*, 13, 401-420.

Travis, F., Haaga, D., Hagelin, J., Tanner, M., Arenander, A., Nidich, S., … Schneider, R. (2010). A self-referential default brain state: Patterns of coherence, power, and eLORETA sources during eyes-closed rest and the Transcendental Meditation practice. *Cognitive Processing*, 11(1), 21-30.

Waddock, S. & Rasche, A. (2012). *Building the Responsible Enterprise*. Stanford, CA: Stanford Business Books.

12

Developing responsible managers through service-learning at Goa Institute of Management, India

Ranjini Swamy
Goa Institute of Management, India

Sheila Keegan
Independent consultant, UK

Earn your crores[1] by all means. But understand that your wealth is not yours; it belongs to the people. Take what you require for your legitimate needs, and use the remainder for society… As soon as a man looks upon himself as a servant of society, earns for its sake, spends for its benefit, then purity enters into his earnings and there is Ahimsa in his Trusteeship venture. Moreover, if men's minds turn towards this way of life, there will come about a peaceful revolution in society, and that without any bitterness (Mahatma Gandhi, 1942).

1 One crore is 10 million rupees.

Introduction

The above excerpt describes Mahatma Gandhi's concept of Trusteeship. Gandhi exhorted business to act as a trustee of society—much like parents are trustees of their children—and conduct itself in a socially responsible manner. However, in the decades following liberalization of the Indian economy, trusteeship has been severely tested. For instance, the drive to reduce costs has resulted in increased use of child labour by several organizations. Again, some international businesses operating in India resist adopting the advanced waste-minimization systems that they adopt in more developed countries (Galliara, 2010). Consequently, rapid economic development has been accompanied by social and environmental challenges. There are renewed calls for business to revisit Gandhi's notion of Trusteeship.

To facilitate this we argue that business schools must help students think and act like trustees of society. The curriculum must include courses and modules that develop appropriate behavioural, intellectual and moral competences that will help them create sustainable value for business and society. Importantly, newer educational processes, such as self-directed, project-based learning, must be explored to inculcate responsibility towards society.

This chapter describes the context of Indian business schools, the imperatives for inculcating trusteeship and some initiatives in response to these imperatives (Principles 1 and 3 of the Principles for Responsible Management Education). It then describes the experience and outcomes of introducing service-learning projects, called GiveGoa projects, at Goa Institute of Management (GIM): First, it describes the context in which service-learning was implemented at GIM. Second, it describes the background of service-learning and the choices made in the design and conduct of the service-learning projects at GIM. Third, it details the qualitative research undertaken to explore the reactions to the projects. Fourth, it explores some of the findings of this research and supplements it with a graduate's perspective on his experience of the project and its outcome. The chapter ends with some reflections on the experience of introducing service-learning projects.

The context of business schools in India

Like many other emerging economies, India has made steady progress towards social and economic development since liberalization. Government data suggests that the absolute number of people in poverty has declined and there has been good progress in achieving universal primary education, reducing gender disparities in primary education, and reducing incidence of diseases like HIV/Aids (UN India, 2015). Yet there is more to be done. India continues to be home to a significant 33% of the extremely poor people in the world (Olinto *et al.*, 2013). Poverty is much higher in rural areas and among excluded groups such as Scheduled Castes,

Scheduled Tribes and religious minorities.[2] Addressing this social challenge is critical for sustaining the country's economic growth.

While liberalization was expected to improve economic growth and thereby reduce poverty, there is reason to believe that the growth strategy since the 1990s has not been entirely pro-poor.

First, access to good quality education still appears to be a challenge. In 2009–10, about 29% of the working age population was illiterate, 24% was educated up to primary school, 17.6% up to middle school, 12% up to secondary school and 17% up to college level (Mehrotra *et al.*, 2013).[3] Even those who attend schools were not able to demonstrate learning achievement in English and mathematics (CRISIL Centre for Economic Research, 2010). These trends suggest that significant sections of the working age population do not have the technical, social and analytic capabilities to participate in the rapidly growing sectors of the economy.

Second, greater economic growth has largely been accompanied by a decline in employment growth. While this is debated, it appears that when GDP grew at 4.7% per annum during 1973–1983, employment growth was 2.4%; when the GDP growth increased to 5% per annum during 1983–1993, employment growth declined to 2.0%; when the GDP growth accelerated to 6.3% per annum during 1993–2004, employment growth declined to 1.8%; and when GDP growth was 9% per annum during 2004–2010, employment grew at an insignificant rate of 0.22% (largely in the informal, unorganized sector). The decline in employment rate has been steeper in the rural areas (Papola and Sahu, 2012). Significant sections of the working age population continue to be employed in agriculture and construction sectors, where working conditions are poor (Papola and Sahu, 2012).

Third, limited and low-wage employment options are driving the poor towards greater dependence on the natural resource systems for their livelihood (Bauman, 2002). However, rapid urbanization and industrialization has reduced their access to high-quality natural resources. In 2005, India's more industrialized states generated about 4.4 million tonnes of hazardous waste, of which about 60% was not recyclable. This has adversely affected the quality of natural resources—such as land and water—on which the poor depend for their livelihood. The water quality of most major rivers in India has deteriorated so much that the Central Pollution Control Board has instituted studies on urban wastewater management (Khan, 2013). Again, new thermal plants commissioned to meet the energy requirements

2 The Scheduled Castes (SCs) and Scheduled Tribes (STs) are official designations given to various groups of historically disadvantaged people in India.
3 Examining these statistics, one observes the dip at secondary school level. One possible explanation for the smaller population with secondary school qualifications than college qualifications is that in many government schools students are promoted automatically to the next grade until they reach secondary school. On reaching secondary school, some students (those struggling to perform) perhaps prefer dropping out to avoid the humiliation of being retained in a class and studying with their juniors. Those who continue into secondary school are likely to be children who have a higher chance of pursuing college education.

of an expanding urban population require the submergence of large tracts of forests that are the source of livelihood for the poor. As a result, the access of the poor to productive and healthful natural resources has declined. This has implications for their ability to participate in the economy.

Thus, despite economic growth, poverty levels continue to be of concern. Given this context and the vast resources available to business, it is imperative that business accepts increased responsibility for the welfare of society, especially its poor.

Corporate responses to poverty

Philanthropy has always been a part of Indian business. In early times, it often took the form of one-time relief to the poor in times of distress. During and after independence, there was a shift towards activities that brought progress to society: for example through the creation of educational institutions. A few enlightened companies believed that it was the duty of business to create wealth, promote ethical behaviour and help attain the social goals of the community. Social development occurred through corporate-run foundations or trusts that worked independently of business. Many initiatives, though well-intentioned, tended to be ad hoc and person-driven (Galliara, 2010).

More recently, some companies have integrated the concern for society and environment into their core business strategies. For instance, Jain Irrigation Systems Limited provides irrigation solutions to the small Indian farmers, so that they can improve land productivity, income and quality of life while minimizing water consumption (Goldberg *et al.*, 2012). Ikea—a global furniture company "offering a wide range of well-designed, functional home furnishing products" at affordable prices—has invested considerably to reduce the incidence of child labour in its supply chain (Bartlett *et al.*, 2006).

Leaders of these companies share a commitment to uplift the poor. They realize that they need employees with a similar commitment to integrate and sustain the concern for the poor in their business. For instance, Jain Irrigation Systems Ltd needs employees who are willing to meet, understand, communicate with poor farmers and help change their mind-set towards farming. Employees must share a high level of commitment to deliver service to the farmers and protect the company's reputation as a brand that can be trusted (Goldberg *et al.*, 2012).

Implications for business schools

If this commitment to serve the poor is the beginning of a trend, business schools in India must develop managers with a concern for and responsiveness towards society, especially the poor. A critical issue for business schools is how to inculcate such a concern. Fundamentally, it could require sweeping changes in the values underlying the curriculum, such as profit maximization and instrumentality (Vaara and Fay, 2011). Profit maximization draws from a widely shared belief that shareholders' interests should prevail over the interests of other less powerful but impacted stakeholders. Instrumentality suggests that actions can only be justified by their outcomes, not by their inherent value. Over time, managerial actions *exclusively based* on these values could generate profits at the cost of a country's economic growth (Asian Development Bank, 2007). Little wonder that business schools are accused of supplying firms with the "tools of their destruction"; that is, "unethical managers" who help ruin firms and the lives of many stakeholders in the desire for short-term profits (Giacalone, 2007).

Changes in the underlying values have implications for the content of the curriculum and the educational process. The curriculum needs to explore alternative paradigms—such as sustainability and shared value—that recognize and include the interests of other stakeholders. Educational processes need to encourage students to think about the prevailing values and explore the need for change. Experiential and other self-directed learning approaches could be more effective in facilitating a review of the values and attitudes underlying MBA education.

Business schools in Asia have responded with various curricular and co-curricular interventions. In the recently concluded 6th PRME Asia Forum, speakers from Asian business schools said they had introduced compulsory courses on ethics, corporate social responsibility and sustainability. A few business schools had integrated sustainability into function-specific courses such as marketing and human resource management *(PRME, 2015)*. However, a shared foundation of the curriculum was yet to emerge within and across business schools (O'Byrne *et al.*, 2015). Existing pedagogies such as case studies, in-class exercises and visiting lecturers have been adapted to promote a concern for other stakeholders (Brundiers *et al.*, 2010). A few business schools—in India, Japan and Hong Kong for instance—were also exploring new pedagogies such as service-learning projects to achieve this purpose. These initiatives could appear piecemeal; however they could also serve as experiments that lead to a questioning of the values underlying MBA education at a later stage.

Service-learning

Background

Service-learning is "an experiential approach to education that involves students in meaningful, real-world activities that can advance social, emotional, career, and academic curricula goals while benefitting communities" (Wilczenski and Coomey, 2007, p. 8). Typically, students work with a community partner to serve a specific need of the community. Based on the experiences, students report their findings and recommendations, along with reflections on what they have learned from their service experiences, and how it relates to the curriculum (Wilczenski and Coomey, 2007). Service-learning is rooted in David Kolb's experiential learning theory (ELT) where learning is:

conceived as a four-stage cycle... Immediate concrete experience is the basis for observation and reflection. These observations are assimilated [*by the learner*] into a "theory" from which new implications for action can be deduced. These implications or hypotheses then serve as guides in acting to create new experiences (Kolb, 1976, p. 21).

The central features of the ELT theory are that: (a) the learner is an active participant in the learning process; (b) the learner's here-and-now experience is an important source of learning; and (c) feedback processes are integral to continuous learning and action.

Several educational institutions seek to improve the welfare of society through service-learning projects. This is accomplished in several ways: by addressing problems of the community; inculcating an ability to participate in the democratic process; and promoting deeper thought about society. For these educational institutions, the purpose of education is to provide students with "the skills and attitudes that will support sustainable development, sustainable democracy, civil society and the peaceful resolution of disputes" (Berry and Chisolm, 1999, p. 14).

Service-learning has become an integral part of the undergraduate curriculum in the United States (Kenworthy and Fornaciari, 2010). It has a modest presence among educational institutions in Asia. Perhaps because of its more recent debut, it remains relatively less researched in this region (Snell *et al.*, 2014). In India, service-learning projects appear to be prevalent in some postgraduate (Vyas *et al.*, 2011) and undergraduate education programmes (Sugumar, 2009). A few business schools are now implementing service-learning projects. There is limited published work on how service-learning is included in the curricular or co-curricular activities of Indian business schools. Anecdotal evidence suggests that business schools implement service-learning through summer internships, as part of core courses or through student clubs.

Service-learning at GIM

GIM is an autonomous institute providing management education through several programmes. The institute is committed to creating responsible managers through high quality education. In its early years, the institute attracted a small number of promising students (about 120 per year) from across India. In the late 2000s, a higher demand for managers from the IT and IT-enabled services sector resulted in a steep increase in the demand for MBA education. By 2007, there was a rapid increase in the number of business schools catering to this demand (Arouje, 2010). Significant investments were made in land and infrastructure to set up these schools. A representative MBA applicant had completed his engineering degree and worked for 1–2 years in a software company (Arouje, 2010). Applicants typically expected the MBA education to quickly improve their career prospects, besides significantly improving salaries. They were willing to pay higher fees for this assurance.

GIM invested in a large campus to accommodate about 240 students per year and shifted to the new campus by 2009. Considerable investments were made to provide good infrastructure in the new campus. Given the increased competition for students, the board of GIM felt the need to differentiate the institute from its competitors. Creating responsible managers was one approach to differentiate the institute among prospective students. This was in line with the mission of the institute: "To educate managers with the knowledge, skills and creativity to manage our nation's enterprise competently and confidently with personal integrity and social responsibility and so provide value to and for the organisation for which they work" (GIM, 2014).

Organization of the course

In 2011, GIM piloted a compulsory course on Social Responsibility and Action, as part of the first year of its two-year Post Graduate Programme in Management. The course was made compulsory to help differentiate GIM's programme and signal the institute's commitment to create socially responsible managers.

The objective of the course was to help students become aware of and responsive towards society, especially the poor (i.e. become socially responsible managers). This was expected to manifest itself in: (a) an enhanced awareness of the circumstances of the poor; (b) positive feelings towards helping them; and (c) an intention to help them in the future. It was assumed that this concern for the poor would express itself in more responsible managerial decisions. The course design differed from that of other courses in that learning: (a) was largely field-based and student-driven; and (b) required reflection and integrative thinking. The course had two components: a 1-credit (10 hours) classroom-learning component and a 3-credit service-learning project component.

- The classroom-learning component explored the notion of social responsibility and why organizations and managers needed to be responsible towards society. Social responsibility of an organization was defined as conducting business in a manner that ensured profitability, while being accountable for the impact of the organization on society. Examples of responsible and irresponsible behaviours were explored in class through case studies and films. The case studies were either procured from Harvard Business School Publishing or developed by the faculty member based on secondary sources. (See Appendix 1 for a description of resources used.)

- The service-learning projects offered students an opportunity to help the poor address some of their problems. Students worked in groups over 20 days (once a week over 20 weeks) with a group of relatively poor people in the local community under the guidance of the client organization. On average, each group had one student who was familiar with the local language. Projects were largely in the field of education and community development. A few projects entailed assisting entrepreneurs in their business. Examples of projects include: (a) explaining bank schemes to farmers, identifying relevant bank schemes and enabling farmers' access to the schemes, and (b) assisting self-help groups in improving the quality of their produce.

A coordination team was set up to plan and implement the service-learning projects. The team developed a broad focus of the projects based on interactions with the client organization. Generally, projects were designed to address the client's concerns while permitting students to apply their classroom learnings from the programme. The client organizations then presented the projects to the student body. Based on the client presentations, students formed six-member groups and communicated their top three project preferences to the coordination team. The latter assigned one of the preferred projects to each team, though not necessarily their most preferred one.

Each student group was assisted by a faculty guide and a mentor from the client organization. Altogether, about 20 faculty guides and 40 client mentors guided the students in serving the community. A few meetings were organized to help students and faculty guides understand the purpose and requirements of the service-learning projects. The projects were largely funded by GIM, with a few receiving support from the client organization or external donors. In the first three years, GIM spent an average of about $20,000–25,000 annually, largely towards arranging transport for the groups to and from the project sites. The groups were graded by the respective stakeholders: peers, faculty guides, client representatives and an independent panel of faculty members. Each stakeholder evaluated the group on criteria that he or she could observe (see Appendix 2 for details of evaluation criteria).

During the projects, the stakeholders became "partners in a reciprocal service learning relationship" (Jacoby, 2014, p. 4). Together, they defined the work to be done. Some of our clients, such as the banks, did not have much contact with the rural community whom they were supposed to serve. Many of our newer clients had a limited understanding of our students' constraints. Specific project objectives therefore emerged from discussions among the client, the community and students over the life of the project. The faculty guides influenced these discussions through weekly meetings organized between faculty and the students.

Early survey data on students' perceptions of the outcomes

Given the considerable investment of time and money, GIM's management was concerned about the effectiveness of the course. The GiveGoa coordination team frequently assessed students' perception of whether the course objectives were met. These were complemented by surveys conducted by an independent team of administrators and faculty members of GIM. Over the years, the coordination team supported the placement committee's initiative to make service-learning projects a "point of difference" while marketing GIM to potential recruiters.

We conducted surveys among students to assess their (self-perceived) awareness of and responsiveness towards the poor (see Table 12.1). Surveys conducted suggest that the experience of doing the projects increased awareness about the poor and generated or reinforced responsiveness towards the poor.

Table 12.1 **Student responses to survey about perceptions of learning**

Source: Swamy (2014). Reproduced with permission.

	2011–12 (n=132)	2012–13 (n=82)
Developed a better insight into the lives of the community members	90%	94%
Felt more concerned about the community	75%	93%
Would like to take up the concerns of the community in the future	60%	96%

Anecdotal interactions with students and observations of their initiatives in the second year of the programme suggest that this concern found expression through donations and charitable activities such as fulfilling the (material) wishes of under-privileged children and conducting classes on hygiene for children from neighbouring schools.

While data from the surveys were useful, there was need to complement it with data from more dialogic interactions with students and faculty. Such interactions would help elicit students' expectations of, and reactions to, many facets of their experiences that might not have been tapped by the surveys and yet were more salient to them.

The research

Research objectives

Our research study was a step towards exploring in more depth the reactions of two important stakeholders—the faculty guides and the students—towards the Give-Goa projects. The purpose was to help us better understand their expectations, salient experiences and significant perceived outcomes of the experience that we might not have tapped in the surveys. Broadly, the objectives of this research were to explore:

- The expectations of faculty guides and students from GIM's postgraduate programme and therefore from GiveGoa projects. Students entered the MBA programme with certain expectations. These expectations would operate as standards against which the service-learning experience would be evaluated. We felt the reactions to the projects would be affected by the programme expectations.

- The reactions of faculty guides and students to the experience of doing the GiveGoa projects.

- The perceptions of faculty guides and students about the outcomes from the project.

Research sample and methodology

Respondents comprised seven faculty members and five students who had completed the course requirements in 2014 (about a year prior to this study). To enable a frank discussion, Dr Sheila Keegan, an external consultant for this project and co-author of this chapter, conducted interviews and group discussions with the respondents. The first author, Professor Ranjini Swamy, who had led the design and conduct of the service-learning projects, was not present during the interactions.

Given the time constraints of the interviewer and respondents, a mix of group discussions and in-depth interviews was carried out. Two focus groups, lasting approximately an hour each, were conducted with students who had worked on education and community development projects. Besides these, four individual interviews and one focus group, each lasting half an hour to an hour, were conducted with GIM faculty members. Participation in the study was voluntary and all participants were assured of confidentiality. Questions were open-ended and designed to elicit a rich description of their experiences during the service-learning projects.

Qualitative analysis was carried out manually by Dr Sheila Keegan using grounded theory. The narrative data were read and re-read, analysed and regularly reviewed. This approach enabled the researcher to be reasonably confident of the veracity of the themes. The analysis reflected the frequently illogical and contradictory nature of human thinking, while respecting the significance, relative importance and priorities of ideas and opinions which respondents related spontaneously.

Findings from interviews

Student reactions

The expectations

Students' expectations from the general programme broadly fell under two categories: process and outcome. Students expected an education process with one or more of the following attributes: (a) individualized attention from faculty; (b) opportunities for peer-learning, collaborative learning; (c) freedom to learn many disciplines (not being "pigeonholed"); (d) experiential, practical learning; and (e) certainty and predictability. A recurrent theme was the expectation of certainty especially among students with limited work experience. This was reflected in the desire for quantifiable targets in the service-learning experience: goals such as conducting a defined number of training programmes were preferred over goals such as building confidence among girl children in a school.

Students expected one or more of the following programme outcomes: (a) confidence in execution; (b) skills for the "world of work", including exposure to industry, soft skills and academic skills; (c) (*enhanced*) résumé value; and (d) an understanding of business and society, of people living in circumstances unfamiliar to the students.

The experience of the project

Students referred to the projects as corporate social responsibility (CSR) and philanthropy, words traditionally associated with charity in the Indian context. Their experience of the projects ranged from excitement about engaging in practical learning to feelings of disorientation (at least initially). Prior education had not prepared students for experiential learning. They felt out of their depth in the project and felt the need for guidance. They reported feeling abandoned by guides/ mentors.

During the projects, they faced uncertainties on several fronts. Initially there was uncertainty about which project would be allotted to them. Certain projects—such as teaching schoolchildren or educating the poor about banking services—were in high demand and oversubscribed. Students who did not get these projects despite indicating their preference felt they had "missed out". Later, the project objectives and strategies, client expectations, community response and even mentors kept changing. There was need for self-reliance and constant adaptation. Students grappled with the demand for initiative, for exploring/taking risks and dealing with ambiguous and conflicting goals. Only a minority of respondents actually enjoyed the uncertainty. Some illustrative quotes are shared below:

> Initially...we didn't actually know...how to go about the project. I think it would have helped if we could have had some homework as to how we could go about it...I felt that...the base that we had was not that good.

> You have everything you have done, all the homework, but sometimes the ground changes. GiveGoa reality is slightly different...That's the fun part actually...the unpredictability. So that is why I like CSR more than the courses we already have.

During the project, their first instinct was to view GiveGoa as another "graded" assignment. They worried that they may fail, they worried about grades. They had learned that success was important. While the projects offered opportunities for peer learning and collaboration, this was not always realized. The following quotes are illustrative of their concerns:

> We are graded based on work we do. But we need a quantifiable output. The college needs a quantifiable output whereas our clients do not need this measure!

> ...the learning part was great...at times...learning takes the back seat and there's more attention to grades...

> Everybody was thinking about the grading...they were...trying to impress people who were going to grade them...

The outcomes

Respondents mentioned one or more of the following outcomes: (a) a broadening of perspective through exposure to different groups of people living different lifestyles in different circumstances; (b) a greater ability to manage uncertainty and unpredictability; and (c) better skills (having "résumé value") such as persuasion, meeting timelines, learning to adapt and compromise when needed. There was recognition among the respondents that they were indeed privileged.

They believed that "CSR type thinking" was here to stay and was therefore a necessary part of their résumé preparation. However, there was also scepticism about the value of such projects. They felt the purpose and the long-term benefits of such projects were not clear. Some quotes are shared below:

> ...what I think Business School adds to you is in growing more as a person, due to the kinds of exposure you have...and CSR [i.e. GiveGoa projects] is one aspect.

> I will need to be aware of charitable and CSR-type activity if I'm going to be a successful senior manager in a large corporation...and also in a personal development sense.

Faculty reactions

Expectations

Faculty respondents expected the projects to provide the following benefits: (a) for students, a broadened perspective and improved résumé value; and (b) for GIM, building useful relations with the local population, improving its status among peers and attracting students. They also expected the client organizations and the targeted community to benefit, but did not elaborate on this.

Experience of guiding the projects

Faculty members took issue with the nature of projects. They observed that students appeared to be doing the work of a labourer and were not understanding the context. What could students learn from that? To quote a faculty member:

> ...students have got a project...pests are coming onto the palm trees and they are getting diseased...they have to trap those pests, have to set traps. So they go there. They are like labourers, cleaning and putting in traps... I tried to tell them to take a bigger thing...[t]hey have to understand the context.

They felt that the schedule of the projects—once a week for 20 weeks spread out over the year—made it difficult for students to engage with the project. During the week, students were initially pulled away from their projects by academic pressures which led to comments from faculty members that "projects were in competition with academic studies". When the project visit was due, the students had to re-engage with the project and then leave it again after the visit. As a result, they could not get engrossed in the projects.

Student ability and motivation to do the projects was another concern expressed by faculty. Students sometimes ended up with projects that did not interest them or for which they were ill-equipped. For example, the students' inability to speak the local language got in the way of understanding community concerns and building a relationship with the community members. Some projects appeared burdensome, leading to tiredness and reduced enthusiasm among students. There was a danger of "lost lessons" due to time pressure at the end of the course. The grading of the projects was confusing to students. Given that the students lacked agency over the outcome of projects, and depended on cooperation from many people across different institutions, the experience (of grading) seemed unfair.

Outcome

Faculty detailed the outcomes of the projects for the students and for GIM but not for other stakeholders. They described the outcomes for students as "an experience", an opportunity to become more aware of and sensitive to the circumstances of the poor, an exposure to different communities. However, they described the projects as "too much effort for insufficient return". The projects took away a great deal of time that should have been spent on more orthodox teaching.

For GIM, the outcomes included an appreciation from peer institutes and an ability to attract students who sought a "diverse business perspective". There were, however, questions about whether the projects fit with the business school curriculum. Moreover, the discontinuation of projects after a year compromised the outcomes for GIM. As one professor put it: "…if we work on a particular project and…do some good job for a particular beneficiary, next year I feel that [it] needs to be sustained and maybe another group could be given the project to take [it] forward…".

In sum, the service-learning projects were an opportunity for students to increase their exposure to society and enhance some résumé-oriented skills. They helped the institute gain appreciation from its peers and attract students who sought "diverse business perspectives". However, there were concerns about their fit with the purpose and curriculum of the MBA programme and whether the returns were worth the effort. There was little evidence of more socially responsible business decisions and actions.

A graduate's perspective

In this section, we present the reactions of Swapnil, a student who graduated from GIM in mid-2015. It offers insight into his reflections on the project experience subsequent to graduation and its impact on his actions in the workplace. At GIM, Swapnil was a member of Samarthan (the student club) and was actively involved in coordinating the service-learning projects. On graduation, he joined a reputed IT firm as an executive. He described his experience during and after the programme as follows:

> As part of the GiveGoa projects, I was dealing with special children. The client organization was "Sethu", which means "a bridge" to connect two worlds—the world of these special children and the world of those "normal" people who tend to avoid them. The programme for special children was well designed. As assistants, we helped practically and observed and suggested improvements.

> The beginning of the programme was a little tough…as it was the first time we were interacting with the special children. Some of us had worked with small children before … But this situation was a little different. We were first told about the psyche of these children… This was very tough to understand …when they threw "tantrums" we were trying to get the situation under control by raising our voice or showing some gesture. In general…all those tactics would fail, as these children could not understand our behaviour.

> Adaptation was the key. I can proudly say we developed a connection with those children at the end of the programme. I specifically learnt a lot about a section of society which I was totally unaware of. I now understand the experiences of parents of these children who have to care for them day and night. This experience has changed my life at many levels and I would say I have started appreciating the gift of life itself…

> … in the corporate environment [in India] today, I strongly feel the need for combining sustainability with business strategy, and that is the way forward if we want everyone to win… Growth should not come at the cost of one and benefit of another. The toughest part is to do business understanding this scenario, because the business practices are ruthless and biased towards the organization.

> While working or taking any decision I always keep in mind the impact of my actions on the society and environment … I have educated peers not to throw garbage on the street … to help the underprivileged and be sensitive towards the lower classes of society. As I work in the rural parts of India now, I see there is need for making people aware and sensitive towards … cleanliness and hygiene. I see a huge gap between cities and villages … in even understanding the importance of cleanliness. I am trying to do my bit by asking people to…keep the environment clean and hygienic.

CSR has left a mark on [my] mind and made me sensitive as well as sensible to work for the larger good of society and believe me, your tiny contribution matters a lot.

Swapnil's response suggests that the experience of serving special children through the service-learning projects made him more aware of their circumstances and those of their parents. It also generated positive feelings towards helping others and improving society. This is expressed through exhorting peers to be responsible citizens outside the workplace. He acknowledges that organizations are ruthless and biased towards protecting their own interests. Incorporating a concern for others into business decisions appears challenging. Perhaps it is premature to expect this so soon. Nevertheless, it provides an opportunity to review the course design.

Reflections on the experience

In this section, we share our reflections on the experience of designing and conducting service-learning projects at GIM. We discuss several challenges that need to be addressed to improve their effectiveness. These could serve as pointers for others who attempt to introduce service-learning projects in the course curriculum. However, as March (2010) suggests, experience is often characterized by small samples, weak signals (of relationships between variables) and substantial "noise". Attempts to establish causality in and generalize from initial experience must therefore be done with great caution.

Establishing a fit between service-learning projects and the institute's purpose

In many universities that introduced service-learning projects, the purpose of education was to prepare students to serve society in a responsible manner. Service-learning projects were a good fit with this longer-term purpose.

For our respondents, the primary purpose of education was to prepare students for managerial careers and to improve their immediate job prospects. Both students and faculty emphasized the acquiring of skills that improved "résumé value".

At GIM, the "fit" with this purpose was attempted by: (a) developing projects which allowed students to apply their classroom learnings and acquire "résumé enhancing" knowledge/skills; and (b) supporting the placement committee's initiative to make service-learning projects a "point of difference" while marketing GIM to potential recruiters. The major challenge was to devise projects that met the short-term expectations of internal stakeholders. Perhaps this could explain the scepticism about the relevance of the projects to the MBA curriculum.

Generating a shared understanding of social responsibility

At GIM, service-learning projects were part of the course "Social Responsibility & Action". The objective of the course was to help students become aware of and responsive towards society, especially the poor (i.e. become socially responsible managers). Several stakeholders—the management, students, faculty guides, client organizations and the coordination team—worked together to help achieve this objective. A shared understanding among all stakeholders about the notion of social responsibility was critical.

However, it appears that the notion of social responsibility was not agreed across stakeholders. Some phrases used by respondents to describe the GiveGoa projects—such as "philanthropic" and "CSR"—indicated that they associated social responsibility with charity. The classroom sessions, however, associated social responsibility with greater accountability of business for the impact of its decisions and actions on society, including the poor. Clearly the notion of social responsibility was not agreed upon. This could have affected the stakeholders' response to and expectations from the projects. A major challenge was to arrive at such a shared conception within the time constraints.

Aligning the service-learning project with the course curriculum

When service-learning projects form part of a core course, they need to be aligned with the course curriculum and the other course components (Robinson *et al.*, 2010). At GIM, the course "Social Responsibility & Action" had two components: a classroom component and a service-learning component. The classroom component created awareness about why companies (and managers) must be socially responsible. The service-learning component promoted an awareness of and concern for society, especially the poor. However, the link between the two components was weak: the projects did not demonstrate the need for business to engage with the poor or the potential benefits of such an engagement. For example, students who served special children felt concerned for the welfare of those children. However, they did not see why business should help improve the welfare of these children or the potential benefits of such an engagement. This could explain why students saw the projects as charity. Even the graduate's commentary highlights his initiatives to help the community outside the workplace.

Greater alignment between the classroom and project components could require the redesign of projects and/or the classroom component. Projects could be redesigned to emphasize the need for business to take responsibility for the welfare of the poor and the benefits that could accrue therefrom. For example, GIM students could help local companies gain acceptance of the local community affected by their operations and document the benefits. The classroom component could be redesigned to help students make business decisions in a socially responsible manner.

Adapting the project design to the students' expectations

Instructional strategies adopted in a course—for example, case studies, classroom simulations, real-time projects—are likely to influence the effectiveness of student learning. These strategies need to be adapted to the local context for greater effectiveness (Du-Babcock, 2006). The students' preferred modes of learning are an important element of the local context. In this study, GIM students voiced their desire for individualized attention, collaborative and practical learning and certainty during the education process. Assuming these expectations are generalizable, they could indicate a preference for more guided, cooperative, less risky modes of learning. How could the design of service-learning projects adapt to these expectations?

We thought that if students worked in teams under the supervision of guides/mentors, they would get the requisite guidance and cooperation. This would help them to better cope with the inherent project uncertainties. However, student-respondents said that some of their team members were not cooperative and that they sometimes felt unsupported by the mentors/guides in dealing with the project-related ambiguities and uncertainties.

Given that the programme curriculum emphasizes classroom-, discipline-based learning, students and faculty guides in such contexts could need much more preparation before implementing the service-learning projects. For instance, students could need preparation to transit from: (a) discipline-based to more integrated thinking; and (b) individualistic learning to team learning.

Summary and conclusion

The chapter starts with Mahatma Gandhi's notion of Trusteeship and suggests that, in pursuing rapid economic growth, Indian business has stepped away from being a trustee of society. If business has to re-commit itself to being a trustee of society, business schools must help potential managers conduct themselves in a socially responsible manner. Business schools in India have responded by introducing several changes (e.g. service-learning projects) in their curriculum.

This chapter describes GIM's experience of introducing service-learning projects into the core curriculum of its Postgraduate Programme in Management and the reactions of a small sample of students and faculty guides to the project experience.

GIM introduced service-learning projects to promote an awareness of and responsiveness towards society, especially the poor. These projects were part of a course called "Social Responsibility and Action" that was compulsory for all first-year students. The projects gave students an opportunity to work with the poor and learn about their circumstances through the experience. We expected that such a concern for society, especially its poor, could translate into more responsible business decisions that protect the welfare of the poor while pursuing profits.

In early surveys, students reported a greater awareness of and concern for the poor. In our interviews for this chapter, respondents shared mixed reactions to the projects. Students felt that the service-learning projects broadened their perspective, helped them develop a greater ability to manage uncertainty and improved their résumé-relevant skills. However, the purpose and the long-term benefits of such projects were not clear to them. Faculty guides said that the projects helped the students to broaden their perspectives and helped GIM attract students and gain appreciation from its peers. However, there were concerns about whether the projects fit with the MBA curriculum and whether the returns were worth the effort.

Given the mixed reactions to the projects, should the service-learning projects be continued as part of the MBA curriculum? The chapter presents some of the national imperatives—notably the continued existence of poverty despite economic growth—to argue that Indian business must conduct itself in a socially responsible manner. If this is accepted, business schools must inculcate the spirit of Trusteeship among their students.

How can trusteeship be inculcated in business schools? Service-learning projects could be one method of inculcating a responsibility and responsiveness towards society, especially the poor. GIM's experience of introducing service-learning projects as part of the course curriculum suggests that these could be more effective under the following conditions: (a) the projects are perceived as useful in preparing students for managerial careers or in improving their immediate job prospects; (b) the projects are aligned with the classroom component of the course; (c) stakeholders involved in the design and conduct of the projects have a shared understanding of social responsibility; and (d) the design and conduct of the projects is adapted to the students' expectations from the programme. For those opting to introduce service-learning projects as part of a core course of the MBA programme, these could be points for reflection.

Appendix 1

Examples of some India-specific materials used in the class discussions of the course "Social Responsibility & Action":

1. Caselets which described decisions that managers in Indian companies had to make:

   - Cipla's decision in the context of the AIDS epidemic in Africa and the unwillingness of multinationals to provide AIDS vaccines at lower costs. *Source*: "Fire in the Blood" documentary.

- Vedanta's decision in response to public outcry against bauxite mining in Niyamgiri hills. *Source*: materials published online on the Niyamgiri agitation

- A small entrepreneur's decision in response to the demand for a bribe in return for a large government order for his products. *Source*: an entrepreneur based in Goa.

- A nylon manufacturer's response to public concern about pollution of their water sources. *Source*: materials published online on the "Nylon 6,6" agitation in Goa against DuPont's project to manufacture nylon for the domestic tyre manufacturers in India.

The caselets were presented sequentially in the classroom. Each caselet was presented as a decision situation and students were asked to discuss in small groups and communicate their decision and its rationale. The potential impact of the decisions on business and society was discussed in the class. Then I presented what the companies actually did and the consequences for the company and society. In all cases, the financial consequences and brand impact were highlighted.

2. Case of Coca-Cola's plant in Plachimada, Kerala, which described the company's response to complaints from the community about water scarcity and the consequences. *Source*: Cedillo Torres *et al.* (2012).
3. IKEA Case: Bartlett *et al.* (2006).
4. Article/videos on Monsanto's strategies. Example: Glover (2007).

Appendix 2

Stakeholders involved in evaluating GiveGoa projects and criteria used for evaluation

Stakeholder	Evaluation criteria
Client organization Why? Evaluation of work at site Weightage: 20%	Contribution to client organization; Contribution to the community Discipline
GIM panel of faculty (excluding faculty guide) and client representative Why? Evaluation of presentations (mid- and end-term) Weightage: 10% + 15%	Scope Strategy Learning about the community Project outcomes
GIM panel of faculty (excluding guide) Why? Evaluation of reflection reports Weightage: 15%	Reflection about working with the community Reflection about working with peers Reflection about working with the client organization Personal learnings

Stakeholder	Evaluation criteria
Faculty guide Why? Evaluation of the weekly preparation Weightage: 30%	Discipline (in attending meetings with faculty guides) Commitment to project Quality of weekly reports
Student peers in the same group Why? Evaluation of involvement and contribution Weightage: 10%	Effort put into project Quality of contribution to the project discipline

References

Arouje, S. (2010). *India's leading Business Schools*. Short Hills, NJ: Dun & Bradstreet. Retrieved from https://www.dnb.co.in/IndiasLeadingBusinessSchool/Trends.asp

Asian Development Bank (2007). *Inequality in Asia: Key Indicators 2007. Special Chapter Highlights*. Manila: Asian Development Bank.

Bartlett, C., Dessain, V.M. & Sjoman, A. (2006). *Ikea's Global Sourcing Challenge: Indian Rugs and Child Labor (A)*. Harvard Business Case no. 906-414. Brighton, MA: Harvard Business Publishing. Retrieved from https://hbr.org/product/ikea-s-global-sourcing-challenge-indian-rugs-and-child-labor-a/906414-PDF-ENG

Bauman, P. (2002). *Improving Access to Natural Resources for the Rural Poor: A Critical Analysis of Central Concepts and Emerging Trends from a Sustainable Livelihoods Perspective*. LSP Working paper 1. Rome: Food and Agriculture Organization of the United Nations Livelihood Support Programme (LSP).

Berry, H.A. & Chisholm, L.A. (1999). *Service-Learning in Higher Education around the World: An Initial Look*. New York: International Partnership for Service-Learning; New York: Ford Foundation.

Brundiers, K., Wiek, A. & Redman, C.L. (2010). Real-world learning opportunities in sustainability: From classroom into the real world. *International Journal of Sustainability in Higher Education*, 11(4), 308-324.

Cedillo Torres, C.A., Garcia-French, M., Hordijk, R., Nguyen, K. & Olup, L. (2012). Four case studies on corporate social responsibility: Do conflicts affect a company's corporate social responsibility policy? *Utrecht Law Review*, 8(3). Retrieved from http://ssbea.mercer.edu/blanke/Four%20Case%20Studies%20on%20CSR.pdf

CRISIL Centre for Economic Research (2010). *Skilling India: The Billion People Challenge*. Mumbai: CRISIL Centre for Economic Research.

Du-Babcock, B. (2006). Reflections on teaching Chinese MBAs in a compressed-time course. *Business Communications Quarterly*, 69(1), 70-76.

Gandhi, M.K. (1942). *Trusteeship. Harijan*, 1-2-1942, p-20. Ahmedabad: Jitendra T Desai. Retrieved from http://www.mkgandhi.org/ebks/trusteeship.pdf

Galliara, M. (2010). Corporate social responsibility in India. In G. Williams (Ed.), *Responsible Management in Asia: Perspectives on CSR*. Basingstoke, UK: Palgrave Macmillan.

Giacalone, R.A. (2007). Taking a red pill to disempower unethical students: Creating ethical sentinels in business schools. *Academy of Learning and Education*, 6(4), 534-542.

GIM (Goa Institute of Management) (2014). Mission. Retrieved from http://www.gim.ac.in/new/content.php?name=Mission&id=52

Glover, D. (2007). Monsanto and smallholder farmers: A case study in CSR. *Third World Quarterly*, 28(4), 851-867.

Goldberg, R.A, Knoop, Carin-Isabel & Preble, M. (2012). *Jain Irrigations Systems Limited: Inclusive Growth for India's Farmers*. Harvard Business School Case no. 912-403. Brighton, MA: Harvard Business Publishing.

Jacoby, B. (2014). *Service Learning Essentials: Questions, Answers, and Lessons Learned*. San Francisco: Jossey-Bass.

Kenworthy, A.L. & Fornaciari, C. (2010). Guest editorial: No more reinventing the service-learning wheel: Presenting a diverse compilation of best practice "how to" articles. *Journal of Management Education*, 34(1), 3-8.

Khan, U. (2013). *Emerging Trends of Urbanization in India: An Evaluation from Environmental Perspectives*. Thesis submitted to Economics Department of Aligarh Muslim University, India.

Kolb, D.A. (1976). Management and the learning process. *California Management Review*, 17(3), 21-31.

March, J.G. (2010). *The Ambiguities of Experience*. Ithaca, NY: Cornell University Press.

Mehrotra, S., Gandhi, A. & Sahoo, B.K. (2013). Estimating the skill gap on a realistic basis for 2022. Occasional Paper no. 1/2013. New Delhi: Institute of Applied Manpower Research.

O'Byrne, D., Dripps, W. & Kimberley, A.N. (2015). Teaching and learning sustainability: An assessment of the curriculum content and structure of the sustainability degree programs in higher education. *Sustainability Science*, 10, 43-59. doi:10.1007/s11625-014-0251-y

Olinto, P., Beegle, K., Sobrado, C. & Uematsu, H. (2013). The state of the poor: where are the poor, where is extreme poverty harder to end and what is the current profile of the world's poor? *Economic Premise Notes No. 125*. Washington, DC: World Bank Poverty Reduction and Economic Management Network.

Papola, T.S. & Sahu, P.P. (2012). *Growth and Structure of Employment in India: Long Term and Post-Reform Performance and the Emerging Challenge*. New Delhi: Institute for Studies in Industrial Development.

PRME (2015). *6th PRME Asia Forum, Goa, India, 27–28 November 2015*. Internal report on the proceedings.

Robinson, D.F., Sherwood, A.L. & DePaolo, C.A. (2010). Service learning by doing: How a student-run consulting company finds relevance and purpose in a business strategy capstone course. *Journal of Management Education*, 34(1), 88-112.

Snell, R.S., Chan, M.Y.L., Ma, C.H.K. & Chan, C.K.M. (2014) A roadmap for empowering undergraduates to practice service leadership through service-learning in teams. *Journal of Management Education*, 39(3), 372-399.

Sugumar, R.W. (2009). Role of service-learning in water quality studies. *New Horizons in Education*, 57(3), 82-90.

Swamy, R. (2014). Inculcating social responsibility at Goa Institute of Management. *Management and Change*, 18(1), 123-136.

UN India (2015). *India and the MDGs: Towards a Sustainable Future for All*. Bangkok: UNESCAP.

Vaara, E. & Fay, E. (2011). How can a Bourdieusian Perspective aid analysis of MBA education? *Academy of Management Learning & Education*, 10(1), 27-39.

Vyas, R., Zachariah, A., Swamidasan, I., Doris, P. & Harris, I. (2011). Integration of academic learning and service development through guided projects for rural practitioners in India. *Medical Teacher*, 33, 401-407.

Wilczenski, F.L. & Coomey, S. (Eds.). (2007). *A Practical Guide to Service-learning: Strategies for Positive Development in Schools*. New York, NY: Springer.

13

The Global Integrative Module

A competence-based online learning experience to help future managers understand complex, global, social challenges

Anna Iñesta, Maika Valencia, Xari Rovira, Josep Francesc Mària,
Josep Maria Sayeras, Ricard Serlavós, Jose Luis Marin, Carlos Obeso
and Jaclyn Wilson
ESADE Business School, Ramon Llull University, Spain

Leonardo Caporarello
SDA Bocconi, Italy

Jang Choi
Sogang University, South Korea

Matt Statler
Stern School of Business, New York University, USA

Gianmarco Gessi
Gruppo Mediolanum, Italy

Companies that have decided to compete on a global scale have revised their business models and organisational structures, but beyond this have they developed skills and a culture that are truly "global"? Have organisations actually "taken in" the cultural revolution brought about by the Internet and the advent of the digital era, the growth of web-based technologies and the overwhelming success of social networks? Has this led them to change the way they operate as a result of the development of new processes and capabilities? Today more than ever, globalisation and digitisation are an indivisible whole. The world is becoming digital, albeit at different speeds in various countries (Dr Gianmarco Gessi, Gruppo Mediolanum).

Introduction

The manager quoted above articulates the basic motivation for the efforts described in this chapter. In the current socioeconomic environment, with rising globalization and rapid advances in information and communication technologies (ICT), management professionals participate in a complex, multicultural, competitive and flexible labour market that requires continuous learning. Such demands render traditional teaching methods obsolete and invite business schools to adapt their curricula and educational practices to train future competent managers. The Global Integrative Module (henceforth GIM) is an elective course that aims to respond to this challenge by offering an international learning experience led by ESADE, and with the participation of students from three business school partners: NYU Stern School of Business (United States), SDA Bocconi (Italy) and Sogang University (South Korea). GIM is a competence-based module in which students work together in multicultural teams via an online learning ePlatform to develop solutions to global social challenges. It provides students with opportunities to equip themselves with the knowledge and competences necessary to confront the challenges facing managers in a complex global environment.

This chapter begins with comments from our practitioner commentator, Dr Gianmarco Gessi, an executive in Mediolanum Group (Italy) who raises challenging questions about contemporary business. According to Dr Gessi:

> The most innovation-oriented companies have understood [that the world is becoming digital] and have started to invest millions of euros to digitise their organisations through the creation of a digital workplace, i.e. a virtual place where all the stakeholders (employees, associates, sales networks, suppliers, customers and so on) can interact remotely, exchanging information, generating and sharing knowledge, communicating, cooperating, carrying out processes, exchanging goods and services. The real challenge for companies is not investing in technology, but activating and completing this cultural turnaround faster

than their competitors. In this perspective, the true critical success factor is human resources.

The managers of the future must be open to the world. They must be able to make the most of their experience and values, and at the same time absorb and take in the stimuli constantly provided by others. They must have the ability to work in a digital organization (i.e. a digital workplace) where the very concept of team is destined to change because the number and identity of the team members are variable, rather than predetermined according to the traditional organizational model. If they want to compete on a global scale, they must "think global", which means identifying and qualifying as citizens of the world: a highly interconnected world, where interaction, information, communication, learning, exchange and use of goods and services are changing more rapidly than people normally wish them to.

The educational innovation experience we present in this chapter contributes to a number of the themes proposed in this book. Specifically, it most importantly connects with the Principles for Responsible Management Education (PRME) Principle 3, "Method: We will create educational frameworks, materials, processes and environments that enable effective learning experiences for responsible leadership". To describe our method we begin by presenting the background and context of the experience to then provide detailed information regarding our process. The chapter then covers the assurance of learning followed by student, practitioner and faculty reflections before outlining how this approach could be replicated in other educational settings.

Background and context

Foundational principles and assumptions

The GIM project is an evolution, or global version, of a course entitled "Integrative Module", which has successfully been put into practice several times as an active innovation element in the Bachelor of Business Administration (BBA) undergraduate programme at ESADE. The idea of designing and implementing an Integrative Module within the curriculum of the BBA emerged as part of the reflection that Spanish higher education is going through in the context of the European Higher Education Area (EHEA).[1] More specifically, the Integrative Module aimed at responding to one of the most important challenges European universities are currently facing: the need to articulate the curricula on the basis of competence

---

1 In 1999 the EHEA was launched along with the Bologna Process with the objective to ensure more comparable, compatible and coherent systems of higher education in Europe. The Bologna Declaration (19 June 1999), http://www.ehea.info/Uploads/about/BOLOGNA_DECLARATION1.pdf

development.[2] This articulation requires reflection on the learning situations (that is, the contexts, tasks, dynamics and teaching-learning strategies) that promote the development of those competences which will prepare students for the best possible professional performance in the context of current global labour markets.

The term "integrative module" can be applied to those formative units which organize around a problem or challenge instead of around contents specific to a knowledge field and whose complexity requires students to apply knowledge and competences acquired in different courses in an integrated way. In this sense, this innovative course format may be considered one of the most appropriate ones to train future competent professionals. In this sense, modules go beyond the traditional organization of the courses, thus overcoming the deeply rooted disciplinary division which has prevailed over many universities. Because of that modules can be designed to be complex learning environments where students acquire new knowledge and competences by confronting the resolution of archetypal or emerging problems (Monereo and Castelló, 2009) similar to those they will encounter in their future professional activity.

Integrative modules, in this context, are curriculum units of a more global nature than traditional courses, which allow for the design of innovative learning tasks and dynamics. Such innovation lies in the characteristics of the tasks which articulate the students' learning process and which we may summarize as being:

- **More complex**: from the point of view of cognitive complexity (they require profound knowledge of concepts from different knowledge fields), personal complexity (tasks which promote the development of students' awareness as individuals/future professionals by requiring from them a clear positioning regarding the analysed question) and relational complexity (teamwork, influence, leadership).

- **More authentic**: in that task resolution requires from students the application of learning processes similar to those which take place in the context of real professional activity.

- **Transversal**: not restricted by the disciplinary conventions found in courses.

Therefore, owing to the above dimensions/qualities we will claim that the kinds of tasks and learning dynamics that can be proposed in Integrative Modules contribute to the integral formation of students (i.e. involving the participant in the holistic sense of the term) and allow for authentic competence-based assessment (Gielen *et al.*, 2003), characterized by the fulfilment of the conditions detailed below (Wiggins, 1990, p. 220):

---

2 The European Commission's Communication of 20 April 2005 on the reform of universities in the framework of the Lisbon Strategy to respond to globalization and the need to create a new knowledge-driven economy, stresses to universities to ensure the mix of disciplines and competences in curricula, among other actions (EUR-Lex, 2006).

- Students' achievement is examined on the basis of relevant tasks.
- It requires students to apply the learned knowledge in situations which are as similar as possible to professional situations.
- The proposed problems are ill-structured, intentionally ambiguous, reflecting the complexity of the professional world.
- The group of knowledge and competences necessary to solve the specific situation/task is evaluated simultaneously.
- A justified argumentation of the students' answers to the questions designed to solve the problem is required.
- The ability to act intentionally in social contexts is evaluated.

According to Monereo and Castelló (2009), these types of tasks bring the following benefits to students' learning:

- Students adjust their learning strategies: If participants realize that the central objective of the task proposed in the module is to allow for the knowledge and competences learned to be available for the successful resolution of future problems and authentic tasks, they will approach the learning process in a deeper way.
- Students' motivation increases: the resolution of the tasks involves a challenge, a new situation which allows students to position themselves in the professional's shoes, approaching their learning to the professional reality.
- Different retroactive effects upon the teaching-learning process (that is, upon the way professors approach the teaching process) may be observed: If professors become aware that students will need to face complex and authentic tasks, they may adjust the way in which they articulate their formative proposals so as to improve students' achievement and performance in this kind of task.

Learning objectives

The Global Integrative Module is designed to promote students':

- Development of a professional approach that allows them to feel capable of confronting and successfully solving problems, no matter how complex these might be.
- Development of competences to solve complex problems by applying pragmatic as well as socially responsible criteria, catering for both global and local perspectives.
- Shared decision-making and information search through strategic ICT use.

- Development of competences to collaborate in the construction of a community of practice (simulation of professional consultancy situation) in virtual environments.

In the section on "Assurance of learning results" below, the specific instruments that will allow us to assess achievement of the learning objectives will be detailed.

Institutional conditions that enable the experience to become a reality

We identified three key enabling conditions. First, external funding in the form of the grant obtained from the Graduate Management Admission Council (GMAC)[3] Management Education for Tomorrow (MET) Fund, an initiative that formalizes and enhances the GMAC's long-standing commitment to investing in strategic philanthropic initiatives that benefit business and management education globally. In the i2i Challenge 2012,[4] this support has been decisive and essential to make the GIM project a reality, helping us develop the educational and technological tools and create the team involved in the design and implementation of the project. Second, the leadership vision of ESADE's President and Business School Dean, and the Deans at the different partner institutions of SDA Bocconi, NYU Stern and Sogang University was essential. Third, critical personal networks ensured the full commitment of the participating business schools. Without the support of the corresponding departments at each of the schools the fruitful partnership would not have been possible.

With regard to constraining conditions, we naturally found some budget constraints. Unlike traditional lecture courses which have minimal costs, we encountered additional expense of necessary resources to ensure the adequate follow-up of students' and tutors' work (which needs to be monitored at all times to ensure excellent learning experience). Furthermore, given the challenging nature of the learning experience, the minimum number of students enrolled (which is usually considered necessary for an elective not to be cancelled) may not be reached.

Finally, integrative modules are also an opportunity to promote the interdisciplinary view and collaboration among the professors who teach the different courses

---

3 The GMAC serves as the leading source of research and information about quality graduate management education. They are also the owner and administrator of the GMAT® exam, the premier standardized test specifically designed for graduate business and management programmes and the most widely used assessment for graduate management admissions. http://www.gmac.com/about-us.aspx

4 In April 2012, GMAC presented Ideas to Innovation (i2i) Challenge grantees focusing on social responsibility, technology, and veterans' education. This challenge proposed a series of big ideas designed to improve management education and called for projects which could help make them a reality for students worldwide. The GIM was identified as one of the projects capable of doing so. For more information: http://www.gmac.com/why-gmac/giving-back-met-fund/met-fund-i2i-challenge.aspx

of a programme. In our experience participation in the joined design of the GIM's task and the assessment architecture allowed faculty to: a) reflect upon the complementarities and differences of the teaching approaches of colleagues from other disciplines; and, more importantly, b) reflect upon the impact of their coordinated intervention in the learning process of students.

Alignment of the GIM experience with the educational missions of participating schools

The Global Integrative Module was designed in line with ESADE Business School's vision to inspire and prepare global-minded individuals so that they become highly competent and innovative professionals capable of successfully addressing the social challenges of the future. Its implementation has been made a reality as a result of the fruitful collaboration and partnership with NYU Stern (US), SDA Bocconi (Italy) and Sogang University (South Korea).

Founded in 1958 in Barcelona when a group of entrepreneurs and the Society of Jesus members joined forces, ESADE Business School is an independent non-profit university institution with an approach dedicated to personal development and social responsibility. The mission of ESADE Business School is to educate and undertake research in the fields of management for: the comprehensive training of professionally competent and socially responsible people, knowledge creation relevant to the improvement of organizations and society, and contribution to the social debate regarding the building of free, prosperous and just societies.

New York University has for the last several years been positioning and branding itself as a "global network university", with its primary location in New York City, with full, four-year, degree-granting campuses in Abu Dhabi and Shanghai, and with academic centres in 11 different locations around the world. NYU Stern has been playing a major role in this international effort. All third-year undergraduate students participate in the International Studies Programme; many students spend at least one semester studying abroad; and some students enrolled in the Business and Political Economy Programme spend two semesters abroad. Thus the GIM project supports and extends an ongoing effort to provide students with global experiences.

SDA Bocconi is the Università Bocconi's School of Management, whose mission is to foster knowledge and innovation to contribute to the development of individuals and organizations. With reference to the innovation dimension, it includes both content and process. In this context, SDA Bocconi Learning Lab (@SDAB-LearningLab) has been created with the aim to conduct research and experiments on innovation and learning methods. Thus, the GIM project is coherent with this mission.

One of the missions of Sogang University is to provide outstanding education grounded in the Jesuit educational principle that cultivates students to become responsible, competent and ethical global leaders who will promote the welfare of all global citizens. Based on this mission, Sogang Business School established its vision which is "A Leading Business School in Asia". With this mission and vision in mind, Sogang University takes part in the GIM to reinforce students' collaborations with colleagues around the world.

Describing the experience

Number of editions of experience that have been implemented

A small-scale pilot edition (involving only ESADE students) was implemented in the academic year 2012–2013 in order to rehearse the dynamics and functioning that were planned for the global edition. The first global edition was implemented in the academic year 2013–2014 and the second in the academic year 2014–2015.

Participants

Number and profile of students involved

The pilot local edition held in 2012–2013 involved the participation of eight students from three different ESADE programmes and four different nationalities. The innovative approach was already present in that pilot edition, and the inclusion of students from the Bachelor of Business Administration, the MSc and the MBA programmes enriched student learning experiences within the teams.

The first international edition held in 2013–2014 involved the participation of 74 students representing 24 different nationalities. Of these students, 33 of which were undergraduates, 26 came from diverse MSc programmes and 15 were studying an MBA; 39% of students were from ESADE, 31% came from NYU Stern, 11% from SDA Bocconi and 19% were from Sogang University.

The second international edition held in 2014–2015 involved the participation of 63 students; 32 of these students were undergraduates, while 15 came from different MSc programmes, and the remaining 16 were MBA students; 22% of the participants came from ESADE, 16% from SDA Bocconi, 22% were New York Stern students and 40% came from Sogang University.

Number and profile of faculty members involved

The team involved in the design and implementation of the project numbered 15 participants, including representatives of each of the business schools involved in the GIM. This included five project leaders (whose profile ranged from faculty members to directors of their school's management team, all of whom developed a leading role in the educational terrain of their institution), five members of an academic team at ESADE Business School (representing the different knowledge areas involved in the integrated resolution of the challenge proposed) and one project manager. Both project leaders and academic team formed the Academic Committee in charge of making final decisions regarding the design, implementation and assessment of the project. Furthermore, a team of four tutors, each one based at one of the participating institutions was formed. One PhD candidate from each partner school acted as a tutor and each of them was assigned a number of teams to supervise closely and their role was to be the first reference point for teams when doubts appeared or when it was the moment to submit any of the assignments proposed.

Ensuring adequate coordination and communication among the different members of the team have been key to the success of the experience and, aware of this, it was carefully planned and orchestrated. First, video-conference distance meetings were held between project leaders every two or three weeks to share views and reach agreements before and during the implementation of the project. The members of the ESADE academic team participated in some of these video-conference distance meetings (which therefore constituted Academic Committee meetings) whenever necessary, for example when assessing and grading students' performance. Email messaging was used before and after each of the meetings to share agendas and minutes of the meetings accordingly, something that proved a very helpful tool for coordination. Tutors held regular parallel meetings during the implementation of the GIM, and used a tutors' website to share materials and discuss approaches via an online forum, and they also participated in video-conference distance meetings at specific moments.

Description of the experience

The task

The GIM confronts students with the resolution of a challenge that is of current international social, political and economic relevance. The challenge is defined and proposed by the academic team and project leaders. Participating students are required to construct a personal and yet conceptually and practically justified action-oriented position that takes the form of a report that proposes recommendations for how companies, organizations and governments can make a difference in solving the challenge. For example, in the first two editions of GIM instructors proposed to students the challenge of presenting to companies, governments, NGOs and/or business schools recommendations regarding how companies can contribute to reducing economic inequality in the world (see Fig. 13.1).

The learning experience is based on collaborative dynamics where students work in diverse teams. Participating students have diverse academic backgrounds in undergraduate, Master of Science (MSc) and Master in Business Administration (MBA) programmes, in one of four business schools from across the globe: ESADE (Spain), NYU Stern (USA), SDA Bocconi (Italy) and Sogang University (South Korea). In this sense, the learning task and the need for students to work together within the constraints of different time zones and the consequent asynchronous coordination provide an excellent opportunity for them to become aware and experience the limitations experienced nowadays by multinational companies.

Figure 13.1 **The learning task**

Content and assignments

As can be seen in Figure 13.1, students were provided with material to address the challenge applying knowledge from three different perspectives, economics, people management and corporate social responsibility (CSR). A team of professors at ESADE created video lectures dealing with the main concepts from each of these fields of knowledge.

From the point of view of economics, students were provided with information regarding:

- How to define inequality from an economics perspective

- How to measure inequality

- The causes or drivers of inequality, taking into account economic policies, governments, social changes and globalization and, finally, economic elite

- The effects of inequality, at individual, social, cultural, political and economic levels of analysis

From a CSR perspective, students were informed about:

- How to define and measure inequality, including terms related to inequality

- Ways to promote equality at macro and micro levels

- Suggested methods to address inequality in their project
- Historical outlook on the importance of the state as an agent that promotes equality

As for people management, students were provided with information about:

- How people management policies and practices influence economic inequality
- What kind of contribution people management can make to resolve the problem on inequality
- The goals of the people management system, in terms of efficiency, fairness and compliance
- Equality vs. equity
- Differences in salaries, working conditions, benefits and labour opportunities and factors that influence these variations
- Perceptions of procedural justice, attributes of fair procedures and attitudes towards economic inequality

These lectures were complemented by an introductory video lecture on economic inequality in the world from the project leader at NYU Stern, as well as a video lecture on project management for international teams from the project leader at SDA Bocconi and an outline on creating shared value from the project leader at Sogang University.

To enhance their learning process we provided assignments that were designed to help students progress in the resolution of the challenge. These assignments constituted different drafts of the final deliverable to be submitted and so they provided opportunities to obtain feedback on their work.

Resources

In order to solve the challenge presented to them, teams have the following resources at their disposal:

- Introductory video lectures from three different fields of knowledge (people management, corporate social responsibility and economics)
- Suggested subtopics to address the general challenge of economic inequality (see Appendix 1)
- Readings and other materials provided by the committee and tutors (see Appendix 2)

- Access to their team's Virtual Studio, an online learning platform where they could work collaboratively to elaborate the various deliverables required before the submission of the final reports

Virtual workspace

The global aspect of the GIM makes online communication a key component of the learning experience. The project's learning ePlatform was created as an informative web space which serves as a base in which students have access to the necessary information and material for the project and external links to the participants' personal biography pages and each team's virtual studio. This ePlatform was created with the Moodle Learning Management System (LMS) because its open source nature was considered to allow for an easy transfer to other schools interested in incorporating the GIM in the curriculum of their programmes. The objective of catering for transferability is in line with the aim of the GMAC MET Fund of contributing to advance management education globally.

Each team is assigned to a specially designed web-based virtual studio where they are given an editing role allowing them full control to decide how, and for what purpose, their studio should be used. The objective of these studios is to enhance shared knowledge-construction and problem-solving among the members of the international teams. Moreover, the studios were equipped with tools allowing for effective intercontinental communication. Existing communication and document-sharing tools that students are familiar with and use regularly were linked to the virtual studios.

Assurance of learning results

The sections below present the different approaches applied and tools used to measure the students' attainment of the expected learning results.

Assurance of learning measurement

The assessment process involved the participation of all stakeholders collaborating in the project. Following specific rubrics gives participants' assurance of learning, as the grade that students received for team deliverables was the accumulation of grades assigned by project leaders and tutors from each of the business schools, as well as the academic team of professors at ESADE. The assessment breakdown, weight of each deliverable and stakeholders responsible for the evaluation of each assignment is detailed in Table 13.1.

Table 13.1 **Assessment breakdown of the GIM edition 2013–14**

	Who evaluated?	% of final grade	Detail of % distribution in deliverables	% break- down	Who evaluated?	Comments
Collaboration and development of tasks (individual focus)	Tutors	20%				Active participation in the virtual studio (including ice-breaker activities)
Collaboration in team work (individual focus)	Peers (peer and self-evaluation)	20%				
Deliverables: Final and preliminary reports/ presentations/ team working plan/reflection paper (group focus)	Tutors Committee	60%	Definition of scope of work	20%	Committee	The agreed-upon rubrics were applied across all the other tasks
			Team strategy plan	–	Committee	Team strategy plan was a requirement but was not graded
			Video progress report	10%	Tutors	
			Final team presentation	10%	Tutors	
			Final group report	20%	Committee	
			Final individual reflection paper	–	Committee	Reflection paper was a requirement but was not graded

Assessment rubrics were developed for each of the team deliverables and shared with students so they could see how their work would be graded. Students were given a grade out of a total of five for each of the criteria considered in the rubrics. After the assessment of each deliverable, the grades were analysed across all teams and they were ranked from the highest to the lowest obtained grade. Following the submission of the final deliverable, the evolution of the teams' overall scores was analysed and categorized according to their performance.

In order to assess students' collaboration in the project, students' final grades were also based on the peer and self-assessment questionnaires made available via the ePlatform in which they were asked to consider understanding of the topic as well as team dynamics. Furthermore, tutors were also required to provide a grade based on students' attitude and active participation in the project.[5] Table 13.2 presents the final report's rubric as an example of the rubrics applied.

Also, students were required to elaborate a final reflection paper (see Appendix 3) as a final task designed to elicit the reflection upon their learning experience.

To summarize: 60% of assessment was allocated to delivered project work, 20% to peer evaluations and 20% to tutor evaluation of individual students' attitude and participation.

Students' feedback on their learning experience

The results compiled in the following sections include the feedback obtained from students participating in the 2013–14 and 2014–15 editions of the Global Integrative Module via the final reflection paper (see Appendix 3). These comments were selected taking into consideration the frequency with which they were cited by students in their reflection papers.

Strengths of GIM

Working in international teams provided positive outcomes, especially regarding:

- The possibility of learning from diversity
- The richness derived from the different levels, views and perspectives of team members
- The richness of meeting and working with new people
- The possibility of developing skills for team work
- The chance to work across different time zones and the corporate atmosphere within the team

From a professional standpoint, the takeaways mentioned included:

- Becoming aware and managing the logistics of working in different time zones
- The perception of usefulness of the experience for professional life
- The acquisition of knowledge on economic inequality
- The experience of international collaboration and dealing with diversity
- The possibility of learning about project work/project management

5 More detail is provided in the GIM project website: http://www.esade.edu/gim/eng

Table 13.2 Assessment criteria (rubrics) applied in the GIM edition 2013–14 final report

Criteria	1	2	3	4	5	Comments
Conceptualization: Theory background Dealing with complexity	No understanding of the underlying theories and unable to grasp the complexity of the problem	Poor theoretical approach and low understanding of the complexity of the problem	Appropriate theoretical approach and limited understanding of the complexity of the problem	Good understanding of the underlying theories, which contributes to understanding the complexity of the problem	Insightful theoretical approach and discussion about the complexity of the problem. In-depth problem analysis helps discover the limits of the theory and provides ideas as to how to expand it	
Focus: Focus Economic inequality	Highly dispersed and lack of awareness of the relevant social issues at stake	Weak focus on relevant issues	Partial focus on relevant issues and some awareness of the companies' social responsibility	Focus on relevant issues and addresses basic questions about the companies' social responsibility	Highly focused and addresses very relevant issues about the companies' social responsibility	
Feasibility	The proposals cannot be produced or executed	Vague or unrealistic proposals with many questions about feasibility	Clear but rather unrealistic proposals with some questions about feasibility	Clear and quite realistic proposals with minor questions about feasibility	All proposals can be produced and executed affordably	
Quality of outputs: Final project	Quality is very poor/ deliverable is incomplete	Quality is poor and/or deliverable is not developed fully	Quality is appropriate but with room for improvement	High quality with room for some minor improvements	Excellent quality, creative editing	
Reflection: Individual Reflection Paper	Incomplete reflection	Lacks basic reflection	Appropriate reflection is provided	High quality, well-structured and offers a profound	Excellent quality, well-structured and offers a highly profound reflection	

From a personal standpoint, the takeaways mentioned were the same as in the professional standpoint plus the richness of forming new friendships and developing flexibility to work effectively in a virtual team. Some of the feedback from students, obtained from their reflection papers or the end of course survey, is quoted below:

> This project has been an exciting and interactive opportunity which gave me the opportunity to apply hard and soft skills and reflect on a fundamental issue, such as economic inequality (MSc student at SDA Bocconi).

> I am motivated to work with different people, different backgrounds, universities and cities around the world (MSc student at ESADE).

> It has opened my eyes to the actual problem of inequality that exists. Being the business leaders of tomorrow, it's much easier now to start working after this (MBA student at ESADE).

> Professionally, this has been a valuable experience on understanding how different people from different cultures work. It is inevitable and important to work internationally in the future. Having this experience prepared me for what to expect and how to handle situations that may arise (undergraduate student at NYU Stern).

> I'd love to work in a global firm that has branches all over the world and the experience to work with virtual team through online communication has helped me to deal with the problems with time delay and cultural difference (undergraduate student at Sogang University).

> The course helps me prepare to enhance my future career progression and improve professional competence. As globalization becomes more prevalent, companies are trying to increase cultural diversity within the workforce. Through the GIM, I got to work interculturally and work in online virtual team (MBA student at Sogang University).

Our practitioner commentator Dr Gessi reinforces the value of the GIM experience by urging students to make the most of all the initiatives offered, as the GIM helps them to open up to the world and leave their comfort zone. Once they begin a career, they will have to compete in a global market that, today more than ever, offers great opportunities for them to distinguish themselves to those who really deserve them. In the digital era talent can achieve maximum visibility, but at the same time there is more competition than ever before. Hence, universities and business schools should integrate in their academic courses "global and learning collaboration" programmes, designed to train the managers of the future and help them interact with companies, so as to engage them in the development and, most importantly, the implementation of these programmes.

Areas for improving the students' learning experience

As detailed in the previous section, and based on the issues most frequently mentioned by students in their reflection papers, while working in an international

Table 13.3 **Areas of improvement, suggestions and solutions**

Areas of improvement	Obstacles (feedback from 2013–14 edition)	Student solutions/ suggestions	Coordination team solutions for 2014–15 edition
Student team coordination	Establishing fruitful coordination among the team members was complex, as was finding an appropriate communication tool	*Implemented solution:* Appointment of a team leader and division of roles and tasks	Students were requested to communicate the name of their team leader one week after the beginning the module
Dealing with different time zones	Finding a suitable time for meeting and setting deadlines proved challenging	*Implemented solution:* Find consensus among all team members regarding the communication means or tools to be used	Students were provided with further communication/ coordination tools, e.g. Facebook page and Google Drive in addition to the forum available on the ePlatform
Communication	There was little contact between students, tutors, coordinators and the academic team between deliverables	*Suggestion:* Tutors become more involved, via online or face-to-face sessions	Communication between students and tutors, coordinators, and the academic team between deliverables was encouraged and enhanced Tutors were provided with a more proactive role on the ePlatform via the forum Optional weekly face-to-face tutorials were introduced at each of the different schools Synchronous sessions with the academic team were held via the forum on the ePlatform
Different levels of commitment among the participating students	The GIM did not have the same weight in the final assessment of students in the courses proposed in the different schools	*Suggestion:* Make students aware of the different levels of participation from the beginning of the module	The conditions whereby the GIM was proposed were changed to make participation elective in all schools Encourage students at all times to get in contact with the coordinators should any members of their team cease to participate effectively Create a more active presence of the coordinators on the ePlatforms and other communication tools

Areas of improvement	Obstacles (feedback from 2013–14 edition)	Student solutions/ suggestions	Coordination team solutions for 2014–15 edition
Varying academic schedules	Adapting to the different academic calendars, including holidays and exam weeks, was difficult	*Suggestion:* Start and end the module on the same day at all of the schools. Have a common academic calendar	The start and end dates were made common to all schools and students were provided with a clear timeline of the module and the deliverables required, including a fully detailed calendar in which all holidays and exam weeks of each of the participating business schools are noted

team was a positive learning experience, it was also a source of challenge. Table 13.3 details: a) the issues that students participating in the first international edition emphasized as being the most challenging ones; b) the solutions that students suggested and/or put into practice in order to overcome these obstacles; and c) the solutions put forward by the coordinators during the second international implementation of the module.

Academic Committee reflection on the experience

This section details the Academic Committee's key learnings and team process reflections.

Making the learning experience possible

In general, the GIM has been an enriching experience from which the team involved has learned a lot. The main learnings can be defined as follows:

- The value of true teamwork among the faculty participating in the learning experience. Confidence, trust and flexibility are a must to ensure the kind of shared decision-making that is necessary for a project like this to advance and improve with each new edition. Such trust, confidence and flexibility resulted from the orchestration of coordination among the different actors involved, which we referred to in the section. on faculty participants, above.

- The importance of producing up-to-date and relevant academic material (guidelines, video lectures, assessment rubrics and so on) and a how-to handbook specifically designed to present an explicit layout of everything that a business school would need to know and put into action in order to start offering the GIM as a learning experience for their students.

- The need for well-designed and implemented ePlatforms. For practical purposes, it is key that, when designing eLearning tools, they are accessible and compatible with the ICT systems of each of the business schools partners. On the other hand, the ePlatforms should integrate existing social networks as well as communication and document-sharing tools so as to facilitate interaction between participants in a user friendly way. Considering all the aforementioned elements we managed to ensure the assimilation of the GIM eLearning Platform into the other schools' systems. All the management involved with the ePlatform was centralized from ESADE's ICT team; stakeholders from other schools (students, tutors and project leaders) used an ESADE account to access it.

Main challenges and strategies used to overcome them

Some of the challenges faced and the strategies that we followed to overcome them can be divided into the following two dimensions:

Institutional dimension:

- The challenge of finding strategic support to make this project a reality was a crucial one. The submission of the project to the i2i Challenge was the strategy that allowed us to access the funding from the GMAC MET Fund award.

- The challenge of sharing a common institutional vision was vital when identifying the right partners to develop this innovative project. The strategy of using personal networking was essential to be able to count on the institutional vision of each of the potential partners. And it was particularly important to have the support of the ESADE President and the Business School Dean, as well as of the Deans from the partner schools.

Academic dimension:

- The challenge of finding the right balance between conceptual rigour and value-added practice when proposing the task for students to solve, given the time and energy constraints students face during programmes, and also given the truly challenging nature of the learning experience was addressed thanks to the strategy of orchestrating coordination detailed above.

- The challenge of reaching a consensus on the start and end of the project/ course, due to the varying academic calendars and administrative requirements of the different participating schools was also addressed via the orchestrating coordination strategy.

- The challenge of finding agreement on the number and characteristics of the tools applied to measure students' learning, given the complex nature of the processes and the need to find a balance between the amount of information obtained (the more the better) and sustainability (we should avoid loading students with unnecessary added work so only the essential surveys or tasks were considered), was also addressed via the orchestrating coordination strategy. Coordination of the academic calendars of each of the four schools involved as well as the knowledge acquired from the implementation of the local and the first international edition also contributed to resolving this challenge.

Implications for educational practice

In this section we present the key success factors and the key recommendations for those schools interested in introducing a module such as GIM in their curricula. Our involvement in the design and implementation of the Global Integrative Module has been a fascinating experience from which we have learned a lot. As possible guidelines for those schools interested in incorporating a similar course in the curriculum of any of their programmes as a learning experience capable of providing students with an opportunity to contribute to the PRME endeavour, there follows a list of factors we consider key to the success of the experience and a list of recommendations.

Key factors for the success of this experience

Considering the insights of all stakeholders (students, academic committee, tutors) we would like to emphasize the following key success factors:

- Reaching a shared understanding of the GIM project's role in each of the business school participants' courses, specifically regarding the level of commitment or dedication required of students.

- Establishing a dynamic of true teamwork among the faculty (project leaders, academics, tutors and coordination) participating in the project.

- Clearly and explicitly sharing with students the objectives and methodology of GIM, together with making all resources available from day one of the course.

- Designing academic materials with a variety of elements to enhance their learning experience, including guidelines for each deliverable and rubrics for each assessment method.

Key recommendations for schools

First, acknowledging the level of dedication required from a faculty perspective is key to the successful design and implementation of a learning experience such as the one proposed in the GIM. The time and energy investment may be considerably more important during the planning stage and this must be taken into account when forming the team of coordinators and professors at the school leading the experience.

We would suggest that schools consider the possibility of gradually implementing the course by beginning with a small-scale pilot edition before moving on to the global experience. In this respect, we suggest starting with a local edition including students from the same school before progressing to an international edition. Depending on the number of faculty available to take part in this experience, one could even consider proposing this as an elective course in one sole programme, controlling the scope by limiting the number of students participating in the experience.

Tables 13.4 and 13.5 provide more details for planning a small-scale pilot edition and a global edition, respectively.

Table 13.4 **Internal planning**

		Recruitment of internal support
Year 1	Selection of coordination team	Two full-time staff members involved in educational innovation who must be able to dedicate the required time to the project. A part-time project assistant must be recruited to provide essential support in project day-to-day management tasks
	Selection of academic team	The faculty selected should be experts in each of the knowledge fields students will need to take into account when solving the challenge. Furthermore, it would be positive if they have previously been involved innovative educational projects
	Selection of ePlatform developer	An open source learning management system (LMS) is advised so as to ensure ease of implementation and potentiality for access from other business schools

Another key condition has to do with whether the school, its students and its faculty are ready to embark on a project that will pull them out of their comfort zone. This was important to bear in mind when identifying and selecting possible partners.

From our perspective and in light of our experience, it is essential to manage change gradually, in such a way that the actors involved find the necessary scaffolding to experience the project within their zone of proximal development, thus ensuring the fruitfulness of the experience (Vigotsky, 1978; Zimmerman, 1990). Details of the evolution of the GIM at ESADE are presented in Appendix 4.

Table 13.5 **External planning**

		Partner business schools
Year 2	Selection of business school partners	Schools whose mission refers to training students to become socially responsible leaders
	Selection of project leaders	Faculty members should have been involved in educational innovation and should be engaging in some way or other in courses dealing with social corporate responsibility or project management
Year 3	Organization of face-to-face meetings	Project leaders should participate in face-to-face coordination meetings at the school leading the experience where important executive decisions can be taken and the sense of community among the team starts to be constructed
	Organization of online distance meetings	Project leaders at the participating schools must hold online distance meetings fortnightly throughout the academic years to plan and follow the international editions and deal with any challenges that may arise

Postscript: The value of the GIM for future managers

This section features Dr Gianmarco Gessi's views on the ways in which the GIM can contribute to the formation of future managers. Dr Gessi mentions that academics, economists, managers and entrepreneurs have been debating on globalization for years, some to acclaim its benefits, others to emphasize its drawbacks.

> Businesses that pursue success on a global scale must invest in their employees, developing their digital skills, i.e. their ability to interact, operate, learn and communicate effectively and efficiently within a context where spatial, temporal, linguistic and cultural barriers no longer exist. People are therefore required to act in a world that is really "global", in the sense that it has no boundaries, although this is true only virtually. As for the future, besides businesses, universities and business schools will also play a key role.

Dr Gessi comments that he learned about the Global Integrative Module programme when he was the Head of the Organization, Information Systems and Human Resources Department of a banking group undergoing the digitization process. He thought that the academic world was finally experimenting with something truly innovative to train the new generations, the future managers, in solving highly complex and practical business issues, resorting to a digital, border-free organizational model; a model within a "global" context where young people of different backgrounds, ages, languages and education levels were called upon to work together and produce high quality output within a challenging timeframe.

Based on the way it has been structured, he thinks, the GIM is a training and organizational experience that meets the need to develop the digital-global skills and culture that companies are already seeking or will be seeking in the near future. The value of the project lies in its experimenting with a new organizational paradigm, in the broad sense of the word, as well as in the content of the issues that the students are asked to address, whose significance in today's business environment is undeniable.

> The great opportunity that the initiative offers students is to use their creativity, put their knowledge to use, acquire new information and boost their "intellectual energy", coming out of the comfort zone in which their culture, mind set and habitual modus operandi risk confining them. It will enrich them with a very powerful, priceless intellectual and human experience.

> The GIM is an excellent experimental programme. Its limit lies in the fact that, for the moment, it is only experimental! My hope is that the academic world will adopt this educational methodology in a more pervasive and structured manner, integrating it within its study programmes. All graduates in Business Administration should take a "global learning and collaboration" course. Also, for full success of this type of programme, it would be essential for universities and business schools to liaise with the world of enterprises on a consistent basis, so as to understand their needs, stimulate them, support them if necessary, and engage them.

According to the PRME Principle 3 to create environments that enable effective learning experiences for responsible leaders, the GIM was designed to inspire and prepare global-minded individuals to become highly competent and innovative professionals within a continuously changing and globalized society. By sharing decision-making methodologies and information search through strategic ICT use, students were required to go beyond reflection and elaborate a personal and yet conceptually practical justified position on a specific matter, by producing a technical report which had to answer some specific questions. Consequently, the experience drove students into the development of competences to collaborate in the construction of a community of practice (simulation of professional consultancy situation) in virtual and international environments, making the most out of the opportunities at their disposal. To summarize, the GIM offers an innovative learning process for future responsible leaders that allows students to feel capable of confronting and successfully solving social and economic problems, no matter how complex these might be.

References

EUR-Lex (2006). Reform of the universities in the framework of the Lisbon strategy. Retrieved from http://eur-lex.europa.eu/legal-content/EN/TXT/?uri=uriserv:c11078

Gielen, S., Dochy, F. & Dierick, S. (2003). Evaluating the consequential validity of new modes of assessment: The influence of assessment on learning, including pre-, post- and true assessment effects. In M. Segers, F. Dochy & E. Cascallar (Eds.), *Optimising New Modes of Assessment: In Search of Qualities and Standards* (pp. 37-54). Dordrecht: Kluwer Academic.

Monereo, C. & Castelló, M. (2009). La evaluación como herramienta de cambio educativo: evaluar las evaluaciones. In C. Monereo (Ed.), *PISA como excusa: Repensar la evaluación para cambiar la enseñanza*. Barcelona: Graó.

Vigotsky, L.S. (1978). *Mind in Society: The Development of Higher Psychological Processes*. Cambridge, MA: Harvard University Press.

Wiggins, G. (1990). The case for authentic assessment. *Practical Assessment, Research & Evaluation*, 2(2). Retrieved from http://PAREonline.net/getvn.asp?v=2&n=2

Zimmerman, B.J. (1990). Self-regulated learning and academic achievement: An overview. *Educational Psychologist*, 25(1), 3-17.

Appendix 1. Suggested subtopics to address the general challenge of economic inequality

Gender inequality:

- Gender inequality

- Are job evaluation systems "gender neutral"?

Education inequality:

- Economic inequality due to differing educational opportunities

Wage inequality:

- Analyse some critical aspects in the deepening of the wage gap

- Wage inequality (workers and managers)

- Should companies introduce a cap in top executives' compensation?

- Should companies have a minimum wage policy at company level?

Economic inequality effects:

- The relationship between inequality and economic growth

- A study on the inequality of rural and urban incomes

- Inequality within countries

- Inequality between countries

- A cross-national analysis on social causes of suicide: the effects of economic inequality

- Inequality between conglomerates and SMEs (small and medium-sized enterprises) in some countries

Managers' skills:

- What are the skills that managers should possess in order to make their organizations contribute to an economically equal environment?

Appendix 2. Readings and other materials provided

Core readings

Economics:
Alvaredo, F., Atkinson, A.B., Piketty, T. & Saez, E. (2013). The top 1 percent in international and historical perspective. *Journal of Economic Perspectives*, 27(3), 3-20.
Levy, F. & Temin, P. (2007). *Inequality and Institutions in 20th Century America*. NBER Working Paper No. 13106. Cambridge, MA: National Bureau of Economic Research.
Piketty, T. & Saez, E. (2006). *The Evolution of Top Incomes*. NBER Working Paper No. 11955. Cambridge, MA: National Bureau of Economic Research.

Sociology and corporate social responsibility:
Antonacopolou, E.P. (2010). Making the business school more "critical": Reflexive critique based on phronesis as a foundation for impact. *British Journal of Management*, 21, S6-S25.
Cavero, T. & Poinasamy, K. (2013). *A Cautionary Tale: The True Cost of Austerity and Inequality in Europe*. Oxfam Briefing Paper. Oxford: Oxfam International.
de Sebastián, L. (2000, January 24). The plea against economic inequality. *El País*.
Fuentes-Nieva, R. & Galasso, N. (2014). *Working for the Few. Political Capture and Economic Inequality*. Oxfam Briefing Paper. Oxford: Oxfam International.
Gilman-Sevcik, T. & Statler, M. (2012). What does it mean to occupy? *Continent*, 5(1), 39-42.
Klugman, J. (2010). Innovations in measuring inequality and poverty. In *Human Development Report 2010. The Real Wealth of Nations: Pathways to Human Development* (pp. 85-100). New York: United Nations Development Programme.
Porter, M.E. & Kramer, M.R. (2011). Creating shared value. *Harvard Business Review*, January-February, 1-17.
Shaheen, F. (2011). *Ten Reasons to Care about Economic Inequality*. New Economics Foundation (NEF) Briefing. London: NEF.

People management:
Berry, D. & Bell, M.P. (2012). Inequality in organizations: Stereotyping, discrimination, and labor law exclusions. *Equality, Diversity and Inclusion: An International Journal*, 31(3), 236-248.
International Labour Organization (2008, June 10). *ILO Declaration on Social Justice for a Fair Globalization*. Geneva: ILO.

International Labour Organization (2015). *Global Wage Report 2014/15: Wages and Income Inequality.* Geneva: ILO.

Morand, D.A. & Merriman, K.K. (2012). "Equality Theory" as a counterbalance to equity theory in human resource management. *Journal of Business Ethics*, 111, 133-144.

Complementary readings

Acker, J. (2006). Inequality regimes: Gender, class, and race in organizations. *Gender & Society*, 20(4), 441-464.

Aquino, K. (1995). Relationships among pay inequity, perceptions of procedural justice, and organizational citizenship. *Employee Responsibilities and Rights Journal*, 8(1), 21-33.

Castilla, E.J. (2011). Bringing managers back in: Managerial influences on workplace inequality. *American Sociological Review*, 76(5), 667-694.

International Food Policy Research Institute (2014). *Global Hunger Index: The Challenge of Hidden Hunger.* Washington, DC: IFPRI.

McGauran, A.M. (2001). Masculine, feminine or neutral? In-company equal opportunities policies in Irish and French MNC retailing. *International Journal of Human Resource Management*, 12(5), 754-771.

Zentner, E. & Campbell, P. (2014, September 22). Inequality and consumption. *US Economics*. New York: Morgan Stanley.

Appendix 3. The final individual reflection paper guideline

Final individual reflection paper

Objectives	
Produce a final reflection on your learning experience in the project in terms of the content	
Produce a final reflection on your learning experience so far in the project in terms of team dynamics	
Evaluate your own performance and that of your team mates so far in working in culturally diverse teams	
Content	
Reflection on the topic	How has your understanding of the topic changed since the start of the GIM? In what areas do you feel you have developed your knowledge most? Has anything in particular surprised you? Which of the cases you focused on proved most relevant?
Reflection on team dynamics	How efficiently has your team worked together? Did all members fulfil their assigned role? What have been the main advantages of working in your culturally diverse team? What have been the main challenges of working in your culturally diverse team? How were conflicts within the group resolved? Looking back, what would you have done differently, if anything?
Reflection on personal + professional experience	In what ways has the GIM contributed to your learning on a personal level (i.e. working interculturally, working in online virtual teams)? In what ways has the GIM contributed to your learning on a professional level (i.e. working interculturally, working in online virtual teams)?
Reflection on the module	What aspects of the course do you feel should be changed? What aspects of the course did you like most? Is there anything that you feel was missing from the course?

Appendix 4. Evolution in the implementation of GIM

Local edition 2012–2013

October–January	Preparation of academic material and online ePlatforms		Online distance coordination meetings
	Selection of ESADE-based tutor		
January	Recruitment of students	MBA	Elective
		MSc	Elective
		Undergraduate	Embedded in the dissertation course
February–May	Module	2 Teams	
		3 Team deliverables	
		70% online	
		30% face-to-face (tutorials)	
May	Collection and analysis of students' feedback and incorporation into the planning of the 1st international edition of GIM		

1st international edition 2013–2014

October–January	Preparation of academic material and online ePlatforms		Online distance coordination meetings
	Selection of tutors (1 per business school)		
January	Recruitment of students	ESADE	MBA and MSC elective course
		NYU Stern	Embedded in undergraduate Experiential Learning Seminar course
		SDA Bocconi	Embedded in MSc Project Management course
		Sogang	MBA and undergraduate elective course
	Provision of ESADE usernames	Non-ESADE students required a username and password to enter the online ePlatform	
February–May	Module	12 teams	
		4 team deliverables and 2 individual deliverables	
		95% online	
		5% face-to-face (opening session)	
May	Collection and analysis of students' feedback and incorporation into the planning of the 2nd international edition of GIM		

2nd international edition 2014–2015

October–January	Preparation of academic material and online ePlatforms		Online distance coordination meetings
	Selection/Confirmation of tutors (1 per business school)		
January	Recruitment of students	ESADE	MBA and MSC elective course
		NYU Stern	Undergraduate elective course
		SDA Bocconi	Embedded in Project Management course
		Sogang	MBA and undergraduate elective course
	Provision of ESADE usernames	Non-ESADE students required a username and password to enter the online ePlatform	
March – May	Module	10 teams	
		2 team deliverables and 2 individual deliverables	
		70% online	
		30% face-to-face (opening session)	
May	Gathering of students' feedback		

14

Management education and social class
Can managers do more to encourage social equality and meritocracy in the workplace?

Kristi Lewis Tyran and Joseph E. Garcia
College of Business & Economics, Western Washington University, USA

with practitioner commentary by Debbie Ahl
Edgewater Advising, USA

Introduction

Discrimination related to social class exists in organizations (Ashley and Empson, 2013), and is often justified by prioritizing the need for employees to have social capital and networks to achieve business success. The "myth" of meritocracy (Lipsey, 2015) assumes free and easy access to social mobility, but class divides are often the result of structural barriers that prevent individuals from moving upward in the social class system.

Globally, social class divides are historical and still difficult to challenge. University education is commonly seen as a path towards upward mobility. In the UK, the path from primary to secondary to university education has, in the past, been clearly and persistently driven by a student's social class (Boliver, 2011). While recent efforts to widen higher education participation have increased university applications from poorer families, challenging this historical norm is still difficult. In the United States, many university students—especially students from more privileged backgrounds—believe the "myth of meritocracy" and are not aware that they are privileged in their social class or that social class is an issue at all (Martin, 2012).

Social class is ubiquitous and it impacts how people interact, how resources are allocated and how organizations identify, select and promote talent (Baker, 2010; Kogan, 2007). It also impacts the way different industries operate and how they identify and treat customers and employees. For example, as a general rule the financial services sector largely operates at a higher class level (middle or upper) than the construction industry, with manual labourers who are largely working class participants. This impacts the structure and culture of firms in their respective sectors.

In this chapter, we argue for raising awareness of social equality and meritocracy as core elements of social justice. With the gap between wealthy and poor individuals expanding and with more attention being paid to social justice issues, and in particular, social class inequities, we contend that management educators have a responsibility to include social class in the curriculum. In this discussion, we define social justice as the moral obligation to work towards equal opportunities for all individuals (Gaetane *et al.*, 2009).

Increasing awareness of social class may facilitate the development of managers who empathize and understand the perpetuation of social stratification that can occur in organizations, and help them in their efforts to succeed through gathering the best and brightest employees. These efforts must be coordinated with practitioners, as education without validation at the organizational level will falter. In this chapter, in addition to the academic voices of the first two authors, Kristi Lewis Tyran and Joe Garcia, the former CEO of Sterling Life Insurance, Debbie Ahl, provides commentary on how integrating attention to social class in management education might well affect organizations and their managers in the future.

While we do not claim that social class is not currently discussed in management courses, in our review of four leading introductory textbooks (Griffin and Moorhead, 2014; Nahavandi *et al.*, 2015; Nelson and Quick, 2015; Robbins and Judge, 2015) and three leading managing diversity textbooks (Bell 2012; Cañas and Sondak, 2014; and Harvey and Allard, 2015) we found just one instance of a treatment of social class that went beyond a mere mention of the phenomenon. That these leading textbooks remain rather silent on the issue is worthy of conversation as social class impacts organizational life in many ways. We believe that ignoring social class is a disservice to our students and the organizations they will work in and lead as they will have little understanding of how organizations perpetuate class systems and create barriers to entry for new talent or underutilize existing talent.

We will argue that even though social class is not a "protected class" (Hemphill *et al.*, 2012), it is a relevant aspect of identity that we as management educators should address in preparing the managers of the future, despite the fact that popular organizational behaviour textbooks are silent on the topic (Colquitt *et al.*, 2015; Griffin and Moorhead, 2014; Nahavandi *et al.*, 2015; Nelson and Quick, 2015; Robbins and Judge, 2015; Uhl-Bein *et al.*, 2014).

The specific responsible management behaviours that we advocate in this chapter relate directly to the six Principles for Responsible Management Education (PRME) and are driven directly by Principle 1: Purpose, which states "we will develop the capabilities of students to be future generators of sustainable value for business and society at large and to work for an inclusive and *sustainable global economy*" (emphasis added). Our recommendations, based on Bloom's taxonomy, are designed to help management students recognize their moral responsibilities to ensure everyone has access to equal economic, political and social rights and opportunities; in other words, to promote social justice in their organizations and with the individuals they interact with (Anderson and Krathwohl, 2001; Bloom *et al.*, 1956).

In the following sections, we first discuss the current state of issues related to social class globally. We then discuss the relationship between diversity and social class—this is a complex relationship, not a simple one. We then talk about how social class relates to responsible management and provide suggestions for how management educators can responsibly address issues of social class in responsible management education. Finally, we provide a practitioner's view. Debbie Ahl, former CEO of Sterling Life Insurance Company, provides a perspective on the importance of responsible management education in addressing issues of social class as a way to expand social mobility opportunities in organizations.

The current state of social class globally

Income and social inequality in every country and culture is historical and richly studied in the disciplines of sociology, psychology and anthropology. These inequalities go back thousands of years. To begin our discussion of the relevance of the role of social class in management education, exploring the findings in other disciplines provides a solid base for our recommendations.

Social class is defined by sociology and psychology researchers Kraus and Keltner (2013, p. 247) as "a social category that is defined by an individual's access to available material resources (e.g. education, income, social capital) and perceptions of rank in society relative to others". Psychologists view social class as a relatively stable individual characteristic, corresponding to such resources as income, education and profession, wherein individuals have subjective perceptions of their own and others' rank in terms of social status (Cote *et al.*, 2013; Kraus *et al.*, 2012). Social class has different relationships with social constructs depending on the global context (Hamamura, 2012). Research has found social class is associated with multiple factors, including lifestyle choice (Petev, 2013), generalized trust (Hamamura, 2012), moral judgement (Cote *et al.*, 2013), and access to higher education (Boliver, 2011).

In contrast to common belief, social mobility (movement from one socioeconomic class to another) is actually very limited in most societies. When surveyed,

80% of US respondents said that they believed that anyone—regardless of family or community of birth—could be where they were today. However, a longitudinal study of family income over time found that 53.3% of families in the lowest income quintile stayed there between 1988 and 1998 (Bradbury and Katz, 2002). During that time, only 10.7% actually experienced social mobility to the highest two quintiles. In addition, they found that 53.2% of those in the highest income quintile stayed there during the same time period. More discouraging, only 6% of individuals born into the lowest quintile are able to achieve movement to the highest quintile (Fahy, 2015). According to Fahy, "the odds of reaching the top 5 percent of income earners is **less than 2%** for anyone starting out in the bottom 3 quintiles" (2015, p. 184; original emphasis).

Improving socioeconomic status mobility is often attempted through improving access to education, but we argue here that more mobility can be achieved through the workplace if managers are proactive in addressing how social status creates differential access to opportunity, leading to inequality (Bolivar, 2011). Managers can support more mobility by providing opportunities to employees of all social class levels. Managers will only do this if awareness is increased, partly through responsible management education.

More specifically, management educators can draw attention to social class issues for future managers, encouraging social class mobility through discussions of social justice, and linking issues of social justice to increased mobility from lower to middle to higher social class. This is reinforced by understanding the consequences for social class in terms of occupational opportunities, social networks, professional skills and self-efficacy regarding skills and abilities (Fahy, 2015). Higher socioeconomic status—and the privilege that comes with this status—has consequential advantages that often go unnoticed by those who have spent their lives with that higher social class privilege. Increasing awareness of privilege for university students will have benefits for organizations in the future. For example, university students who go on to be managers will be more sensitive to the impact of social class and be better prepared to guarantee access to opportunities for all employees.

Diversity and social class

In this section, we introduce the topic of diversity into our discussion. Organizational diversity and social class intersect in so far as class is a concept that describes the stratification of people within an economic system. Diverse members of specific categories of people or identity groups (e.g. ethnic, racial, gender, ability, age) are not distributed evenly across levels of the economic hierarchy, with some groups being more likely to experience poverty, discrimination and lack of access to education. As a consequence, group membership is correlated with social class status and the associated access to opportunities and resources. However, the correlation is not perfect and as Ellis Cose (1993) documented in the case of African Americans, it is not unusual for members of a specific group to be misidentified on the basis of class. For example, while in the US African-Americans are dispropor-tionally represented in the lower economic strata of society, individuals such as Oprah Winfrey, Barack Obama, Condoleezza Rice and Colin Powell could not legiti-mately be described as members of the lower class. However, they run the risk of being viewed and responded to as a member of a lower social class, a social identity group, by a bystander who met them out of context on the street. This phenom-enon is not limited to race, however, as it occurs in relation to gender (e.g. females being assumed to have lower level positions in an organization) and with members of selected ethnic groups who experience being stereotyped into low level service positons and hence lower class status in spite of real membership in the middle class or higher (Bell and Nkomo, 2001).

This correlational relationship adds complexity to the issue of how social class operates in society in a way that challenges organizational leaders and management educators to be more mindful of social class and identity group membership(s). Managers would be well advised to be aware of the fact that what social class and social identity group membership seem to have in common is that both are linked to a person's access to resources and opportunities and privilege (Thomas and Azmitia, 2014).

Additional complexity is generated by the fact that individuals have phenotype characteristics (e.g. skin colour, facial features) that are synonymous with group membership and are in public view and undeniable, versus other equally impor-tant social identity/cultural characteristics (e.g. sexual orientation, religion) that an individual can privately manage (Cox, 1993). For example, diversity models by Loden (1996) and Gardenswartz and Rowe (1994) conceptualize an individual's more static and public characteristics as deeper personal elements (e.g. personal-ity, age, ethnicity, race, gender) at the core and more fluid characteristics, such as income and occupation, which contribute to social class at a relatively more super-ficial level. More recent work, however, has challenged this framework and places more static and public characteristics at the surface and more fluid but organi-zationally relevant characteristics as deep organizational identity characteristics (Tyran and Gibson, 2008). For example, Cena *et al.* (2002) state that SES (socioeco-nomic status), or class, primarily depends on occupation, income and educational attainment (Nickens, 1995) and that race and class status are conflated as they fre-quently co-occur and together are the determinants of health, occupational and other significant experiences. Darvin and Norton (2014, p.114) further argue that:

> Social class, however, is more complex than socioeconomic status and can no longer be understood as simply a person's relation to the means of production. While social class has always been recognized as an economic position, it has also increasingly been regarded as a cultural process, marked by consumption patterns, identity formations, and bodily attributes like accent, behavior, and dress (Kelly, 2012, cited in Darvin and Norton, 2014).

Which of these interpretations of the role of class in understanding identity should be accepted—surface versus deep—remains open to debate. Indeed, it may be best interpreted in a particular social context, as social class may operate as both static and fluid in actual situations.

At the practical level, there are many social class indicators. Kraus *et al.* (2012) describe how social class can be identified in terms of various attributes and behaviours (e.g. wealth, education, dress, personal hygiene, healthcare practices, leisure activities, social club memberships, language style, accent and grammar usage), access to information that represents social capital (e.g. knowledge of music, the arts, sports, the economy and politics) and relationships (e.g. associations with significant individuals) which signify an individual's place within a social hierarchy.

An alternative approach to addressing this complexity is the concept of intersectionality, defined as the study of the processes and impacts of membership in multiple groups that have been exploited and/or marginalized (Cole, 2008; Settles, 2006).[1] Therefore, in the United States context, gender and race can lead to differential results. While an African-American female and a Caucasian female have some similar identity-based commonalities, they are manifested differently; the African-American female has to incorporate what it means to be black in addition to what it means to be female in a society where race and gender are differentially associated with privilege and hence class (Bell and Nkomo, 2001). As an example, an African-American female has the special opportunity to be selected as the "diversity" representative for both females and African-Americans in committees in organizations where diversity is being sought. This is an added, and unjust, burden as the African-American female is being asked to serve as the representative for both groups where that would not be the case for white females. In other words, race and gender both matter and they both have the potential to impact social class. Ignoring class is problematic because the individual experience of access to privilege is impacted by class membership and attenuated or enhanced by characteristics such as race and gender. In recognition of these issues, instead of assuming a uniform model of the human experience in organizations, management educators can highlight the nuanced complexities associated with social class and multiple identity affiliations in the workplace.

Furthermore, these complexities are amplified by the ongoing demographic shifts in the labour market via the movement of people across borders and the resulting impact on the composition of the workforce. We argue that management educators need to be cognizant of the impact of these new workers, who are most frequently taking jobs at the lower levels of the socioeconomic class spectrum (e.g. agricultural labour, domestic work, service jobs) and who bring with them cultural traditions, religious affiliations, experiences and world-views that create a more heterogeneous workplace than was previously the case (Farnsworth Riche and Mor Barak, 2014). To this end, management educators should have a firm grasp of the

1 Definition of "intersectionality" from Definitions.net. Retrieved from http://www.definitions.net/definition/intersectionality

role migration plays in workforce composition as well as its broader societal effects and integrate into the curriculum material that addresses developing intercultural competences and frameworks for enhancing inclusion as a strategic approach to managing diversity.

Social class as it relates to responsible management

In this section we identify three key issues related to social class and management: hiring, training and development, and managing employees. We provide suggestions for how managers can advocate for positive change in the workplace with regards to social class related to these three key managerial responsibilities.

Managers influence everything in organizations, from hiring to training programmes to promotion and development opportunities. Successful responsible management includes achieving goals and objectives that help organizational success. This success in part comes from responsibly hiring, developing and managing employees. Responsible managers want employees to succeed. They see the potential for success in all applicants, even potential that is not obviously there, and they help each employee achieve their potential by developing their unique strengths, as well as addressing weaknesses associated with social class background through mentoring and training (Thomas and Gabarro, 1999).

Managers hire employees using many criteria. *Responsible* managers understand that the wrong criteria may exclude qualified candidates because of their social class background. For example, managers may use strict educational criteria or high-level references when screening applicants. If managers only consider applicants from certain types of schools (i.e. Ivy League in the US, Russell Group in the UK), then they may inadvertently exclude many qualified lower social class applicants who likely had fewer opportunities to gain entry into elite universities (Armstong and Hamilton, 2013; Larew, 2008; Sacks, 2003).

Managers often ask, "How will this person fit in to our culture?" Questions of organizational "fit" often justify hiring people who are just like those doing the hiring, and while discrimination on surface diversity (i.e. gender, race, age) may be consciously avoided, subconscious attention to fit may lead to cultural reproduction and excluding people of a different social class. In addition, professionalism is a set of skills that is often important in successful job applicants and thus is used as a screening tool by managers. The extent to which professionalism can be learned (for example, in a professionalism training seminar) is ignored, disadvantaging many applicants with high potential who because of their social class did not have opportunities to learn or practise professionalism. Written and interpersonal communication skills are often judged based on middle and upper class norms that some individuals may not be familiar with. These skills can be improved through training and practice in the workplace.

Once a person is hired, there are many issues related to social class that can affect a person's performance at work. For example, conditions associated with lower social class can influence employee success as individuals cope with more stress in their daily lives (Reuss, 2008). Social class affects the availability of social safety nets that provide help with issues ranging from caring for a sick child to dependence on public transportation or a low quality vehicle. Many individuals need multiple jobs to make ends meet, and this can affect work performance (Ehrenreich, 2001).

Based on our review of the literature, we have several recommendations for developing managers who are more responsible and responsive to issues of social class:

- **Hiring**:

    Responsible managers will consider a more extensive, open and detailed evaluation of applicants where criteria that may be biased by social class background are either eliminated or critically evaluated (Hewlett *et al.*, 2005).

    When evaluating applicants, change the focus on organizational fit to a focus on the potential for each applicant to contribute to the organizational mission.

    Develop strong orientation programmes for new employees that provide both passive and experiential opportunities to learn about the culture of the organization and its environment.

    Consider a broader set of educational background and reference sources.

- **Training, development, coaching and mentoring**:

    Provide a wide range of training and development that makes middle and upper class norms of professionalism more transparent for all employees. Examples of such training include professional work practices, networking, conflict management, business writing and effective communication.

    Assign mentors to coach individual employees to plan how to meet their needs for development.

    Provide resources and coached assignments so individual employees can gain skills and confidence in networking situations.

- **Managing employees**:

    Focus on problem-solving rather than discipline. Be aware of the many challenges individuals may experience due to their social class background.

    When there are issues with an employee, have a dialogue with the person regarding potential causes of negative performance with an emphasis on empathy.

Integrating social class into the management curriculum using Bloom's learning model

What can we offer to the field of management education, including textbook authors and educators, in terms of including social class in the management curriculum? Above, we provide recommendations to managers related to hiring, training and development, and managing employees. We now introduce Bloom's model of thinking, feeling and acting to better understand the role of responsible management—and responsible management education—as it relates to issues of social class (Anderson and Krathwohl, 2001; Bloom *et al.*, 1956). We believe this model shifts the focus from profitability and productivity exclusively to the responsibility of managers to act in ways that demonstrate a moral responsibility for social justice in their organization.

Based on our analysis of social class in industry and academia, and our interest in applying Bloom's model to improving management education as it relates to social class, we asked ourselves the following questions:

- Why is social class not part of the accepted and available curriculum?

- Are business school academics predominantly from middle and upper class backgrounds and not aware of the full impact of social class?

- How do business school academics accept that, owing to social class differences, meritocracy and free market systems are not perfect?

- How does the general orientation of the corporate world to gloss over individual experience and homogenize people lead to ignoring class distinctions and perpetuating existing class structures?

- Is meritocracy a sacred and unassailable ideology in the culture of business and management education? How so?

In answering these questions, we found Bloom's notions of thinking, feeling and acting useful in gaining a deeper understanding of how to effectively educate managers to embrace their responsibilities to promote social justice in their role as leaders in their organizations and communities (Anderson and Krathwohl, 2001). This is not just a logical imperative—to make future managers more effective—but a moral imperative for managers to address all issues of social justice, including social class inequities. In order to prepare more responsible managers, we start with recommendations for management educators.

We recommend first that faculty consider getting "in touch" with the experience of another social class as a means of opening up avenues for conversation with individuals of diverse social class backgrounds (Ehrenreich, 2001). Certainly there are opportunities for faculty to gain this knowledge such as by incorporating service-learning experiences in socioeconomic class diverse communities into their classes, or on a more personal level engaging in the diversity, inclusion and equity training opportunities that are offered to staff on most university campuses.

Another way for academics to address these questions is to ask more research questions that inform our understanding of social class and examine the rich literature on class in sociology, race and ethnic studies, gender studies and other related disciplines. For example, more research into how social class impacts hiring, promotion and development would provide more knowledge and understanding of how responsible managers can be more inclusive with regard to social class. Faculty development towards a higher understanding of how social class impacts organizations is needed and should be based on this research.

Once management educators prepare themselves, they can now focus on preparing students. Using the thinking, feeling and acting approach, we make the following suggestions:

Thinking

Addressing what is social class and what we know about the impacts of social class and how it relates to other organizational concepts such as diversity is a sound beginning to enhancing student knowledge of social class. Examples of strategies to use include:

- Using literature which describes the impact of social class and how social class challenges commonly held assumptions about business and society (Fahey, 2015). This approach helps in addressing the issue of social class-based bias in hiring decisions.

- Assigning students to research firms who serve different social classes of society and analyse how they position themselves to better serve those segments. This type of assignment focuses on training and development of employees.

- Organizing a panel or series of guest executives from industries that are associated with different social classes to talk about their firm's culture, talent acquisition and promotion practices and customer and community relations. Guest speaker panels will address hiring, training and managing from a working manager's perspective.

- Using cases which feature social class issues (e.g. Chesler and Beale, 1997; Garcia, 1995) to illustrate how social class-based norms impact responses to managerial directives. While no repository of cases that address social class (to the authors' knowledge) has been formally developed, many cases exist in which social class can be highlighted in the case analysis.

Feeling

Social class impacts people's feelings of inclusion and place in society and in an organization's hierarchy. Examples of strategies to use include:

- Asking students to read real accounts of people and or dramatizations (film, plays) from different levels of society about their work life (e.g. Terkel, 1974; Ehrenreich, 2001) to evoke feelings about the impact of social class.

- Engaging students in self-awareness activities such as assessments (e.g. Christian Science Monitor, n.d.) or experiential activities (e.g. "Walk of Privilege" exercise;[2] BBC News Magazine, 2013) which highlight their own level of social class and how that impacts their feelings about who they are and their future as professionals. Through increasing empathy related to social class issues, future managers learn to more effectively manage employees from all social classes.

Acting

This can be the most challenging learning objective to achieve as shaping behaviour is a longer-term enterprise. Some suggestions include:

- Asking students to develop plans on how they would interact and then role play situations with people from different social classes (cf. Garcia and Hoelscher, 2008; Powell, 2011).

- Asking students to develop a plan for creating a firm that is sensitive to matters of class and diversity which will be judged by professionals from several different industries.

- Introducing courses that focus on professionalism (e.g. etiquette dinners, interviewing and networking skills seminars) in a way that is more sensitive to and appreciative of social class, the social classes represented in the student population, and how professionalism, often a code word for upper middle class values and ways of interacting, is a means of accessing privilege. In addressing managerial behaviour from an experiential perspective, all aspects of our manager recommendations benefit.

In summary, we suggest that management educators begin to share pedagogical resources and tools addressing social class in management such as cases, role-plays and experiential exercises, as well as drawing upon literature in diversity, gender studies and immigration studies, to name a few, from disciplines outside of management to inform the development of new materials. Our aim here is to better inform and prepare students to be more aware of class and better at making decisions that take into account the impact of class in their organizations and beyond. As such, our challenge to readers is to generate more content that enables students to know more, develop sensitivity to and perform more effectively

2 "Walk of Privilege" exercise. Retrieved from https://www.youtube.com/watch?v=hD5f8 GuNuGQ

in relation to class issues as organizational leaders. This would include culturally specific resources that tackle intersectionality in different global contexts.

In addition to scholarship focused on social class, we view the role of a responsible management educator to include enabling her students to be clear about their values and ethics surrounding fairness and equity in organizations. As such, social class is experienced by all people, although many of our students are unaware of how they are impacted by social class or the privilege or lack thereof they derive from their social class relative to others. They may not acknowledge that the social class system exists in their current or future workplace organization. Providing students with conceptual frameworks to help them understand the role of social class in organizations as well as developing a personal awareness of its impacts on the people who live, work and are served by organizations will develop managers and leaders who will be more informed about the moral and ethical choices they will be making as professionals.

By addressing social class issues through thinking, feeling and acting in the curriculum, future managers will be better prepared for hiring, training and development, and managing all employees. Is this feasible in real organizations today? Our next section addresses this issue. We asked Debbie Ahl, former President and CEO of Sterling Life Insurance Company and founding partner of Edgewater Advising, to comment on how increasing attention to social class may benefit organizations and managers.

Continuing the conversation

A practitioner's perspective from Debbie Ahl

When I was first asked to provide a business perspective on the need for improved management education on social class as a barrier to mobility, my reaction was immediate: "Absolutely!" Ironically, this stemmed from the realization that I, as a business leader who encourages the development of a diverse employee base, had never once identified social class as a specific element of diversity. Let me explain.

As President/CEO of Sterling Life Insurance Company, I had the honour of leading a US company specializing in health plans for the Medicare eligible population. Medicare is a US Government programme offering healthcare coverage to individuals who meet the following criteria: age 65 and older or with a qualifying disability. At the time, we had 250,000 enrolees in a variety of Medicare Advantage, Medicare supplement, Prescription drug and employer group plans. The core of our business was Medicare Advantage and Medicare supplement. Our enrolees were distributed across the United States, predominantly in suburban and rural markets, and were diverse in terms of their age (we once had three generations of Medicare enrolees on our system: one age 65, her mother age 82 and her grandmother age 92), race, cultural heritage, religion and socioeconomic status. We had many low income seniors and individuals eligible for Medicare due to disability. To serve our enrolees, Sterling had about 750 sales agents and management in markets across the country, and another 700 employees providing customer service, enrolment, premium and claims processing, clinical case management, marketing and financial services in Bellingham, Washington State (in the United States). We worked hard to hire and promote a diverse employee base to serve our enrolees, and to train our team to the unique needs of the Medicare population. We also felt that a diverse employee population would provide greater perspective into decision-making at all levels of the organization.

But never did we specifically identify social class as an element of diversity that might benefit from a unique approach from a management perspective. We likely addressed this element by virtue of our general desire to hire a diverse employee base and to promote where possible from within, but it is likely we could have done so much more.

Many job skills for entry level positions or promotion to higher positions include those that may not come as easily to individuals of a lower socioeconomic class. The ability to communicate well either verbally or in writing, an ease of presentation even in terms of initial introductions, the ability to feel comfortable engaging in discussion with peers or supervisors; these are skills that might come more naturally to those with higher socioeconomic status than to those of lower socioeconomic class where education and role models were not accessible. Such skills, however, can be developed within the workplace.

Earlier in my career I was a single mom, and my three children were often called upon to help me when entertaining for our growing business. This gave them an opportunity to interact with adults who were gathering for business purposes (albeit informally), and they learned to "meet and greet" and developed conversation styles at an early age. Later, when I was CEO of the company, my daughter would be dropped off in our lobby at the end of the day. Exiting the elevator early one evening to meet her, I found her surrounded by a group of 30–40 incoming market managers, who had identified her as my daughter. I was amazed to see this 13-year-old, still in braces, reach out to individually greet each manager, asking them to tell her which market they were from and a little about themselves. While my children were not raised in an extremely high socioeconomic class, they clearly benefited from my role with the company and the opportunities to grow social and communication skills.

Managers can seek to mitigate the inequities of social class through training and mentorship programmes, offering an opportunity to learn such skills in order to qualify for promotions. At Sterling, we saw the benefit of hiring individuals from diverse backgrounds, but I believe we could have added further benefit by consciously integrating people from different socioeconomic backgrounds into our infrastructure, including supervisory, management and even executive positions. I believe this type of diversity adds value to an organization, by offering different perspectives to complement the broad customer base, and by providing role models from all socioeconomic backgrounds for individuals to see the possibilities for their own futures.

Enhancing awareness of social class as an element of diversity is the first step to expanding mobility opportunities, and doing this within the management curriculum provides a foundation upon which to develop responsible managers. Storytelling of individuals who have achieved success with lower socioeconomic backgrounds is a great place to start to reinforce the fact that great intelligence and abilities exist under the surface of those who have not had the opportunities of education.

Conclusion

Social class is an important, yet often neglected, issue for responsible managers. Debbie Ahl makes a good case that this is not always intentional, meaning that increasing awareness for managers and students of management may provide increased motivation to address issues of inequality related to social class. Benefits from making a concerted effort to address issues that may result from social class difference can be both economic and moral.

Economic benefits mean more efficient use of the social capital and talent of all members of the organization by addressing challenges individuals of lower social class may have. **Moral and ethical benefits** mean that members of lower social classes have increased access to economic and educational opportunity and the means to enhance their lives. Expanding opportunities to all potential employees by addressing biases related to social class increases social justice in all areas of society.

In general, managers—and their organizations—will benefit from increased awareness of barriers to social mobility and how issues of social class may affect their workplace. A deeper understanding of how to develop individual employees has the potential to increase performance and provide a deeper sense of community within the organization. Most importantly, however, attention to social justice through addressing issues of social class means that managers are more responsible.

More needs to be done to ensure that social class—low, middle or high—is not a predictor of the level of success an individual achieves in an organization. Responsible management education can support efforts towards equal access to opportunities in the workplace by increasing attention to issues of social class through research, curriculum, faculty development, managerial training and community engagement. The recommendations introduced here encourage management educators to take into account social class—and social justice issues related to social class—in achieving "an inclusive and sustainable global economy" as outlined in Principle 1 of the PRME initiative. Stories, as Debbie Ahl mentions earlier in the chapter, have power. So perhaps in the end responsible management educators, through research and practice, will generate a new narrative about how social class impacts the workplace, leading to broader opportunities for all people regardless of social class background.

References

Anderson, L.W. & Krathwohl, D.R. (eds.) (2001). *A Taxonomy for Learning, Teaching, and Assessing: A Revision of Bloom's Taxonomy of Educational Objectives.* New York, NY: Longman.

Armstrong, E.A. & Hamilton, L.T. (2013). *Paying for the Party: How College Maintains Inequality.* Boston, MA: Harvard University Press.

Ashley, L. & Empson, L. (2013). Differentiation and discrimination: Understanding social class and social exclusion in leading law firms. *Human Relations,* 66(2), 219-244.

Baker, J. (2010). Great expectations and post-feminist accountability: Young women living up to the "successful girls" discourse. *Gender and Education,* 22(1), 1-15.

BBC News Magazine (2013, April 3). The Great British class calculator. Retrieved from http://www.bbc.com/news/magazine-22000973

Bell, E.L.J.E. & Nkomo, S.M. (2001). *Our Separate Ways: Black and White Women and the Struggle for Professional Identity.* Cambridge, MA: Harvard Business School Press.

Bell, M.T. (2012). *Diversity in Organizations* (2nd ed.). Mason, OH: Southwestern—Cengage Learning.

Bloom, B.S., Engelhart, M.D., Furst, E.J., Hill, W.H. & Krathwohl, D.R. (1956). *Taxonomy of Educational Objectives: The Classification of Educational Goals. Handbook I: Cognitive Domain.* New York: David McKay Company.

Boliver, V. (2011). Expansion, differentiation, and the persistence of social class inequalities in British higher education. *Higher Education,* 61, 229-242.

Bradbury, K. & Katz, J. (2002). Are lifetime incomes growing more unequal: Looking at the new evidence on family income mobility. *Regional Review,* 12(4), 3-5.

Cañas, K.A. & Sondak, H. (2014). *Opportunities and Challenges of Workplace Diversity: Theory, Cases and Exercises* (3rd ed.). Boston, MA: Pearson.

Cena, L., McGruder, J. & Tomlin, G. (2002). Representations of race, ethnicity, and social class in case examples. *American Journal of Occupational Therapy,* 56(2), 130-139.

Chesler, M. & Beale, R.L. (1997). Is the plaintiff's social scientist off the wall? In T. Cox & R.L. Beale (eds.), *Developing Competency to Manage Diversity: Readings, Cases and Activities.* San Francisco, CA: Berrett-Koehler Publishers.

Christian Science Monitor (n.d.). What is your social class? Take our quiz to find out! Retrieved from http://www.csmonitor.com/USA/Society/2013/1017/What-is-your-social-class-Take-our-quiz-to-find-out/How-did-you-score

Cole, E.R. (2008). Coalitions as a model for intersectionality: From practice to theory. *Sex Roles,* 59, 443-453.

Colquitt, J.A., LeaPine, J.A. & Wesson, M.J. (2015). Organizational behavior: Improving performance and commitment in the workplace (4th ed.). New York, NY: McGraw-Hill Education.

Cose, E. (1993). *The Rage of a Privileged Class.* New York, NY: HarperCollins.

Cote, S., Piff, P.K. & Willer, R. (2013). For whom do the ends justify the means? Social class and utilitarian moral judgment. *Journal of Personality and Social Psychology,* 104(3), 490-503.

Cox, Jr, T. (1993). *Cultural Diversity in Organizations: Theory, Research and Practice.* San Francisco, CA: Berrett-Koehler Publishers.

Darvin, R. & Norton, B. (2014). Social class, identity, and migrant students. *Journal of Language, Identity & Education,* 13(2), 111-117.

Ehrenreich, B. (2001). *Nickel and Dimed: On (not) getting by in America.* New York, NY: Henry Holt.

Fahy, C.A. (2015). Social class: The fiction of American meritocracy. In C.P. Harvey & M.J. Allard (Eds.), *Understanding and Managing Diversity: Readings, Cases, and Exercises* (6th ed.) (pp. 182-195). Boston, MA: Pearson.

Farnsworth Riche, M. & Mor Barak, M.E. (2014). Socioeconomic transitions: The new realities of the global workforce. In Mor Barak (ed.), *Managing Diversity: Toward a Globally Inclusive Workplace* (3rd ed.). Thousand Oaks, CA: Sage Publications.

Gaetane, J., Normore, A.H. & Brooks, J.S. (2009). Leadership for social justice: Preparing 21st century school leaders for a new social order. *Journal of Research on Leadership Education*, 4(1), 1-31.

Garcia, J.E. (1995). Underground chemicals: The case of the bloodied bins. In A.M. Whiteley (Ed.), *Managing Change: A Core Values Approach*. South Melbourne, Australia: Macmillan Education Australia.

Garcia, J.E. & Hoelscher, K.J. (2008). *Managing Diversity Flashpoints in Higher Education*. Westport, CT: Praeger Publishing, American Council on Education Series.

Gardenswartz, L. & Rowe, A. (1994). *Diverse Teams at Work: Capitalizing on the Power of Diversity*. New York, NY: McGraw-Hill.

Griffin, R.W. & Moorhead, G. (2014). *Organizational Behavior: Managing People and Organizations* (11th ed.). Stamford, CT: Cengage Learning.

Hamamura, T. (2012). Social class predicts generalized trust but only in wealthy societies. *Journal of Cross-Cultural Psychology*, 43(3), 498-509.

Harvey, C.P. & Allard, M.J. (2015). *Understanding and Managing Diversity: Readings, Cases, and Exercises* (6th ed.). Boston, MA: Pearson.

Hemphill, T.A., Lillevik, W. & Cullari, F. (2012). The long-term unemployed: A new protected class of employee? *Business and Society Review*, 117(4), 535-553.

Hewlett, S.A., Luce, C.B. & West, C. (2005). Leadership in your midst: Tapping the hidden strengths of minority executives. *Harvard Business Review*, November 2005, 74-82.

Kelly, P. (2012). Migration, transnationalism, and the spaces of class identity. *Philippine Studies: Historical and Ethnographic Viewpoints*, 60(2), 153-186.

Kogan, I. (2007). A study of immigrants' employment careers in West Germany using the sequence analysis technique. *Social Science Research*, 36(2), 491-511.

Kraus, M.W. & Keltner, D. (2013). Social class rank, essentialism, and punitive judgment. *Journal of Personality and Social Psychology*, 105(2), 247-261.

Kraus, M.W., Piff, P.K., Mendoza-Denton, R., Rheinschmidt, M.L. & Keltner, D. (2012). Social class, solipsism, and contextualism: How the rich are different from the poor. *Psychological Review*, 119, 546-572.

Larew, J. (2008). Why are droves of unqualified, unprepared kids getting into our top colleges? Because their dads are alumni. In K.E. Rosenblum & T.C. Travis (Eds.). *The Meaning of Difference: American Constructions of Race, Sex, and Gender, Social Class and Sexual Orientation* (5th ed.) (pp. 300-305). New York, NY: McGraw-Hill.

Lipsey, D. (2015, February 27). The meritocracy myth: The meritocracy myth—and what ever happened to the old dream of a classless society? *New Statesman*, 23.

Loden, M. (1996). *Implementing Diversity: Best Practices for Making Diversity Work in Your Organization*. New York, NY: McGraw-Hill.

Martin, N.D. (2012). The privilege of ease: Social class and campus life at highly selective, private universities. *Research in Higher Education*, 53, 426-452.

Nahavandi, A., Denhart, R.B., Denhart, J.V. & Aristigueta, M.P. (2015). *Organizational Behavior*. Thousand Oaks, CA: Sage Publications.

Nelson, D. & Quick, J.C. (2015). *ORGB: Organizational Behavior*. Stamford, CT: Cengage Learning.

Nickens, H. (1995). The role of race/ethnicity and social class in minority health status. *Health Services Research*, 30, 154-161.

Petev, I.D. (2013). The association of social class and lifestyles: Persistence in American sociability, 1974 to 2010. *American Sociological Review*, 78(4), 633-661.

Powell, G.N. (2011). *Managing a Diverse Workforce: Learning Activities* (3rd ed.). Thousand Oaks, CA: Sage Publications.

Reuss, A. (2008). Cause of death: Inequality. In K.E. Rosenblum & T.C. Travis (Eds.). *The Meaning of Difference: American Constructions of Race, Sex, and Gender, Social Class and Sexual Orientation* (5th ed.) (pp. 297-300). New York, NY: McGraw-Hill.

Robbins, S.P. & Judge, T.A. (2015). *Organizational Behavior* (16th ed.). Upper Saddle River, NJ: Pearson Education.

Sacks, P. (2003). *Class rules: The fiction of egalitarian higher education. Chronicle of Higher Education*, 49(46), B7.

Settles, I.H. (2006). Use of an intersectional framework to understand Black Women's racial and gender identities. *Sex Roles*, 54, 589-601.

Terkel, S. (1974). *Working: People Talk About What They Do All Day and How They Feel About What They Do.* New York, NY: The New Press.

Thomas, D.A. & Gabarro, J.J. (1999). *Breaking Through: The Making of Minority Executives in Corporate America.* Cambridge, MA: Harvard Business School Press.

Thomas, V. & Azmitia, M. (2014). Does class matter? The centrality and meaning of social class identity in emerging adulthood. *Identity: An International Journal of Theory and Research*, 14(3), 195-213.

Tyran, K.L. & Gibson, C.B. (2008). Is what you see, what you get? The relationship among surface- and deep-level heterogeneity characteristics, group efficacy, and team reputation. *Group and Organization Management*, 33(1), 46-76.

Uhl-Bein, M., Schermerhorn, Jr, J.R. & Osborn, R.N. (2014). *Organizational Behavior* (13th ed.). Hoboken, NJ: John Wiley & Sons.

15

Drivers, barriers and enablers of institutionalizing responsible management education

Charlotte Warin and Eshani Beddewela
The Business School, University of Huddersfield, UK

with practitioner commentary by Christopher Cowton

Introduction

Responsible management education (RME) is increasingly appearing in both the curricula and strategies of business schools around the world. In this instance we define RME as any teaching, research or enterprise surrounding the areas of ethics, sustainability and responsible corporate practices. As the corporate world rallies in the aftermath of the economic and financial crises of 2007/2008 and society reflects on the scandals and turmoil sustained by a number of multinational companies, the need for a manager to participate in "responsible" management education becomes ever more apparent. Business schools have been blamed for contributing to the crisis due to the lack of responsible management education, choosing instead to perpetuate the more profit-focused approach which was considered the norm historically (Blasco, 2012).

It is imperative that students are taught the appropriate skills and tools to be able to make responsible and ethically minded decisions that will contribute to a sustainable future. Equally important, students need to be educated within a responsible environment and business schools must be seen to "walk the talk".

Consequently, the need for RME activities under the teaching, research and enterprise remit to be present within a business school is increasing in terms of both awareness and demand (Rasche and Escudero, 2010).

This chapter aims to examine from an institutional perspective what the key drivers, barriers and enablers are for business schools within the UK that are intending to institutionalize RME. This initial research forms part of a doctoral study and suggests there are both implicit and explicit drivers, barriers and enablers that can, and will, affect business schools to varying degrees. By exploring these factors it can be argued this will help business schools and other higher education institutions to understand the role they play in the creation of sustainable value. A further aim of this chapter is to provide a guideline for business school staff members which can assist them when they begin the institutionalization of RME.

The framework will offer a number of suggestions for different levels of staff members and how they could respond to the drivers, barriers and enablers present throughout the implementation of RME, as suggested above. This will allow managers and deans of business schools within the UK to be readily aware of the challenges and opportunities facing them when considering the development of RME activities within their institution, which we argue is an imperative in order for corporate organizations to lead us into a sustainable future. Finally, this chapter contributes to the Principles for Responsible Management Education (PRME) Principle Four—Research: "We will engage in conceptual and empirical research that advances our understanding about the role, dynamics, and impact of corporations in the creation of sustainable social, environmental and economic value" (see p. 10).

Corporate social responsibility (CSR) has grown almost exponentially with UK and US companies in the Fortune Global 500 spending $15.2 billion a year on CSR activities (*Financial Times*, 2014). However research commissioned by the Business Backs Education campaign recently found that only $2.6 billion (13%) of the CSR budget is spent on CSR education-related activities (Silvera, 2015) with less than half (218) of the 500 companies spending any of the budget on CSR-related education. It is here that we can observe the gap between CSR within businesses and the increasing prominence and relevance of CSR and other ethical, responsible and sustainable issues within higher education. The corporate world now more than ever needs business schools to produce ethically and responsibly educated students who must implement responsible management education (RME) curriculum reforms.

The chapter begins by reviewing internal and external factors; thus, identifying drivers, barriers and enablers that could play a majority or minority role when business schools are implementing and increasing RME activities. Second, we introduce theory to explain how these three factors act within an institutionalization process. Third, the chapter then assesses empirical data and incorporates a number of practitioner voices. Here the research takes three case studies that are considered to be "advanced", in the "middle" and in the "initial" stages of institutionalizing RME. The empirical data is drawn from a number of sources including interviews with three members of staff, one from each case study, including one director, a senior lecturer and a principal lecturer, all of whom have a connection to the PRME agenda present within their institutions. We assess two other complementary data sources: the biannual Sharing Information on Progress (SIP) reports from PRME and the business school websites focusing on what they communicate about their RME agenda.

Fourth, we discuss these case studies following a table of the key drivers, barriers and enablers drawn from the data. Fifth, we provide application ideas of these key factors with suggestions tailored to deans, senior and junior staff regarding each of the driver, barrier and enabler categories. Finally, in addition to the application that we as researchers suggest, we provide a commentary from a dean of a UK business school which extends the application that we offer, and postulates how the drivers, barriers and enablers taken from the data will act in practice.

Responsible management education in the UK context

RME is predominantly implemented by business schools through their curricula, in the form of either a core module, an elective module or via an interdisciplinary approach. Research suggests that European schools favour the elective option (Matten and Moon, 2004; Nicholls *et al.*, 2013). Rasche *et al.* (2013) found that, while courses on responsibility are being added to the curricula, 75% of these courses are electives and detached from core disciplines, suggesting a "bolt on" effect (Louw, 2015). Matten and Moon (2004) advocate that in order for CSR education to be successful it needs to be fully integrated and embedded within the core strategic approach of a business school. Critics also postulate that overloading RME across a curriculum can dilute its effectiveness with students (Sharland *et al.*, 2013) and at times even become a barrier for the teaching of other topics (Exter *et al.*, 2013).

There are other areas that can also promote and raise awareness of RME activities beyond the curriculum such as faculty research in the areas of ethics and sustainability within a school. Further activities that encourage RME cognizance can include voluntary projects for staff and students, community work and more organizational policy-related aspects such as environmental policy, carbon plans and recycling schemes. Blasco (2012) speaks of the hidden curriculum and the implicit impact of educational settings beyond the curricula that play a pivotal role in improving students' sense of responsibility within business.

It is important to understand the drivers, barriers and enablers of RME, in order to assist and embark on the institutionalization process. While such terms are not well defined within the literature, many authors have sought to examine the forces that help or hinder the implementation of RME within business schools (see for example: Maloni *et al*, 2012; Barber *et al*, 2014; Sobczak and Mukhi, 2015). Through this previous work and in line with the Oxford Dictionary definitions[1] we surmise that driving factors are those that cause and guide a particular phenomenon to develop. A barrier is any restraint or obstruction that prevents access and an enabler is a factor that gives power and ability to an action to make it possible. In connection to the RME agenda, drivers can be seen as those stakeholders/stakeholder actions that are leading to the institutionalization of RME, any actions that are hindering or apprehending the process can be regarded as barriers, whereas enablers are those stakeholder/stakeholder actions that are allowing and helping business schools to engage with the RME process. The following sections discuss the key internal and external factors that can play a role within the higher educational environment in the UK in relation to the area of responsible management education. We define internal factors as those stakeholders or actions operating internally within a business school and making an impact from the "inside-in". External factors are regarded as any initiatives, bodies or stakeholders that are established and operate externally to a business school having an "outside-in" impact.

Internal factors

The internal factors that we discuss here include faculty staff interest and expertise, the role that management plays, students, institutional philosophy and the increasing presence of a "research agenda" within higher education.

Often the suggestion of embedding RME-type modules across a curriculum can be met with resistance from faculty staff members who do not see it as an imperative or who do not wish to alter their course to adopt new approaches (Doh and Tashmann, 2014). However, research by Matten and Moon (2004), when looking at CSR education within Europe, found that faculty members were considered to be the top driving force, followed by business school leadership. This finding is echoed by Cowton and Cummins (2003) who describe teachers of business ethics as having a large personal interest in the topic, and argue that individuals with enthusiasm will pioneer a change in business school policy. These motivated faculty members can thus help to disseminate the uptake of RME issues within a curriculum (Fukukawa *et al.*, 2013). A further point to note is that few business school faculty members are trained to teach in the area of RME and so often do not feel comfortable in doing so (Podolny 2009 as cited by Sharland *et al.*, 2013). It is therefore suggested here that faculty staff members, while possibly creating the strongest influence through personal passion and enthusiasm, can also create the greatest resistance, especially due to their professional interpretation of RME (Reay *et al.*, 2013).

While personal interest and enthusiasm towards RME can be a large part of a positive driving force, if administrative processes do not support a new strategy, then institutionalization processes will struggle. Zell (2005) explains how deans of business schools can have conflicting priorities, trying to simultaneously balance

1 http://www.oxforddictionaries.com

the need to preserve core institutional activity and the need to transform and change in order to remain relevant. Interestingly, work by Exter *et al.* (2013) found that one school director had engaged with the PRME initiative *without* an extensive debate with faculty members knowing that this would make it difficult to secure an agreement, suggesting possible disinterest or rejection of involvement from faculty in becoming a PRME signatory.

Students are a further internal stakeholder group that can help to drive the institutionalization process as they can help promote course development (Christensen *et al.*, 2007). Research conducted by the British Sky Broadcasting Group (BSBG, 2012) found that 70% of UK graduate trainees working in business agreed that sustainability is important to business yet only 35% believed that they had received sufficient training in this area (BSBG, 2012). Further research by Kolodinsky *et al.* (2010) showed that business students had a more favourable attitude towards CSR, and therefore RME, if they held ethically idealistic views—something which may not be under the control of a business school strategy. It can be contested here that while student interest in the topic can be an essential driver promoting the RME agenda, disinterest and low enrolments on elective or optional modules can result in a rejection or hindering of the institutionalization process.

In some instances it is simply the case that the university and/or business school has a strong sustainability or responsibility value within their ethos and philosophy. Many business schools are now incorporating terminology associated with RME into their mission and vision statements and this can give the school impetus and a drive to make changes to curriculum and strategies (Rasche and Gilbert, 2015).

A final factor within the internal environment is the "research agenda" that is often promoted within UK institutions. The suggestion is that faculty staff members need to research and publish in disciplines, and of a quality, that will help the institution develop within the league tables and benchmarking initiatives such as the Research Excellence Framework (REF) within the UK.[2] Staff members that already research within the RME area can contribute in this manner; however faculty staff members with other interests will have no impetus or imperative to promote RME research. Alternatively, faculty members with interdisciplinary research interests would face pressures and expectations for publishing within their discipline, potentially acting as a strong deterrent from focusing on RME-specific issues (Sharland *et al.*, 2013). Similarly, faculty who spend time actively implementing RME-related activities into a business school's practice, such as the development of a module or a research group, will not advance their career (Rasche and Gilbert, 2015) or their "research agenda".

---

2 The Research Excellence Framework (REF; http://www.ref.ac.uk/) is a system for assessing the quality of research in UK higher education institutions.

External factors

The above internal factors will affect different institutions in various ways and there is the potential for each of them to act as either a deterrent or an opportunity. Next we examine five factors that affect the institutionalization of RME from outside the business school environment: the PRME, accreditation and professional bodies, business and society, and the Research Excellence Framework, alluded to above.

The PRME is a voluntary initiative established in 2007 for business schools around the globe seeking to advance social responsibility, and any institution can become a signatory. PRME is considered by many to be a soft mechanism for regulatory change (Burchell *et al.*, 2014) and only requires a small membership fee and a biannual "Sharing Information on Progress" (SIP) report in which schools highlight how they are implementing RME. There are numerous criticisms of the PRME initiative and many argue that by becoming a signatory to PRME a business school may simply be operating a "tick box" approach and consider this their commitment as opposed to making any real changes within their operations. The viewpoint taken on the PRME initiative can vary considerably between schools and individuals but nevertheless it is still an active driving force and is gaining momentum with membership numbers rising annually.[3]

Further external driving forces include accreditation bodies, and many UK business schools are striving towards the "triple [accreditation] crown" of the Association for the Advancement of Collegiate Schools of Business (AACSB), European Quality Improvement System (EQUIS) and the Association of MBAs (AMBA). All three have ethical benchmarks within their standards and aim to incorporate more (Cooper *et al.*, 2014). Accreditation bodies can be considered a coercive force on business schools that wish to attain and retain an accredited status. However the question of the "tick box" approach can again be considered, and Sharland *et al.* (2013) make reference to the notion that, even though the AACSB has required ethically related content in their criteria since 1974, the way this is to be achieved is not evident and there is the potential that business schools could be construing their activities to reflect more RME actions than are actually present. The main way in which the accreditation bodies will act as a driver is to force business schools to incorporate RME-related activities in line with their standards; management understands the importance of achieving accredited status and so will strive to maintain and implement these measures.

Alongside accreditation bodies, there are several discipline-specific professional bodies that often govern the content of a curriculum, and this will have an effect on the ability to execute new areas (Doherty *et al.*, 2015). Within the UK, the Association of Chartered Certified Accountants (ACCA) provides a professional ACCA accredited qualification that has a professional ethics module, and claims to put

---

3 PRME home page. Retrieved from http://www.unprme.org/

ethics at "the heart of the qualification".[4] The implementation of new modules and different pedagogical techniques to assist these all vie for space within a curriculum. The autonomy to embed topics of ethics, sustainability and responsibility can be limited for business schools whose curriculum is governed by a professional body.

Employers are a key constituency within the society that business schools must engage. Universities need to respect that they do not work in isolation and the graduates they are developing need to be able to procure a job within the current economic market. As a consequence, businesses are in a position to be able to dictate the skills and competences that need to be taught within business school curricula (Doherty *et al.*, 2015).

As previously mentioned within the internal factors section, the Research Excellence Framework (REF) and other benchmarking or league table type initiatives affect the practices of UK business schools. Education is an increasingly competitive industry (Pfeffer and Fong, 2004) and the introduction and increase in awareness and prestige of initiatives such as the REF, has resulted in business schools altering their strategies to include more practices that adhere to their criteria in order to improve reputation, status and to gain funding. Maintaining ranking positions requires a significant amount of input (Cornuel and Hommel, 2015) and business schools strive to retain or improve their positions, as they do with the accreditation bodies.

As can be observed, there are a number of internal and external factors that may impact business schools aiming to institutionalize RME. The next section reviews the theoretical connections of these factors and the relevance and significance of how these operate together.

Institutionalization of responsible management education

Institutionalization

Berger and Luckmann (1967) identified institutionalization as a core process of creating and perpetuating social reality among organizational actors. Maheshwari *et al.* (2010) describe institutionalized innovations as relatively widely diffused practices, technologies or rules that have become normatively and cognitively entrenched. With regard to the institutionalization of RME, many UK business schools are striving to diffuse RME practices and related activities so they become entrenched within the everyday processes of the stakeholders involved and also day-to-day operations. The process of institutionalizing a practice is regarded as

---

4 ACCA Qualification, Retrieved from http://www.accaglobal.com/gb/en/qualifications/glance/acca/details.html#prof

an effort to acquire legitimacy (Green *et al.*, 2009); however without an explicit measure of the legitimacy it is difficult to tell if this has been attained or not. When considering RME institutionalization, it is important to note the status an "institutionalized" business school is aiming for in order to identify when the goal has been achieved. Within the current UK context there are no dominant benchmarking or league table processes that can act as a measure of legitimacy, and so the notion of having achieved institutionalization will be down to the individual school and the level that they have set themselves to reach, dependent upon their circumstances and aspirations.

In relation to the higher educational context, it is noted that institutionalized practices are particularly evident in professionalized settings (Reay *et al.*, 2013) and that education plays an important role in the transmission of societal norms and values from one generation to the next (Trevino and Thomas, 2008). In this respect the need for RME is paramount so that the educational system within the UK can socialize the values (Trevino and Thomas, 2008) espoused by this new strategic direction, and assist in them becoming institutionalized and therefore legitimate as an important way forward. When an institution such as an educational system promotes a "correct" way to behave, that institution influences organizational and individual actions by normative processes (Trevino and Thomas, 2008).

Institutional change

Institutional change is described by Khavul *et al.* (2013, p. 32) as "a dynamic and an interactive process that occurs over time with actors both being shaped by and shaping the institutional environment". It is a complex process (Leca *et al.*, 2009) which can occur at any level from a micro-interpersonal and sub-organizational level to the most macro and societal level (Dacin *et al.*, 2002). Institutional change processes can also take a significantly varied amount of time dependent upon the final outcome, and the change process can last from days to years.

The amount of time taken for a business school to institutionalize RME will depend on the *level* of RME that they are aiming to achieve. For instance, a school aiming to achieve a strong commitment to the RME agenda, and thus a higher level of RME, would require a substantially longer amount of time and level of investment, as they would have to establish new research groups, potentially recruit new staff members specialized in RME-related subject matter, become a signatory to PRME and introduce or restructure their curriculum to incorporate ethics, sustainability and responsibility related features. In contrast, a business school aiming for a low level of RME can do so within a shorter time span and with considerably less investment, for instance by becoming a PRME signatory and/or creating an elective module.

With this brief review of institutionalization theory and RME, the chapter now reviews the empirical data and offers suggestions on how to apply the findings within other business school environments.

Case studies

To select cases we began with all 134 universities within the UK and reduced this number to 90 by utilizing only those schools that were members of both the Chartered Association of Business Schools (CABS) and the British Accounting and Finance Association (BAFA). Schools were then further categorized by dividing them into eight categories within two groups as noted in Figure 15.1: those schools that are signatories to PRME and either triple, double, single or not accredited, and the same for those schools that are not signatories to PRME—triple, double, single or not accredited.

Figure 15.1 **Categorization of business schools**

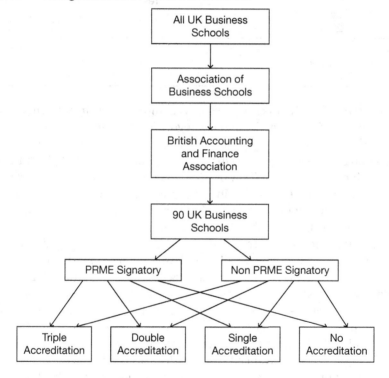

The total number of interviews stood at 19 from 17 different institutions, 13 of those were signatories to PRME, and of those 13, 11 had submitted a SIP report. The interviews were conducted via Skype and transcribed verbatim as soon after the event as possible. The transcripts were then analysed using NVIVO and a thematic analysis technique identifying core and sub themes.

From this data schools were then divided into those that were regarded as having either an "advanced", a "middle" or an "initial" level of RME activities within their operations. Schools were initially divided into levels using the date they signed up to PRME as a proxy indicator for level of perceived institutionalization. They were then further categorized using accreditation status and it can be seen from Table 15.1 that all three case studies for this research were PRME signatories and that the advanced school was triple accredited, the middle double accredited and the initial singly accredited.

Table 15.1 **Case study characteristics**

University/ Business school	Signatory to PRME	AACSB	EQUIS	AMBA	Russell Group member[5]	Pre/Post 1992[6]
Advanced	Yes, 2 July 2008	Yes	Yes	Yes	No	Pre
Middle	Yes, 20 September 2011	No	Yes	Yes (pending)	No	Post
Initial	Yes, 31 October 2014	No	Yes	No	No	Post

As there are no benchmarks available within the literature in relation to the institutionalization of RME, after the initial categorization via secondary data was complete, the next step was to utilize the interview data to create benchmarks through which schools can be categorized further in line with their level of institutionalization. In line with our definition of RME, we then used four further categories: teaching, research, enterprise (mainly green agenda) and faculty staff positions. Within each of these four areas we defined levels (that were created subjectively) as a comparison with each school analysed through data collection. For example, when looking at the Green Agenda, those schools that are engaged in a range of activities would be considered at a higher level than a school that is engaged in a lower number of activities as a comparison. See Table 15.2 for the specific categorization of the schools chosen for this chapter.

The analysis includes a variety of sources including primary data collected from semi-structured interviews conducted with staff members associated with RME or PRME within a business school. Secondary data analysis was conducted on the PRME SIP reports by the advanced and middle institutions; the initial level institution has not yet produced a report as they are new signatories to the PRME. Lastly, we audited business schools' webpages as an extension to the SIP reports to review how and where schools display their RME information.

5 The Russell Group universities within the UK are a group of 24 institutions which are committed to maintaining the very best research, an outstanding teaching and learning experience and unrivalled links with business and the public sector.
6 A manner by which UK universities are split into those that achieved university status post-1992 and were previously known as polytechnics.

Table 15.2 **Categorization of case study schools**

	Advanced	**Middle**	**Initial**
Teaching	Specialist Master's course titled "Social Responsibility and Sustainability" *(Interview)*	Selection of undergraduate and postgraduate core and elective modules with RME-related content *(Interview)*	Limited modules offered with RME-related content; aiming to have an overhaul and rewrite in line with PRME Principles *(Interview)*
Research	Ethics, Governance and Sustainability Research Group *(SIP Report)*	Centre for Sustainable Communities *(Interview)*	"Responsible Business" research based on nine areas *(Website)*
Enterprise (Green Agenda)	High number of activities supporting the green agenda such as schemes and policies *(SIP Report)*	High number of activities supporting the green agenda listed *(SIP Report)*	Weak level of Green Agenda with limited activities *(Interview)*
Staff	Director of Sustainability and Responsibility position *(Interview)*	Senior Lecturer has role of PRME Champion *(SIP Report)*	Senior Lecturer recruited to implement PRME *(Interview)*

Advanced institution

The advanced institution chosen for study was one of the first signatories to the PRME initiative signing up in July 2008 and becoming a PRME Champion school in 2013. The advanced institution case highlights two external factors, PRME and management support for RME advances, and four internal factors: RME-related module and course provision, the strategic direction of the university, evidence of sharing practices among faculty and staff and the common terminology used as a result of course audits.

From this institution's 2012 SIP report *strategic* aspects of the school were highlighted including a pledge to be one of the first universities to sign up to PRME in a university capacity with an aim to have *all* students regarded as sustainably literate by 2020.

The SIP report highlights several "Green Agenda" activities including a sustainability week on campus, a Gold Eco-Campus award and a variety of campus initiatives including a cycle to work scheme, furniture reuse and electric vehicles. The SIP report also identifies a number of courses and modules including a full-time specialist MSc in Social Responsibility and Sustainability. These activities and commitments are reflected on the business school's website which hosts a large section for "Environment and Sustainability", "Policies and Reports" and a "2020 Strategy" section.

The interview for the advanced institution held with the Director of Social Responsibility and Sustainability, which as a role itself demonstrates a commitment by the university to the agenda, described the number of processes available for *staff members* to share information, practices and resources within the RME agenda including away days/staff development workshop days and seminars. Additionally, the university has implemented new human resource policies and an "Ethics Framework" that integrates the ethical issues or problems that could occur while working within an academic environment and support in how to handle or discuss these. A video was made to help explain ethical issues in real time settings.

> [W]e used actors to show ethical dilemmas that staff and students might face which brought it to life a lot more, so you know it wasn't just about having a policy it was actually how do we make this real (Director of Social Responsibility and Sustainability, 2015).

An interesting area that emerged from the interview was the impact and focus on the *terminology* used: for example ethics as opposed to sustainability or corporate governance as course or module titles. This staff member led two audits, one conducted within the business school and the second across all other schools within the university. The aim of the audit was to assess the level and areas where RME-type topics were already being taught. Prior to the audit a list of terms were developed which would be used to search within the analysis of the documents; all documents relating to the curriculum were reviewed such as module handbooks and learning objectives as well as all documentation from the virtual learning environment. The terms chosen were regarded as reflecting the full range of issues that covered this area and represented the diverse ways in which the different disciplines defined and focused in this area.

> [We] tested 9 titles (for an MSc) … and it doesn't sound very imaginative but as you know the kind of naming of this area is quite contested and we wanted something that would reflect the fact that it did cover a range of things … we had a whole range of things that were tested but that seemed to cover what people expected to be in the course (Director of Social Responsibility and Sustainability, 2015).

One of the reasons why the presence of RME is so strong within this advanced institution can be identified as relating to personal enthusiasm. The Vice Chancellor's personal support and passion for the RME agenda is evidenced in positive allocation of time and resources: "[I] took the plans to her and she was very supportive of that" (Director of Social Responsibility and Sustainability, 2015). Having managerial support is essential for the development and changes of any policy and RME is no exception

Middle institution

The middle institution business school signed up to the PRME initiative in September 2011 and has submitted one SIP report to date. There are two external factors discussed: PRME and community work. The internal factors are fourfold: management support, strategic focus, the "research agenda" and staff.

The process for this school becoming a PRME signatory was not a simple one and the idea kept being put forward and pushed back, and after approximately a year of trying the *management* finally took the decision after an *accreditation* body visited suggesting that PRME membership would be a positive addition. Since becoming a signatory to PRME it has been described as a process giving legitimacy to their actions and forcing the business school to be more organized and more focused. It was suggested that becoming PRME signatories was a sensible step. "[B]ecause I think we have been doing so much in that area it was only logical that we had some kind of a framework that would pull it all together" (Principal Lecturer, Director of Social Enterprise Unit, 2015).

What was suggested within the interview is that the main kick-starter of introducing these types of activities into the middle level institution was the creation of a social enterprise unit which focused a lot on giving back to the *community*. Equally, *management support* from the dean, as with the advanced business school, has continued potential for a change in faculty leadership that could essentially "make or break" the focus of future RME activities; new management could enter the system that are not as dedicated to this area.

> [So] we could become exceptionally responsible all of a sudden, you know the dean will say that no module will come out of this business school without at least thinking about demonstrating that you have thought about responsibility and how you think about responsible education, or it could be a dean who will ... probably no one will stop it and no one will be openly against responsibility. But it could be a dean that it's not their agenda (Principal Lecturer, Director of Social Enterprise Unit, 2015).

The SIP report for this institution is heavily focused on the "Green Agenda" aspects of the university and business school including a number of different plans such as a sustainable procurement plan, a carbon management plan, a travel plan and a waste and resource management *strategy*. Information in the report surrounding the curriculum highlights a number of modules in both undergraduate and postgraduate curricula and a mixture of core and elective options.

The Principal Lecturer interviewed suggested that perhaps there was too much emphasis on the Green Agenda because it is measurable, and the university can promote the results should they be favourable; the interviewee felt that other areas within the RME remit should be focused on more, which have perhaps less tangible or measurable aspects but are equally important.

The institution's website suggests that it has a "Centre for Sustainable Communities" which contributes to the commitment to this *research agenda*. With regard to *staff*, this middle level institution was open in discussing the resistance that was met when trying to incorporate these topics into the curriculum alongside other aspects of RME. It was described not as an overt pressure, more of a struggle with disengaged staff members who did not see the changes as relevant or relating to their courses. A main feature of staff engagement was described as simply how busy academics are and their nature and aversion to change from a professional standpoint.

> [I] wouldn't say its overt resistance you know, no one says it's not important to us, no one said we don't want our students to be responsible but I have some problem with … and the answer from that programme tutor would be "well, on my programmes it's not relevant" (Principal Lecturer, Director of Social Enterprise Unit, 2015).

It is evident from this business school that changes are being made which are making a difference but these are coming up against a number of barriers and therefore the *timescale* in making these changes and the commitment to them is fluctuating. With engagement from management and continued support in terms of both *resources* and commitment, this business school should be able to develop practices that are regarded as "everyday" activities and institutionalize RME.

Initial institution

The initial institution is a relatively new signatory to the PRME initiative in November 2014. As a result there is currently no SIP report to review, but after reviewing their website and an interview with a Senior Lecturer in Business Ethics that is leading in this area, there were some interesting areas to report. The three external factors identified in the initial institution case are: accreditation, changing needs of students and commitment to business and society. The internal factors are: administrative and pedagogical processes, management addressing strategic needs, staff and common terminology. The interviewee was recruited to the specific role of implementing RME and signing up to the PRME initiative; this school describes itself as being in the very early stages but about to embark on a complete overhaul of all modules and to rewrite them with a sustainability core based on the PRME principles. The website of the initial institution has a section describing their commitment to sustainable and responsible business and management.

In this case there was a very clear passion and enthusiasm from the member of staff who was interviewed. This is reflected in their confident ability to lead these important changes and their personal belief and high standards. "[T]his is my life, so I kind of think that if I am happy with it … then we are ok. My standards are extremely high, so if I believe we've done that then I'll be happy" (Senior Lecturer in Business Ethics, 2015).

Interestingly, one of the challenges that was identified within the initial institution's business school was a *pedagogical issue* that arose from both an organizational structure and *administrative* perspective; in order to teach RME this staff member saw a need for new creative and innovative teaching methods, such as experiential learning, that will enable a better learning environment in which to raise awareness. The issue, however, is that when teaching on large modules that may incorporate over 500 students in addition to the virtual learning environment that teaches the same material to students within three other countries, the logistics and practicalities of engaging in novel and new pedagogical techniques such as experiential learning are just not possible. A further barrier was again resistance from staff members. In this instance it was viewed as a practical resistance as opposed to an ideological resistance, and that staff members see the importance of these changes but are reluctant to take the time and energy to make the required alterations within their module or course.

> [M]ost people are positive but there are a core of resistors if you like, but I don't feel like it's an ideological resistance, I think it's a practical resistance to having to put more things in that they are maybe not comfortable with, into their teaching (Senior Lecturer in Business Ethics, 2015).

With respect to the Green Agenda it is seen as weak and something else that needs to be worked on within this institution to ensure that they are "practising what they preach" and that they cannot expect to educate graduates in this manner if their "own houses are not in order".

> I think we need to be demonstrating to our students and our stakeholders that we are not just teaching this, we are actually living this and doing this and I think that's a focus for responsible management education, we need to get our own houses in order, be sustainable businesses, sustainable campuses, be sustainable organizations—otherwise we have no legitimacy (Senior Lecturer in Business Ethics, 2015).

A similarity between the advanced and initial case is a focus on shared *terminology*; while an explicit shared definition was not regarded as important, the need to ensure that definitions and terminology were translatable was a clear issue. The data suggest student understanding of the term "ethics" differs immensely based on culture, country and orientation. While still in the early stages of implementing RME activities, this institution appears to have a keen interest, the appropriate faculty in place, and a very clear business plan for making these changes.

After a review of the webpages for all three institutions, there was no evidence of RME language within the mission or vision statements. The data investigated and analysed from the case studies is presented in the Appendix. How this information can be applied in practice will now be explored.

Guidance for practitioners

From the analysis above we can identify a generic list of drivers, barriers and enablers (see Table 15.3) which affect the institutionalization process of RME. Not of all the factors listed within this table affected all three of the institutions identified within the case study, and further characteristics will play an important role as to the level of success of the implementation process. It is dependent upon a business school's characteristics and the organizational environment within which they operate as to which of the variables will play a more dominant role in the institutionalization of RME into their operations and strategies. However the leading factors are discussed here.

Table 15.3 **Drivers, barriers and enablers for institutionalizing RME in UK business schools**

Drivers	Barriers	Enablers
Accreditation *EQUIS and AACSB specifically*	Administrative processes *Pedagogical difficulties: delivering course content to high numbers of students via different mediums*	Strategic direction *Business school ethically based values intertwined with strategic direction will add weight to the change process*
Dedicated staff members *Passionate and enthusiastic staff that want to make the difference*	Resources (time and money) *The research agenda affects the ability and willingness of staff to make changes*	PRME *Becoming a signatory validates processes*
Management support *Schools with deans and vice chancellors that support this make more changes*	Staff resistance *Relevance and commitment Inherently busy staff with other schedules*	Mission/vision terminology *Using words such as "responsible" gives leverage within the school*
Student interest *Take up of RME-related modules*	Timescale *Potential lengthy period to change curriculum*	

Sharma and Hart (2014) argue that institutional change is difficult for business schools for four main reasons:

1. Tenured faculty members are typically researchers focused on established functions; untenured staff are left to deal with the "grey" area of sustainability (or RME) and lack influence within a school.

2. Career progression is based on high level publications which do not promote "messy" research on complex issues such as sustainability (or RME).

3. Staff have little interest or incentive to alter the content of their courses or to add in new content related to RME.

4. Leadership at dean level is weak, often with limited knowledge on sustainability or RME.

As noted from the case study analysis, the data supports points 2 and 3 suggesting that the research agenda limits possible RME research and that, while some staff support the RME agenda, there is evidence that competing priorities remain a barrier to change. However, contrary to the difficulties suggested by Sharma and Hart (2014), our research found that as RME becomes a stronger presence within higher education, although there are still clear silos within business school functions, it is not necessarily untenured staff members handling RME activities. In relation to point 4, our data questions this finding as varying degrees of leadership and commitment impact RME activities in different institutions.

The predominant driver came from management within a school and whether or not the individuals driving the institutionalization process had an adequate amount of managerial support. Management control the resources and can help or hinder the process by allocating time or financial resources to the RME agenda. Respondents in two of the three case studies commented on how a change in management can either strengthen a RME approach or lose its momentum. " [You] know there are changes in management, and you know when changes happen … you know by and large initially the first couple of deans were very supportive" (Director of Social Responsibility and Sustainability, 2015).

For the initial and advanced institutions the notion that management were supportive of the idea but had no knowledge with regard to direction was raised, or how individuals were recruited to guide the process. The passion and enthusiasm of individuals is often needed as a prerequisite to push on the management and develop the assistance required.

For the barriers, the main challenge to overcome stems from both lack of managerial support as an opposition to the above driver and staff resistance. Resistance was described as being presented in a number of different formats including ideological, practical and relevance. In order for management and those engaged staff members to overcome this resistance, communication skills are required to persuade other members of staff of the advantages of the institutionalization of RME.

> [O]ne of my strengths has always been engaging people, I kind [of] know how to press people's buttons quite quickly and so I talk to my team and say, you know this is a hearts and minds exercise rather than a technical exercise, we need to win over staff (Senior Lecturer in Business Ethics, 2015).

PRME was never commented on as a driver but often described as a lever for change and subsequently seen as a key enabler that allowed staff members to push processes and sign up to the initiative. Again, this requires resource allocation and commitment from management. "[Getting] PRME wasn't a main thing it was vehicle to lever everything else in" (Senior Lecturer in Business Ethics, 2015).

A further enabler can be seen as RME-related terminology within mission and vision statements. While this was not evidenced within the case studies, from the website analysis it was noted that a lack of RME language was evident, but the initial institution made reference to making changes to a mission statement in order to position the school within the wider academic environment.

> [W]e are talking about changing our mission statement at the moment and I'm trying to get the words "responsible management" kind of inserted into our mission statement, the idea being well if you say "ok well you know

where do you want to go as a student, I want to go and learn more about responsible business or social business or sustainable business where do I go" … we kind of see that we can maybe position ourselves in there for people making that choice (Senior Lecturer in Business Ethics, 2015).

After evidencing the key drivers, barriers and enablers, we now offer some practical suggestions for facilitating the institutionalization of RME.

Application

In order for RME to be institutionalized successfully to the level the school chooses, management need to support the process in terms of both authoritative decision-making and resource allocation. Faculty members need to gain an understanding and appreciation of the requirements of the RME agenda, even when it does not fall within their active discipline, and driven, enthusiastic staff with new ideas will help to diffuse the new strategies and practices.

It is here that we offer practical suggestions for three different staff levels, deans, senior lecturers and junior lecturers, making recommendations for areas in which they can engage in order to improve the institutionalization of RME, promote the drivers and enablers and combat the barriers.

Drivers

- **Deans**:

  Actively recruit staff who have specialisms within the RME remit

  Initiate engagement with accreditation bodies to enforce RME-related standards

  Input RME-related terms within the strategic direction and plans of the business school

- **Senior staff**:

  Create committees to support raising the RME agenda, e.g. PRME steering committees or recruiting more RME focused participants to other committees such as advisory boards and research groups

  Push for RME-related terms to be present within business school literature, e.g. mission/vision, induction proceedings and web pages

- **Junior staff**:

  Require knowledge and understanding of RME as a prerequisite for all new staff via job descriptions

  Make the signing off of a probationary period reliant on satisfactory engagement with RME

- **All**:

  Engage with volunteering programmes that encompass RME activities, e.g. collaborating with schools or colleges within the community, partnerships with local businesses to offer consultancy

Barriers

- **Deans**. Provide resources, such as time and finance allocation, to faculty who are working on the RME agenda

- **Senior staff**. Understand and support the need for change towards a responsibility agenda—even if this affects teaching structures and is not explicitly within their area of research

- **Junior staff**. Bring in new pedagogical methods for teaching RME to large numbers of students and/or through virtual learning environments

Enablers

- **Deans**. Initiate the conduct of curriculum audits to determine where the gaps lie

- **Senior staff**:

  Acquiring knowledge of organizational structures will help to get changes pushed through quicker

  Sharing their expertise in RME with other staff and students

- **Junior staff**. Promote the RME-related courses and modules to increase student take up

- **All**:

  Support the PRME initiative by providing resources for SIP reports, allowing module reviews and creating space to implement new features, and assist the PRME Champions. This will help raise the agenda quicker and with fewer obstacles.

  Engage with the Green Agenda present within universities' strategies and campus actions, e.g. recycling, energy saving and sustainable transportation methods

By offering this guideline we hope to enable staff members to understand how they can apply the actions in relation to the drivers, barriers and enablers derived from this research to improve the success and efficiency of the institutionalization of RME.

Commentary

Professor Christopher Cowton
Dean of University of Huddersfield Business School

Those of us with management responsibilities need to think carefully about how we exercise our leadership of RME, learning from our experiences. The way the RME agenda plays out will vary from organization to organization, but this chapter provides a valuable framework for directing our attention to key issues to consider as the RME agenda is taken forward in business schools.

The analysis of drivers, barriers and enablers of RME in this chapter resonates well with my experience as a business school dean, as a professor who introduced business ethics to the school's curriculum many years ago, as a long-standing researcher in business and financial ethics, and as someone involved in professional ethics. In commenting further on the chapter, though, I don't want to draw explicitly on this background but instead reflect on an episode at my university.

I was recently concerned to see some student feedback critical of recycling on campus. This particular episode and subsequent investigation generated some useful learning. First, in addition to the teaching, research and enterprise remit, to which the authors refer in their chapter, the operation of our facilities and more generally how we carry out our activities, is also significant. It is a key part of "walking the talk". Second, the ability of a business school to "walk" the PRME "talk" will be influenced, and to some extent constrained, by the wider context when the school is part of a multi-faculty university. Conversation revealed that the university's approach to recycling was, because of the way it was carried out, much better than students—or staff—might appreciate. Thus the third lesson was that it is important to communicate what we do. This is not just to inform (or placate) our stakeholders though; a sound understanding of what we currently do can provide the basis for better informed dialogue as we seek to make progress on RME.

Conclusion

Our findings suggest that business schools have a variety of activities they can engage in, in order to institutionalize RME and equally a number of drivers, barriers and enablers that can help or hinder this process. In order for a school to embed the RME agenda with success they must be consciously aware of the challenges and opportunities presented to them in order to act proactively and educate the next generation of managers ethically, responsibly and sustainably.

Instead of managers emulating an "act first, think later" mentality, there is a need for managers to understand CSR, sustainability and other similar issues prior to their development within an organization's operations and to operate proactively as opposed to the reactive scenarios found in the current economic climate. Thus, there is an increasing need for RME to be present within a school's strategy and daily activities.

A summary of the results show that management support and motivated faculty members were regarded as key drivers. Both access to and allocation of resources, as well as staff resistance, were seen as the main barriers to the institutionalization process with PRME seen as the strongest enabling factor.

Possible future research needed in line with Principle 4 of the PRME could include further investigation of the suggested drivers, barriers and enablers, potentially across the UK higher education sector. Furthermore, comparative case studies of business schools at different stages of the RME institutionalization process could be monitored and evaluated in order to explore how they implement and handle the challenges and opportunities encountered. A final further research option could include focusing at the specific staff level to investigate if the suggested actions and application of this research are pertinent.

Given the current economic climate and increasingly negative responses and actions to a number of situations, it is imperative that RME is raised not only within business schools but also universities and other higher education institutions across the world in order to lead the next generation into a more sustainable future.

References

Barber, N.A., Wilson, F., Venkatachalam, V., Cleaves, S.M. & Garnham, J. (2014). Integrating sustainability into business curricula: University of New Hampshire case study. *International Journal of Sustainability in Higher Education*, 15(4), 8.

Berger, P.L. & Luckmann, T. (1967). *The Social Construction of Reality: A Treatise in the Sociology of Knowledge*. London: Allen Lane.

Blasco, M. (2012). Aligning the hidden curriculum of management education with PRME: An inquiry based framework. *Journal of Management Education*, 36(3), 364-388.

BSBG (British Sky Broadcasting Group) (2012). *Annual Report 2012*. Retrieved from https://corporate.sky.com/documents/publications-and-reports/2012/annual-report-2012.pdf

Burchell, J., Murray, A. & Kennedy, S. (2014). Responsible management education in UK business schools: Critically examining the role of the United Nations Principles for Responsible Management Education as a driver for change. *Management Learning*, 1(19), 1-19.

Christensen, L.J., Peirce, E., Hartman, L.P., Hoffman, W.M. & Carrier, J. (2007). Ethics, CSR, and sustainability education in the Financial Times Top 50 Global Business Schools: Baseline data and future research directions. *Journal of Business Ethics*, 73(4), 347-368.

Cooper, S., Parkes, C. & Blewitt, J. (2014). Can accreditation help a leopard change its spots? Social accountability and stakeholder engagement in business schools. *Accounting, Auditing & Accountability Journal*, 27(2), 234. doi:10.1108/AAAJ-07-2012-01062

Cornuel, E. & Hommel, U. (2015). Moving beyond the rhetoric of responsible management education. *Journal of Management & Enterprise Development*, 34(1), 2-15. doi:10.1108/JMD-06-2014-0059

Cowton, C.J. & Cummins, J. (2003). Teaching business ethics in UK higher education: progress and prospects. *Teaching Business Ethics*, 7(1), 37-54.

Dacin, M.T., Goodstein, J. & Scott, W.R. (2002). Institutional theory and institutional change: Introduction to the special research forum. *Academy of Management Journal*, 45(1), 45-56.

Doh, J.P. & Tashmann, P. (2014). Half a world away: The integration and assimilation of corporate social responsibility, sustainability, and sustainable development in business school curricula. *Corporate Social Responsibility and Environmental Management*, 21(3), 131-142.

Doherty, B., Meehan, J. & Richards, A. (2015). The business case and barriers for responsible management education in business schools. *International Journal of Management & Enterprise Development*, 34(1), 34-60.

Exter, N., Grayson, D. & Maher, R. (2013). Facilitating organizational change for embedding sustainability into academia: A case study. *International Journal of Management & Enterprise Development*, 32(3), 319-332.

Financial Times (2014, October 12). Fortune 500 companies spend more than $15bn on corporate responsibility. *Financial Times*. Retrieved from http://www.ft.com/cms/s/0/95239a6e-4fe0-11e4-a0a4-00144feab7de.html#axzz3mSl5hZ1t

Fukukawa, K., Spicer, D., Fairbrass, J. & Burrows, S.A. (2013). Sustainable change: Education for sustainable development in the business school. *The Journal of Corporate Citizenship*, 49, 71-99.

Green, S.E., Li, Y. & Nohria, N. (2009). Suspended in self-spun webs of significance: A rhetorical model of institutionalization and institutionally embedded agency. *Academy of Management Journal*, 52(1), 11-36.

Khavul, S., Chavez, H. & Bruton, G.D. (2013). When institutional change outruns the change agent: The contested terrain of entrepreneurial microfinance for those in poverty. *Journal of Business Venturing*, 28(1), 30-50.

Kolodinsky, R.W., Madden, T.M., Zisk, D.S. & Henkel, E.T. (2010). Attitudes about corporate social responsibility: Business student predictors. *Journal of Business Ethics*, 91(2), 167-181. doi:10.1007/s10551-009-0075-3

Leca, B., Battilana, J. & Boxenbaum, E. (2009). How actors change institutions: Towards a theory of institutional entrepreneurship. *The Academy of Management Annals*, 3(1), 65-107.

Louw, J. (2015). "Paradigm change" or no real change at all? A critical reading of the U.N. Principles for Responsible Management Education. *Journal of Management Education*, 39(2), 184-208. doi:10.1177/1052562914547965

Maheshwari, B., Kumar, V. & Kumar, U. (2010). Delineating the ERP institutionalization process: go-live to effectiveness. *Business Process Management Journal*, 16(4), 744-771. doi:10.1108/14637151011065982

Maloni, M.J., Smith, S.D. & Napshin, S. (2012). A methodology for building faculty support for the United Nations Principles for Responsible Management Education. *Journal of Management Education*, 36(3), 312-336.

Matten, D. & Moon, J. (2004). Corporate social responsibility education in Europe. *Journal of Business Ethics*, 54(4), 323-337.

Nicholls, J., Hair, J.F., Ragland, C.B. & Schimmel, K.E. (2013). Ethics, corporate social responsibility, and sustainability education in AACSB undergraduate and graduate marketing curricula: A benchmark study. *Journal of Marketing Education*, 35(2), 129-140. doi:10.1177/0273475313489557

Pfeffer, J. & Fong, C.T. (2004). The business school "business": Some Lessons from the US experience. *Journal of Management Studies*, 41(8), 1501-1520.

Rasche, A. & Escudero, M. (2010). Leading change: The role of the Principles for Responsible Management Education. *Journal of Business and Economic Ethics*, 10(2), 244-250.

Rasche, A. & Gilbert, D.U. (2015). Decoupling responsible management education: Why business schools may not walk their talk. *Journal of Management Inquiry*, 24(3), 239-252. doi:10.1177/1056492614567315

Rasche, A., Gilbert, D.U. & Schedel, I. (2013). Cross-disciplinary ethics education in MBA programs: rhetoric or reality? *Academy of Management Learning & Education*, 12(1), 71-85. doi:10.5465/amle.2011.0016A

Reay, T., Chreim, S., Golden-Biddle, K., Goodrick, E., Williams, B. E., Casebeer, A, … & Hinings, C.R. (2013). Transforming new ideas into practice: An activity based perspective on the institutionalization of practices. *Journal of Management Studies*, 50(6), 963-990. doi:10.1111/joms.12039

Sharland, A., Fiedler, A. & Menon, M. (2013). Ethics in the business curriculum: Does delivery need to be revisited? *Southern Journal of Business and Ethics*, 5, 55-69.

Sharma, S. & Hart, S.L. (2014). Beyond "saddle bag" sustainability for business education. *Organization & Environment*, 27(1), 10-15. doi:10.1177/1086026614520713

Silvera, I. (2015, January 14). Global Fortune 500 spend "fraction" of corporate social responsibility budget on education. International Business Times. Retrieved from http://www.ibtimes.co.uk/global-fortune-500-spend-fraction-corporate-social-responsibility-budget-education-1483348

Sobczak, A. & Mukhi, U. (2015). The role of UN Principles for Responsible Management Education in stimulating organizational learning for global responsibility within business schools: An interview with Jonas Haertle. *Journal of Management Inquiry*, 1-7.

Trevino, L.J. & Thomas, D.E. (2008). The three pillars of institutional theory and the FDI in Latin America: An institutionalization process. *International Business Review*, 17(1), 118-133. doi:10.1016/j.ibusrev.2007.10.002

Zell, D. (2005). Pressure for relevancy at top-tier business schools. *Journal of Management Inquiry*, 14(3), 271-274. doi:10.1177/1056492605279097

Appendix

Case study data and correspondent drivers, barriers and enablers identified

	Drivers	Barriers	Enablers
Advanced	Passionate Vice Chancellor (*Interview*) Specialist MSc (*Interview/Webpage/SIP*) Audit, see where gaps are (*Interview*) UG/PG RME-related modules (*SIP*)	Terminology (*Interview*) No RME language within mission/vision (*Webpage*)	Processes for staff sharing information (*Interview*) Strategy, sustainably literate graduates by 2020 (*Interview/Webpage/SIP*) Social responsibility and sustainability as one of eight key strategic aims (*SIP*)
Middle	Social enterprise unit (*Interview*) Management support (*Interview*) Estimated 80% take up on module (*Interview*) UG/PG RME-related modules (*SIP*)	More focus on "Green Agenda" as it is measurable (*Interview*) SIP report heavily focused on "Green Agenda" (*SIP*) PRME sign up resistance (*Interview*) Staff resistance (*Interview*) Timescale (*Interview*) No RME language within mission/vision (*Webpage*)	PRME sign up (*Interview*) Management support (*Interview*) Resources (*Interview*) Good student response (*SIP*)
Initial	Accreditation (*Interview*) Student needs (*Interview*) Passionate staff (*Interview*)	Pedagogical issues (*Interview*) Staff resistance (*Interview*) No RME language within mission/vision (*Webpage*)	Translatable terminology (*Interview*) Having a sustainability section promoting their RME engagement (*Webpage*)

16

Teaching methods and the Kolb learning cycle
Pedagogical approaches in the Principles for Responsible Management Education domain

Jeanie M. Forray
Western New England University

Jennifer S.A. Leigh
Nazareth College of Rochester

Janelle E. Goodnight
Western New England University

with practitioner commentary by Dean Cycon
Dean's Beans Organic Coffee Company

I am often approached after talks at business schools and undergraduate management programmes around the country by students who say that they had been ready to quit school until they heard me speak about how a business could (and should!) deeply integrate ethics and sustainability into its core operations and still be profitable. These students consistently say that even though they are exposed to ethics, social and environmental responsibility in specific classes, these concepts are drowned in a tsunami of the pedagogy of profit. I have personally witnessed this both as a guest lecturer and in conversations with faculty who bemoan the same dynamic in their universities. What's going on here? (Dean Cycon, Founder and CEO, Dean's Beans Organic Coffee Company).

This chapter is an attempt to respond to the concern and pointed question in the above story. As Dean tells us, current efforts to educate students as responsible managers are insufficient to overcome the dominant business narrative of profit. If we are to make a difference in business conduct, we must do more to expose and overcome this dynamic. In other words, we must change the way we educate future managers about and for responsible management practice. In addition, the Principles for Responsible Management Education (PRME) require us to consider how we can be more effective in integrating responsible management education (RME) topics and processes into our classrooms. The approach we take to addressing this challenge is to report on research examining common teaching methods used during "exposure" to RME topics, connect these methods to a noted learning framework, and use insights derived from that connection to offer suggestions for expanding and enhancing RME integration in business education.

We define RME as both content (knowledge) and pedagogy (process) that emphasizes corporate social responsibilities, stakeholder relationships and the firm's impacts on stakeholders and the natural environment. This domain includes, but is not limited to, education focused on corporate citizenship, sustainability, social entrepreneurship and business ethics. RME is part of a long-standing and growing reform movement within management education. As noted in many chapters within this book and elsewhere, and based on the year after year global decline of trust (Edelman, 2015) and confidence (Gallup, 2015) in business, it is increasingly clear that Dean's voice is one of many and that management education is in dire need of transformation.

As we discuss the research study and RME, you will hear two different voices. The first voice you have already heard, that of Dean Cycon, who represents the business world. After the main study report, Dean will offer additional thoughts on RME practices. In the middle of the chapter, you will read the blended voices of the three academic researchers—Jeanie Forray, Jennifer Leigh and Janelle Goodnight—describing the conceptual framework of the research project, the method used and the findings.

In the last few years, we have seen a surge in responsible management education resources such as textbooks, teaching resource guides, book reviews and special issues in scholarly journals. This surge is due, in part, to increased interest in the topic based on the PRME initiative and is built upon a sustained trend in this domain for the last 30 years. This content is fundamental for helping teach a new generation of managers. However, content alone is insufficient for this task and, based on our decades of experience as educators and entrepreneurs, we argue that the *process* of educating for responsible management is as central as the content we cover in lectures and readings. To date there have been no comprehensive global surveys on the pedagogical practices of RM educators, and we believe that establishing a starting point for RME will be beneficial for many reasons, such as understanding what is actually happening in our classrooms, identifying priority areas for faculty development and as benchmark for development in the domain. By reviewing the main findings readers can reflect on their own RME teaching practices and opportunities for growth.

This study investigates two questions about teaching and learning within the PRME domain.

- What is the extent to which educators covering PRME-related topics use instructional methods that represent multiple learning opportunities in their classrooms?

- What differences exist in instructional methods at different levels (undergraduate, Master's and Executive), in different disciplines (management or non-management) and in varied teaching locations (US and non-US) among those teaching within the PRME domain?

This study attempts to provide an understanding of PRME Principle 3, our educational methods, from a broad perspective. In contrast to other chapters focused on Principle 3 which offer valuable specific strategies and methods, this chapter investigates Principle 3 methods themselves. We offer that the findings from this study will help RM educators in two ways. First, the findings allow us to reflect on our standard RME pedagogy repertoire. Second, the findings allow us to understand the teaching and learning methods utilized at different educational levels and by colleagues in different disciplines which can assist with school-wide conversations about learning priorities and professional development.

We categorize nine common teaching methods in management education according to the Kolb learning cycle and survey business educators to identify the most commonly used instructional methods for teaching PRME-related topics. The researchers selected the Kolb Cycle model as it is one of the best known experiential learning theory models in management education. Findings suggest an unequal distribution of instructional methods across the Kolb Cycle, several significant differences in instructional methods used at undergraduate, Master's and Executive levels, and differences in instructional methods across disciplinary training but not geographic region.

Our chapter begins with a literature review addressing RME-related teaching, teaching and learning evaluation and debates, and the Kolb cycle model. After considering the research methods employed in this study, the key research findings are discussed with commentary from both managerial and academic perspectives.

RME-related teaching resources

Six core principles drive the PRME's large-scale business school curricular reform framework: Purpose, Value, Method, Research, Partnership and Dialogue. The third

Principle—Method—asks educators to "create educational frameworks, materials, processes and environments that enable effective learning experiences for responsible leadership". With respect to this aspiration, a growing set of resources for RME-related teaching already existed before PRME, including dedicated websites and newsletters from academic societies such as the Academy of Management (cf. Social Issues in Management, SIM) as well as a wide and growing range of pedagogical articles for specific RME topics such as sustainability, business ethics and poverty, among others, in well-known management education journals. Recently PRME Working Groups have released publicly a range of teaching resources such as the Anti-Corruption guidelines "Toolkit", the Gender Equity Global Resource Repository[1] and a number of Inspirational Guides for the Implementation of PRME (PRME, 2012, 2013; Escudero *et al.*, 2012; Murray *et al.*, 2015). We should note that special issues on PRME have appeared in both management education and responsibility management journals such as the *Journal of Management Education* (Forray and Leigh, 2012a), *Journal of Corporate Citizenship* (McIntosh, 2013) and *Journal of Management Development* (Cornuel and Hommel, 2015).

Notwithstanding the above, much of the PRME literature has focused primarily on six areas:

- Explaining the initiative and its evolution (Haertle and Miura, 2014; Weber *et al.*, 2013; Rasche, 2011; Kell and Haertle, 2011; Alcaraz and Thiruvattal, 2010; Rasche and Escudero, 2010)

- Highlighting institutional change with respect to PRME (Fougère and Solitander, 2009; Horwitz and Grayson, 2010, Godemann *et al.*, 2011)

- Employing PRME as part of the broader critique of management education (Verbos and Humphries, 2015; Mette and Rovira, 2012, Fougère *et al.*, 2014)

- Exploring executive views of PRME (Gitsham, 2008, Gitsham and Clark, 2014)

- Describing specific pedagogies such as international study trips (Viswanathan, 2012; Sroufe *et al.*, 2015), pragmatic inquiry (Kelley and Nahser, 2014), action research (Lavine and Roussin, 2012), benevolent leadership development (Karakas *et al.*, 2013), internships and live case studies (Baden and Parkes, 2013), real-life student projects (Prandini *et al.*, 2012), and comparative case studies (Solitander *et al.*, 2012; Dickson *et al.*, 2013)

- More recently, critiquing PRME (Cornuel and Hommel, 2015; Louw, 2015; Perry and Win, 2013)

In addition, there is now an increasing amount of traditional management education resources such as PRME textbooks (Lawrence and Beamish, 2012; Laasch and Conaway, 2015). Yet despite the content advances relatively little is known

1 Wikispace of the PRME Working Group on Gender Equality. Retrieved from http://prmegenderequalityworkinggroup.unprme.wikispaces.net/Welcome+to+the+Wikispace

about the bigger "pedagogical picture" of RME-related teaching methods and the learning process.

Teaching practices and student learning

A common approach to linking teaching to learning is to use student outcomes assessment as a proxy for arguing that a particular approach leads to particular outcomes. Such evidence of learning is a requirement for articles in most pedagogical journals in our field, and outcomes assessment is used to measure and evaluate student learning across higher education in general (cf. Astin and Antonio, 2012) and in management education in particular (cf. Moskal *et al.*, 2008; Michlitsch and Sidle, 2002). While the impetus in journal articles for evidence of learning via outcomes assessment is consistent with a social science domain, much of outcomes assessment more generally is driven by issues of accountability. A 2006 report by the US Department of Higher Education "criticized higher education for its limited demonstration of student learning and called for more sophisticated assessment in the name of public accountability" (Astin and Antonio, 2012, p. 2). This sentiment has been particularly salient for business programmes, especially those that are subject to assurance of learning standards established by accrediting bodies such as AACSB International (2012) and others. Links between teaching and learning with respect to RME-related areas follow a similar outcomes-oriented model, often focusing on a particular approach and its efficacy (for recent examples, see Dufresne and Offstein, 2012; Shrivastava, 2010; Litzky *et al.*, 2010).

While an outcomes assessment model does provide evidence of what is learned, often in the context of a particular teaching approach, it does not address the relationship between teaching methods and the learning process. In other words, outcomes assessment does not address the aforementioned interest of the PRME in "processes and environments that enable effective learning experiences". To begin to explore these processes and environments, our study is designed to examine the extent to which educators covering RME-related topics in their classrooms are using instructional methods that represent multiple learning opportunities as represented by the Kolb learning cycle. In addition, we are interested in the extent to which differences exist in instructional methods among those teaching at different levels (undergraduate, Master's and Executive), in different disciplines (management or non-management) and in varied teaching locations. These interests led to two broad research questions: based on the Kolb learning cycle, 1) what are the most commonly used instructional methods for teaching PRME topics and to what extent are they distributed across the Kolb cycle? 2) What, if any, are the differences in instructional methods used among those teaching different student populations (undergraduate, Master's and Executive levels), in different disciplinary domains (management, non-management) and in different geographic regions (US/non-US)? Our aim is to examine the methods and approaches used in the classroom for complex interdisciplinary RME topics, such as sustainability, gender and diversity inclusion, and serving the base-of-the-pyramid. Our contribution allows for reflection at the personal and organizational levels based on a well-known typology of teaching and learning practices and global findings. Accordingly, our hope is to foster examination of one's personal teaching and learning repertoire and to structure institutional RME conversations.

This project builds upon the global research study conducted by the Ashridge Business School in the United Kingdom (Gitsham, 2008). In that study, researchers interviewed CEOs and other senior executives regarding the importance of RME-related topics to the conduct of their business. The results highlighted the standing that senior executives give to having the necessary knowledge and skills to respond to RME trends yet which are slow to be adopted as is poignantly illustrated by Dean Cycon in our opening quote. With respect to teaching methods, that study assessed executives' opinions about different approaches to learning that they viewed as being required to develop corporate social responsibility (CSR) and sustainability knowledge and skills. Our study extends that research to include data from the instructor perspective and links instructional methods to a learning theory conceptual framework. Linking methods into a framework allows for a systematic review of what is occurring in our RME classrooms.

Teaching practices and learning theory

Admittedly, there are a variety of learning theories and numerous classification systems that link particular theories to various instructional methods (see Neumann and Koper, 2010 for an extensive discussion). One learning theory commonly referred to in the management education literature is Kolb's Experiential Learning Theory (ELT) (Kolb, 1984), which has been used extensively as a framework for methodological innovation in the management education field (see MacNab, 2012 and Borredon *et al.*, 2011 for recent examples). While we acknowledge that Kolb's ELT conceptualization and operationalization has been critiqued by scholars using a variety of stances, including conceptual (Webb, 1980), epistemological (Vince, 1998) and practical (Rogers and Horrocks, 2010), ELT remains a widely accepted and useful model of the learning process within management education (Kayes, 2002).

Experiential Learning Theory posits a learning cycle made up of four elements representing ends of two diametrically opposed learning situations (Kolb *et al.*, 2001): Concrete Experience (CE)/Abstract Conceptualization (AC) and Reflective Observation (RO)/Active Experimentation (AE) (see Fig. 16.1). The first dimension (CE/AC) represents the nature of information input, either from experience or from abstractions, while the second dimension (RO/AE) represents information processing either by internal reflection on the experience or externally acting upon conclusions drawn (Svinicki and Dixon, 1987). ELT also suggests that individuals have a predisposition for particular forms of information input and information processing, known as their learning style, and that effective learning environments provide opportunities for learners to encounter all phases of the experiential learning cycle (Svinicki and Dixon, 1987; Kolb, 1984).

Figure 16.1 **Four elements of Experiential Learning Theory**
Source: from Dennison (2012), based on Kolb (1984).

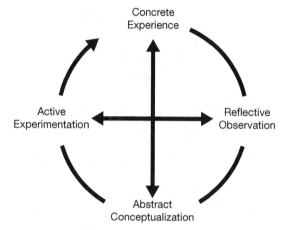

A number of authors have categorized different pedagogical activities according to the experiential learning cycle (Dede, 2009; Svinicki and Dixon, 1987). These schemes assign different educational activities to a phase of the learning cycle according to the predominant orientation of the activity. Dede (2009, p. 156) notes that Concrete Experience (CE) is based on feeling, Reflective Observation (RO) is based on watching, Abstract Conceptualization (AC) is based on thinking, and Active Experimentation (AE) is based on doing and living. So, for example, lectures presenting a theoretical model or conceptual material are categorized as AC because they foster the categorization and organization of theories and concepts; simulations are categorized as CE because they involve students integrating and building upon theoretical or mental models in example situations.

Utilizing categories from the Ashridge Business School study of executives (Gitsham, 2008), common teaching methods within management education (cf. Burgoyne and Cooper, 1976), and drawing upon the work of Dede (2009), we categorize nine commonly used teaching methods in terms of their position in the Kolb ELT cycle (see Fig. 16.2). These methods are: action learning, case studies, class discussion, experiential, lecture, project-based, service-learning, simulations and small group discussions. While no categorization scheme of learning activities aligns perfectly to the learning cycle model, ours reflects a high degree of consensus concerning the types of activities most commonly found in management education environments and their placement within each of the four components of the experiential learning cycle. We acknowledge that any categorization of teaching methods is subject to challenge, and that any particular method may not "fit" exclusively within only one quadrant. However, based on our understanding of the conceptual framework provided by Kolb, confirmatory discussions with a small sample of management education experts, and drawing upon other existing categorization schemes, we assert that the dominant features of each teaching method as commonly practised are most strongly affiliated with the quadrant shown.

Figure 16.2 **Teaching methods aligned to the Kolb ELT cycle**

	Concrete Experience **Feeling**: *learning through integrating information with individual values or feelings* Small group discussion Simulations/games Experiential (role plays, in-class exercises)	
Active Experimentation **Doing**: *learning through manipulating and testing to obtain answers* Action learning Project-based learning Service-learning		Reflective Observation **Watching**: *learning through observation and contemplation* Class discussion Case studies
	Abstract Conceptualization **Thinking**: *learning through organizing information into concepts, theories and principles* Lectures	

Methods

Survey design

We developed our survey to determine the teaching methods used by business educators when addressing PRME-related areas of ethics, social responsibility, sustainability/environment and social entrepreneurship for different populations of students (undergraduate, Master's, Executive). These methods are: action learning, case studies, class discussion, experiential, lecture, project-based, service-learning, simulations, small group discussions and "other". Brief descriptions of some of the methods were provided (see Appendix). The survey asked respondents whether they taught a particular population of students and, if so, to indicate the type(s) of teaching methods used for that population. The survey also asked for information on whether the respondent's institution was a PRME participant, country in which they teach, their business discipline or area, and provided space for respondents to make additional comments.

Sample

The survey was conducted online in English and gathered information about the methods used by instructors in all business disciplines when covering issues of ethics, social responsibility, sustainability/natural environment or social entrepreneurship in their courses. It took approximately 20 minutes to answer all questions if the respondent taught at all levels and somewhat less for those teaching at only one or two levels. A link to the survey was distributed to various electronic discussion lists within business academe and posted on the PRME website. Respondents were told the survey was confidential and that personal information not voluntarily provided by the respondent would not be collected. There were 280 responses to the online survey, of which 239 were usable.

While most respondents were from the United States (n=119 or 57%), many other countries were represented in the study. Of those indicating their primary business discipline, 43.3% were management, followed by18.3% indicating "other", 14.4% in marketing, and from 1.4% to 7.2% for all other business fields (accounting, business administration, finance, information systems, international business, and operations). Some of the "other" responses were reclassified as management fields, yielding an overall distribution of 51.9% management and 48.1% non-management disciplines. For those respondents who indicated whether their institution was affiliated with PRME, 46.9% designated yes, 21.1% no, and 31.9% "I don't know".

Respondents were asked to rate, on a 5-point Likert scale of 1= "Always Use", 2= "Often Use", 3= "Sometimes Use", 4= "Rarely Use", and 5= "Never Use", the extent to which they employ various teaching methods in their classes for different populations of students when covering RME-related topics of ethics, CSR, sustainability/natural environment or social entrepreneurship. When calculating results, we combined the entire population for "always" and "often" because the numbers for "always" were very low. This approach is consistent with the absence of extreme scale indicators among survey populations in general (Miller, 1956; Kerlinger and Lee, 2000). Figure 16.2 shows the various teaching methods queried clustered according to the Kolb learning cycle.

Findings

In this section we begin with data that addresses the first research question: What is the extent to which educators covering RME-related topics use instructional methods that represent multiple learning opportunities in their classrooms? After the review of the most commonly used teaching methods for RME instructors in the survey, we then continue to the results which address the second research question: What differences exist in instructional methods at different levels, in different disciplines and in varied teaching locations among those teaching within the PRME domain?

Teaching methods commonly used

There were two broad trends in the most common methods and Kolb quadrants. First, the top three utilized methods overall were: class discussion 93.3% (RO), case studies 79.5% (RO) and small group discussion 71.1% (CE). The least utilized methods included service-learning 21.8% (AE) and simulations 23.8% (CE).

When comparing methods used by those who exclusively teach undergraduates (n=49) with those who teach only graduate students (Master's and Executive=55), the use of action learning (AE) is significantly different between these populations; those teaching only undergraduates are far less likely to use this method (p=.001) (see Fig. 16.3). Further, while at least half of each respondent group "Always" or "Often" use small group discussion (CE) and case studies (RO), those who teach graduate students exclusively are significantly more likely to utilize these methods (p=.022 and p=.035, respectively). Over half of both populations use class discussion (RO) and lecture (AC). And, while there is no statistical significance between them, over half of those who teach graduate students exclusively use experiential (CE) methods (56.4%), while under half (42.9%) of those who teach only undergraduates use this method.

Figure 16.3 **Distribution of methods and Kolb quadrants by teaching level**

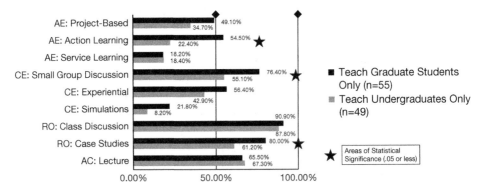

Reflecting on this finding we ask ourselves the following: What is the collective impact if undergraduates experience fewer teaching and learning methods compared with graduates?

Teachers in management vs. non-management disciplines

With respect to undergraduate teaching, over half of respondents in both populations (management, n=77; non-management, n=78) "Always" or "Often" use small group discussion (CE), class discussion (RO), case studies (RO) and lecture (AC). While these populations indicate similar teaching methods used for undergraduates, those in management are statistically more likely to use action learning (AE) (p=.023) and small group discussion (CE) (p=.003) (see Fig. 16.4).

Figure 16.4 **Teachers of undergraduates: MGT/non-MGT in usage of teaching methods**

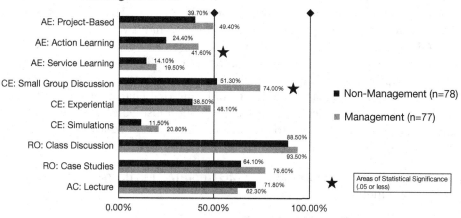

When teaching Master's students, over half of respondents in both populations (management, n=85/non-management, n=76) use the same methods "Always" or "Often": small group discussion (CE), class discussion (RO), case studies (RO) and lecture (AC). Those in management are significantly more likely to use small group discussion (CE) (p=.030). In addition, over half of those in management indicated use of action learning (AE) and experiential (CE) methods at "Always" or "Often" levels, while fewer than half in non-management disciplines indicated those levels of use for these methods; these differences were statistically different across the two populations (p=.037 and p. 009, respectively) (see Fig. 16.5).

Figure 16.5 **Teachers of Master's: MGT/non-MGT in usage of teaching methods**

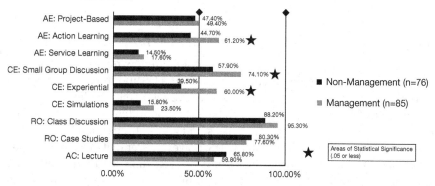

For those respondents teaching Executive students, over half "Always" or "Often" use class discussion (RO), small group discussion (CE), case studies (RO) and action learning (AE) (see Fig. 16.6). While over half of respondents in management (n=39) use experiential (CE) methods, and fewer than half of respondents in non-management disciplines (n=28) use experiential (CE) methods, the difference is not statistically significant. Similar conclusions are noted for lecture (AC); even though over half of respondents in non-management disciplines use lecture (AC) and fewer than half of those in management do so, the difference is not statistically different. Interestingly we see similar Kolb learning cycle differences for CE and AE methods for non-management and management disciplines as we did for undergraduate vs. graduate populations. Disciplinary differences in the breadth of teaching approaches and learning styles as they are connected to the Kolb learning cycle are of particular relevance to RME internal change agents, academic administrators and curriculum coordinators, who must work to provide a broad and comprehensive approach to responsible management education throughout their programme.

Figure 16.6 **Teachers of executives: MGT/non-MGT in usage of teaching methods**

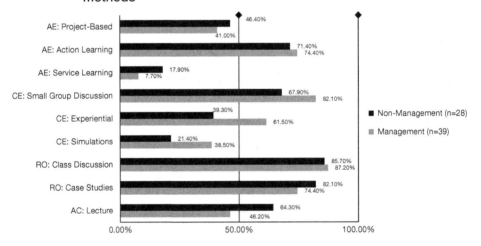

Teaching in the United States vs. teaching in non-US countries

Generally speaking, regardless of level taught, there are few differences between methods used by those teaching predominantly in the US and those teaching predominantly outside the US. Even where there is a difference in the level taught, it is only a matter of degree; for example, those teaching undergraduates primarily outside the US (n=63) are more likely to use small group discussion (CE) (p=.022) than those teaching undergraduates in the US; however, over half of each respondent group uses this method "Always" or "Often" (see Fig. 16.7). For undergraduates, methods used "Always" or "Often" by over half of those teaching predominantly inside or outside the US are class discussion (RO), lecture (AC), case studies (RO) and small group discussion (CE).

Figure 16.7 **Teachers of undergraduates: US/non-US in usage of teaching methods**

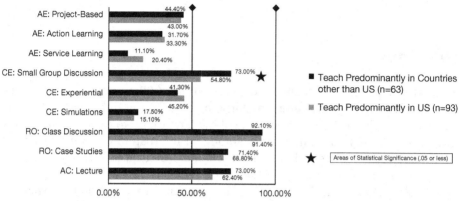

This is also true of both groups of respondents teaching Master's students. The methods for which half or more of both groups indicate "Always" or "Often" are class discussion (RO), case studies (RO), lecture (AC) and small group discussion (CE). Over half of those teaching predominantly in the US (n=90) indicate "Always" or "Often" for two additional methods, project-based (AE) and action learning, while those teaching predominantly outside the US (n=70) indicate experiential (CE), although none of these differences is statistically significant (see Fig. 16.8).

Figure 16.8 **Teachers of Master's: US/non-US in usage of teaching methods**

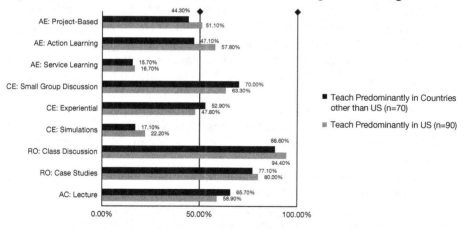

In the case of those teaching Executive students, no overall statistical differences exist between those teaching predominantly in the US and those outside the US, and over half of both groups of respondents indicate use of class discussion (RO), case studies (RO), action learning and small group discussion (CE) as "Always" or "Often". However, in the case of project-based (AE), lecture (AC) and experiential (CE), more than half of US respondents (n=25) indicate that they "Always" or "Often" use all of these methods but this difference is not statistically significant for the two respondent populations.

Discussion

While the educational domains of business ethics, CSR and sustainability have been the subject of research attention for some time (Forray and Leigh, 2012b), the current research project represents one of the few studies to examine wide-scale instructional practices in these areas among an international population across numerous student levels and business disciplines. As such, this research contributes to an understanding of actual faculty practices in classrooms when covering PRME-related topics and the extent to which these practices represent engagement with learning theory.

Learning populations

Our findings suggest that while instructional methods used by faculty across all student population levels represent all learning cycle quadrants, the teaching methods of Reflective Observation (class discussion, case studies, lecture) and Concrete Experience (small group discussion) dominate classroom engagements. Further, there are stark differences between those teaching only upper level students and those teaching only undergraduates. The difference in methods used for these two groups is most notable with respect to action learning (AE quadrant), small group discussion (CE quadrant) and case studies method (RO quadrant), with those who teach only graduate populations significantly more likely to use each of these methods than those who teach only undergraduates. Also, while instructors from all levels report using methods from the Active Experimentation (AE) quadrant, instructors teaching only graduate student populations reported using them more frequently than those teaching only undergraduates, with a significant difference between these two teaching groups in the use of action learning.

Of additional interest is a difference in the use of Concrete Experience (CE) methods among those who teach graduate students exclusively (Master's and Executive) and those teaching only undergraduates. More than half of those who teach only graduate students indicated that they use CE methods while under half of those teaching only undergraduates indicated such use. The handful of studies on PRME pedagogies confirm the value and need for concrete experience (CE) learning opportunities such as live case studies (Baden and Parkes, 2013) and real-life student projects (Prandini *et al.*, 2012). Also of note is the diversity of methods used by those teaching only upper level populations and those teaching only undergraduates. The former group reported frequent use of six of the nine methods surveyed, representing all four Kolb quadrants, while those teaching only undergraduates reported frequent use of four of the nine methods, representing only three Kolb quadrants. These findings suggest that those who teach exclusively at the upper level employ a wider repertoire of teaching methods than those who teach only undergraduates.

Implications for practice

Taken together, and given the importance of creating multiple learning opportunities for students in addition to the powerful potential of experiential and active learning both inside and outside the classroom (Kolb and Kolb, 2005), there is a clear need for faculty development efforts in teaching methods directed towards those who teach only undergraduates. These could include but are not limited to the following:

- Creating mentoring relationships between Master's and Executive faculty members and those teaching undergraduates exclusively

- Incentivizing more concrete experience methods (CE) by paying for training or stipends for course redesigns that incorporate these approaches

- Working with faculty developers to identify appropriate simulations, games and experiential exercises that fit course objectives

- Helping undergraduate faculty extend their networks to practitioners committed to responsible management practices for guest visits, site visits and even experience-focused assignments such as managerial interviews

Disciplinary differences

Disciplinary differences in teaching methods exist between faculty in management and those in non-management disciplines. While both populations use the same four methods extensively (small group discussion (CE), class discussion (RO), case studies (RO) and lecture (AC)), management instructors were significantly more likely to utilize service-learning (AE) and small group discussion (CE) at the undergraduate level and action learning (AE), small group discussion (CE) and experiential (CE) at the Master's level than their non-management colleagues. What these findings suggest is that not only do management faculty employ a wider range of teaching methods, reflecting more engagement with the Kolb learning cycle, but their use of small group discussion is more common at both the undergraduate and graduate levels in management classrooms than in non-management classrooms.

Implications for practice

These findings suggest that greater attention to learning theory and its relationship to classroom practices will be useful for those both within and outside the management domain. Learning theory provides an interdisciplinary common ground for understanding why students can leave their business programmes without a clear connection to responsible management practices across domains or an ability to act in ways consistent with them regardless of content area. The Kolb ELT cycle provides a useful diagnostic tool for schools and institutions to evaluate their teaching practices with a shared framework. We suggest the following:

- Institutions reflect by conducting an audit that examines RME content and process together to assess their own strengths and areas for development based on the model and knowledge of student populations.

- Faculty can identify points for potential synergies throughout the curriculum and gaps by assessing pedagogical practices by disciplines paired simultaneously with a school's learning objectives.

- Areas for improvement can be addressed in the short term by internal workshops and strategic planning of new hires with different pedagogical approaches.

US vs. non-US instructors

Interestingly, there were few notable differences between US and non-US instructors in teaching methods utilized for PRME topics. We admit to being surprised by this finding, having expected that cultural and historical differences in educational environments would be represented in our exploration of common teaching practices. Yet, with the exception of a significant difference between US and non-US faculty in the use of small group discussion at the undergraduate level, the teaching methods used for PRME-related topics are remarkably similar for each group. This finding may, in fact, be attributed to the international focus and collaborative nature of the PRME initiative. Faculty teaching in PRME-related areas may be more likely to use the same resources and approaches as their colleagues in this area regardless of geographical location.

Implications for practice

While the results of this study need additional replication, the current lack of differences still provides validation for current RME development opportunities. We suggest the following:

- Global networks for RME scholars from all disciplines, with increasing attention to disciplines outside of management, offer professional development workshops at international convenings and meetings, particularly ones related to high impact and less utilized active experimentation (AE) and concrete experience (CE) pedagogies.

- Regional PRME and UN Global Compact chapters can work to identify ways to support these teaching approaches in a way that is mutually beneficial for students and companies.

We now turn again to Dean Cycon's views on responsible management education reform from the perspective of a small business owner, change agent and social entrepreneur actively involved in mentoring the next generation of responsible management leaders. His extensive business experience, along with interactions with students in the classroom and in his organization, provides the basis for his critique of management education and suggestions for RME reform.

The Godfather, Breaking Bad and RME: cultures in need of change

At the beginning of the chapter, I raised the issue of student and faculty concern with the dominant content of business school education. Why—after 40 years of Earth Days, Love Canals, Bhopals and Enrons—are these issues still being raised? To me it is largely a cultural dynamic.

If you have ever seen *The Godfather* (or more currently, *Breaking Bad*) the question that arises is: how can these guys who are so loving to their families and giving to their communities also be capable of going out and murdering people? The answer is simple—that is the culture they live in, where such are norms of acceptable behaviour. Similarly, we can ask: how is it possible that a man or woman who is loving to his or her family and generous to his or her community is also capable of polluting the environment and poisoning people as a by-product of their business? How can they purchase raw materials from child labour, slave labour or from factories that regularly collapse on workers either directly or through independent contractors? How does the simple act of slipping on a business suit bring forth a set of business behaviours so at odds with personal behaviours? The answer? Business schools and undergraduate education exists in a vibrant and very real culture of its own. The obvious cultural imperatives in business are profit, growth and efficiency, as seen in the opening statement of the chapter. These cultural imperatives become manifest in organizational structures where ethics, social and environmental responsibility are relegated to afterthoughts or "highest goals" in mission statements, but are rarely foundational to the business. The easiest way to see this is to look where these functions are housed within complex business organizations. Generally they can be found in marketing departments or at best some vice-president position that is reactive to company behaviours rather than proactive and effective in their creation and implementation. These values become part of the commodity chain, rather than core or foundational beliefs. And that is exactly where they are in many business schools—side dishes to the main menu. Even noble attempts to quantify these values so that they can be evaluated on a level playing field with more crunchable variables (profit, job creation, efficiency, etc.) are problematic, as the very act legitimates the business-friendly cost/benefit approach where such values are inherently second class.

How can the culture of business as usual be changed? How can business schools and undergrad programmes integrate PRME as foundational for the future crops of business leaders in this hyper-globalized world? In the academic realm studies like this that provide an initial view of the RME landscape are a start. In the working world, a few examples from my experience give hope that it can happen.

At my company, we offer internships to students from around the US to live with our cooperative farmer partners in Peru, Nicaragua and Indonesia, among others, where the students participate in real world problems and processes of trade and justice. Internships are one type of Active Experimentation (AE) approach but, as noted in the survey results, are used more commonly with graduates and executives. We presently limit our internships to undergraduates. In my experience, the earlier students are in the field the more meaningful the coursework and degree becomes. Also, to be frank, I find that by the time students are in graduate school they are very far down the road of closing their minds to new paradigms—after all, they just spent the last four or five years in the business education system that represents that certain set of values we are discussing here, and it is very difficult to get students so educationally and emotionally invested in their paradigm to challenge it.

Internships for undergraduates can be meaningless exercises in frustration for both sides. If the practitioner does not understand what the educational purpose of the internship is, the internship may be nothing more than a series of tasks unrelated to a higher calling. It is imperative that internships be sculpted by the school and the practitioners together, so that the practitioner can become a true contributory partner in the education process. Otherwise the internship may be just a summer warehouse or technique building exercise for the student. In my experience, few if any partnerships regarding internships are based on a deep connection around ethics and structure as well as the subject matter of the internship. At Dean's Beans, our paradigmatic challenges to the interns are conscious, but they come from our commitment, not from a pre-designed strategy worked out with the host institution. Practitioner involvement in business education is an endeavour whose promise has yet to be realized. I think that there should be studies of the structure and substance of those potential relationships. Practitioners are not accustomed to being brought into an educational framework and need to be invited in (hopefully in a jargon neutral setting!) and engaged in sculpting programmes that meet educational as well as vocational objectives.

Along these lines, and given that case studies (RO) continue to be one of the most common teaching tools, we have talked to several universities about using our company for real-time case studies of how ethics and social and environmental concerns are an inextricable part of our decision-making fabric. These kind of real world experiences demonstrate to the students that such concerns are neither secondary nor ephemeral and this sentiment is echoed in some of the other studies mentioned in this chapter.

While it is heartening to see responsible management teaching across the disciplines in business schools, I see this as just the first step. Several years ago, Antioch Graduate School in New Hampshire set up a team of faculty, community leaders and practitioners (I was one) to see how social justice issues could be integrated into every aspect of the school's behaviour—not just in every offering in the curriculum, but in the institution itself (buying practices of the school, relations with workers, etc.). After a two-year study the school did a great job of acting on the recommendations, so that the school actually began to live the values it was professing. I participated in similar initial discussions with faculty and administration at Northeastern University regarding how social justice values could be represented throughout the curriculum, in every offering, not just as a smattering of elective classes that give the students a clear signal that these concerns are secondary in their education and to their lives as business people.

In conclusion, I strongly believe that the challenges of transforming business school and management culture are those of breadth and of depth. We need to understand the baseline of what RME topics are being offered and the teaching and learning strategies for delivering them. It is clear from the findings that much more exploration is needed of RME methods in non-management disciplines. However, this is just the first step. RME must be injected into the core of business and management education and across a very broad spectrum of courses, not remain as secondary offerings or tolerated by administration like some embarrassing adolescent visitor. This broadening must be combined with a deepening of teaching and exposure to PRME through the more engaged pedagogies described in this chapter and this edited book. Our Earth, our globalized business community and our humanity depend upon it.

Challenges of new pedagogical strategies research

We acknowledge two main limitations in this study's design and findings. First, we did not closely define instructional methods for respondents. For instance, class discussion, one of the most commonly used instructional methods, can be enacted very differently by different instructors. A related limitation is the use of one learning theory as the basis for methods categorization. While we believe the insights derived from the Kolb scheme are useful, other theories of experiential learning may yield different results. Building from these gaps and key findings, we see several avenues for future research related to instructional methods and RME topics.

- Given the significant differences observed in this sample with respect to management and non-management disciplines, we see the need for research on teaching methods that addresses business disciplines more specifically. It would be extremely useful to have a more differentiated understanding of pedagogical strategies with respect to RME-related topics for the different business administration disciplines, as well as an understanding of these differences irrespective of specific topic area. Understanding the starting point of pedagogical methods within the entire business school would provide a context for understanding what is happening and where critical necessity exists for faculty development and pedagogical innovation.

- Qualitative studies could explore why there are particular learning cycle quadrants that are less utilized than others in the management education process. Likewise, qualitative studies could explore in more fine-grained detail why some instructors opt for single methods and others multiple methods. Greater understanding of the basis for faculty selection of teaching methods would assist those responsible for faculty development, deans, professional associations and the PRME Secretariat with further RME integration across the entire business curriculum.

- We encourage a broader discussion within management education of learning theories and teaching methods classification, and encourage additional refinements in the categorization of teaching methods. As noted above, while our research was based on Kolb's learning cycle, that is not the only theory of learning that may be useful in understanding the relationship between teaching methods and student learning opportunities.

- Given Dean Cycon's experiences, we suggest future research focus on how to best leverage academic–practitioner relationships that support a wide range of teaching and learning experiences.

Conclusion

This research sought to illuminate an element of PRME Principle 3 by using the Kolb learning cycle model in documenting a global baseline of instructional practices among those teaching within RME domains. The study identified two main findings regarding RME teaching methods: 1) a wide range of teaching and learning methods spanning the entire Kolb learning cycle are utilized to some extent in RME education; and 2) the breadth of learning cycle methods varies based on instruction level—a wider range of learning cycle methods are used at the graduate level compared with the undergraduate level—and on discipline (management vs. non-management). From these findings we ask instructors to consider two questions: 1) For your RME classes, what is your balance of instructional practices at the undergraduate, graduate and executive levels, and what are the implications for learning within your classroom? 2) For your RME institutions, how do the disciplines utilize or underutilize the various instructional practices, and what are the implications for learning within your RME curriculum? We know from empirical studies about business schools that there is a need for conversation about curriculum, as disciplinary silos are the norm in leading business schools (Navarro, 2008). Additionally, Teece (2011, p. 499) has argued "there is a great need to interrelate the social science disciplines and business sub-disciplines; in most cases this does not take place". RME offers unique opportunities for integration and we suggest that reflections on RME instructional processes provide an opportunity for institutions to move beyond disciplinary content silos and towards further innovation through deeper curricular integration.

With the increasing number of schools becoming signatories to PRME—nearly 600 from over 80 countries—there is clearly a demand to understand both the emerging instructional "responsibility" content areas as well as learning approaches needed to educate the next generation of global managers. In addition, this study opens the door to other content domains and their teaching practices. As responsible management educators, we believe it is our obligation to design pedagogy that reaches as many learning styles as possible within our student populations and to reflect and constructively respond to the challenges and opportunities for RME across different delivery platforms such as face-to-face, hybrid and online instruction.

The practitioner commentary also pushes us to go further in our management education reform and work towards more integration of real experiences into the classroom, more integration of disciplines and more integration of urgency in our roles as educators and consumers. We hope that this research endeavour will be taken up by others in the pursuit of greater knowledge about our common practices and learning approaches. Such a knowledge stream contributes to a growing demand for evidence-based teaching practice and enhanced integration of learning theory and practice and social and ecological sustainability.

References

AACSB (Association to Advance Collegiate Schools of Business) (2012). AACSB Sustainability Conference. Retrieved from http://www.aacsb.edu/sustainability/, accessed 1 September 2013.

Alcaraz, J.& Thiruvattal, E. (2010). An interview with Manuel Escudero. The United Nations' Principles for Responsible Management Education: A global call for sustainability. *Academy of Management Learning & Education Journal*, 9(3), 542-550.

Astin, A.W. & Antonio, A.L. (2012). *Assessment for Excellence: The Philosophy and Practice of Assessment and Evaluation in Higher Education*. Lanham, MD: Rowan & Littlefield Publishing.

Baden, D. & Parkes, C. (2013). Experiential learning: Inspiring the business leaders of tomorrow. *Journal of Management Development*, 32(3), 295-308.

Borredon, L., Deffayet, S., Baker, A.C. & Kolb, D. (2011). Enhancing deep learning: Lessons from the introduction of learning teams in management education in France. *Journal of Management Education*, 35(3), 324-350.

Burgoyne, J. & Cooper, C.L. (1976). Research on teaching methods in management education: Bibliographical examination of the state of the art. *Management International Review*, 16(4), 95-102. Retrieved from http://www.jstor.org/stable/40227294

Cornuel, E. & Hommel, U. (2015). Moving beyond the rhetoric of responsible management education [Special issue]. *Journal of Management Development*, 34(1).

Dede, S. (2009). The teacher's educational leadership roles according to Kolb's theory of learning. *Humanity and Social Sciences Journal*, 4(2), 153-163.

Dennison, P. (2012). Reflective practice: The enduring influence of Kolb's Experiential Learning Theory. *Compass: Journal of Learning and Teaching*, 1(1). Retrieved from: https://journals.gre.ac.uk/index.php/compass/article/view/12/28

Dickson, M.A., Eckman, M., Loker, S. & Jirousek, C. (2013). A model for sustainability education in support of the PRME. *Journal of Management Development*, 32(3), 309-318.

Dufresne, R.L. & Offstein, E.H. (2012). Holistic and intentional student character development process: Learning from West Point. *Academy of Management Learning & Education*, 11(4), 570-590.

Edelman (2015). *Edelman Trust Barometer Executive Summary*. Retrieved from: http://www.edelman.com/insights/intellectual-property/2015-edelman-trust-barometer/trust-and-innovation-edelman-trust-barometer/executive-summary/

Escudero, M., Albareda, L., Alcaraz, J., Weybrecht, G. & Csuri, M. (2012). *Inspirational Guide for the Implementation of PRME: Placing Sustainability at the Heart of Management Education*. Leeds, UK: GSE Research Limited (Leigh House).

Forray, J.M. & Leigh, J. (Eds.) (2012a). Principles of Responsible Management Education [Special issue]. *Journal of Management Education*, 36.

Forray, J.M. & Leigh, J.S.A. (2012b). A primer on the Principles of Responsible Management Education: Intellectual roots and waves of change. *Journal of Management Education*, 36(3), 295-309.

Fougère, M. & Solitander, N. (2009). The global moral management of business schools: A governmentality perspective on the principles for responsible management education. *Proceedings of the 5th International Critical Management Studies, University of Warwick, Warwick, UK, July 2009*.

Fougère, M., Solitander, N. & Young, S. (2014). Exploring and exposing values in management education: Problematizing final vocabularies in order to enhance moral imagination. *Journal of Business Ethics*, 120(2), 175-187.

Gallup (2015). Confidence in institutions. Retrieved from http://www.gallup.com/poll/1597/confidence-institutions.aspx

Gitsham, M. (2008). Developing the global leader of tomorrow. Presented at the *1st Global Forum for Responsible Management Education, United Nations Headquarters, New York, December 2008.* Retrieved from http://www.unprme.org/resource-docs/developingthegloballeaderoftomorrowreport.pdf

Gitsham, M. & Clark, T.S. (2014). Market demand for sustainability in management education. *International Journal of Sustainability in Higher Education,* 15(3), 291-303.

Godemann, J., Herzig, C., Moon, J. & Powell, A. (2011). *Integrating Sustainability into Business Schools: Analysis of 100 UN PRME Sharing Information on Progress (SIP) Reports.* ICCSR Research Paper Series No. 58-201. Nottingham, UK: Nottingham University Business School. Retrieved from http://www.nottingham.ac.uk/business/ICCSR/research.php?action=single&id=77

Haertle, J. & Miura, S. (2014). Seven years of development: United Nations-supported Principles for Responsible Management Education. *SAM Advanced Management Journal,* 79(4), 8-17.

Horwitz, F. & Grayson, D. (2010). Putting PRME into practice in a business school. *EFMD Global Focus,* 4(2), 26-29. Retrieved from http://www.networkedcranfield.com/doughty/Document%20Library/Practitioner%20publications/Putting%20PRME%20into%20practice%20in%20a%20business%20school.pdf

Karakas, F., Sarigollu, E. & Manisaligil, A. (2013). The use of benevolent leadership development to advance principles of responsible management education. *Journal of Management Development,* 32(8), 801-822.

Kayes, D.C. (2002). Experiential learning and its critics: Preserving the role of experience in management learning and education. *Academy of Management Learning & Education,* 1(2), 137-149.

Kell, G. & Haertle, J. (2011). UN Global Compact and Principles for Responsible Management Education: The next decades. *EFMD Global Focus,* 5(2), 14-16.

Kelley, S. & Nahser, R. (2014). Developing sustainable strategies: Foundations, method, and pedagogy. *Journal of Business Ethics,* 123(4), 631-644.

Kerlinger, F.N. & Lee, H.B. (2000). *Foundations of Behavioral Research.* (4th ed.). Fort Worth, TX: Harcourt College Publishers.

Kolb, A. & Kolb, D. (2005). Learning styles and learning spaces: Enhancing experiential learning in higher education. *Academy of Management Learning & Education,* 4(2), 193-212.

Kolb, D. (1984). *Experiential Learning: Experience as the Source of Learning and Development.* New York, NY: Prentice Hall.

Kolb, D., Boyatzis, R.E. & Mainemelis, C. (2001). Experiential learning theory: Previous research and new directions. In Sternberg, R.J. & Zhang, L.F. (Eds.), *Perspectives on Thinking, Learning, and Cognitive Styles* (pp. 193-210). NJ: Lawrence Erlbaum.

Laasch, O. & Conaway, R.N. (2015). *Principles of Responsible Management: Glocal Sustainability, Responsibility, and Ethics.* Stamford, CT: Cengage Learning.

Lavine, M. & Roussin, C. (2012). From idea to action: Promoting responsible management education through a semester-long academic integrity learning project. *Journal of Management Education,* 36(3), 428-455.

Lawrence, J.T. & Beamish, P.W. (Eds.) (2012). *Globally Responsible Leadership: Managing According to the UN Global Compact.* Thousand Oaks, CA: Sage.

Litzky, B.E., Godshalk, V.M. & Walton-Bongers, C. (2010). Social entrepreneurship and community leadership: A service-learning model for management education. *Journal of Management Education,* 34(1), 142-162.

Louw, J. (2015). Paradigm change or no real change at all? A critical reading of the U.N. Principles for Responsible Management Education. *Journal of Management Education,* 39(2), 184-208.

McIntosh, M. (Ed.). (2013). Creating global citizens and responsible leadership [Special issue]. *Journal of Corporate Citizenship*, 49.

MacNab, B.R. (2012). An experiential approach to cultural intelligence education. *Journal of Management Education*, 36(1), 66-94.

Miller, G.A. (1956). The magical number seven, plus or minus two: Some limits on our capacity for processing information. *Psychological Review*, 63, 81-97.

Mette, M. & Rovira, A. (2012). *Business Schools and their Contributions to Society*. Thousand Oaks, CA: Sage.

Michlitsch, J.F. & Sidle, M.W. (2002). Assessing student learning outcomes: A comparative study of techniques used in business school disciplines. *Journal of Education for Business*, 77(3), 125-130.

Moskal, P., Ellis, T. & Keon, T. (2008). Summary of assessment in higher education and the management of student learning data. *Academy of Management Learning & Education*, 7(2), 269-278.

Murray, A., Baden, D., Cashian, P., Haynes, K., & Wersun, A. (2015). *Inspirational Guide for the Implementation of PRME: UK and Ireland Edition*. Sheffield, UK: Greenleaf Publishing.

Navarro, P. (2008). The MBA core curriculum of top ranked US business schools; a study of failure? *Academy of Management Learning & Education*, 7(1), 108-123.

Neumann, S. & Koper, R. (2010). Instructional method classifications lack user language and orientation. *Educational Technology & Society*, 13(2), 78-89.

Perry, M. & Win, S. (2013). An evaluation of PRME's contribution to responsibility in higher education. *The Journal of Corporate Citizenship*, 13(49), 48-70.

Prandini, M., Isler, P., Vervoort, & Barthelmess, P. (2012). Responsible management education for 21st century leadership. *Central European Business Review*, 1(2), 16-22.

PRME (Principles for Responsible Management Education) (2012, July). *Anti-corruption Guidelines ("Toolkit") for MBA Curriculum Change*. Retrieved from http://www.unprme.org/resource-docs/ComprehensiveAntiCorruptionGuidelinesforCurriculumChange.pdf

PRME (2013). *Inspirational Guide for the Implementation of PRME: Second Edition: Learning to Go Beyond*. Sheffield, UK: Greenleaf Publishing.

Rasche, A. (2011). The Principles for Responsible Management Education: A call for action for German universities. In Haase, M., Mirkovic, S. & Schumann, O.J. (Eds.). *Stand und perspektiven der unternehmens—und wirtschaftsethischen ausbildung in Deutschland* (pp. 1-20). Hampp: Mering. Retrieved from http://ssrn.com/abstract=1709873

Rasche, A. & Escudero, M. (2010). Leading change: The role of the Principles for Responsible Management Education. *Journal of Business and Economic Ethics (zfwu)*, 10(2), 244-250.

Rogers, A. & Horrocks, N. (2010). *Teaching Adults* (4th ed.). New York, NY: Open University Press.

Shrivastava, P. (2010). Pedagogy of passion for sustainability. *Academy of Management Learning & Education*, 9(3), 443-455.

Solitander, N., Fougère, M., Sobczak, A. & Herlin, H. (2012). We are the champions: Organizational learning and change for responsible management education. *Journal of Management Education*, 36(3), 337-363.

Sroufe, R., Sivasubramaniam, N., Ramos, D. & Saiia, D. (2015). Aligning the PRME: How study abroad nurtures responsible leadership. *Journal of Management Education*, (39)2, 244-275.

Svinicki, M.D. & Dixon, N.M. (1987). The Kolb model modified for classroom activities. *College Teaching*, 35(4), 141-146.

Teece, D. (2011). Achieving integration of business school curriculum using the dynamic capability framework. *Journal of Management Development*, 30(5), 499-518.

Verbos, A. & Humphries, M. (2015). Indigenous wisdom and the PRME: inclusion or illusion? *Journal of Management Development*, 34(1), 90-100.

Vince, R. (1998). Behind and beyond Kolb's learning cycle. *Journal of Management Education*, 22(3), 304-319.

Viswanathan, M. (2012). Curricular innovations on sustainability and subsistence marketplaces: Philosophical, substantive, and methodological orientations. *Journal of Management Education*, 36(3), 389-427.

Webb, M. (1980/2003). A definitive critique of experiential learning theory. Doctoral dissertation. Retrieved from http://web.archive.org/web/20061109200729/http://www.cc.ysu.edu/~mnwebb/critique/TheCritique_final2_wtp.pdf

Weber, J., Green, S. & Gladstone, J. (2013). Responding to the call: Changes in graduate management curriculum's attention to social and environmental issues. *Teaching Ethics*, 13(2), 137-157.

Appendix: Survey

This survey is being conducted in cooperation with the OBTS Teaching Society for Management Educators to gather information about the methods used by instructors in all business disciplines when covering issues of ethics, social responsibility, sustainability/natural environment or social entrepreneurship in their courses. We are grateful for your participation. The results of the survey will be presented at the Global Forum of the Principles for Responsible Management Education (PRME) and published at a later date. The survey should take no more than 15 minutes to complete. This survey is confidential and no personal information not voluntarily provided by you will be collected. Your participation is entirely voluntary and may be discontinued at any time.

I. **Teaching level**. Please indicate which of the following business student populations you teach:

a) Undergraduate only

b) Master's only

c) Executive only

d) Undergraduate and Master's

e) Undergraduate and Executive

f) Master's and Executive

g) Undergraduate, Master's and Executive

II. **Teaching methods** (response tree structure; one complete and discrete set of Teaching Methods questions for each level based on answer to Q I)

Please indicate the extent to which you use the following teaching methods in your classes at the [undergraduate/Master's/Executive] level when covering issues of ethics, corporate social responsibility, sustainability/natural environment or social entrepreneurship.

a) Action learning (based on problems from students' work organizations)

b) Case studies

c) Class discussion

d) Experiential (role plays, in-class exercises)

e) Lecture

f) Project-based learning (multiple activities to solve problem or answer question)

g) Service-learning (community service projects, volunteering, etc.)

h) Simulations

i) Small group discussion

j) Other (please specify)

III. **PRME question**

The Principles for Responsible Management Education (PRME) is a voluntary initiative through which business schools and management-related academic institutions express their commitment to integrating universal values of sustainability and corporate citizenship into curriculum, research and learning methods. Is your institution a PRME participant?

a) Yes

b) No

c) Don't know

IV. In what country do you conduct the majority of your teaching? (text box)

V. What is your primary business discipline (area)? (drop-down selection box)

a) Accounting

b) Business administration

c) Finance

d) Information systems

e) International business

f) Management

g) Marketing

h) Operations

i) Other (please specify)

VI. What is your primary teaching area within your discipline? (text box)

VII. Comments? (text box)

17

Conclusion
Managing our students' learning through our professional practice

Jennifer S.A. Leigh
Nazareth College, USA

This book enhances our understanding of responsible management education and the PRME Principles by deeply considering the *process of educating* the next generation of responsible managers within and beyond the boundaries of higher education. The authors—both academics and practitioners—share their perspectives on responsible management pedagogy from a variety of geographies (10), several academic and private organizations (over 50), numerous industry sectors and a wide range of theoretical orientations.

As a whole, the chapters in this book cover each PRME Principle and offer a variety of innovative strategies available to integrate responsible management education (RME) into existing classes, RME classes, modules, courses, curricula and co-curricular. Furthermore the authors address not just the "how", but the "why" and "so what" through the practitioner voices seen throughout the text. Some of the pedagogical ideas are well established through the long-term work of dedicated instructors, and some examples are early experiments with mixed results pointing us towards new possibilities and flagging areas for concern. One steadfast feature is that each chapter offers specific ideas for adaptation to different courses, classrooms and institutional contexts.

The chapters remind us about the numerous opportunities to innovate responsible management education by bringing attention to new pedagogies and change strategies that enhance responsible management content. As we know, specialized RME classes are not enough and the responsibility management complexities facing managers in all sectors—as highlighted in the Sustainable Development

Goals—urgently demand that we find even more approaches like these to help develop responsible management competences while learning responsible management content.

In this chapter we begin with a discussion of the "So what?" including a reflection on the process of integrating theory and practice with our academic and managerial voices. Second, we identify the common and distinct educational philosophies, research traditions and theoretical models seen in the chapters. Third, we discuss opportunities for further responsible management education research in the various scholarships (Boyer, 1990). Finally, in the spirit of application incorporated in all the chapters, we close with two reflection questions for the book that support self-directed professional development and inquiry.

What were our aspirations for this book? We started with the idea that the book's unique selling proposition (USP), modelling Principles 5 and 6, Partnership and Dialogue, offered a new integration of management scholarship. This was our deliberate attempt to address the theory–practice division commonly complained about by managers and academics alike. What came of this notion included a variety of chapter structures and, more importantly, the emergent themes that we captured in the introduction: Out of the comfort zone—into the learning zone; Risk taking; Ambiguity; Engagement; Interdisciplinary intersections and integration; and Mind-sets. We acknowledge that these themes are the typical fodder of conclusion chapters, yet proved too insightful to hold back and thus created the new organizing structure for the book set forth in the introduction. These themes tell us that similar challenges are faced around the globe and responsible management educators benefit from specific abilities such as emotional and social intelligence, creativity, risk taking, managing uncertainty, co-learning, holistic thinking, and reflecting and interrogating one's fundamental teaching philosophy.

Management education is a constantly evolving field needing to react to new trends within our globalized business environment and adapting to the constant innovation and technological revolutions. We offer that RME must be both reactive to global trends and more proactive in terms of responding to the world's needs as were articulated in the first chapter within the Principles for Responsible Management Education (PRME) framework, as well as the new Sustainable Development Goals (SDGs) adopted by the United Nations. For a cohesive educational experience responsive to these dynamics we now conceptualize RME quite broadly: content (what), process (how), instructors (who) and the location (where). The "what"—as covered briefly in the Introduction and in Chapter 2, illustrated the dramatic growth of the RME field, which is providing more content on a monthly basis. The "how"—as demonstrated in numerous ways across chapters—detailed a wide range of possibilities at several levels: activity, course/module, curricular and institutional. The "who" is evidenced in the passionate commitment of responsible management educators to teaching and learning throughout the chapters. Furthermore, we have a broader understanding of the institutional side—the context and "where" the instruction happens and the type and scope of innovation needed and what's possible. Indeed, from these chapters we see plenty is possible within resource-rich and resource-constrained contexts.

Theory–practice challenge

We experimented with a new format for knowledge development in this book by utilizing the theory–practice chapter framework, and it is important to share our reflections on this experience, as we feel that it has the potential to influence the way we undertake management education. As captured in PRME Principle 5, Partnership, and Principle 6, Dialogue, PRME's fundamental opportunity is moving business schools towards broader engagement with society in their curriculum and in their organizing structures. Our notion was that bringing managers and leaders into the conversation about responsible management pedagogy would provide a direct validity test if you like. Furthermore, we sought to directly address the common critique of relevance, which is often a criticism of responsibility management topics: does learning social responsibility, ethics, stakeholder management or any of the myriad RME concepts really matter in the "cut-throat" world of business? It turns out, yes, it does matter, practically and urgently! This reality testing is a necessary part of keeping RME relevant, which is often challenging because it goes against institutional values, practices and reward systems.

Combining the academic and practice voices, however, proved difficult at times, despite our awareness of the challenges of the theory–practice divide (Rynes *et al.*, 2001; Van de Ven and Johnson, 2006). Initially we prepared for the uncertainty by creating an academic–practitioner template for chapters and then realized quickly that discussing alternative authoring options presented by authors would expand that framework further. Next, we developed a structured style of evaluating chapters. Yet it was hard to know initially when we were there, when chapters had achieved a point of integration between research insights and practical know-how. From our perspective, there were no current models for this style of writing within management education. Sure there were case studies that honoured and centred the storytelling of practitioner voices and, yes, there were textbooks with excellent highlighted boxes of best practice stories of responsible management leaders—but nothing quite like our vision.

Academic authors, including ourselves, needed to find ways to speak about our teaching and learning practices with managers without our typical jargon and assumptions about knowledge base. We also needed to reflect on our networks with managers and assess who might have the interest, ability and time to engage in such an endeavour. Managers needed to step back and reflect on the basis of their opinions and justifications, remembering to include both personal experience and research. We observed that managers typically do not get opportunities to comment and critique academic teaching, and this new territory required coaching and discussion.

All the chapter authors, even us co-editors, experienced challenges weaving these two voices into a harmony—new understanding for responsible management educators which is reflected in the various implications for practice sections. Despite these challenges and numerous revisions the nearly 20 practitioners working across many sectors and many organizational forms (non-governmental organizations, social enterprise B Corps, worker owned, small business, large corporations) all willingly engaged with the academics. They urged us to continue experimenting with new approaches in the classroom and in our management education reform initiatives.

We hope that both academics and practitioners are motivated by this joint scholarship and continue to find other ways to integrate real world realities with systematic inquiry, through co-authorship such as in this book, practitioner peer review of academic scholarships and designing joint research projects. Based on our experience of academic–practitioner co-authorship, we acknowledge that this is a time-intensive commitment. While we would advocate this approach to readers, we acknowledge this is not possible in some circumstances.

Underpinning theoretical and educational frameworks

Educational philosophy

We can gain further insights by reflecting on the unifying and distinct educational philosophies, research traditions and theoretical models in the book. Broadly speaking, most of the authors approach their chapters from a constructivist perspective, which is an epistemology (theory of knowledge) popular in the humanities and social sciences, offering that humans generate understanding from their experiences and their ideas notably described by Jean Piaget among others. Not surprisingly, many authors explicitly claim the influence of pragmatism, an educational philosophy that values dialogue, joint knowledge development with students, and embraces ambiguity building (Ornstein and Levine, 1997). These educational philosophies have direct implications for the personal and teaching competences needed by RME instructors—those with strong facilitation skills, emotional and social intelligence, and ability to manage ambiguity.

Research traditions

This book included chapters positioned within different research traditions and for the purposes of this chapter, we discuss these distinctions in terms of first-, second- and third-person research practices. Starting with third-person research practice, this approach "aims to take small scale projects to create a wider impact" (Reason and Bradbury, 2006, p. 6). Third-person research practice includes familiar social science research approaches. In the book this included chapters covering survey research (Chapter 16 by Foray, Leigh, Goodnight and Cycon), comparative case analysis (Chapter 15 by Warin and Beddewela), the state of the literature in the field (Chapter 2 by Hayes, Parkes and Murray) and field critique (Chapter 14 by Tyran and Garcia). Collectively these pieces provide foundational information about our applied practices in the classrooms, in our institutions and emerging scholarly conversations to which all of the chapters can be connected. We see that this type of structured descriptive research is important for us to reflect on responsible management education—what is actually happening (or not), how disciplines engage RME and emerging ideas.

Our book's structure, with the theory–practice voices, is a type of hybrid second-person research approach since some of the chapter authors met together in person and others worked collaboratively, but virtually. Formally, second-person research practice, "addresses our ability to inquire face-to-face with others into areas of mutual concern" (Reason and Bradbury, 2006, p. 6). Within the context of this book, RME process formed the mutual concern for academics and practitioners, and numerous chapters highlight a variety of second-person research including the following: Swamy and Keegan's focus group interviews of faculty in their service-learning course (Chapter 12), Wagenberg and Gutiérrez's joint reflection on their responsible entrepreneurship course (Chapter 5), Sunley and Coleman's discussion about responsible learning mind-sets (Chapter 3), and Glaser and Sunley's chapter with the opening section that describes their transformative "Level III" conversation (Chapter 7). Additionally, the two in-depth case studies of the Global Integrative Module (GIM) and the Daniels Compass focus on the local and global levels, respectively. Mayer and Hutton with their alumni voices provide the readers with the long-term view of RME reform, as the chapter discusses the numerous iterations of a RME curriculum over the past several decades (Chapter 10). The GIM chapter evidences the possibilities of how mutual concern for social impact education can be delivered in a virtual platform (Chapter 13).

At the individual level, several chapters provide models and suggestions on how to enhance the first-person research practice, which is defined as "address[ing] the ability of the researcher to foster an inquiring approach about his or her own life, to act choicefully and with awareness and to assess effects on the outside world while acting" (Reason and Bradbury, 2006, p. 6). We observe this awareness taking many forms through student orientation to consciousness-based education (CBE in Chapter 11 by Heaton, Schachinger and Laszlo), pragmatic inquiry as a philosophy-based learning approach (Chapter 8 by Kelley and Nahser), and the sustainability mind-set (Chapter 9 by Rimanoczy). Of note, Humphries, Casey-Cox and Dey (Chapter 4) integrate both first- and second-person research practices by combining their own personal reflection on their identities and their community conversations about the role of plastic in food production.

Theoretical traditions

Theoretically, there is a wide range of conceptual traditions utilized in the book from traditional management education models to more normative and humanistic ones. For instance, Humphries, Casey-Cox and Dey (Chapter 4) introduce *mihis* that stem from indigenous traditions and these insights alerts us to the dialogic richness and new frontier possibilities for responsible management education. The notion of consciousness-based education (CBE) in the chapter by Heaton, Schachinger and Laszlo (Chapter 11) alerts us to the power and potential of personal reflective practices such as the wisdom tradition of Transcendental Meditation. While present in management research, we see need and potential for these practices steeped in millennia of experiences in various parts of the world.

Several chapters emphasize the concept of holism and holistic educational practices as fundamental for student development. Holism is a concept which offers that systems, whether biological or social, must be viewed as a whole and not the sum of discrete parts. Holism is pointedly observed in all the first-person research chapters which take a systemic view of learning, incorporating personal discovery, cognitive knowledge, emotional intelligence and learning through doing. This integrative notion is seen in Sunley and Coleman's consideration of the "Relational Model of the Learning Self" (Chapter 3) and in Rimanoczy's notion of sustainability mind-set in "A holistic learning approach for responsible management education" (Chapter 9). Given that the main challenges facing RME are quite complex, we see that comprehensive learning that includes holistic concepts and systems thinking will be needed more and more by future managers.

Beyond management theory

The notion of learning from the humanities and other non-management social science research is a powerful focus in many chapters as our authors fused insights from numerous disciplines. Sunley and Coleman model this in their responsible learning chapter by synthesizing liberal learning with human spiritual growth and students as agents in their own developing narratives (Chapter 3). Kelley and Nahser demonstrate the utility of moral philosophy in their detailed chapter on pragmatic inquiry (Chapter 8). Finally, the practitioner-based research and insights from neuroscience informed Glaser and Sunley's chapter on communication (Chapter 7). Now more than ever new knowledge and enduring knowledge from humanities, social sciences and natural sciences should inform new ways of thinking in responsible management education.

Interdisciplinary starting point

As mentioned in the introduction, a handful of the courses discussed in the book began with an explicit interdisciplinary framework such as the introductory business class at Babson where integrative learning is enhanced with behavioural ethics in the "Giving Voice to Values" framework detailed by Manwaring, Greenberg and Hunt (Chapter 6). Likewise, the GiveGoa service-learning projects presented by Swamy and Keegan highlight the universal and particular challenges for community-based learning in emerging market contexts (Chapter 12). The Global Integrative Module (GIM), another type of social impact-focused project-learning, stretches our imaginations to think about how to move impact from local to glocal context with the technology mediated, team-based project learning (Chapter 13). Again, we emphasize that integrative and interdisciplinary thinking is essential for management education reform because the challenges do not begin or end within disciplinary boundaries.

Future research opportunities

Responsible management education inherently pushes us to the edge of current knowledge and practices. To successfully teach RME topics we must stay in touch with current and emerging themes from a wide range of disciplines as the various responsibilities we seek to prepare our students for become increasingly complicated and urgent. To use a US metaphor, RME educators are creative outliers, proverbial "cowboy and cowgirl" instructors. What new knowledge, resources and competences will these educators need to push forward the frontier?

The premise of the book suggests that what we consider scientific knowledge (i.e. scholarship that identifies new discoveries or "Scholarship of Discovery") is not enough and we must have a deeper understanding of pedagogical process, known as the "Scholarship of Teaching and Learning", in order to deliver our important and compelling responsible management content. Furthermore, we offer that these scholarships in sum should promote skilful and useful application in the real world. We provide our suggestions by unpacking these "scholarships" popularized in Boyer's (1990) influential essay, "Scholarship Reconsidered".

In this work, Boyer argued persuasively that academic knowledge production can be considered beyond our narrow conception of new scientific discoveries and instead be reconceptualized into four broader domains: 1) Scholarship of Discovery, 2) Scholarship of Integration, 3) Scholarship of Application, and 4) Scholarship of Teaching and Learning. First, Scholarship of Discovery focuses on adding new information to human knowledge. For example, in the responsible management domain we draw upon the essential work done by scientists who have come to understand the role of CO_2 in global climate change.[1] Scholarship of Integration involves making connections between disciplines for new insights—for instance, the rapidly developing field of environmental psychology. This is where interdisciplinary understanding is developed through synthesis. Boyer offers that integration stems from "new intellectual questions and pressing human problems" (1990, p. 21). Third, Scholarship of Application moves from knowledge development into more direct engagement by addressing the question: "Can social problems themselves drive an agenda for scholarly investigation?" (1990, p. 21). Scholarship of Application turns knowledge into action by addressing real-world issues. For responsible management educators, this can be taking water consumption

---

1 See http://climate.nasa.gov/scientific-consensus/ for a summary.

research and developing a simulation or assessment tool to determine an individual's or institution's water footprint.[2] Lastly, the Scholarship of Teaching and Learning (SoTL) is making public research on student learning to advance teaching. This book is an example of SoTL. In sum, these four types of scholarship are very relevant for responsible management educators as our competences relate to being able to access the latest scholarship of discovery and scholarship of integration in order to present relevant content to our students.

Of note, a few years later, Boyer extended his notion of scholarships to include an additional category "Scholarship of Engagement". In his essay he contended that: "[t]he academy must become a more vigorous partner in the search for answers to our most pressing social, civic, economic, and moral problems, and must affirm its historic commitment to what I call the scholarship of engagement" (1996, p. 11).

Scholarship of Engagement (SoE), also known as public scholarship or community-engaged scholarship, disrupts conceptions of faculty work as research, teaching and service and instead encourages faculty to bring any of the scholarship categories together to address pressing social, civic and ethical problems. At its core SoE is about collaboration between academics and the lay public. Within the context of this book SoE is represented by the academic authors and the working managers and practitioners. Below we build upon these categories as a framework to encourage the development of new RME scholarships.

Scholarship of Discovery research: change focus

RME as it innovates educational practices, also contests long-standing practices and traditions as highlighted in Mayer and Hutton's chapter on three decades of RME reform (Chapter 10) and Warin and Beddewela's chapter on RME institutionalization barriers, drivers and enablers (Chapter 15). Thus, for deep change and systematic adoption of RME throughout an institution or, as PRME advocates, across all business schools, new insights are needed regarding organizational change within a higher education context. Therefore, we see that more research is needed to evaluate such questions as:

- What are the shared challenges for business schools creating sustainable economic, social and environmental value?
- What challenges are distinct in different regions of the world, economic contexts or institutional settings?
- How is institutional change similar and different in higher education institutions (HEIs) compared with other sectors?
- Which factors facilitate change towards more RME integration from the position of different internal stakeholder advocates (students, untenured faculty, tenured faculty, administrators, alumni, etc.)?

2 e.g. http://waterfootprint.org

- What are the challenges and obstacles to values-based education/management practice in politically and ideologically mixed contexts?

- How can external organizations accelerate change (i.e. accrediting agencies, government, NGO think-tanks [cf. Aspen Institute] and advocacy groups [cf. People & Planet], chambers of commerce, ranking organizations, etc.)?

- How do institutional resources impact RME change (i.e. doctoral granting institutions, teaching-intensive institutions, "Global North" vs. "Global South" HEIs)?

- Which stakeholders, constituencies and actors benefit from resisting RME?

- What can be learned from the history of management education and other large curriculum shifts in the last century?

Scholarship of Integration research

Given our modern social, economic and ecological interconnection, scholarship of integration, and its emphasis on knowledge synthesis, is critical for preparing responsible managers for the unknown complex challenges they will face. The following questions relate to practical dimensions of scholarship of integration.

- How can best practices for interdisciplinary and trans-disciplinary education from the humanities and other professions be utilized in RME?

- What PhD training and professional development is needed to help cultivate more integration between managerial and organization studies and other social sciences, humanities and natural sciences?

- What incentive systems, policies and organizational structures facilitate scholarship of integration research and use of scholarship of integration in the classroom?

Scholarship of Application research

We believe that the Scholarship of Application (SoA) with its focus on turning knowledge into action holds tremendous untapped potential for responsible management education. Our questions focus on applying managerial and organizational knowledge through course or module settings, although we acknowledge that SoA can occur in many other ways.

- What are the similarities and differences between the wide range of application-focused learning approaches such as problem-based learning, student consulting, design thinking, workplace learning, service-learning and action research? Which approaches are better suited for various student populations, development contexts and instructor ability or experiences?

- What changes are needed in policies and organizational norms to encourage more scholarship of application through class assignments and projects?

- What educational best practices support positive and fruitful application experiences by students within real organizations? Are there differences based on the organizational sector or size such as students working in family run organizations vs. larger corporations, students collaborating with NGOs vs. businesses, or students working with start-up ventures?

Scholarship of Teaching and Learning research

Scholarship of Teaching and Learning (SoTL) is the intent of this book, to make public research on student learning to advance teaching, especially as it relates to responsible management. Given the burgeoning RME literature and the contributions here, we sense that management education is on the edge of a fundamental shift and that many research opportunities remain for RME SoTL.

- What are the key RME skills and competences needed for future managers? Which pedagogies best support their development?

- How does co-curricular learning influence RME learning?

- What global differences exist in teaching RME?

- What competences do instructors need to teach RME?

- How do different learning platforms impact RME education (i.e. face-to-face, hybrid, virtual, MOOC [massive open online course])?

- How can gamification, virtual laboratories and other online technologies be harnessed to support RME learning?

- What is the state of affairs for undergraduate access to RME courses? How does access to RME courses at the bachelor level impact early career decisions and opportunities?

- What ethical values underpin education for socially responsible leaders? How are the values of social responsibility incorporated into academic and business activities? What are the challenges and obstacles to values-based education/management practice in politically and ideologically mixed contexts?

Scholarship of Engagement research

While similar to Scholarship of Application, Scholarship of Engagement (SoE) seeks to fundamental redefine the nature of academic work and knowledge development. In the SoE framework faculty reorient their focus on creating social impact through their research, teaching and service. This shift cannot come fast enough based on the global needs specified in the UN SDGs. Numerous questions, conceptual and practical, remain in this domain.

- What models exist for faculty blending responsibility management research that impacts scholarship, practice (application), and teaching and learning?

- How can business schools learn from institutions that have institutionalized SoE at the department, unit, school or university level? How might institutional arrangements (public vs. private, unionized vs. at will contracts) and national rules and regulations impact policy changes?

- Which fundamental skills and competences are needed for SoE beyond the traditional social science training of typical business school faculty?

- How should faculty evaluation and reward systems be adjusted in business schools to allow for SoE?

As seen from the suggested research questions, responsible management education reform with Boyer's model provides a structured approach to considering where we need to proceed as a field. A unique aspect of this book—academic and practitioner co-authorship—provided a RME laboratory where we observed multiple scholarships simultaneously. The book's focus is on providing knowledge to advance RME teaching—SoTL, Scholarship of Integration (SoI) with the introduction of non-management disciplines and models, and Scholarship of Engagement (SoE) with the examples of faculty reworking their activities, courses and entire curriculum—to ensure a direct connection between business schools and society.

Challenges and suggestions

As responsible management educators, we are keenly aware that numerous challenges impede faster progress towards the types of innovative and integrative educational practices we advocate. We summarize them here to raise awareness and at the same time, point out how the pedagogies described in this book managed to negotiate with, out run and incorporate some of these barriers.

Over the years we have heard reoccurring complaints from responsible management educators and academic leadership favouring reform. The first is time constraints. With the changing and increasing demands on academics, time is our ultimate currency. Academics at all types of institutions struggle with finding space to refresh, renew and realign courses and curricula. Second, institutional policies and practices do not always support RME needs. For instance, many faculty have to choose between attending "research" (a.k.a. Scholarship of Discovery) conferences and pedagogy conferences (SoTL), specialized responsible management conferences (SoI) or practitioner conferences (SoE and SoA). Third, there is often a large gap between the espoused value of RME and the enacted value of how faculty is rewarded. This relates to what "counts" (SoD) and does not count (SoTL, SoI, SoA, SoE) in faculty promotion. Finally, RME reforms can disrupt the power and politics within institutions, as such changes can contest the taken-for-granted arrangements (what classes are taught and how) and disciplinary assumptions (how fields contribute to sustainability or foster corrupt practices).

We offer that this book provides educators with several snapshots of RME pedagogy in action from a wide variety of settings. While individuals can work to identify RME resources strategically, more structural support is needed from academic administrators in two key areas: policy and culture.

To begin, institutional policies define the implicit and explicit values of institutions. Many business schools prioritize Scholarship of Discovery (SoD) by publishing in top tier journals. We agree that this is important; however it should not be the exclusive focus for faculty if RME is to be taken seriously. Therefore, institutions that seek to deeply integrate RME must consider adopting a wider view of scholarship and seek to translate these into policies such as travel reimbursement (i.e. allowing attendance at pedagogy conferences and RME convenings), professional development (i.e. supporting faculty with funds and time to develop RME skills), internal research grants (i.e. including RME SoTL as a valid category), and all other resources that support faculty training and networking. Additionally, all faculty reward and promotion policies need to be reconsidered in light of any RME reform so that the different scholarships, especially SoTL, are properly valued by incorporating inclusive language within faculty governance documents. A related action is assessing current institutional metrics in place at institutions, such as course evaluations and student evaluation of teaching (SET) which can provide useful information. However, the more innovative RME teaching practices are not always measurable and conceptually commensurate with traditional institutional metrics which are based on a positivist, within-the-classroom-walls view of learning. For instance, SETs prioritize structure and order, whereas experiential learning practices require different skills such as facilitation, improvisational lectures and co-instruction, which are often not measured. Steps such as these will help the next stage of RME reform by creating structural alignment between RME values and actual institutional priorities and desired outcomes.

Personal reflection

Following best practices for education and a core theme from several of our chapters, we invite you to reflect on your reading.

- **Theory**: Which of these concepts, themes and approaches resonated the most with your pedagogy and why?

- **Practice**: What will you now apply in your classroom practice?

The purpose of the concluding reflection was fourfold. First, we sought to offer our thematic integration, emerging from our small collective of global pedagogy innovators. Second, we aspired to share our reflections on the theory–practice authorship model. Third, we worked to prioritize research directions for responsible management education through the lens of Boyer's types of scholarship. Fourth, we developed opportunities to reflect on the book through the discussion questions. We believe this textbook complements the existing PRME scholarship by emphasizing the process, the how, the pedagogy for responsible management education. It calls attention to the creativity, resources and time needed to innovate and why we should. As spotlighted in these chapters, RME opportunities exist in all types of institutions and in all types of courses across the globe.

As we prepare the next generation of thought-leaders as managers and citizens, we as instructors must follow the insights from the (un)learning literature and to remain agile and adaptive we must "manage unlearning", which is a shedding of organizational schemas and routines in order to provide space for new ideas. For RME this process relates to our fundamental beliefs about teaching, historic practices and preferences (de Holan and Phillips, 2004, p. 1611).

We contend that managing unlearning will permit the transformation needed to broaden our perspectives. Helena Barnard, Director of Research at the Gordon Institute of Business Science, University of Pretoria, summarizes this situation for RME educators (Wright and Brown, 2014, p. 8):

> Thought leadership requires an even wider understanding of different worlds. This challenges us, the faculty, to be brave and open doors to worlds where our students may be scared to venture alone. We need to guide future leaders to engage more fully with the world. We need leaders who can look at the "margins" and not just the "centre" of business; leadership who can question those categorizations. The mechanisms of deprivation—poverty, poor education, crime—shape economies and business as much as mechanisms of privilege and excellence. We need to connect both those worlds.

It is our hope that the models provided in these chapters, and ideas generated by reading and applying them in your learning environments, will help build those connections and cultivate the new generation of responsible managers and leaders.

References

Boyer, E. (1990). *Scholarship Reconsidered: Priorities of the Professoriate.* Stanford, CA: Carnegie Foundation for the Advancement of Teaching.
Boyer, E. (1996). The scholarship of engagement. *Journal of Public Service & Outreach,* 1(1), 11-20.
de Holan, P.M. & Phillips, N. (2004). The dynamics of organizational forgetting. *Management Science,* 50(11), 1603-1613.

Ornstein, A.C. & Levine, D.U. (1997). *Foundations of Education*. Boston, MA: Houghton Mifflin.

Reason, P. & Bradbury, H. (2006). *Handbook of Action Research*. London: Sage Publications.

Rynes, S.L., Bartunek, J.M. & Daft, R.L. (2001). Across the great divide: Knowledge creation and transfer between practitioners and academics. *Academy of Management Journal*, 44, 340-355.

Van De Ven, A. & Johnson, P. (2006). Knowledge for theory and practice. *Academy of Management Review*, 31(4), 802-821.

Wright, R.P. & Brown, K.G. (Eds.) (2014). *Educating Tomorrow's Thought-Leaders: Distinguished Scholars Answer a Burning Question*. Chicago, IL: Strategic Management Society. Retrieved from http://strategicmanagement.net/ig/pdf/Educating_Tomorrow_s_Thought-Leaders_from_SMS_Teaching_Community_28th_Aug2014.pdf

About the contributors

Editors

Jennifer S.A. Leigh is an associate professor of management at Nazareth College in Rochester, NY, USA where she teaches courses on business ethics, strategy and social entrepreneurship. Her research addresses responsibility management education, cross-sector partnerships and the scholarship of engagement. She is a senior editor for the *Annual Review of Social Partnerships* and an associate editor for the *Journal of Management Education* (JME) and *Business Ethics: A European Review*.

Roz Sunley teaches responsible management at the Winchester Business School, UK, where she combines teaching with research into transition into higher education. In 2015 she was awarded a National Teaching Fellowship in recognition of her contribution to student learning and the wider teaching profession. This combination of theory and practice has helped her develop innovative approaches to study that are reflected in her contributions to this book.

Contributors

Eshani Beddewela is a senior lecturer in corporate social responsibility (CSR). She received her PhD in CSR and international business from Bradford University School of Management on the complex nature of implementing CSR within multinational enterprises in Sri Lanka. Eshani is a past Commonwealth Scholar and a Fellow of the Higher Education Academy. Eshani's research interests are: corporate social responsibility in the multinational corporation, political dimensions of CSR and micro-foundations of CSR. She has published in journals such as the *Journal of Business Ethics* and *Accounting Forum*, and contributed to edited collections.

Leonardo Caporarello is the Director of the Learning Lab at SDA Bocconi School of Management and SDA Professor of Leadership & Managerial Development. Leonardo specializes in negotiation and influencing at Harvard Law School. His main research, teaching and advisory topics are in the field of organizational transformation and change management. Leonardo has extensive experience on graduate and executive education programmes. He is faculty member of the SDA Bocconi Global Executive MBA and of the Bocconi Mumbai International School of Business. Leonardo has published in journals and books, at both national and international levels.

Anna Casey-Cox is a Pākehā New Zealander of Irish and English decent. Anna is a community organizer and social researcher. She has significant experience in managing and organizing community projects, including community-based research. Anna studied at the University of Waikato and has a Master's degree in health development and policy and a PhD in organizational studies.

Jang-Ho Choi is a professor of Sogang Business School at Sogang University in South Korea. He also currently serves as a Director of the Center for Social Enterprise Development. He received a BA and an MS in management from Seoul National University and received his PhD in human resource management from the University of Wisconsin-Madison. His research interests centre on improving organizational performance through high commitment work systems.

Michael Coleman is a learning program manager at IBM with responsibility for the internal project management learning curriculum. Prior to this he held a range of technical and managerial roles in the company, primarily in software development. He is also a part-time student on the University of Winchester's Doctoral Business Administration (DBA) degree programme.

Dean Cycon is an environmental and indigenous rights attorney and social entrepreneur in Massachusetts, USA. He is the co-founder of Coffee Kids, Inc, the first international development organization in the coffee industry. Dean founded Dean's Beans Organic Coffee Co. in 1993 to model business as a vehicle for positive economic, social and environmental change in the coffee lands. His unique business model has received numerous national and international awards, including the Oslo Business for Peace Award, the United Nations Women's Empowerment Principles Leadership Award for Community Engagement and the Specialty Coffee Association of America's Sustainability Award. His book, *Javatrekker: Dispatches from the World of Fair Trade Coffee*, was awarded the Gold Medal by the Independent Publishers Association as the Best Travel Essay Book of 2008, and has been published in English, Chinese and Korean.

Kahurangi Dey (Ngāti Pūkenga, Ngāi Te Rangi) is a PhD student at Waikato University, New Zealand. Concerned with issues of social justice and management education, Kahu has an affinity for critical perspectives and her academic interests include integrative, holistic and relational aspects of a shared humanity.

Jeanie M. Forray is Professor of Management and Director of the Management Institute at Western New England University in Springfield, Massachusetts (US). She received her PhD in organization studies from the University of Massachusetts-Amherst and her undergraduate degree in history from the University of California at Berkeley. Dr Forray teaches organizational behaviour, business and society, international management and other management-related topic areas at the undergraduate and graduate level. Dr Forray's current research agenda addresses issues in management education, including ethics in experiential teaching approaches, teaching methods and corporate social responsibility, and factors influencing first year programme success. She co-edited a 2012 special issue of the *Journal of Management Education* on the Principles for Responsible Management Education (PRME) and a special section cluster in 2015 on responsible management education for Academy of Management Learning & Education.

Joseph E. Garcia is a professor of management at Western Washington University. He also serves in a leadership role for the Society for the Advancement of Chicano/a/Hispanic and Native American Scientists' (SACNAS) Leadership Institutes. He previously was Associate Dean and Founding Director of the College of Business and Economics' Center for Innovation and Education and then served as the Bowman Distinguished Professor of Leadership Studies and Founding Director of the Karen W. Morse Institute for Leadership. In addition to leadership, Dr Garcia's scholarship and teaching interests include management education, diversity in organizations and organizational behaviour.

Gianmarco Gessi graduated in business administration at Bocconi University in Milan, majoring in finance. After three years at Merrill Lynch, he moved to the Mediolanum Banking Group, first as General Manager of Mediolanum Communications S.p.A. He was appointed Director of Equity Holdings in January 2016, a role that covers coordination of the financial, organizational and operational activities of the various entities controlled by the parent company, as well as business development in new foreign markets. Gianmarco is a lecturer on planning & control and business administration at the Mediolanum Corporate University. Together with Bocconi, he has created the Executive Master in Business and Banking Administration, exclusively aimed at Mediolanum managers, in which he also lectures. He is occasionally a guest lecturer at both Bocconi and Politecnico Universities.

Judith E. Glaser is an Organizational Anthropologist. She is the CEO of Benchmark Communications, Inc., and the Chairman of The Creating WE Institute. She has also served as an Adjunct Professor at The Wharton School of the University of Pennsylvania, a visiting guest speaker at Harvard School of Business, the Keynote Speaker at MIT's Innovation Conference, a guest speaker at the Kellogg School of Management at Northwestern University, at Loyola University, University of Chicago Booth School of Business, NYU, IIT, University of Stellenbosch in South Africa, Etisalat Academy in Dubai, Tsinghua University in China, and others.

Janelle Goodnight has been with Western New England University since 1999. Her background interests are marketing research, e-commerce, consumer behaviour, teaching pedagogy and programme development. Dr Goodnight has received numerous awards for research in statistics, buyer behaviour and teaching pedagogy. Her students have received awards from School-to-Career and the State of Massachusetts for outstanding work in marketing research with paying clients.

Danna Greenberg is a professor and holder of the Carpenter Chair of Organizational Behavior at Babson College. Professor Greenberg's research focuses on two scholarly areas. In the field of work–life integration, she is especially interested in work–life transitions such as pregnancy, return to work, negotiating flexible work arrangements and enacting different work paradigms, and how individuals experience and manage these transitions in today's demanding work world. Professor Greenberg is also passionate about the scholarship of teaching and learning and is particularly interested in innovation and changing paradigms in management education. Professor Greenberg received her BA from Wellesley College and her PhD from Boston College, Carroll School of Management.

Roberto Gutiérrez has a PhD in sociology from Johns Hopkins University and has been an associate professor in the School of Management at the Universidad de los Andes (Bogotá, Colombia) since 1995. He has published articles about alliances, social enterprises, education and development in popular media and academic journals—among them the *American Sociological Review*, the *Review of Educational Research, Stanford Social Innovation Review*, the *Journal of Business Ethics* and *Long Range Planning*.

Ross Hayes is a full-time PhD student at Winchester Business School, University of Winchester (UK). His thesis is using critical realism to explore the application of PRME in European business schools. Prior to starting his thesis Ross spent two years teaching management at a business school in Burma and has, more recently, been teaching on undergraduate programmes at Winchester Business School.

Dennis Heaton is Director of the Management PhD programme at Maharishi University of Management (MUM) in Fairfield, Iowa, USA, which focuses on consciousness and sustainability. Dennis has explored the interface of psychological models from Western developmental psychology and Eastern models of higher states of consciousness, and he is a proponent of consciousness-based management education, which includes the Transcendental Meditation technique. He is a member of the PRME Working Group on the Sustainability Mindset.

Maria Humphries is an associate professor at the Waikato Management School in Hamilton, New Zealand. Her interests are in the critical consideration of diversity management.

James Hunt is Associate Professor of Management at Babson College where he teaches organizational behaviour and leadership. In 2009 he received Babson's Deans' Award for Excellence in Teaching in All Programs. James is the co-author of two books, *The Coaching Manager: Developing Top Talent in Business* (2nd edition) and *The Coaching Organization: A Strategy for Developing Leaders* (Sage Publishing). James is a former chair of the management division at Babson, a member of the Babson Faculty Senate, and Babson Graduate and Undergraduate Policy Committees. James chaired the faculty committee charged with redesigning Babson's flagship undergraduate course, Foundations of Management.

Bruce Hutton is Professor and Dean Emeritus at the Daniels College of Business, University of Denver. He holds the Piccinati Chair in Teaching Innovation. He has served as dean of the college (1990–1994, 2007–2008), founder and director of off-site MBA programmes (1986–1989), and Chairman of the Department of Marketing (1980–1985). He is the recipient of the Faculty Pioneer Institutional Leadership Award from the Aspen Institute Business and Society Program. Dr Hutton received his PhD from the University of Florida with a major in marketing and minors in social psychology and social research methods.

Anna Iñesta is Director of the Center for Educational Innovation at ESADE Business and Law School, Ramon Llull University in Barcelona, where she has developed other responsibilities such as Associate Director of the Bachelor of Business Administration and Associate Director of Educational Innovation. She holds a BA in English, an MA in multimedia pedagogies and a PhD in educational psychology. Her main areas of research are related to educational innovation and leadership at a course and programme level, as well as academic writing regulation.

Sheila Keegan holds a doctorate of management and is a chartered psychologist. She has been Principal of Campbell Keegan Consultancy—a qualitative research and organizational change consultancy firm working on public and private sector projects—for 32 years. She is trained in the practical application of qualitative research approaches and has published several books on the topics. She has also been a visiting teacher at Bath Business School, Cambridge University and many other universities in the UK.

Scott Kelley is Assistant Vice-President for Vincentian Scholarship in the Office of Mission and Values and Assistant Professor in the Religious Studies Department at DePaul University, USA. His research focuses on pragmatic inquiry as a method for sustainable strategy development in management education. He co-authored *Alleviating Poverty through Profitable Partnerships: Globalization, Markets, and Economic Well-Being* and has published articles on for-profit contributions that alleviate poverty. He teaches courses at the graduate and undergraduate levels in sustainable development and labour abuses in the collegiate apparel industry.

Chris Laszlo is a managing partner of Sustainable Value Partners LLC, which provides advisory services to help companies create competitive advantage by integrating sustainability and CSR into their core businesses. Chris is also Professor of Organizational Behaviour and Faculty Director for Research and Outreach, Fowler Center for Business as an Agent of World Benefit at Case Western Reserve University, USA. Chris's book *Flourishing Enterprise: The New Spirit of Business* has advocated cultivating a consciousness of connectedness to enable individuals to advance sustainability into flourishing.

Melissa Manwaring is a lecturer in management at Babson College, where she teaches negotiation and organizational behaviour. She has a special interest in adult learning and curriculum design. As an independent trainer and consultant, she has worked with a wide range of corporate and non-profit clients to build individual and institutional negotiation capacities. She has served as Babson's Director of Learning Assessment and as the Director of Curriculum Development at Harvard's Program on Negotiation. Prior to her education career, Melissa practised law, focusing on commercial litigation, intellectual property transactions and dispute resolution. She received her JD from Harvard Law School and her MEd from the Harvard Graduate School of Education.

Josep Francesc Mària is a Jesuit. He is Associate Professor at ESADE Business and Law School. He teaches sociology, corporate social responsibility and spirituality in management. He holds a degree in theology and a PhD in economics. His main areas of research are CSR of mining companies and spirituality in management.

Jose Luis Marin holds an Advanced Studies Diploma in Management from ESADE, an MBA in international business from the University of Texas at Austin and industrial engineer from the ITESM, Campus Monterrey. His main areas of expertise are strategy, entrepreneurship and international business. He has also collaborated in many research projects in different universities in Europe and America. He is an expert in the case method for teaching management. His main research field is international entrepreneurship.

Don Mayer is Professor of the Practice of Business Ethics and Legal Studies at the Daniels College of Business, University of Denver. Before coming to Daniels in 2007, he was Professor of Management at Oakland University in Rochester, Michigan. He is lead author of *Foundations of Business Law* (Flatworld Knowledge, 2011) and co-author of *International Business Law: Cases and Materials* (Prentice Hall, 2008). He has written frequently for law journals and business ethics journals. At Daniels, and as a visiting professor, he teaches globalization, business ethics, business law and public policy, and sustainability. He holds a JD from Duke University and an LLM in international and comparative law from Georgetown University Law Center.

Alan Murray holds the Hoare Chair in Responsible Management at Winchester Business School, UK, where he is Head of Research and Knowledge Exchange, in the Faculty of Business, Law and Sport. Alan has been closely connected to the PRME initiative right from the beginning having been part of the original UN Global Compact Taskforce which developed the Principles in 2006/2007. In 2006, he also instigated the establishment of the British Academy of Management Special Interest Group in Corporate Social Responsibility (now renamed as the Sustainable and Responsible Management SIG), and became its founding chair. In subsequent years he ran, with colleagues in what is now the UK and Ireland Regional Chapter, a succession of events both to promote PRME and also to offer support in the teaching and researching of subjects connected to the wider notion of responsible management.

Ron Nahser is Managing Partner of Corporantes, Inc. Over the past 25 years, Ron has developed the Pathfinder Pragmatic Inquiry® and the accompanying Corporantes Pathfinder Notebook© proving its effectiveness from corporate, academic, organizational and personal perspectives. He is the author of *Learning to Read the Signs* and *Journeys to Oxford*, and co-editor of *Praxiology and Pragmatism*. He has also contributed articles for books such as the *Value Inquiry Book Series* as well as numerous journals including *Perspectives: The Journal of the World Business Academy* and *The Journal of Business Ethics*. Ron lectures worldwide on the subjects of business values, vision, branding and marketing strategy and social responsibility.

Carlos Obeso is a lecturer in the Department of People Management and Organization at ESADE Business School. He holds a BA in management sciences and an MA in industrial relations. He has spent the last 10 years researching and studying in depth the so-called "knowledge society" and the characteristics that work ecology should have for the development of this society. Since its creation, ESADE's Institute for Labour Studies (IEL), which he currently runs, has been used as an instrument of applied research in this work ecology.

Carole Parkes is Professor of Management—Global Issues and Responsible Management, Winchester Business School, UK, Chair of the regional PRME Chapter—UK & Ireland, member of the PRME Advisory Committee and co-editor of the PRME Working Group on Fighting Poverty. With a background in business and academia, Carole regularly speaks, publishes and participates in academic and practitioner events, locally and globally.

Isabel Rimanoczy developed the concept of the Sustainability Mind-set based on her research on business leaders who champion sustainability initiatives. She designed a course to develop that mind-set, adopted or adapted by members of the PRME Working Group on the Sustainability Mindset on five continents, which she coordinates. She teaches at Nova Southeastern University, and is a member of the core team of the Aim2Flourish prize, which celebrates profitable innovations that support the UN Sustainable Development Goals. She is a licensed psychologist (University of Buenos Aires), has an MBA from the University of Palermo and obtained her doctorate at Teachers College, Columbia University.

Xari Rovira has been Associate Professor in the Operations, Innovation and Data Science Department and Director of Quality and Program Development at ESADE, Universitat Ramon Llull since 2014. She holds a BA and PhD in mathematics, an MBA from ESADE and an MA in mathematics for financial instruments. She was Associate Director of the PhD programme (1995–2004), Director of the Bachelor of Business Administration—BBA (2004–2012) and Vice-Dean of Programmes and Educational Innovation (2012–2014) at ESADE. Her areas of interest are the applications of qualitative reasoning and fuzzy reasoning to business management, and the study of the mathematical aspects of qualitative calculus in order-of-magnitude models.

Josep Maria Sayeras is Associate Professor at the Department of Economics, Finance and Accounting at ESADE. He holds a BA in management sciences, a BA in humanities, an MBA and PhD from ESADE, and he currently holds the position of Associate Dean of the Master of Science Programmes in Management at ESADE. He was Visiting Scholar at Columbia University and he worked as a lecturer at the Universidad Centroamericana José Simeón Cañas in El Salvador (UCA). His research focuses on prevention, prediction, solution and handling of financial crises and, in particular, how the various configurations of institutions in different countries affect the handling of exchange rate crises.

 **Emanuel Schachinger** is currently a PhD student at Maharishi University of Management, where he has taught conceptual maps for change-makers, covering models of human development and tools for system thinking, for the Sustainable Living Department at MUM. He received his MBA in sustainable business from MUM. His research interest is human development and organizational change in relation to sustainability.

 **Ricard Serlavós** is Lecturer in the People Management and Organization Department at ESADE Business School. He served as Chair of the same department and Vice-Dean of Educational Innovation. He has also worked as an HR director and consultant. His main areas of research are strategic HRM and leadership competences development. He holds a BA in business administration and an MBA.

 **Matt Statler** is the Richman Family Director of Business Ethics and Social Impact Programming and a Clinical Associate Professor of Business and Society at NYU Stern School of Business. Previously, Matt served at NYU's Center for Catastrophe Preparedness and Response as the Director of Research and as Associate Director of the International Center for Enterprise Preparedness. He worked as the Director of Research at the Imagination Lab Foundation in Lausanne, Switzerland following several years as a management consultant in New York City. His research focuses on ethics, leadership and strategy. He completed a PhD in Philosophy from Vanderbilt University, spent a year as a Fulbright Scholar at the University of Heidelberg, and obtained Bachelor's degrees in Spanish and philosophy from the University of Missouri.

 **Ranjini Swamy** is a Fellow from the Indian Institute of Management, Ahmedabad, India. After obtaining her Fellowship, she has taught courses in the area of organizational behaviour at various business schools in India. Her research interests include responsible management education and ethical behaviour in organizations. She has published several case studies and book chapters and a few journal articles in the area.

Kristi Lewis Tyran is Associate Professor of Management at Western Washington University. Dr Tyran's research interests focus on exploring the roles of values, emotion and technology in leadership and teams, as well as improving management education. She received her PhD from the University of California, Irvine. In 2014, Dr Tyran received the Dennis Murphy Research Award. In 2012, she was honoured as the CBE Distinguished Teaching Fellow. In 2005 and 2015, Dr Tyran received the Allette and Cayden Chase Franklin Excellence in Teaching Award. She has served on the Whatcom Educational Credit Union Board of Directors since 2006.

Maika Valencia-Silva holds a PhD in management sciences (ESADE Business School), a Master's degree in finance (Tec of Monterrey), a BS in business administration (Tec Monterrey) and a BS in accounting (University of Colima). Her teaching and research interests are in entrepreneurship and accounting. Her research has been published in international refereed journals such as *Journal of Business Ethics, European Management Review* and Babson's conference proceedings.

Alan Wagenberg has been a consultant for Fortune 500 companies, multilaterals and not-for-profits in corporate social responsibility, strategy and entrepreneurship. He has also been teaching these topics at various universities since 2009. Additionally, he has co-founded various organizations such as Impact Hub Bogotá (a co-sharing space for social entrepreneurs) and La Arenera (a not-for-profit that promotes collective action), among other initiatives.

Charlotte Warin is a doctoral researcher at the University of Huddersfield. Her research interests include responsible management education, corporate social responsibility and the use of institutional theory. Charlotte also teaches on a number of undergraduate modules to a wide range of national and international students. She is also an active member of the British Academy of Management Council acting as a representative for doctoral students.

Jaclyn Wilson is project assistant at the Global Integrative Module and PhD candidate at the Graduate School of Psychology, Educational and Sports Sciences Blanquerna, Ramon Llull University.

Printed in the United States
By Bookmasters